EU Law and the Harmonization of Takeovers in the Internal Market

EUROPEAN MONOGRAPHS

Editor-in-chief Professor David O'Keeffe

In this series *European Monographs* this book *EU Law and the Harmonization of Takeovers in the Internal Market* is the seventy-first title. *The titles published in this series are listed at the end of this volume.*

Kluwer Law International

EU Law and the Harmonization of Takeovers in the Internal Market

Thomas Gr. Papadopoulos

Wolters Kluwer
Law & Business

AUSTIN BOSTON CHICAGO NEW YORK THE NETHERLANDS

Published by:
Kluwer Law International
PO Box 316
2400 AH Alphen aan den Rijn
The Netherlands
Website: www.kluwerlaw.com

Sold and distributed in North, Central and South America by:
Aspen Publishers, Inc.
7201 McKinney Circle
Frederick, MD 21704
United States of America
Email: customer.service@aspenpublishers.com

Sold and distributed in all other countries by:
Turpin Distribution Services Ltd.
Stratton Business Park
Pegasus Drive, Biggleswade
Bedfordshire SG18 8TQ
United Kingdom
Email: kluwerlaw@turpin-distribution.com

Printed on acid-free paper.

ISBN 978-90-411-3340-3

Speech by Jacques Delors

(Luxembourg, 9 September 1985)*

The large market is not just for European businessmen; it is to serve the people too. And this raises extremely thorny problems, particularly on security and health protection grounds. We have to harmonize the rules because there can be no internal market with a reasonable degree of competition unless at least a few of them and hence to some extent business costs as well have been brought into line.

* On 9 Sep. 1985, President of the European Commission Jacques Delors delivers a speech at the first Intergovernmental Conference (IGC) to be held in Luxembourg.
Source: Speech by Jacques Delors, in Bulletin of the European Communities. September 1985, No 9, pp. 7–10.

About the Author

Thomas Papadopoulos is a visiting researcher at Harvard Law School. He received his DPhil in Law (PhD in Law) from the Faculty of Law, University of Oxford. He received a degree of Magister Juris(MJur/LLM) and a degree of MPhil in Law from the Faculty of Law, University of Oxford. He also received his LLB with Distinction (ranked 1st) from the Department of Law, Aristotle University of Thessaloniki, Greece. He is an alumnus of the Anatolia American College of Thessaloniki, Greece. Furthermore, he is Attorney at law (Greece), North Atlantic Treaty Organization (NATO) Scholar and Scholar of the A.G. Leventis Foundation, Paris. He is a part-time law lecturer at the Law School, University of Buckingham and a law tutor at the Oxford University Programme for Undergraduate Studies(OPUS), University of Oxford, UK. Additionally, he was Academic Student Coordinator of the Financial Law Discussion Group, Faculty of Law, University of Oxford. Moreover, he is a contributor to 'Law of the European Union' edited by D. Vaughan, A. Robertson, P. Eleftheriadis and published by Oxford University Press (2008). He participated in workshops of the Technical Assistance and Information Exchange instrument (TAIEX) managed by the Directorate-General Enlargement of the European Commission. E-mail: thomas.papadopoulos@yahoo.com or thomas.papadopoulos@bnc.oxon.org.

Table of Contents

Foreword by Derrick Wyatt

Corporate takeovers can have profound effects on the interests of shareholders, and employees, as well as on society at large. Particularly when they are contested, takeovers can provoke vigorous debate in the financial press, and attract the critical attention of national governments. The phenomenon of the corporate takeover has long been the subject matter of a prolific literature examining its implications from the financial, economic, social and legal perspectives. This book makes a new and distinct contribution to the legal literature on takeovers, since it places the EU Takeover Bid Directive in the context of the EU company law harmonization programme, and of the fundamental freedom of corporate bodies under EU law to establish themselves in other Member States. The book examines the freedom of establishment of companies, and explains how it is this freedom which provides the rationale and framework for the EU company law harmonization programme, as well as providing the specific logic underpinning the Takeover Bid Directive. The author offers a clear and readable explanation of the relationship between freedom of establishment and takeover bids, and devotes a chapter to the significance of the corporate mobility case law of the Court for the takeover process. The regulation of takeovers is then discussed in the context of the relationship between company law and capital markets law. One of the most impressive chapters in the book comprises an overview of the Takeover Bid Directive in the context of the EU internal market, which includes examination of provisions of the Directive which deal with mandatory bids, board neutrality, and breakthrough, as well as the controversial rules on reciprocity which allow companies which apply the board neutrality and breakthrough rules to opt out if they are the target of a bidder that does not apply the same takeover provisions. As well as analysing the Takeover Bid Directive, the author examines in light of recent case law the potential horizontal effect of EU Treaty provisions on freedom of establishment and the free movement of capital. Thoughtful and provocative questions are raised as to the extent to which the corporate constitution and the conduct of the board in a takeover situation might in themselves constitute restrictions on the freedom of establishment (and of capital movement) of a bidder. It was a very great pleasure to supervise the thesis which has provided the basis for this monograph, and I recommend it without hesitation to the reader as a valuable and original contribution to legal literature.

Professor Derrick Wyatt QC
May 2010

Foreword by Mads Andenas and Philip R Wood

Thomas Papadopoulos has written an important book about the Takeover Directive. His conclusion is that the Directive will have a more limited impact than originally intended but that this impact may yet be important to the development of the law of the Internal Market relating to companies and capital.

Takeover Directive not only spent some thirty years in gestation but went through much false labour. It started out as a proposal by Professor Robert Pennington, mainly codifying the City Code on Take Overs and Mergers in the form of an EU Directive. EU regulation of take overs seemed a wholly reasonable ambition. If all the Member States established different forms of national take-over regulation, that could create restrictions to an Internal Financial Market. But the Germans feared that a European market in corporate take overs would threaten both their employee representation and *Konzernrecht* or group law. The Swedes started to fear that fair take over rules would challenge the dominating position of the Wallenbergs in Swedish industry and finance. In the UK, it was the City Panel on Take Overs that opposed the Directive. This seemed to be a paradox, as the Directive would codify the City Code on Take Overs and Mergers. But the Panel and the Code had no direct statutory basis, and the Panel wished to defend its 'self-regulatory' status. An intermediate stage was to herald a new version of the Directive as a 'framework directive'. Then a few UK companies, including the Daily Mail Group as controlled by Viscount Rothermere, joined in the opposition as the proposed break through rule could weaken the family's hold over the company where they sat on voting stock and the majority of the share capital was issued as non-voting stock. In the end national regulators in some countries wanted to keep national jurisdiction and got a form of host country control in through some rather unclear jurisdictional rules, with various opt-in and opt-out regimes.

Each new round resulted in a watering down of the provisions and the scope of the Directive. It did not become shorter, more concise or clearer.

There is much work to be done in sorting out the problems that the legislative process has accumulated in this way. The European Court of Justice has an important role here. The Commission will certainly propose amending directives. Scholarship can assist courts and the Commission. This book will do so, and it will also be of practical use for lawyers who have to advise on the law under the Directive.

The main text of this book has fifteen chapters which broadly fall into three broad sections. The first places the Takeover Directive in the context of the harmonization objectives of EU law. The second reviews specific articles of the Directive, and the third is mainly concerned with the direct effect of the fundamental freedoms and the Directive in EU law, followed by a conclusion. It follows that the book properly places the Directive in the much wider setting of EU law and shows a fine understanding of this wider perspective.

The first part deals principally with the intersection between EU law and the Takeover Directive. There is a concisely written overarching review of the four fundamental freedoms of the EU internal market as the cornerstone concepts and a sound discussion of discriminatory and non-discriminatory restrictions with pertinent case law, followed by chapters on the legal basis for harmonization (a chapter which convincingly demonstrates the importance of company law and securities regulation in the achievement of the internal market), on the various degrees of harmonization and the obstacles to freedom of establishment, on the scope of the Financial Services Action Plan for a single financial market, on subsidiarity issues in Article 5 of the EC Treaty, on the weaknesses and defects in the harmonization efforts and on the barriers to market integration. This latter chapter contains a well-debated argument explaining the importance of the market for corporate control as an indispensable element of the internal market. There is in this section a comprehensive review of the relevant case law.

A chapter focuses on the Takeover Directive as a company law instrument with strong links to capital markets law and shows deftly how the market for corporate control is a part of regulated capital markets. The section concludes with the essential definitions of the market of corporate control showing a good grasp of the tensions which arise.

In our view this section shows a most commendable understanding of the broader issues and the essential themes at this level and goes through the arguments and the principles with great perspicacity and attention to both policy and legal detail.

The next chapter considers certain specific articles on the Takeover Directive. Dr Papadopoulos reviews the provision in Article 5 as to mandatory bids and exposes the drawbacks and deficiencies of the provision, especially areas of vagueness. There is a perceptive discussion of the squeeze-out and sell-out rights in Articles 15 and 16 with well-supported criticism in relation to circumvention techniques. The author then discusses the non-frustration rule in Article 9, the breakthrough rule in Article 11 and the reciprocity rule in Article 12.

In cogent paragraphs Dr Papadopoulos criticizes the various opt-in and opt-out regimes in relation to these rules and convincingly argues why they detract from the objectives of a harmonized regime and lead instead to legal diversity and lack of uniformity in essential aspects. At the same time he reviews why these articles proved so troublesome by reason of differing philosophies about corporate takeovers in the EU which effectively prevent a level-playing field. The section concludes with a well-written and succinct discussion of the supervisory authority and applicable law, the information for and consultation of employees' representatives and the transposition of the Directive.

In our view this chapter reveals a scholarly and incisive approach to the objectives and deficiencies of the particular articles examined and how they might work in practice.

The final section covers mainly the direct effect of the fundamental freedoms in EU law and reviews the extent to which conduct of the board and the articles in the corporate constitution might be said to constitute restrictions on the freedom of establishment and the free movement of capital. Dr Papadopoulos discusses the distinction between vertical and horizontal direct effect and demonstrates the resulting legal position by ample reference to leading EU case law.

In his conclusion Dr Papadopoulos cites the remark of the former Commissioner F. Bolkenstein that the Takeover Directive is not worth the paper it is written on. He cogently summarizes the opposing arguments that on the one hand the aim was to consolidate not only financial markets but also to achieve integration of EU industry and to boost competition, while, on the other hand, the arguments in favour of regulatory competition and diversity. He views the opt-in opt-out regime as a blow to the efficacy of the Directive and to a harmonized market in corporate control.

Dr Papadopoulos nuanced conclusion is that the Directive in its current form is not capable of altering decisively cultural or institutional objections to the creation of a single market but that it can contribute to a movement in this direction so that, despite it imperfections, it is not completely not worth the paper it is written on.

In our view the book as a whole shows great strengths in percipient legal analysis and is eloquent in marshalling the points. It shows a scholarly attention to the jurisprudence and the theoretical side of the topic, as well as a mastery of the practical implications. Dr Papadopoulos is as much aware of the policies as the fineness of legal detail and intricate interpretation.

The arguments are presented in a well-organized and thoughtful manner. The text is well-backed up by careful analysis of the case law and by relevant citation from the literature. Throughout there is a high standard of legal intelligence and intellect. There is a first-class bibliography which cites just under 170 books and over 380 articles – a comprehensive and useful list of the leading works on the subject.

In our view the book is an original contribution to knowledge. As the examiners for the University of Oxford D.Phil., we were satisfied that the thesis fully met the standards and criteria required for the degree. We had no reservations nor did we note any corrections which we thought should be made. We were therefore glad to recommend that the degree of DPhil be conferred on this candidate, as the University subsequently did. It is only left to us to congratulate Dr Papadopoulos and his supervisor, Professor Derrick Wyatt, QC, on the publication of the dissertation in this book.

Prof. Mads Andenas and Prof. Philip R Wood, QC (Hon.)
July 2010

Acknowledgements

This monograph derives from my doctoral thesis (DPhil in Law) which was written during my time as a member of the Faculty of Law and of Merton College, University of Oxford, UK between 2007 and 2009. I transformed my doctoral thesis into a book while I was a visiting researcher at Harvard Law School, USA. This monograph analyses the Takeover Bid Directive in the light of EU Law, and examines the extent to which this Directive facilitates the exercise of the fundamental freedom of establishment and the free movement of capital in the internal market. Other monographs and articles on thc Takeover Bid Directive and on the regulation of takeovers in Europe tend to favour different approaches. For example, they follow a comparative perspective (e.g., comparisons between the EU and the US, or among the different Member States of the EU), a law and economics perspective, an environmental/sustainable development perspective, etc. My monograph follows an EU Law approach – although, of course, when necessary company law, capital markets law and financial law considerations are taken into account.

I would like to acknowledge the gratitude that I owe to all those who helped and supported me directly or indirectly during the conduct of this research. I would like to thank my father, Grigorios, my mother, Evdokia, my grandmother, Vivi, and the rest of my family, without whose love and support this doctoral thesis would not have been possible. I would also like to thank my supervisor, Professor Derrick Wyatt, QC, for his patience and for his encouragement during the supervision of my thesis. I would also like to thank my DPhil examiners, Prof. Mads Andenas and Prof. Philip Wood, QC. Moreover, I would like to thank Dr Pavlos Eleftheriadis for his interest in my research and for his moral support.

Furthermore, the Scholarship of the Graduate Assistance Fund of the Faculty of Law, University of Oxford, UK, the North Atlantic Treaty Organization (NATO) Research Scholarship, granted by the Greek Ministry of Foreign Affairs, the Scholarship of the Tsagka-Despotidou Foundation and the Scholarship of the A.G. Leventis Foundation, Paris facilitated my research significantly. Opportunities to present one's research in conferences and workshops and to receive comments are vital for the young researcher, and the various Research Travel Grants received from the University of Oxford allowed me to present my research at many interesting conferences and to receive precious feedback. I would also like to thank the Greek Foundation of State Scholarships (IKY) for the awards that it granted to me during my undergraduate studies at the Aristotle University of Thessaloniki, Greece.

My research benefited notably from discussions with various persons. These persons expressed an interest in my research and discussed my arguments with me. Grateful acknowledgement is made of: John Armour (Oxford), Bart De Meester (KU Leuven, Belgium), Georg Ringe (Oxford), Phil Syrpis (Bristol), Antonis Antoniadis (Durham), Jonathan Black-Branch (Oxford), Federico Mucciarelli (Modena e Reggio Emilia), Emilios Avgouleas (Manchester), Niamh Moloney (LSE), Nicholas Georgakopoulos (Indiana), Anne-Marie Higginson (Buckingham), Paschalis Paschalidis (Oxford), Nigel Foster (Buckingham), Mathias Siems (Norwich), Panagiotis Staikouras (Piraeus), Reinier Kraakman (Harvard), Stavros Gadinis (Harvard), Sofie Cools (Harvard), Harry Papadopoulos (Oxford), Alexandros Tsadiras (Thessaloniki), Marios Papaloukas (Peloponnese), Ioannis Mournianakis (Athens). While doing my research at Merton College, University of Oxford, I benefited from the advice and the care of my college tutors, Mindy Chen-Wishart and Jennifer Payne. Moreover, I would like to thank my students at the University of Buckingham, UK and at the Oxford University Programme for Undergraduate Studies (OPUS), University of Oxford, UK. Student questions about basic points have assisted my knowledge and my critical ability and constituted a fruitful experience. Sometimes going back to the 'basics' and 'fundamentals' of a subject helps the researcher more than does focusing on a special but restricted issue. My interaction with the various guest speakers of the Financial Law Discussion Group of the Faculty of Law, University of Oxford, UK stimulated my mind and moved me to re-think many parts of my research. Of course, the usual disclaimer applies, and none of these persons is responsible for any inconsistencies or mistakes of this book.

Access to libraries with up-to-date collections and to online legal databases is crucial for legal research. The Bodleian Law Library of the University of Oxford as well as the Harvard Law School library constituted perfect environments for legal research, and facilitated my work by offering easy access to bibliography.

I would also like to thank my friends at Oxford who made my research there less dull and monotonous: Spilios Tzouras (London), Spiros Droukopoulos-Demiris (London), John Tzartos (Athens), Bart and Annlies De Meester (Brussels), Konstantinos Delaportas (Cambridge), Savvas Savva (Cambridge), Jon WooJung (Oxford), Philip Atzemoglou (Oxford), Alexandros Grammatikos (Oxford), Eirik Bjørge (Oxford), Mihalis Gousgounis (Brussels) and Antonios Kouroutakis (Oxford). I would also like to thank my various friends in Greece for their friendship all these years.

The structure of the postgraduate courses of the Faculty of Law, University of Oxford, UK played a major role in the completion of this doctoral study. The fact that the degrees of Magister Juris (MJur/LLM) and of Master of Philosophy in Law (MPhil) preceded the degree of DPhil smoothed the way towards the completion of my research. The Faculty's recommended route is the best choice for someone planning to do a DPhil in Law. In my opinion, the structure of the postgraduate taught and research degrees of the Faculty of Law (MJur>MPhil>DPhil) helps the student to develop his or her work up this 'pyramid' to the internationally esteemed DPhil level, the Oxford counterpart to what is more often known as a PhD. Furthermore, my undergraduate legal studies at the Law Department, Faculty of Law, Economics and Politics, Aristotle University of Thessaloniki, Greece provided the necessary foundations for the conduct of postgraduate studies. I must also stress the importance of my studies at the Anatolia American College of Thessaloniki, Greece (1st Gymnasium 1995-98, 1st Lykeion 1998-2001). All these years of study, Anatolia College enhanced significantly my knowledge of English. I would also like to thank the people of Kluwer Law International (Wolters Kluwer Law & Business) and especially Mr Karel E. van der Linde and Ms Hanneke Verbeek, as well as, the editor of the European Monographs Series, Professor David O'Keeffe. Once more, I would like to thank my beloved family and to stress their importance for the completion of my studies at the University of Oxford.

Thomas Gr. Papadopoulos

Oxford (United Kingdom), Cambridge\Boston (Massachussetts, USA), Thessaloniki (Greece)

Preamble

This book analyses the Takeover Bid Directive in the light of EU Law, and examines the extent to which this Directive facilitates the exercise of the fundamental freedom of establishment and the free movement of capital in the internal market. Takeover bids are very important for the internal market, because they contribute to market integration and to business consolidation. According to the Directive's Preamble, it is necessary to protect the interests of the holders of securities of companies (in particular, those with minority holdings). This is in order to create EU-wide clarity and transparency in respect of legal issues to be settled in the event of takeover bids and to prevent patterns of corporate restructuring within the European Union from being distorted by arbitrary differences in governance and management cultures.

At the beginning of this book, there is an analysis of the fundamental freedom of establishment of companies, as well as of the legal bases for the harmonization of company law and capital markets law at EU level. Some other aspects of EU company law harmonization, as well as the permissible limits of harmonization (subsidiarity issues), are discussed. These initial discussions will assist the reader in approaching the Takeover Bid Directive in its EU law context, and in understanding the wider EU legal framework surrounding the harmonization of takeovers in the internal market.

Since the Directive is based on the EC Treaty chapter on freedom of establishment (Articles 43 and 44(2)(g) EC Treaty), it should, in principle, contribute to cross-frontier corporate mobility in the internal market through takeover bids. This was certainly the aim of the Commission in its various proposals. Takeover bids and the EC Treaty provisions on freedom of establishment are closely related. Additionally, the significance of corporate mobility and of the freedom of establishment case law of the European Court of Justice for the takeover process is analysed. The Directive forms part of the EU company law harmonization programme, whose weaknesses and limits are also explored. However, the Takeover Bid Directive is an EU company law instrument with strong links to EU capital market law. The initial aims of the EU legislature were to establish an internal market for companies and to achieve market integration in the field of EU company law. However, the Takeover Bid Directive is a compromise and watered down version of a proposal which the Commission envisaged would lead to a more effective pan-European takeover regime than that which actually proved possible. The need for compromise was the result of the very different legal and policy approaches of the Member States in the field of takeover regulation. Some provisions of the Directive are obligatory for all Member States. These provisions include the mandatory bid rule, the squeeze-out right, and the sell-out right. All these obligatory provisions of the Directive are, in their present form, liable to some criticism.

The two key provisions of the Directive have been made optional for Member States. These are the non-frustration rule, which requires the board to obtain the prior authorization of the general meeting of shareholders before taking any action that could result in the frustration of the bid; and the breakthrough rule, requiring that any restrictions on the transfer of securities or voting rights provided for in the articles of association of the offeree company or in contractual agreements between the offeree company and the holders of its securities or in contractual agreements between holders of the offeree company's securities shall not apply vis-à-vis the offeror during the time allowed for acceptance of the bid. Nevertheless, those Member States that opt out are obliged to allow individual companies to opt in. Moreover, a reciprocity rule was also adopted, which allows Member States to permit those companies that do apply these provisions to opt out again if they are the target of a bidder that does not itself apply the same takeover provisions. Additionally, the non-frustration and breakthrough rules are not fully comprehensive, and, even when a company applies them, it is still possible to evade their application, since some corporate and financial structures remain outside the Directive's scope.

Finally, this monograph discusses the extent to which obstacles to cross-border takeovers addressed by the Directive, or indeed left intact by the Directive, are to be regarded as restrictions on the right of establishment stricto sensu, or simply as obstacles in practice to making a successful takeover bid. More specifically, it scrutinizes the horizontal direct effect of the EC fundamental freedoms and seeks to analyse the extent to which conduct of the board and articles in the corporate constitution might be said to constitute restrictions on the freedom of establishment and on the free movement of capital. At the close of the thesis, there some essential concluding remarks on EU law and the harmonization of takeovers in the internal market.

Chapter 1
The Fundamental Freedom of Establishment of Companies

1.1 INTRODUCTION

This chapter will analyse the various characteristics of the fundamental freedom of establishment of companies. In this analysis, some elements of the freedom of establishment case law on natural persons will be invoked, but only to the extent that these elements fit into the special nature of legal persons, such as companies; arbitrary generalizations will be avoided. This general approach will assist in the understanding of some obscure parts of the exercise of this fundamental freedom by companies and in the drawing of a more complete analysis.

1.2 THE RIGHT OF ESTABLISHMENT: A RIGHT OF NATURAL AND LEGAL PERSONS

The European Community (EC) treaty sets out the four fundamental freedoms of the European Communities: the free movement of goods workers, the establishment and provision of services, and capital. These fundamental freedoms contribute to the development and the evolution of the internal market.[1] The EC Treaty relates to economic activities that are physically carried out by natural persons, either as such or organized in the form of a legal person or persons.[2] The applicable fiscal regime, rules for the limitation of liability, and organizational, commercial,

1. The concept of the internal market will be explained below.
2. I.G.F. Cath, 'Free Movement of Legal Persons', in *Free Movement of Persons in Europe, Legal Problems and Experience*, ed. H.G. Schermers et al. (London: Martinus Nijhoff Publishers, 1991), 450.

and even promotional purposes play an important role in the choice to conduct business as a natural or legal person. The distinction between natural persons and legal persons relates to form, not to substance, and the economic operator should be free to select the form in which to conduct his or her economic activities.[3] This freedom of choice is crucial for market integration and for the most efficient allocation of economic resources; in addition to that, it boosts entrepreneurship and economic initiatives because businesspeople are free to choose and realize their business plans. Intra-community economic activities can be carried out either by the cross-border movement of goods and/or services or by the cross-border movement of the supplier or receiver of such goods and/or services.[4] In the first case, the emphasis is on the movement of the goods and/or services; in the second case, the emphasis is on the movement of the supplier or receiver thereof.[5] From the perspective of rights guaranteed and treatment received under the EC treaty, the form selected should make no difference.[6] The distinctions in the EC Treaty among the fundamental freedoms should be seen as the result of the organization of the subject matter in the EC Treaty rather than of any significant difference in substantive treatment.[7] Except when specifically provided for otherwise under the EC Treaty (or its interpretation by the European Court of Justice (ECJ)), there should be no national exceptions or 'reserved areas' that cannot be affected by the above-mentioned fundamental freedoms on the cross-border movement of economic activities, unless the subject matter is completely harmonized by Community measures that leave no discretion to the Member States.[8]

According to Article 43 of the EC Treaty, freedom of establishment includes the right for nationals of a Member State 'to take up and pursue activities as self-employed persons and to set up and manage undertakings, in particular companies or firms' in the territory of another Member State 'under the conditions laid down for its own nationals by the law of the country where such establishment is effected' (primary establishment).[9] It also includes the right, for nationals of any Member State who are already established in any Member State, to set up agencies, branches, or subsidiaries in another Member State (secondary establishment).[10] According to Article 48 of the EC Treaty, companies or firms, as defined in that provision, are to be treated in the same way as natural persons who are nationals of Member States.[11] Although Article 48 of the EC Treaty requires companies to be

3. I.G.F. Cath (n. 2), 450. Case C-1/93, *Halliburton Services BV v. Staatssecretaris van Financiën*. [1994] ECR I-1137 paras 16–23.
4. I.G.F. Cath (n. 2), 450.
5. *Ibid.*, (n. 2), 450.
6. *Ibid.*
7. *Ibid.*, (n. 2), 451.
8. *Ibid.*
9. A.G. Toth, *The Oxford Encyclopaedia of European Community Law*, vol. 2 of *The Law of the Internal Market* (Oxford: Oxford Clarendon Press, 2005), 242.
10. A.G. Toth (n. 9), 242. C. Gavalda & G. Parleani, *Droit des Affaires del' Union Europeenne*, 5th edn (Paris: Litec LexisNexis, 2006), 126–127.
11. A.G. Toth (n. 9), 242.

treated in the same way as nationals for the purposes of the Treaty provisions on freedom of establishment, this is not strictly possible, given the differences between natural and legal persons.[12] It may be easier, for example, to recognize what is a primary as opposed to a secondary establishment in the case of the registered office of a company and one of its subsidiaries or branches than it is in the case of a professional who has two places of practice in different Member States.[13] Article 44(2)(g) constitutes the legal basis for the harmonization of the area of company law by means of directives.

G. Marenco expresses his objections as to whether nationality and a company's registered office are characterized by common elements and as a result could be treated in the same way. There can never be more than a partial equivalence of the nationality condition and that of the company's registered office on national territory.[14] The former indeed uses a purely formal criterion, with no concrete or substantial content, to exclude equality of treatment.[15] Thus, it cannot be justified on economic grounds, which is where freedom of establishment operates.[16] By contrast, the registered office as a criterion for the connection of a company with a state is simultaneously a concrete situation that might justify a difference in treatment. Thus, it cannot be equated purely and simply with nationality.[17] This argument is underpinned by *Commission v. France*,[18] which examined the legality of a French discriminatory tax provision. The ECJ declared that, by not granting to the branches and agencies in France of insurance companies whose registered offices were in another Member State on the same terms as apply to insurance companies whose registered offices were in France the benefit of shareholders' tax credits with respect to dividends paid to such branches or agencies by French companies, France had breached the freedom of establishment of companies. Nevertheless, the ECJ admitted that a distinction based on the location of the registered office of a company or the place of residence of a natural person may, under certain circumstances, be justified in an area such as tax law.

12. P. Craig & G. De Burca, *EU Law, Text, Cases and Materials*, 4th edn (Oxford: Oxford University Press, 2008), 806.
13. The case law of the ECJ discussing the exercise of the primary and secondary establishment of companies and its influence on takeovers and cross-border corporate restructuring will be analysed in a separate chapter.
14. G. Marenco, 'The Notion of Restriction on the Freedom of Establishment and Provision of Services in the Case-Law of the Court', *YEL* 11 (1991): 113–114. S. Fazio, *The Harmonization of International Commercial Law* (AH Alpen aan den Rijn: Kluwer, 2007), 81. In Case C-369/90, *Micheletti* ([1992] ECR I-4239), the ECJ presumed that the conferal of nationality of a Member State to a natural person is a matter that must be decided solely by that Member State, and that the rest of the Member States have to respect this decision and must not restrict the exercise of fundamental freedoms by imposing an additional condition for the recognition of this citizenship. It is interesting that this case concerned the effective exercise of the freedom of establishment. P. Dyrberg, 'Full Free Movement of Companies at the European Community at Last?', *EL Rev.* 4 (2003): 528.
15. G. Marenco (n. 14).
16. *Ibid.*
17. *Ibid.*
18. Case 270/83, *Commission v. France* [1986] ECR 273.

The registered office is thus compared first with the nationality of the physical person and then with his or her residence.[19] This double comparison reveals that the registered office condition plays a role at once formal and substantial.[20] Hence, the location of the registered office of a company carries a content that could result in justified exemptions from the fundamental freedom of establishment.

1.3 DISCRIMINATORY RESTRICTIONS

Article 43 of the EC Treaty applies to the terms under which business may be carried on.[21] The conditions under which business activities are conducted could often result in discriminatory restrictions treating non-nationals or foreign companies differently on the basis of their nationality. Directly discriminatory restrictions treating non-nationals less favourably than nationals should be distinguished from indistinctly applicable (indirectly discriminatory) measures that ostensibly treat non-nationals and nationals in the same way but in fact disadvantage the non-nationals.[22]

Article 43 of the EC Treaty may be invoked to challenge a national rule, whether in the form of a nationality or a residence requirement, that is discriminatory.[23] Moreover, by prohibiting any discrimination on grounds of nationality resulting from national laws, regulations, or practices, Article 43 of the EC Treaty seeks to ensure that, as regards the right of establishment, a Member State accords to nationals of other Member States the same treatment as it accords to its own nationals. These business terms could also include securities regulation and company law issues of cross-border takeover bids.

1.4 NON-DISCRIMINATORY RESTRICTIONS

As far as the ambit of Article 43 of the EC Treaty is concerned, some of the early cases supported the idea that Article 43 (then 52) of the EC Treaty did not apply to non-discriminatory restrictions. Thus, in *Commission v. Belgium* (*Clinical Biology Services*),[24] the ECJ rejected the Commission's argument that restrictions on the freedom of establishment were not confined to discriminatory measures, but also included measures that were indistinctly applicable to nationals and foreigners

19. G. Marenco (n. 14), 113–114.
20. *Ibid.*
21. J. Steiner, L. Woods & C. Twigg-Flesner, *EU Law*, 9th edn (Oxford: Oxford University Press, 2006), 452. E. Stein, *Harmonization of European Company Laws* (Indianapolis: Merrill, 1971), 26.
22. C. Barnard, *The Substantive Law of the EU*, 2nd edn (Oxford: Oxford University Press, 2007), 312.
23. J. Steiner, L. Woods & C. Twigg-Flesner (n. 21), 452.
24. Case 221/85, *Commission of the European Communities v. Kingdom of Belgium* [1987] ECR 00719.

when they constituted an unjustified restriction for the latter.[25] Furthermore, in *Fearon*,[26] the Court followed the same rationale and found that certain Irish legislation relating to the compulsory acquisition of land applied equally to Irish nationals and non-nationals, and that it did not infringe upon Article 43 of the EC Treaty.[27]

However, non-discriminatory rules may also breach Article 43 of the EC Treaty by obstructing or making less attractive the exercise of this fundamental freedom.[28] Some non-discriminatory (indistinctly applicable) rules are related to market access and to the conditions of penetrating into a new market. This approach was introduced in the field of establishment in *Gebhard*,[29] which examined the requirement to be registered with the local bar. Gebhard was a German citizen and was residing in Italy. The preliminary reference arose out of disciplinary proceedings brought by the Milan Bar against this German member of the Stuttgart Bar for using the term *avocato* contrary to Italian law. National provisions different from those of the home country are suspect and must be justified.[30] Member States must justify these different requirements if they want to continue to apply them. The four requirements of the justification test employed in *Gebhard*[31] and *Centros*[32] apply here with regard to non-discriminatory restrictions. In these cases, the Court held that national measures that are liable to hinder or render less attractive the exercise of fundamental freedoms guaranteed by the Treaty must be applied in a non-discriminatory way, must be justified by imperative requirements in the general interest, must be suitable for obtaining the objective they pursue, and must not go beyond what is necessary to attain it.[33] After *Gebhard*, the ECJ focused very often on whether the national requirements are

25. F. Weiss & F. Wooldridge, *Free Movement of Persons within the European Community*, in *European Monographs*, 2nd edn (Alphen aan den Rijn: Kluwer Law International, 2007), 109.
26. Case 182/83, *Robert Fearon & Company Limited v. Irish Land Commission* [1984] ECR 03677.
27. F. Weiss & F. Wooldridge (n. 25), 110.
28. *Ibid.*, (n. 25), 111. National measures that have direct or sufficiently substantial (possibly exclusionary) effects on the exercise of the Treaty rights stipulated by Arts 18, 39, 43 and 49 EC Treaty constitute prima facie infringements of the EC Treaty and need to be justified. H. Toner, 'Non-Discriminatory Obstacles to the Exercise of Treaty Rights: Articles 39, 43, 49, and 18', *YEL* 23 (2004): 274, 301.
29. Case C-55/94, *Reinhard Gebhard v. Consiglio dell'Ordine degli Avvocati e Procuratori di Milano* [1995] ECR I-04165.
30. P. Kent, *Law of the European Union*, 4th edn (Essex: Pearson Longman, 2008), 240. J. Shaw, J. Hunt & C. Wallace, *Economic and Social Law of the European Union* (Basingstoke: Palgrave Macmillan, 2007), 151.
31. Case C-55/94, *Reinhard Gebhard v. Consiglio dell'Ordine degli Avvocati e Procuratori di Milano* [1995] ECR I-04165.
32. Case C-212/97, *Centros Ltd v. Erhvervs- og Selskabsstyrelsen* [1999] ECR I-01459.
33. In Case C-222/95, *Societe civile immobiliere Parodi v. Banque Albert de Bary et Cie* [1997] ECR I-3899, the Court held that imperative requirements in the general interest could justify compliance with stricter national conditions for mortgage loans than those prescribed by the first Banking Directive ([1977] OJ L33/30). J. Usher, *The Law of Money and Financial Services in the EC*, Oxford EC Law Library, 2nd edn (Oxford: Oxford University Press, 1999), 90. Weiss & F. Wooldridge (n. 25), 112.

liable 'to prohibit, impede or make less attractive' access to the right of establishment (e.g., *Payroll Data Services*[34]).[35]

In *Kraus*,[36] the Court adopted the following propositions: (1) that the right of establishment is a fundamental freedom in EC Law and would not be fully realized if the Member States were able to refuse to grant the benefit of the provisions of Community law to those of their nationals who have taken advantage of its provisions to acquire vocational and academic qualifications in a Member State other than that of which they are nationals, and (2) that Articles 48 and 52 of the EC Treaty (now 39 and 43 of the EC Treaty) prohibited the invocation of national legislation regulating the use of an academic qualification, which applied equally to nationals and non-nationals, but which was 'liable to hamper or render less attractive the exercise by Community nationals, including those of the Member States, which enacted the measures, of fundamental freedoms guaranteed by the Treaty'.[37] This market access proposition constituted one of the harmonization rationales that the European legislature invoked in its European Company Law Harmonization Programme. Although national company laws could possibly treat nationals and non-nationals equally, the various differences among them could hamper or render less attractive the exercise by companies of their fundamental right of establishment. For example, in *Centros*, the measure in question was 'liable to hinder or make less attractive the exercise of fundamental freedoms'.[38]

Non-discriminatory restrictions have sometimes been treated as being outside the scope of Article 43 of the EC Treaty (e.g., Case C-182/83 *Robert Feron*,[39] Case C-221/85 *Commission v. Belgium* (*Clinical Biology Services*)[40]), but it is now clear from cases such as *Kraus*,[41] *Gebhard*,[42] and *Centros*[43] that such restrictions may require justification by imperative requirements in the public interest.[44] Such justification was held to exist in *Pfeiffer*,[45] in which a restriction on the right of establishment brought about by an indistinctly applicable provision of national

34. Case C-79/01, *Payroll Data Services* [2002] ECR I-8923 para. 26.
35. C. Barnard (n. 22), 313.
36. Case C-19/92, *Dieter Kraus v. Land Baden-Württemberg* [1993] ECR I-01663.
37. F. Weiss & F. Wooldridge (n. 25), 111.
38. Case C-212/97, *Centros Ltd v. Erhvervs- og Selskabsstyrelsen* [1999] ECR I-01459 para. 30. J. Shaw, J. Hunt & C. Wallace (n. 30), 151.
39. Case 182/83, *Robert Fearon & Company Limited v. Irish Land Commission* [1984] ECR 03677.
40. Case 221/85, *Commission of the European Communities v. Kingdom of Belgium* [1987] ECR 00719.
41. Case C-19/92, *Dieter Kraus v. Land Baden-Württemberg* [1993] ECR I-01663 para. 32.
42. Case C-55/94, *Reinhard Gebhard v. Consiglio dell'Ordine degli Avvocati e Procuratori di Milano*.[1995] ECR I-04165 para. 37. See also Case C-108/98, *MacQueen* [2001] ECR I-837.
43. Case C-212/97, *Centros Ltd v. Erhvervs- og Selskabsstyrelsen* [1999] ECR I-01459 para. 34.
44. F. Weiss & F. Wooldridge (n. 25), 90. In *Commerzbank* (Case C-330/91 [1991] ECR I-4017), it was stipulated that equality of treatment did not include only discrimination on the basis of nationality or on the basis of a company's seat but all covert forms of discrimination applied through differentiated standards and leading to the same result. T. Tridimas, 'The Case-Law of the European Court of Justice on Corporate Entities', *YEL* 13 (1993): 335. S. Fazio (n. 14), 82.
45. Case C-255/97, *Pfeiffer Großhandel GmbH v. Löwa Warenhandel GmbH* [1999] ECR I-02835 para. 21.

law whose aim was to protect trade names against the risk of confusion was held to be so justified.[46] In *Pfeiffer*, the ECJ examined whether a restraining order that prevented an Austrian subsidiary of a German parent company operating discount stores in Austria from using a trade name used by the German parent company in Germany and other Member States is compatible with Article 43 of the EC Treaty. The restriction operates to the detriment of undertakings whose base is in another Member State, where they lawfully use a trade name that they would like to use beyond the boundaries of that State. However, such a restriction on the right of establishment, brought about by a provision of national law whose primary aim is to safeguard trade names against the risk of confusion, is justified by overriding requirements in the general interest pertaining to the protection of industrial and commercial property. No exception can be made under Community law to the protection granted by a national law against the risk of confusion, since it corresponds to the specific subject matter of a trade name, that is, protection of the proprietor of the trade name against that risk. The fact that non-discriminatory restrictions fall within the scope of freedom of establishment is very important for the examination of defensive actions of a company's board of directors and defensive measures embedded in the articles of association of the offeree company as potential non-discriminatory takeover barriers that obstruct the exercise of the fundamental freedom of establishment.

Furthermore, it is relevant here to mention the case of national rules reinforcing barriers to market entry that hinder market access of subsidiaries (and must be justified if they are going to be preserved).[47] In *CaixaBank France*, the ECJ held that Article 43 of the EC Treaty precludes legislation of a Member State that prohibits a credit institution that is a subsidiary of a company from another Member State from remunerating sight accounts in euros opened by residents of the former Member State. That prohibition hinders credit institutions that are subsidiaries of foreign companies in raising capital from the public by depriving them of the possibility of competing more effectively – by paying remuneration on sight accounts – with the credit institutions traditionally established in the Member State of establishment, which have an extensive network of branches and therefore greater opportunities than those subsidiaries for raising capital from the public. Where credit institutions that are subsidiaries of foreign companies seek to enter the market of a Member State, competing by means of the rate of remuneration paid on sight accounts constitutes one of the most effective methods to that end. Access to the market by those establishments is thus made more difficult by such a prohibition.[48] First, this prohibition enhances a barrier to market entry that is constituted by a prohibition to compete efficiently with already established market

46. F. Weiss & F. Wooldridge (n. 25), 87–90. D.A. Wyatt & A. Dashwood, *European Union Law*, 5th edn (London: Thomson Sweet & Maxwell, 2006), 847.
47. D.A. Wyatt & A. Dashwood (n. 46), 848.
48. Case C-442/02, *CaixaBank France v. Ministère de l'Économie, des Finances et de l'Industrie* [2004] ECR I-8961 paras 13–14. E. Spaventa, 'Case Note, Caixa-Bank', *CML Rev.* (2005): 1151–1168.

operators owning an extensive and well-organized network of branches and subsidiaries.[49] Second, this prohibition lessens the available means of competing with established market operators and obstructs access to the market (which should be justified).[50] Thus, freedom of establishment also includes national measures that reinforce obstacles to market access and render market operators unable to compete with other established market operators with strong and well-organized participation in the specific sector of the market.

The fact that the boundary between discriminatory and non-discriminatory measures is blurred results in an additional problematic situation.[51] The ECJ often applies an obstacle-based test rather than one that examines the notion of direct or indirect discrimination, and, as a result, it does not always clearly characterize a measure as discriminatory or not.[52] One example underpinning this argument in the area of establishment of companies is the corporate taxation case of *Marks and Spencer*. In *Marks and Spencer*,[53] the measure could be categorized as directly discriminatory, as different rules applied depending on place of establishment.[54] However, the ECJ proceeded to examine possible justifications for this law and did not refer solely to the justifications set out explicitly in specific Treaty provisions (Article 46 of the EC Treaty).[55]

1.5 POSSIBLE DEROGATIONS

As far as the 'survival' of a restriction is concerned, if there is a restriction on the freedom of establishment, whether or not this restriction could be justified will be examined.[56] Article 45 (participation in the exercise of official authority) and Article 46(1) (public policy, public security, and public health) of the EC Treaty provide the basis for justification of discriminatory measures.[57] However, Article 46 of the EC Treaty is very narrowly worded and is also narrowly interpreted by the ECJ. As a matter of fact, in the majority of cases, it is quite difficult to successfully invoke this article. Besides that, the possibility of justifying an indistinctly applicable restriction that the ECJ developed within *Cassis de Dijon*[58] – although regarding the free movement of goods – is applicable to the freedom of

49. D.A. Wyatt & A. Dashwood (n. 46), 848.
50. D.A. Wyatt & A. Dashwood (n. 46), 848.
51. J. Steiner, L. Woods & C. Twigg-Flesner (n. 21), 458.
52. *Ibid.*
53. Case C-446/03, *Marks & Spencer plc v. David Halsey (Her Majesty's Inspector of Taxes)* [2005] ECR I-10837.
54. J. Steiner, L. Woods & C. Twigg-Flesner (n. 21), 458.
55. *Ibid.*
56. I. Saenger, 'Recent Developments in European Company and Business Law', *Deakin LR* 10 (2005): 297, 302.
57. I. Saenger (n. 56), 302.
58. Case 120/78, *Rewe-Zentral AG v. Bundesmonopolverwaltung fur Branntwein ('Cassis de Dijon')* [1979] ECR 649.

establishment (see *Thieffry*[59]).[60] According to this case law, restrictions on both foreign and domestic citizens can be justified by the 'general good . . . provided that such application is affected without discrimination'.[61] Thus, non-discriminatory measures must be justified by imperative requirements in the general interest, must be suitable for securing the attainment of the objective that they pursue, and must not go beyond what is necessary to attain it (the so-called *Gebhard*[62] test).

1.6 FREEDOM OF ESTABLISHMENT APPLIES ONLY TO CROSS-BORDER SITUATIONS

The protective scope of freedom of establishment includes only cross-border situations. This is very important in cases of cross-border takeovers and mergers. It is in those specific cases that Members and others fall within the protective scope of freedom of establishment. The national takeover laws follow quite divergent models for the protection of Members and others, and the Takeover Bid Directive does not manage to achieve uniformity in the protection of the various interests during cross-border investment activities (because of the opt-in–opt-out/reciprocity system, which will be examined below). Hence, the fundamental freedom of establishment could still play a very important protective role in this harmonized part of the internal market. The relevant case law of the ECJ is quite interesting. In *Nino*,[63] the ECJ held that the provisions of the Treaty on freedom of establishment do not apply to purely internal situations in a Member State, such as in a situation in which nationals of a Member State engage within its territory in a self-employed professional activity with respect to which they cannot rely on any previous training or experience in another Member State.[64] As the ECJ stated in its judgment in *Bekaert*, the absence of any element going beyond a purely national setting in a given case means, in matters of freedom of establishment, that the provisions of Community law are not applicable to such a situation.[65] Nonetheless, the requirement of a cross-border element seems quite easy to satisfy. This can occur when an individual moves or when a company moves, or sets up a branch, agency, or subsidiary in another Member State. Establishment rights may be exercised against both the home and the host Member State. In *Marks and Spencer*,[66] at issue was

59. Case 71/76, *Jean Thieffry v. Conseil de l'ordre des avocats à la cour de Paris* [1977] ECR 765.
60. I. Saenger (n. 56), 302. E.I. Kaldellis, 'Freedom of Establishment versus Freedom to Provide Services: An Evaluation of Case-Law Developments in the Area of Indistinctly Applicable Rules', *LIEI* 28 (2001): 23, 46.
61. I. Saenger (n. 56), 302.
62. Case C-55/94, *Gebhard* [1995] ECR I-4165 para. 37.
63. Joined cases C-54/88, C-91/88, and C-14/89, *Criminal Proceedings against Eleonora Nino and Others* [1990] ECR I-03537.
64. J. Steiner, L. Woods & C. Twigg-Flesner (n. 21), 450.
65. Case 204/87, *Bekaert* [1988] ECR 2029, Joined cases C-54/88, C-91/88, and C-14/89, *Criminal Proceedings against Eleonora Nino and Others* [1990] ECR I-03537 para. 11.
66. Case C-446/03, *Marks & Spencer plc v. David Halsey (Her Majesty's Inspector of Taxes)* [2005] ECR I-10837.

that British tax legislation did not permit a parent company to deduct losses suffered by its subsidiaries in other Member States, though it could deduct losses made by British subsidiaries. The effect of this rule was to discourage companies established in the UK from establishing subsidiaries (secondary establishments in general) in other Member States. The cross-border element in that case was provided by the impact on a company's choices about whether to set up subsidiaries in other Member States.[67] The discouragement, the limitation of choices, and the sole restriction of the possibility of establishing a secondary establishment of a company in another Member State could satisfy the cross-border criterion. A cross-border takeover bid definitely constitutes a situation fulfilling this cross-border criterion. The aim of a takeover bid is the acquisition of control of an offeree company, which becomes very frequently a subsidiary of the offeror company. Thus, the impact on the offeror company's choices about whether to set up subsidiaries in other Member States by taking them over satisfies the requirement of a cross-border element.

1.7 A FEW CLOSING REMARKS

The right of establishment is granted to natural and legal persons, and, subject to relevant exceptions, it allows all types of self-employed activity to be taken up and pursued on the territory of any other Member State, undertakings to be formed and operated, and agencies, branches, and subsidiaries to be set up.[68] It follows that a person may be established, within the meaning of the Treaty, in more than one Member State – in particular, in the case of companies by the setting up of agencies, branches, or subsidiaries, and in the case of the members of professions by establishing second professional bases.[69] The abolition of national laws constituting restrictions on freedom of establishment also applies to restrictions on the setting up of agencies, branches, or subsidiaries by natural or legal persons of any Member State established in the territory of any other Member State.[70] In addition to that, the ECJ in *Thieffry* held that, under Article 3(c) of the EC Treaty, the activities of the Community include, *inter alia*, the abolition of obstacles to freedom of movement for persons and services.[71]

67. J. Steiner, L. Woods & C. Twigg-Flesner (n. 21), 450. Other cases discussing the cross-border character of freedom of establishment: Case C-134/95, *Unità Socio-Sanitaria Locale n° 47 di Biella (USSL)* [1997] ECR I-195 para. 19; Case C-108/98, *RI.SAN. Srl* [1999] ECR I-5219 para. 23; Case 71/76, *Jean Thieffry v. Conseil de l'ordre des avocats à la cour de Paris* [1977] ECR 765 para. 27; Case C-19/92, *Dieter Kraus v. Land Baden-Württemberg* [1993] ECR I-01663 paras 15–16; Case 115/78, *J. Knoors v. Secretary of State for Economic Affairs* [1979] ECR-399 paras 20–24.
68. D.A. Wyatt & A. Dashwood (n. 46), 750.
69. *Ibid.*, 751.
70. Case 270/83, *Commission of the European Communities v. French Republic* [1986] ECR 273 para. 13.
71. Case 71/76, *Jean Thieffry v. Conseil de l'ordre des avocats à la cour de Paris* [1977] ECR 765 para. 78.

The *Gebhard*[72] case law is crucial in defining the scope of this fundamental freedom.[73] The concept of establishment within the meaning of the Treaty is a very broad one, allowing a Community national to participate, on a stable and continuous basis, in the economic life of a Member State other than his or her State of origin and to profit therefrom, thus contributing to economic and social interpenetration within the Community, in the sphere of activities of self-employed persons.[74] The Court has held that an undertaking of one Member State that maintains a permanent presence in another is covered by the provisions on establishment 'even though presence does not take the form of a branch or agency, but consists merely of an office managed by the undertaking's own staff or by a person who is independent but authorized to act on a permanent basis for the undertaking as would be the case with an agency'.[75] Although the primary objective of these provisions is to guarantee the right of establishment to foreign nationals and companies in, as well as their equal treatment with the nationals of, the host Member State, they also prohibit the Member State of origin from hindering the establishment in another Member State of its own nationals and companies, for example, by preventing them from leaving the national territory so as to establish themselves elsewhere[76] or by applying unfavourable tax measures that discourage them from setting up primary or secondary establishments in another Member State.[77]

The scope of Article 43 of the EC Treaty is quite broad and covers many different areas, from pure economic activities, such as liberal professions, to personal situations, such as family rights of residence.[78] Company law is a distinctive part of the regulatory scope of the fundamental freedom of establishment because of both the special national nature of company laws and the way in which companies or groups of companies can reside in more than one Member State at a time.[79] These special features should be taken into account by the European legislature and by the ECJ when they are dealing with a situation involving the freedom of establishment of companies.

72. Case C-55/94, *Reinhard Gebhard v. Consiglio dell'Ordine degli Avvocati e Procuratori di Milano* [1995] ECR I-04165.
73. Case C-55/94, *Reinhard Gebhard v. Consiglio dell' Ordine degli Avvocati e Procuratori di Milano* [1995] ECR I-4165 paras 23, 24, 25.
74. D.A. Wyatt & A. Dashwood (n. 46), 751.
75. Case 205/84, *Commission v. Germany* [1986] ECR 3801 para. 21.
76. Case 81/87 *Daily Mail* [1988] ECR 5483, 5510.
77. Case C-264/96 *ICI* [1998] ECR I-4695 and Case C-251/98 *Baars* [200] ECR I-2787.
78. J. Steiner, L. Woods & C. Twigg-Flesner (n. 21) 466.
79. J. Steiner, L. Woods & C. Twigg-Flesner (n. 21) 466.

Chapter 2

Legal Bases for the Harmonization of Company Law and Capital Market Law at the EU Level

2.1 INTRODUCTION

This chapter will discuss the available legal bases for the harmonization of company law and capital market law at the EU level. It will also analyse briefly the ECJ's case law on community competence to regulate certain parts of the internal market. This is necessary so as to understand the foundations of this harmonizing instrument and to see how the European legislature perceives and uses the available legal bases.

2.2 HARMONIZING COMPANY LAW AND CAPITAL MARKET LAW: PRELIMINARY ISSUES

Two basic premises underpin the harmonization of company law in the European Union (EU). The first premise stresses the significance of companies as the most important economic actors of the Community, playing a crucial role in cross-border investments and other entrepreneurial activities.[80] The second premise is based on the existence of a strong link between the harmonization of company law and securities regulation, and the progress of market integration as proclaimed by the EC Treaty.[81]

80. R. Buxbaum & K. Hopt, *Legal Harmonization and the Business Enterprise* (Berlin: Integration through Law Series, de Gruyter, 1988), 167.
81. R. Buxbaum & K. Hopt (n. 80), 167.

Company law regulates 'companies' that is, unions or associations of persons for carrying on commercial or industrial enterprises, while capital market law or securities regulation addresses the market for long-term investment funds.[82] The function of capital market law has been viewed as (1) protecting investors, (2) increasing market efficiency, (3) completing the organization of the market 'firms', (4) capturing wealth for some members of the industry, and (5) affecting competition in the industry.[83] The main use of capital markets is to secure financing for companies through equity or bonds. With regard to the scope of these two areas of law, their distinction[84] is blurred by the development of the law of listed companies, a law that is a mixture of traditional company law and traditional capital markets law.[85] The adoption of legislation specifically addressing listed companies, and incorporated into capital market law, shows that capital market law can play an important role in many of the aspects of the regulation of listed companies (e.g., listing standards, disclosure and structure of governance, accounting, auditing, prospectus and proxy rules etc.).[86] Ideas and concepts that have been cultivated in the field of capital market law exercise an influence on company law. One characteristic example is the notion of legal capital deriving from company law; capital market law challenges the effectiveness of this notion and argues that equivalent protection could be provided by transparency and the conduct of business rules.[87] Company law harmonization should also take into account the needs of the capital markets[88] and should not be confined only to company law considerations. It could be argued that the harmonization of company law could enhance capital markets' security, transparency,[89] and efficiency because divergent[90] national company law standards (e.g., special classes of publicly traded securities and information asymmetries) have a negative influence on capital

82. H.C. Black, *Black's Law Dictionary*, 5th edn (St. Paul, Minn.: West Publishing Co, 1979), 190, 255. P.L. Davies, *Gower and Davies' Principles of Modern Company Law*, 7th edn (London: Sweet & Maxwell, 2003), 3.
83. E. Kitch, 'Regulation of the Securities Market', in *Encyclopedia of Law & Economics*, ed. B. Bouckaert & G. De Geest (London: Elgar and the University of Ghent, 1999), 813.
84. The contrast between the company law and the capital market law approaches raises the most important questions in the area of the choice of the relationship that is to be regulated, because this choice will determine the definition of basic concepts (e.g., those of 'insider' and 'inside information' in insider dealing laws). P.L. Davies, 'The European Community's Directive on Insider Dealing: From Company Law to Securities Markets Regulation?', *OJLS* (1991): 92, 93.
85. J. Garrido-Garcia, 'Company Law and Capital Markets Law', *RabelsZ* (2005): 761, 776.
86. J. Garrido-Garcia (n. 85), 777.
87. E. Wymeersch, 'European Company Law and Corporate Governance: Quo Vadis?', *RabelZ* (2005): 789.
88. See also J. Heiser, 'Can Capital Market Law Approaches Be Harmonized with Essential Principles of Company Law?', *EBLR* (2000): 60–82.
89. For the influence of transparency requirements on company law: W. Ebke, 'The Impact of Transparency Regulation on Company Law', in *Capital Markets and Company Law*, ed. K. Hopt & E. Wymeersch (Oxford: Oxford University Press, 2003), 173.
90. I.H.Y. Chiu, *Regulatory Convergence in EU Securities Regulation* (Alphen aan den Rijn: Kluwer Law International, 2008), 185.

markets' transparency.[91] In countries where capital markets are efficient, company law can be less intrusive, relying on markets to exert pressure on market participants and leaving more room for parties to conclude their own arrangements. If capital markets are ineffective, company law has to cope with these problems and the legislature will adopt more mandatory standards.[92] Therefore, there is a potential overlap between the scopes of these two fields of law.

In modern industrialized societies, the company, in a solitary form or as group of interconnected and dependent undertakings, has become the main vehicle of economic organization.[93] Companies are considered to be the central mode for the conduct of business because, apart from being the major traders of goods, they are the major borrowers and lenders of capital flowing between and among countries and the principal conveyors of new technology. Consolidated groups of companies constituted by companies based in different Member States play a crucial role in corporate restructuring and in market integration. Thus, the particular concern of the Community for the regulation of companies is justified.[94] The power of the European legislature to adopt a legislative measure lies in a specific legal basis in the EC Treaty The European legislature is bound to select the most appropriate legal basis for the legislative measures that it plans to adopt; otherwise, if the legislative measure had an incorrect legal basis, there would be a violation of the principle of attributed competence (Article 5 of the EC Treaty),[95] which could be brought before the European Court of Justice. The choice of legal basis will also determine the legislative process that will be followed.[96] The EC Treaty basis for the company law harmonization programme is Article 44(2)(g). The regulatory goal of this provision is provided by Article 44(1) of the EC Treaty and is the attainment of freedom of establishment. Any harmonizing legislation in the field of company law must eliminate obstacles to cross-frontier business activities, mobility, expansion, and investment, and/or it must eliminate appreciable distortions of competition.[97] Additionally, the high degree of competitiveness of EU businesses

---

91. E. Wymeersch, 'About Techniques of Regulating Companies in the EU', in *Reforming Company and Takeover Law in Europe*, ed. G. Ferrarini et al. (Oxford: Oxford University Press, 2004), 158, 173. See also G. Ferrarini, 'Introduction' and R. Dale, 'The Regulation of Investment Firms in the European Union', in *Prudential Regulation of Banks and Securities Firms*, ed. G. Ferrarini (London: Kluwer Law International, 1995), 10, 27.
92. Z. Goshen, 'The Impact of Insider Trading Rules on Company Law', in *Capital Markets and Company Law*, ed. K. Hopt & E. Wymeersch (Oxford: Oxford University Press, 2003), 566.
93. C.M. Schmitthoff, 'The Future of the European Company Law Scene', in *The Harmonization of European Company Law*, ed. C.M. Schmitthoff (London: UKNCCL, 1973), 6–7.
94. E. Stein (n. 21), 23.
95. D.A. Wyatt & A. Dashwood (n. 46), 85.
96. V. Edwards, *EC Company Law* (Oxford: Oxford EC Law Library, Oxford Clarendon Press, 1999), 4. D.A. Wyatt & A. Dashwood (n. 46), 55, 938.
97. Case C-376/98, *Germany v. Council and European Parliament* (Tobacco Advertising ruling) [2000] ECR I-8419. D.A. Wyatt & A. Dashwood (n. 46), 864. The way the aims of market integration are incorporated into the company law directives and are understood by the Community institutions is criticized in R. Buxbaum, G. Hertig, et al. (eds), *European Business Law* (Berlin-New York: de Gruyter, 1991), 131.

and the market proclaimed by Article 2 of the EC Treaty as one of the primary tasks of the Community shall also be pursued by the harmonizing measures, which have to try to reduce the transaction costs involved in cross-border business activity.[98]

Articles 94 and 95 of the EC Treaty have never been invoked in company law directives. Apart from the general legal bases providing the competence to harmonize internal market law in general (Articles 94 and 95 of the EC Treaty), the EC treaty does not deal with company law as such, but rather approaches the position of companies in terms of freedom of establishment in a cross-border framework.[99] Hence, the legal basis for the harmonization of freedom of establishment of companies is found in Article 44(2)(g) (Title III: Free movement of persons, services and capital, Chapter 2: Right of establishment), which requires qualified majority[100] voting in the European Council in accordance with the legislative process of Article 251 of the EC Treaty. It should also be mentioned that the initial Article 47(2) (as it appeared in the original European Economic Community (EEC) Treaty), providing for the harmonization of the taking up and pursuit of activities as self-employed persons, required unanimity. This potential legal basis would add more difficulties in the initial stages of the harmonization process in comparison with Article 44(2)(g), requiring a qualified majority and constituting a more specific legal basis. Article 95 of the EC Treaty, requiring a qualifying majority, operates by way of derogation from Article 94 of the EC Treaty, which enables the Council, acting unanimously, to issue directives for the approximation of national provisions directly affecting the establishment or functioning of the common market. Article 94 of the EC Treaty has been left with a residual role and is available in cases expressly excluded by the second paragraph of Article 95 of the EC Treaty from the scope of that latter Article.[101] Free movement of persons

98. D.A. Wyatt & A. Dashwood (n. 46), 864.

99. E. Wymeersch (n. 91), 161. It should be noted that the founding Member States did not include a specific legal basis for the harmonization of company law only as an instrument to facilitate market integration but also as a political compromise for their agreement to confer the right of establishment on companies because they were afraid that the fairly liberal and lax company law of The Netherlands would attract many companies and would become the 'Delaware of Europe'. R. Buxbaum, G. Hertig, et al. (eds) (n. 97), 132.

100. E. Stein (n. 21), 175. Article 54(3)(g) (now Art. 44(2)(g)) EC Treaty required directives to be adopted by a unanimous vote in the Council until the end of the first stage of the transitional period of the Community's harmonization programme, but they may be adopted subsequently by a qualified majority. C. Villiers, 'Harmonization of Company Laws in Europe: With an Introduction to some Comparative Issues', in *European Business Law*, ed. G. Howells (Aldershot: Dartmouth, 1996), 171. E. Stein (n. 21), 24–25.

101. D.A. Wyatt & A. Dashwood (n. 46), 929. The Commission abandoned its idea to invoke both Arts 44(2)(g) and 94 EC Treaty as the legal bases for company law directives (such as the Eleventh Directive) applying also to companies incorporated in a non-Member State but having an establishment within the Community. The Community considers Art. 44(2)(g) EC Treaty as a sufficient legal basis for these cases. R. Buxbaum, G. Hertig, et al. (eds) (n. 97), 144. The debate on democracy both at the EU level and at the company level is quite important in the legislative process of market integration. At the EU level, democracy should be representative, and at the company level, democracy should be participative. C. Villiers examines the extent to which the harmonization of company law has changed the structure

(and, as a consequence, the freedom of establishment of companies) is among those fields that fall outside the harmonizing scope of Article 95 of the EC Treaty. Those qualifications of the second paragraph of Article 95 of the EC Treaty were probably inserted so as to alleviate the concerns of Member States about the adoption of harmonization measures by a qualified majority and the possibility of being outvoted in the Council.[102] Additionally, Article 95 of the EC Treaty itself constitutes a residual provision because it applies 'save where otherwise provided in this Treaty'. This means that wherever there is a specific legal basis for the harmonization of a specific part of the internal market, such as Article 44(2)(g) of the EC Treaty and the freedom of establishment of companies, Article 95 of the EC Treaty should not be used as a legal basis for the harmonizing measures.[103]

In the area of securities regulation, one can encounter various situations: Article 95 of the EC Treaty constitutes an often invoked legal basis, along with Article 44(2)(g) of the EC Treaty, because those specific directives cover not only companies formed in accordance with a national company law (Article 48 of the EC Treaty), but also, companies established in third countries that issue securities on the capital markets of one or several Member States or that pursue listing on capital markets established in Member States.[104] However, other EC Treaty Articles have also been invoked: Article 47 for the Undertakings for Collective Investments in Transferable Securities (UCITS) Directive,[105,106] Article 94, and, in the

---

(internal and external corporate governance of corporations) and whether or not it has created greater opportunities for participatory democracy within those business structures. C. Villiers, *European Company Law: Towards Democracy?* (Aldershot: Ashgate, 1998), 1, 6. It is also argued that Art. 95 EC Treaty is a *lex specialis* of Art. 94 EC Treaty and also a *lex specialis* of Art. 308 EC Treaty. (Case 45/86, *Commission v. Council* [1987] ECR 1493 para. 13). As a matter of fact, Art. 95 EC Treaty is *lex generalis* of some other Treaty articles (Case 84/94, *United Kingdom v. Council* [1996] ECR 5755 para. 12 and Case 202/88, *France v. Commission* [1991] ECR 1223 para. 25). P. Craig & G. De Burca (n. 12), 1119. A. Knook, 'Guns and Tobacco: The Effect of Interstate Trade Case Law on the Vertical Division of Powers', *MJ* 11 (2004): 347, 348.

102. D.A. Wyatt & A. Dashwood (n. 46), 930. R. Buxbaum, G. Hertig, et al. (eds) (n. 97), 143.
103. D.A. Wyatt & A. Dashwood (n. 46), 929.
104. G. Wolff, 'The Commission's Programme for Company Law Harmonisation: The Winding Road to a Uniform European Company Law?', in *E.C. Financial Market Regulation and Company Law*, ed. S. Kenyon-Slade & M. Andenas (London: Sweet & Maxwell, 1993), 20.
105. Council Directive 85/611/EEC of 20 Dec. 1985 on the coordination of laws, regulations and administrative provisions relating to undertakings for collective investment in transferable securities (UCITS) [1985] OJ L375/3-18.
106. E. Wymeersch, 'Company Law in Europe and European Company Law', University of Ghent, Financial Law Institute Working Papers (2001) 3 and 14–15. E. Wymeersch proceeds to a theoretical analysis and comparison between Art. 44(2)(g) and Arts 94 and 95 EC Treaty as a potential basis for company law harmonization. Insofar as the European legislature had chosen only Art. 44(2)(g) EC Treaty as the legal basis for company law harmonization, this discussion and the comparison between potential legal bases is interesting only from an EU market governance and efficient market-making perspective. Additionally, the argument that Community can adopt directives based on Art. 94 or 95 EC Treaty regulating almost the areas of company law and corporate governance could be strictly scrutinized under the principle of attributed competence and the principle of subsidiarity (Art. 5 EC Treaty) as developed by the

case of the Insider Dealing Directive, Article 95 have been used in some cases as an additional or alternative legal basis for the Directives in the area of securities regulation.[107] These legal bases are capable of producing a harmonized capital-raising regime that is designed to promote the development of a common capital market by boosting investor confidence in capital markets and by removing any regulatory obstacles.[108] Legal diversity in the area of securities regulation amounts to non-tariff barriers with high costs, inhibiting market access. Competition is appreciably distorted and a level playing field cannot be established. Moreover, investor confidence fosters cross-border investment and market integration.[109] An integrated securities market, within which markets are easily accessed by investment services providers, investors, and issuers, could strengthen European capital markets.[110] Since investor protection is a clear objective of all the securities Directives and since it is clear from the Preamble to all these Directives that market integration is a direct and specific aim, there is little room for doubt as to the appropriateness of their legal basis, leading to no objections to the choice of legal basis for capital market Directives.[111]

2.3 ARTICLE 43 AND ARTICLE 44(2)(g) OF THE EC TREATY

Article 43 of the EC Treaty defines freedom of establishment,[112] which is available not only to natural persons, but also, to legal persons and especially companies

ECJ's case law (for an analysis of this case law see: D.A. Wyatt, 'Community Competence to Regulate the Internal Market' Oxford Legal Studies Research Paper No. 9/2007). <http://ssrn.com/abstract=997863>, accessed 21 Aug. 2008 [also published in M. Dougan & S. Currie (eds), *50 Years of the European Treaties, Looking Back and Thinking Forward* (Oxford: Hart, 2009), 93–136.

107. V. Edwards (n. 96), 4. In general, Art. 94 EC Treaty has been used frequently as a legal basis for securities law, worker participation measures, banking regulation, insurance law, and taxation rather than mainstream company law. C. Villiers (n. 101), 18.
108. N. Moloney, *EC Securities Regulation* (Oxford: Oxford EC Law Library, Oxford University Press, 2002), 66.
109. This internal market orientation had affected significantly the substance of the harmonization of capital markets. The place of investor protection rationale in this harmonizing agenda is still discussed in a very interesting constitutional debate, N. Moloney (n. 108), 7, 9. Most of the concerns about the investor confidence rationale are related to Art. 5 EC Treaty (in accordance to *Tobacco Advertising* case law that will be discussed extensively in the chapter on subsidiarity). N. Moloney, 'Confidence and Competence: The Conundrum of EC Capital Markets Law', *JCLS* 1 (2004): 1, 46. N. Moloney, 'New Frontiers in EC Capital Markets Law: From Market Construction to Market Regulation', *CML Rev.* (2003): 809, 812, 833–840.
110. N. Moloney (n. 108), 6–7.
111. V. Edwards (n. 96), 4–5.
112. I. Saenger distinguishes between the factual and the personal scope of the protection that the fundamental freedom of establishment provides. Within the factual scope of protection, it has to be clarified whether the affected activity is indeed an act of free movement. As far the personal scope of the protection is concerned, as a result of Art. 48(1) EC Treaty, the freedom

(Article 43(2) of the EC Treaty). Moreover, the harmonization programme of the freedom of establishment of companies is based on Article 44(2)(g) of the EC Treaty. Article 48 of the EC Treaty provides a definition for companies or firms, which also enjoy freedom of establishment. There is also Article 293 of the EC Treaty, which urges Member States to reach an international agreement on mutual recognition of companies and entities that have legal personalities. We should always keep in mind that the main purpose of harmonization in the area of company law is the realization of an internal market as proclaimed by Article 3(c) and (h) of the EC Treaty.

The EC Treaty Articles dealing with freedom of establishment and, more specifically, with freedom of establishment of companies, are the following:

> Article 43 (EC Treaty)
>
> Within the framework of the provisions set out below, restrictions on the freedom of establishment of nationals of a Member State in the territory of another Member State shall be prohibited. Such prohibition shall also apply to restrictions on the setting-up of agencies, branches or subsidiaries by nationals of any Member State established in the territory of any Member State.
>
> Freedom of establishment shall include the right to take up and pursue activities as self-employed persons and to set up and manage undertakings, in particular companies or firms within the meaning of the second paragraph of Article 48, under the conditions laid down for its own nationals by the law of the country where such establishment is effected, subject to the provisions of the chapter relating to capital.

> Article 44 (EC Treaty)
>
> 1. In order to attain freedom of establishment as regards a particular activity, the Council, acting in accordance with the procedure referred to in Article 251 and after consulting the Economic and Social Committee, shall act by means of directives.
>
> 2. The Council and the Commission shall carry out the duties devolving upon them under the preceding provisions, in particular:
>
> . . . (g) by coordinating to the necessary extent the safeguards which, for the protection of the interests of members and others, are required by Member States of companies or firms within the meaning of the second paragraph of Article 48 with a view to making such safeguards equivalent throughout the Community . . .

> Article 48 (EC Treaty)
>
> Companies or firms formed in accordance with the law of a Member State and having their registered office, central administration or principal place of

---

of establishment should be applicable to companies that comply with Art. 48(2) EC Treaty. I. Saenger (n. 56), 299.

> business within the Community shall, for the purposes of this Chapter, be treated in the same way as natural persons who are nationals of Member States.
>
> 'Companies or firms' means companies or firms constituted under civil or commercial law, including cooperative societies, and other legal persons governed by public or private law, save for those which are non-profit-making.

As far as the scope of Article 44(2)(g) of the EC Treaty is concerned, two views on this issue were developed: a broad view and a narrow one. On one hand, the restrictive view requires harmonization measures only when harmonization is going to abolish a specific discriminatory national law or practice that inhibits companies established in other Member States from exercising their right of establishment by providing equivalent specific safeguards for the protection of the interests of company members and/or others.[113] Taking into account the scope of the restrictive view, it seems that directives seeking in more general terms to harmonize specific parts of company law and corporate governance would not be permitted.[114] On the other hand, the broader view stresses the importance of the existence of a particular legal basis for company law harmonization. Article 43 of the EC Treaty requires a host State to treat equally both members and others of a foreign company exercising its right of establishment in the host Member State and members and others of a company registered originally in the host State.[115] It is easily understood that the majority of areas of company law are open and available for harmonization by the European legislature.[116] Of course, this would not be a viable project for the European legislature, and more moderate approaches should be followed. The evolution of the harmonization of company law and EU Law shows that the restrictive approach did not prevail. Eleven Directives regulating very different parts of company law and corporate governance were adopted and implemented on the basis of Article 44(2)(g).[117] It is obvious that the European Commission envisaged harmonization as a means of promoting more intensively cross-border business activity and of boosting the competitiveness of European enterprises. This approach derived from the fact that the legal basis for company law harmonization was located in the chapter on freedom of establishment. Yet, not all Member States were satisfied with this approach towards company law harmonization because they realized that some of their company law doctrines were under attack.[118] However, this broader view should always be scrutinized by the principles of attributed competence and of subsidiarity, as has been constructed by the ECJ's case law.

113. V. Edwards (n. 96), 6–7. R. Buxbaum & K. Hopt (n. 80), 204.
114. V. Edwards (n. 96), 6–7. Corporate governance is a notion evolved from commercial law through business law and commercial regulation. L. Nottage, 'Commercial Regulation', in *Elgar Encyclopedia of Comparative Law*, ed. J.M Smits (Cheltenham: Elgar, 2008), 135–144.
115. V. Edwards (n. 96), 7.
116. V. Edwards (n. 96), 7. R. Buxbaum & K. Hopt (n. 80), 205.
117. V. Edwards (n. 96) 6–7. R. Buxbaum & K. Hopt (n. 80), 204–205.
118. D.A. Wyatt & A. Dashwood (n. 46), 885.

Although the harmonization of company law is not a self-standing objective and requires the existence of a link between the adopted legislation and the fundamental freedom of establishment, that goal calls for a wide and flexible interpretation in accordance with the general approach of the ECJ over the last five decades to the construction of Treaty Articles.[119] In *Saldanha and MTS Securities Corporation,*[120] the ECJ stated that:

> Article 44(2)(g) EC Treaty empowers the Council and the Commission, for the purpose of *giving effect to the freedom of establishment*, to coordinate to the necessary extent the safeguards which, for the protection of the interests of members and others, are required by Member States of companies or firms within the meaning of the second paragraph of Article 48 of the EC Treaty with a view to making such safeguards equivalent throughout the Community. *It follows that rules which, in the area of company law, seek to protect the interests of shareholders come within the scope of the Treaty and are for that reason subject to the prohibition of all discrimination based on nationality.* (emphasis added).

While Article 44(2)(g) of the EC Treaty refers to 'coordinating' certain areas of company law, other terms are used in other legal bases of the EC Treaty, such as 'approximation' and 'harmonization' of laws.[121] Scrutiny of the EC Treaty supports the common-sense view that no differences exist among these three terms; the Treaty adopts the same content for these terms.[122] The major component of this content is the avoidance of complete unification of national laws. That conclusion is confirmed by the objective described in Article 44(2)(g) of the EC Treaty: 'with a view to making such safeguards equivalent' rather than identical or uniform.[123]

---

119. V. Edwards (n. 96), 7.
120. Case C-122/96, *Stephen Austin Saldanha and MTS Securities Corporation v. Hiross Holding AG* [1997] ECR I-05325.
121. V. Edwards (n. 96), 8.
122. *Ibid.*
123. V. Edwards (n. 96), 8. Cl. Lempereur, 'Myth and Reality in the European Harmonization Process', in *Further Perspectives in Financial Integration in Europe,* ed. E. Wymeersch (Berlin-New York: de Gruyter, 1994), 242. S. Fazio (n. 14), 92. C. Villiers (n. 100), 176–177, C.M. Schmitthoff, 'The Future of the European Company Law Scene'. H.C. Ficker, 'The EEC Directives on Company Law Harmonization', in *The Harmonization of European Company Law,* ed. C.M. Schmitthoff (London: UKNCCL, 1973), 6–7, 67–70. Common rules at the EU level are not only difficult to attain, but they are also considered to be undesirable as contrary to competitive legal and cultural diversity. Harmonization could be 'modernized' and not be characterized as competitive and negative to minority preference and legal diversity. This is related to the debate about the tension between centralization and respect for local autonomy at the EU level. S. Weatherill, 'Why Harmonize?', in *European Union Law for the Twenty-First Century,* ed. T. Tridimas & P. Nebbia (Portland: Hart, 2004), 11–12. Approximation differs from unification. Approximation of laws has the conferred function to bring about adjustment in national company legislations where they obstruct the process of market integration. E. Stein, *Harmonization of European Company Laws* (Indianapolis: Merrill, 1971), 23. There are some academics supporting the idea of uniformity in EU Company Law drawing arguments from the American experience of differences among states' company laws. It was argued that uniform company law, in the sense of company law systems that are

However, in some areas of company law (some of them rather technical ones), unification is the only way forward and coincides with the meaning of harmonization. In parts of company law, in practice, only unification will result in equivalence by imposing a uniform rule that is valid throughout the EU (e.g., mandatory disclosure in favour of third parties).[124] This 'disguised' unification available through harmonization is mainly found in technical aspects of company law, such as disclosure of information, accounting provisions, auditing regulations, etc.

The original EEC Treaty demanded the abolition of various barriers to freedom of establishment in progressive stages during the transitional period. The required secondary legislation on the abolition of restrictions was to be preceded by a General Programme.[125] In *Thieffry*, the ECJ characterized the General Programme on the abolition of restrictions on freedom of establishment,[126] adopted on 18 December 1961, as a mean providing 'useful guidance for the implementation of the relevant provisions of the Treaty'.[127] The main purpose of the 1961 Programme was to set certain minimum requirements so as to promote the freedom of establishment at a cross-border level.[128] Among the beneficiaries of

---

interchangeable and in line with one another, is a practical condition for the exercise of the right of establishment. It was alleged that only unification of company law could result in an efficient regulatory competition as is the case in the US. The European political efforts of the last forty years, the case law of the ECJ, and economic globalization will urge companies in Europe to grow increasingly closer to one another, to become more interchangeable, and to exercise more efficiently the freedom of establishment. However, it is admitted that the Commission's 2003 Company Law Action Plan does not aim at uniformity but at encouraging cross-border cooperation and freedom of establishment. M.J. Kroeze & H.M. Vletter-Van Dort, 'History and Future of Uniform Company Law in Europe', *ECL* 5 (2008): 114, 120–121, K. Hopt, 'Modern Company Law Problems: A European Perspective. Keynote Speech' given at the Conference on Company Law Reform in OECD Countries: A Comparative Outlook of Current Trends (Stockholm, December 2000) 9, 12–13.

124. V. Edwards (n. 96), 8. M. Lutter declared that future company law should not be purely national, nor exclusively European, but is to be conceived as a system with continuing roots in the national traditions and realities, but characterized by largely uniform structure all over Europe (as translated and cited by E. Wymeersch). M. Lutter, 'Perspektiven eines Europaischen Unternehmensrechtes-Versuch eines Summe', *ZGR* (1992): 450, E. Wymeersch, 'The Regulation of Takeover Bids in a Comparative Perspective', in *European Economic and Business Law*, ed. R. Buxbaum, et al. (Berlin-New York: de Gruyter, 1996), 322. M.J.G.C. Raaijmakers, 'Which Way with Company Law Harmonization?', in *Further Perspectives in Financial Integration in Europe*, ed. E. Wymeersch (Berlin-New York: de Gruyter, 1994), 239.
125. D.A. Wyatt & A. Dashwood (n. 46), 763.
126. General Programme for the Abolition of Restrictions on Freedom of Establishment [1962] OJ 2/36–45 and English spec. edn: series II vol. IX/7-15.
127. Case 71/76, *Jean Thieffry v. Conseil de l'ordre des avocats à la cour de Paris* [1977] ECR 765 I.G.F. Cath (n. 2), 453. Other cases referring to the General Programme: Case 182/83, *Robert Fearon & Company Limited v. Irish Land Commission.* [1984] ECR 3677; Case 136/78 *Criminal Proceedings against Vincent Auer* [1979] ECR 437; Case 107/83, *Ordre des avocats au Barreau de Paris v. Onno Klopp* [1984] ECR 2971. D.A. Wyatt & A. Dashwood (n. 46), 764.
128. I.G.F. Cath (n. 2), 453. This programmatic fixation of legislative goals should not undermine the dynamic character of the Community's harmonizing measures and should not neglect the importance of the facts of specific situations. It seems that the 2003 Company Law Action Plans takes into account those considerations. R. Buxbaum & K. Hopt (n. 80), 208.

freedom of establishment, there were also companies, provided that, 'where only the seat prescribed by their statutes is situated within the Community, their activity shows a real and continuous link with the economy of a Member State'. It was further explained that such a link is not permitted to be 'one of nationality, whether of the members of the company or firm, or of the persons holding managerial or supervisory posts therein, or of the holders of the capital, who wish to set up agencies, branches or subsidiaries in a Member State'. If this requirement is met, then Community law prohibits any formal or informal, direct or indirect, difference in treatment between national legal entities and foreign legal entities that have established themselves cross-border on a secondary basis, or any kind of barrier capable of obstructing their access to the market of the host Member State.[129] Title III of the General Programme required the abolition of discriminatory measures that might impair access to the non-wage-earning activities of nationals of the Member States.[130] In addition, Title III of the 1961 Programme provides a long and non-exhaustive list of examples of express or implied 'restrictions' on the freedom of secondary establishments, such as restrictions on access to economic activities in general; licensing or specific document requirements; imposition of specific conditions; prior practical training requirements; financial impediments, such as specific fiscal or other charges; guarantees or security; access to professional training; participation rights in legal entities; compensation in the social security system; different treatment in the event of expropriation, agreements to be concluded, public procurement, administrative concessions, or licenses, purchase, sale, or use of assets and intellectual property rights; loans, State aid; procedural rights; and membership in professional associations.[131] It is quite interesting for EU company law that Title III of the General Programme called for the abolition of national provisions barring or limiting membership in companies, particularly with regard to the activities of their members.[132] The subject matter of takeover bids is closely related to the following restrictions that this Programme tried to abolish: restrictions on access to economic activities in general, financial impediments such as specific fiscal or other charges, and especially the participation rights in legal entities and the purchase, sale, or use of assets. Furthermore, a generic statement of the Preamble of Council Directive 64/225/EEC on the abolition of restrictions on freedom of establishment and freedom to provide services with respect to re-insurance and retrocession[133] is very

129. I.G.F. Cath (n. 2), 453.
130. D.A. Wyatt & A. Dashwood (n. 46), 764.
131. I.G.F. Cath (n. 2), 453.
132. D.A. Wyatt & A. Dashwood (n. 46) 764.
133. Council Directive 64/225/EEC of 25 Feb. 1964 on the abolition of restrictions on freedom of establishment and freedom to provide services in respect of reinsurance and retrocession [1964] OJ 56/878-883. A. McGee, 'The Single Market in Insurance: Breaking Down the Barriers' in G. Howells (ed.) *European Business Law* (Dartmouth: Aldershot, 1996) 223. D. Weber-Ray, 'Harmonization of European Insurance Contract Law', in *The Harmonization of European Contract Law*, ed. S. Vogenauer & S. Weatherill (Portland: Hart, 2006) 207. For a very interesting and up-to-date analysis of insurance law, see: M. Clarke, *Policies and*

important for the aim of the promotion of freedom of establishment at the EU level (even if this Directive addresses re-insurance and retrocession):

> Whereas, for the purposes of applying measures concerning the right of establishment and freedom to provide services, companies and firms are to be treated in the same way as natural persons who are nationals of Member States, subject only to the conditions laid down in Article 58 (now Article 48) EC Treaty and, where necessary, to the condition that there should exist a real and continuous link with the economy of a Member State; whereas therefore no company or firm may be required, in order to obtain the benefit of such measures, to fulfil any additional condition, and in particular no company or firm may be required to obtain any special authorisation not required of a domestic company or firm wishing to pursue a particular economic activity; whereas, however, such uniformity of treatment should not prevent Member States from requiring that a company having a share capital should operate in their countries under the description by which it is known in the law of the Member State under which it is constituted, and that it should indicate the amount of its subscribed capital on the business papers which it uses in the host Member State.

2.4 ARTICLE 293 OF THE EC TREATY

Article 293 of the EC Treaty prompts Member States to conclude an international agreement on mutual recognition of companies and entities with legal personalities:

> Article 293 (EC Treaty)
>
> Member States shall, so far as is necessary, enter into negotiations with each other with a view to securing for the benefit of their nationals:
>
> ... the mutual recognition of companies or firms within the meaning of the second paragraph of Article 48, the retention of legal personality in the event of transfer of their seat from one country to another, and the possibility of mergers between companies or firms governed by the laws of different countries.

As far as the application of Article 293 of the EC Treaty is concerned, it has not contributed much to market integration in the field of EU company law.[134] It could be assumed that this provision for agreements was inserted because the founding Member States were not sure that the Treaty contained a sufficient legal basis for dealing with these substantive areas. Nevertheless, this assumption does not mean that Article 293 of the EC Treaty has a pre-emptive effect and excludes

Perceptions of Insurance Law in the Twenty-First Century (Oxford: Oxford University Press, 2007).

134. R. Buxbaum & K. Hopt (n. 80), 210. E. Stein (n. 21), 41–45, 394–424.

harmonization of these areas on the basis of Article 44(2)(g) of the EC Treaty.[135] The original six Member States had signed in 1968 an agreement on the mutual recognition of companies and legal persons.[136] However, this international agreement never came into effect because it was not ratified by The Netherlands. The agreement has been abandoned, but it had some impact on the domestic case law of the Member States that ratified it (e.g., Belgium).[137] In 1967 and 1972, the EU legislature tried to regulate cross-border mergers by drafting a Convention under Article 220 (now Article 293) of the EC Treaty. However, the regulatory choice of using conventions based on Article 293 of the EC Treaty was finally abandoned, and the EU chose directives as the most appropriate harmonizing legal instrument.

2.5 ARTICLE 308 OF THE EC TREATY

Article 308 of the EC Treaty is supposed to supplement Article 44(2)(g) of the EC Treaty as a basis for market making, and it promotes integration even where the Treaty's basis itself cannot encompass the required measures.[138] The role of Article 308 of the EC Treaty should also be mentioned:

> Article 308 (EC Treaty)
>
> If action by the Community should prove necessary to attain, in the course of the operation of the common market, one of the objectives of the Community, and this Treaty has not provided the necessary powers, the Council shall, acting unanimously on a proposal from the Commission and after consulting the European Parliament, take the appropriate measures.

This Article was used as the legal basis of two EU Regulations, the European Economic Interest Grouping (EEIG) and the European Company Statute[139] (SE Statute). The justification for recourse to Article 308 of the EC Treaty instead of Article 44 of the EC Treaty is that Article 44 constitutes a basis for the adoption of directives requiring Member States to harmonize their national company structures, whereas, in the case of the EEIG and the SE Statute, what was necessary for market integration were directly applicable EU regimes introducing European corporate entities operating in parallel with existing national company

135. R. Buxbaum & K. Hopt (n. 80), 210.
136. C. Schmitthoff, 'Introduction', in *European Company Law Texts,* ed. C. Schmitthoff (New York-London: M. Bender-Stevens & Sons, 1974), 3–4, 44–49.
137. E. Wymeersch (n. 106). C. Villiers (n. 100), 175. R. Schutze, 'Organized Change towards an "Ever-Closer Union": Article 308 EC and the Limits to the Community's Legislative Competence', *YEL* 22 (2003): 79.
138. R. Buxbaum & K. Hopt (n. 80), 212.
139. E. Stein (n. 21), 427, 445. The same legal basis (see Recital 17 of the Preamble) was used for the Worker's Participation Directive completing the SE Statute. Council Directive 2001/86/EC of 8 Oct. 2001 supplementing the Statute for a European company with regard to the involvement of employees, OJ 2001 L294/0022.

law regimes.[140] An additional political argument in favour of this choice of legal basis is that Article 308 of the EC Treaty requires a unanimous decision of the Council.[141] Recourse to Article 308 of the EC Treaty does not mean that these EU vehicles for corporate restructuring should not contribute to the facilitation of the exercise of freedom of establishment, because Article 308 of the EC Treaty applies 'in the course of operation of the common market', while the 'objectives of the Community' applicable in such a context are internal market/common market objectives.[142] In the 1970s, 1980s, and 1990s, the Community institutions had used this legal basis in a broader way than that affirmed by the ECJ in Opinion 2/94.[143] In paragraph 30 of the Opinion, the ECJ characterized this basis as an integral part of the institutional system based on the principle of attributed competence and, as such, cannot broaden the scope of Community competences beyond the general framework created by the provisions of the EC Treaty as a whole and, in particular, by those that define the tasks and the activities of the Community.[144] R. Buxbaum and K. Hopt considered that this broadly worded provision is found in the area between a legal and political definition.[145] The ECJ had the opportunity to discuss the appropriateness of Article 308 of the EC Treaty instead of Article 95 of the EC Treaty as a legal basis for a transnational corporate entity, such as the European Cooperative Society. In *European Parliament v. Council,*[146] the ECJ clarified the purpose of Article 308 and Article 95 as potential legal bases for harmonization measures aimed at market integration. It stated that Article 308 may be used as the legal basis for a measure only where no other provision of the Treaty gives the Community institutions the necessary power to adopt it.[147] Article 95 empowers the Community legislature to adopt measures to improve the conditions for the establishment and functioning of the internal market, and they must genuinely have that objective, contributing to the elimination of obstacles to the economic freedoms guaranteed by the Treaty, which include the freedom of establishment.[148] Recourse to that Article as a legal basis

---

140. D.A. Wyatt & A. Dashwood (n. 46), 864.
141. *Ibid.*
142. *Ibid.*
143. Opinion 2/94, *Accession by the Community to the European Convention for the Protection of Human Rights and Fundamental Freedoms* [1996] ECR I-1759. D.A. Wyatt, 'Constitutional Significance of the Tobacco Advertising Judgment of the European Court of Justice', in The ECJ's Tobacco Advertising Judgment *CELS* Occasional Paper No. 5, 20.
144. S. Weatherill states that the reference in Art. 308 EC Treaty to the 'course of the operation of the common market' has exerted little if any restriction on legislative resort to Art. 308. S. Weatherill, 'Competence Creep and Competence Control', *YEL* 23 (2004): 1, 28 (as cited by D.A. Wyatt,n. 106.
145. R. Buxbaum & K. Hopt (n. 80), 211.
146. Case C-436/03, *European Parliament v. Council of the European Union* [2006] ECR I-3733.
147. Case C-436/03 paras 35–37 referring to Case 45/86, *Commission v. Council* [1987] ECR 1493 para. 13, and Case C-350/92, *Spain v. Council* [1995] ECR I-1985 para. 26. In Case 45/86, *Commission v. Council*, the ECJ stated that the choice of legal basis for a legislative measure has to be based on objective factors amenable to judicial review. N. Moloney (n. 108), 8.
148. Case C-436/03 para. 38.

is also possible if the aim is to prevent the emergence of obstacles to trade resulting from the heterogeneous development of national laws; the emergence of such obstacles must, however, be likely, and the measure in question must be designed to prevent them.[149]

The ECJ proceeded to explain the basic legislative goals of the European Cooperative Society so as to justify recourse to Article 308 of the EC Treaty and not to Article 95 of the EC Treaty. Regulation No. 1435/2003 on the Statute for a European Cooperative Society (SCE) aims to introduce a new legal form in addition to the national forms of cooperative societies, since the SCE must be considered to be a European legal form for cooperative societies that has a specific Community character.[150] The legal form of the SCE is governed first and foremost by that Regulation, the conditions of its formation are specific to that form of society, and the possibility of transferring its registered office from one Member State to another, without that resulting in the dissolution of the SCE or in the creation of a new legal person is also specific to the SCE.[151] In addition, the European cooperative society is a form that co-exists with cooperative societies under national law.[152] In those circumstances, the Regulation, which leaves unchanged the different national laws already in existence, cannot be regarded as aiming to approximate the laws of the Member States applicable to cooperative societies.[153] Consequently, Article 95 of the EC Treaty could not constitute an appropriate legal basis for the adoption of the Regulation, which was thus correctly adopted on the basis of Article 308 of the EC Treaty.[154]

2.6 IMPORTANT ECJ CASE LAW ON REGULATORY COMPETENCE TO HARMONIZE THE INTERNAL MARKET

A very important case, which is relevant to the debate on community competence to regulate the internal market, is the *Tobacco Advertising*[155] case. Article 95 of the EC Treaty, pertaining to the adoption of internal market measures, was used as the legal basis of a Directive prohibiting many forms of tobacco advertising.[156] Germany challenged this Directive. It argued that this measure was adopted

149. Case C-436/03 para. 39 referring to Case C-376/98, *Germany v. Parliament and Council* [2000] ECR I-8419 paras 83, 84, 86, and 95, and Case C-491/01, *British American Tobacco (Investments) and Imperial Tobacco* [2002] ECR I-11453 paras 60–61.
150. Case C-436/03 para. 40.
151. Case C-436/03 paras 41–42.
152. Case C-436/03 para. 43.
153. Case C-436/03 para. 44.
154. Case C-436/03 para. 46.
155. Case C-376/98, *Germany v. European Parliament and Council of the European Union* [2000] ECR I-8419. G. de Burca, 'The Tobacco Advertising Saga: Political Aspirations and Constitutional Constraints', in The ECJ's Tobacco Advertising Judgment *CELS* Occasional Paper No. 5, 5.
156. D.A. Wyatt & A. Dashwood (n. 46), 929–959. An EU-US Comparative Perspective, A. Knook (n. 101), R. Buxbaum, G. Hertig, et al. (eds) (n. 97), 35, 61, and 399. For the recent case law

because of public health issues and not market considerations, and, as a result, should have been enacted under Article 152 of the EC Treaty, which expressly prohibits harmonizing legislation.[157] The ECJ held that a measure based on Article 95 of the EC Treaty must genuinely have as its objective the improvement of conditions for the establishment or functioning of the internal market;[158] other Treaty Articles should not be used as a legal basis to circumvent the express exclusion of harmonization. It was also held that, provided that the conditions for recourse to Articles 95, 47, and 55 of the EC Treaty as a legal basis are fulfilled, the Community legislature cannot be prevented from relying on that legal basis on the grounds that public health protection is a decisive factor in the choices to be made.[159] The Community legislature does not possess a general power to regulate the internal market because this would be in direct opposition to the principle of attributed competence of Article 5 of the EC Treaty.[160] The ECJ also criticized the legislative practice of Community institutions in the 1970s, 1980s, and 1990s by disapproving the rationale of many harmonizing measures[161] and held that if a

---

concerning the scope of Art. 95 EC Treaty: K. Gutman 'Case Not: Case C-66/04 *Smoke Flavourings*, Case C-436/03 *SCE* & Case C-217/04 *ENISA*' [2006] 13 *Col JEL* 147.

157. N. Foster, *EU Law Directions* (Oxford: Oxford University Press, 2008), 114.
158. Case C-376/98 para. 84.
159. Case C-376/98 para. 88. The ECJ does not adopt the 'centre of gravity' argument (paras 32–34) supported by Germany, but it alleges that the definition of competence could not be strictly defined *rationae materiae* or *rationae personae*. The relevance of the measure in the broader context of the internal market could be an important element of that definition. Following this thread, the ECJ contended that the ban on advertising of tobacco products in press (periodicals, magazines, newspapers) could be based on Art. 95 EC Treaty. C. Hillion, 'Case Annotation, Tobacco Advertising: If You Must, You May', *CLJ* (2001): 486, 488–489. It is quite ironic that, in the second *Tobacco Advertising* case (Case C-380/03 [2006] ECR I-11573, the case brought before the ECJ when Germany challenged the new Directive passed after the first *Tobacco Advertising* ruling prohibiting mainly tobacco product advertising in press and in certain categories of mass media), the ECJ held that Art. 95 EC Treaty could constitute the legal basis for harmonizing measures requiring all the Member States to authorize the marketing of the products under specific conditions or definitely prohibiting the marketing of products (paras 43–44). If the ECJ had adopted this approach in the first *Tobacco Advertising* case, the first Directive would have survived. D.A. Wyatt (n. 106) 11, 29. M. Ludwigs, 'Case Note, Case C-380/03 *Germany v. European Parliament and Council of the European Union (Second Tobacco Advertising Ruling)* [2006] ECR I-11573', *CML Rev* 44 (2007): 1159. It should be added that economic and non-economic political pressures to create a rational and sensible accommodation and division of state and federal competences over the same area of law are equally important and can be analysed better and more extensively by a comparative research between the EU and the US. R. Buxbaum & K. Hopt (n. 80), 22–23.
160. N. Foster (n. 157), 114. For an interesting overview and analysis of the debate about EU competence to legislate in the field of contract law: S. Weatherill, 'Constitutional Issues: How Much Is Best Left Unsaid?' and S. Vogenauer & S. Weatherill, 'The European Community's Competence to Pursue the Harmonization of Contract Law: An Empirical Contribution to the Debate', in *The Harmonization of European Contract Law*, ed. S. Vogenauer & S. Weatherill (Portland: Hart, 2006), 89, 105.
161. D.A. Wyatt, 'Constitutional Significance of the Tobacco Advertising Judgment of the European Court of Justice' in The ECJ's Tobacco Advertising Judgment *CELS* Occasional Paper No. 5, 19-21.

mere finding of disparities between national rules and the abstract risk of obstacles to the exercise of fundamental freedoms or of distortions of competition liable to result therefrom were sufficient to justify the choice of Article 100(a) of the EC Treaty as a legal basis, judicial review of compliance with the proper legal basis might be rendered nugatory.[162]

This ruling tried to set a few criteria essential for the delimitation of community competence to regulate the internal market. Any harmonizing initiative of the European legislature should focus on combating appreciable distortions[163] of competition and not on disparities between national laws having a remote and indirect effect on competition.[164] It is easily understood that the ECJ does not consider that all disparities between national laws could constitute an appreciable distortion of competition. The case law of the ECJ on the exercise of the fundamental freedoms would be the most important factor in determining whether legal diversity at the EU level could amount to a barrier restricting trade and/or to distortions of competition; national measures treated by that case law as being incapable of affecting inter-state trade (e.g., *Keck and Mithouard*[165] and subsequent case law) fall outside the scope of the definition of a barrier restricting trade and of a measure appreciably distorting competition.[166] Thus, the existence of a barrier to free movement of goods, persons, services, and establishment is a crucial condition for the justification of harmonization. It should be decided whether a national provision falls within the definition of a trade barrier or not. National measures may be harmonized where their effect on trade is actual or potential, direct or indirect (but not too remote and indirect to inhibit trade).[167] Additionally, the ECJ held that harmonization is permissible even if no disparities in national laws currently exist but it is probable that barriers to freedom of movement will arise in the future.[168] It is quite interesting to consider here the alternative (as opposed to cumulative) character of those two elements' providing the required internal market dimension in

162. Case C-376/98 para. 84.
163. The element of appreciable distortions of competition was referred by the ECJ in Case 300/89, *Commission v. Council (Titanium Dioxide)* [1991] ECR I-2867 para. 23 and Cases 91/79 and 92/79, *Commission v. Italy* [1980] ECR 1099 para. 8. Appreciable distortions of competition, as an aspect of subsidiarity, are related to the identity of the decision-maker; this identity could have an important impact on the content of internal market regulation. This effect depends on competition in the whole market and on the exercise of fundamental freedoms. Competition between the EU and non-Member States is less complicated than competition within the EU because EU possess wider powers to impose restrictions against other non-Member States but is bound by the aims of market integration in trade among the various Member States. F. Easterbrook, 'Federalism and European Business Law', in *European Economic and Business Law*, ed. R. Buxbaum, et al. (New York: de Gruyter, 1996), 2.
164. D.A. Wyatt (n. 106), 22.
165. The 'certain selling arrangements' test. Joined Cases C-267 and C-268/91, *Keck and Mithouard* [1993] ECR I-6097. See also Case C-412/93, *Leclerc-Siplec* [1995] ECR I-179 para. 21 and Case C-292/92, *Huenermund* [1993] ECR I-6787 para. 21
166. D.A. Wyatt (n. 106), 23.
167. *Ibid.*
168. D.A. Wyatt (n. 106), 23. L. Woods, *Free Movement of Goods and Services within the European Community* (Aldershot: Ashgate, 2004), 266.

Article 95 of the EC Treaty. The ECJ stated in both the second *Tobacco Advertisement* ruling (paragraph 67) and in *BAT* (paragraph 60) that, when the existence of obstacles to trade has been established, it is not necessary also to prove distortions of competition to justify recourse to Article 95 of the EC Treaty. Hence, when the first element is fulfilled, the second element is not required to be fulfilled, and presumably vice versa.[169] Moreover, harmonization of national laws aiming at the abolition of trade barriers will be open to question if the harmonized rules do not ensure the free movement of products being in conformity with the harmonized provisions.[170] The barriers that the Directive proposes to abolish should exist both in fact and in law, and the fulfilment of this condition should be scrutinized by the ECJ. The ECJ is willing to accept that the mere likelihood that trade barriers might arise in the future could satisfy the factual existence of trade barriers open to harmonization. It is not a positive development that the ECJ set quite low standards for the establishment of the probability of the emergence of obstacles to trade.[171] As far as the appreciable distortions of competition are concerned, the Community institutions are not required to conduct the detailed analysis used in the field of competition law.[172] It is obvious that this lack of factual assessment and the absence of a more empirical approach toward these potential trade barriers constitute a shortcoming of this case law.[173]

Nevertheless, subsequent case law reached different conclusions from those of the *Tobacco Advertisement* judgment that contradicted or eroded many of its elements. In *Swedish Match,*[174] it was held that obstacles to trade could be confronted by simply banning the trade.[175] In *BAT,*[176] the ECJ found that disparities between national labelling rules result in hypothetical trade barriers that could be addressed by eliminating these disparities, even if this makes no contribution to cross-border trade in the products in question.[177] In *Leitner,*[178] the ECJ confirmed that the lax assessment of the criterion of appreciable distortions of competition could be applied by the European legislature in the regulation of the internal market.[179] In *Rundfunk,*[180] the ECJ stipulated that as long as a measure makes a contribution to the internal market, this measure could regulate situations with no link at all with the fundamental freedoms[181] This conclusion of *Rundfunk* is not in conformity with the *Tobacco Advertisement* judgment but follows the pattern of the case law

169. M. Ludwigs (n. 159), 1159, 1166–1167.
170. D.A. Wyatt (n. 106), 23.
171. M. Ludwigs (n. 159), 1176.
172. D.A. Wyatt (n. 106), 31.
173. D.A. Wyatt (n. 106), 31. Empiricism was also proclaimed as a very important element of market integration if the field of EU Company Law.
174. Case C-210/03, *Swedish Match* [2004] ECR I-11825.
175. D.A. Wyatt (n. 106).
176. Case C-491/01 [2002] ECR I-11453.
177. D.A. Wyatt (n. 106), 1, 29.
178. Case C-158/00, *Simone Leitner v. TUI* [2002] ECR I-2631.
179. D.A. Wyatt (n. 106), 1, 34.
180. Joined Cases C-465/00, C-138/01, and C-139/01, *Rundfunk* [2003] ECR I-4989.
181. D.A. Wyatt (n. 106), 1, 37.

dating from the 1960s, which adopts a broad interpretation of competence to regulate the internal market.[182] The major conclusion of this subsequent case law is that Community competence to regulate the internal market has not in practice been confined to eliminating trade barriers and appreciable distortions of competition, but instead, it has been extended to harmonizing national rules that facilitate freedom of movement and abolishing legal diversity among Member States, which creates uncertainty for those planning cross-border transactions or expansion of their activities.[183] As far as EU company law is concerned, community measures aimed at the promotion of cross-border cooperation and establishment of legal persons, according to Article 308 of the EC Treaty, and the adoption of company law Directives, pursuant to Article 44(2)(g) of the EC Treaty, were based on similar arguments of legal certainty resulting from different national provisions.[184] The approach that the elimination of psychological obstacles caused by legal uncertainty could constitute the reasoning of harmonizing measures regulating the internal market might be also be considered as an aspect of a broader proposition, to the effect that internal market measures could be justified by the need to facilitate the exercise of fundamental freedoms.[185]

2.7 CONCLUSION

The market integration and the economic benefits accrued by companies exercising their right of establishment are revealed by the intra-Community direct-investment flows over the past ten years.[186] The Community's proclaimed regulatory aim was to promote an equivalent level of protection of members of companies and third parties; this development was indeed prescribed by Article 44(2)(g) of the EC Treaty.[187] The Community's company law harmonization

182. See various examples of directives that were adopted under this wide construction of Community competences in D.A. Wyatt (n. 106), 2–9. A wide interpretation of community competence to regulate the internal market (the so-called 'spillover' at the EU level) could also produce a legislative 'spillover' at national level when the directives are implemented. The national legislature could also follow a wide interpretation. The implementation of a directive might involve a choice to extend the relevant regulatory regime beyond the sphere mandated by the EC (through stricter rules in case of minimum harmonization, through introduction of the directive's provisions into new areas beyond the directive's material or personal reach, through more vigorous enforcement or through early implementation before the end of the relevant deadline) S. Weatherill, 'Harmonization: How Much, How Little?', *EBLR* (2005): 533, 538–539.

183. D.A. Wyatt (n. 106), 1.

184. D.A. Wyatt (n. 106), 6.

185. *Ibid.*

186. P. Pelle, 'Companies Crossing Borders within Europe', *Utr. LR* 4 (2008): 6, 7. Law and the Related Institutional Framework Are Fundamental to Economic Development and an Effective Financial Sector Is Essential to Economic Growth. D.W. Arner, *Financial Stability, Economic Growth and the Role of Law* (Cambridge: Cambridge University Press, 2007): 1–2.

187. P. Pelle (n. 186), 7.

programme frequently adopted the lowest common denominator that Member States could agree upon[188] – a minimum that was relatively easy to reach, as it essentially amounted to a replication at the Community level of the main content of existing national laws, albeit with some domestic peculiarities.[189] This is shown by the number of options in some Directives (up to forty in the Accounting Directives[190]) and by the content and intensity of the opt-in–opt-out/reciprocity system in the Takeover Bid Directive (waiving the most important parts of the Takeover Bid Directive).[191]

188. *Ibid.*
189. *Ibid.*
190. The Accounting Regulation 1606/2002 ([2002] OJ L243/1) which implements the International Accounting Standards at the EU level will probably enhance uniformity in this area of law. C. Villiers, 'European Integration and Globalisation: The Experience of Financial Reporting', *CYELS* 8 (2006): 109.
191. P. Pelle (n. 186), 7. S. Fazio (n. 14), 93–94.

Chapter 3

Aspects of EU Company Law Harmonization

3.1 DIRECTIVES

Without entering into a discussion of what 'harmonization' means exactly, or whether there is or should be any differences among the harmonization, approximation, coordination, and so on of laws, harmonization constitutes a form of limited regulatory intervention.[192] The Member States should adopt the necessary provisions only as far as this is necessary for the attainment of the legislative goals of the relevant Treaty provision upon which a directive was based.[193] A directive is an instrument that corresponds very well to this idea of limited intervention. Being binding 'as to the result to be achieved' but leaving the Member States the choice of 'form and methods', it is by its nature very suitable for bringing about the necessary changes in national laws while respecting to the extent possible the national legal systems, with their own conceptions and terminology.[194] Each Member State can use its own method of implementation while implementing a directive. In the Declaration on Article 100(a) (now Article 95 of the EC Treaty) of the then EEC Treaty annexed to the Single European Act, the Member States expressed their preference for directives as instruments of harmonization of laws rather than the use of regulations.[195] The same is also true for Article 44(2)(g) of the EC Treaty which is the legal basis for company law harmonization. At the

192. S. Prechal, *Directives in EC Law*, Oxford EC Law Library, 2nd edn (Oxford: Oxford University Press, 2004), 4. P.J. Slot, 'Harmonization', *EL Rev.* 21 (1996): 378.
193. S. Prechal (n. 192), 4.
194. S. Prechal (n. 192), 4, N. Moloney (n. 108), 17.
195. S. Prechal (n. 192), 4.

Edinburgh Summit,[196] the Member States clarified that the principle of proportionality stipulated in Article 3B (now 5(3)) of the EC Treaty should imply that wherever the European legislature should regulate a specific area, preference should be given to directives over regulations and to framework directives over detailed measures.[197]

3.2 OBSTACLES IMPEDING THE EFFECTIVE EXERCISE OF THE FREEDOM OF ESTABLISHMENT BY COMPANIES

Measures that prima facie have little immediate impact on cross-border establishment would, after empirical study, be found to facilitate the freedom of establishment of companies.[198] The Third[199] and Sixth[200] Directives on domestic mergers and divisions of public companies have a two-fold importance for cross-border activities: (a) they combat psychological obstacles by encouraging foreign investors to establish companies in other Member States and then to expand their activities in these new markets by conducting mergers with other companies established in those other Member States, and (b) they inspired the adoption of the relevant legal instrument for cross-border mergers, that is, the Tenth Company Law Directive on cross-border mergers.[201] The existence of many similar provisions in the regulation of national and cross-border mergers could diminish some of the costs and could facilitate companies' plans to merge with other companies.[202] Similarly, directives with narrow scope and specific, apparently protective goals, such as the Eleventh Directive on branch disclosure and the Twelfth Directive on single-member companies, in fact facilitate cross-border establishment: the former is designed to reduce administrative costs of branches of companies established in other Member States, and the latter to ensure equivalent protection for creditors and enhance credibility of single-member companies.[203]

The barriers inhibiting the effective exercise of the fundamental freedom of establishment by companies could be categorized into the following:

(1) National legal diversity in the same subject matter of company law that discourages cross-border establishment to the extent that economic

196. *Edinburgh European Council*, Bull EC 12-1992, Fifteen confirmed in the Protocol on subsidiarity and proportionality to the Treaty of Amsterdam, in point 6 and by the Commission, in the 'White Paper on European Governance', COM (2001) 428, final, 20.
197. S. Prechal (n. 192), 4.
198. V. Edwards (n. 96), 7.
199. Third Council Directive 78/855/EEC of 9 Oct. 1978 based on Art. 54(3)(g) of the Treaty, concerning mergers of public limited liability companies [1978] OJ L295/36.
200. Sixth Council Directive 82/891/EEC of 17 Dec. 1982 based on Art. 54(3)(g) of the Treaty, concerning the division of public limited liability companies [1982] OJ L378/47.
201. Directive 2005/56/EC of the European Parliament and of the Council of 26 Oct. 2005, on cross-border mergers of limited liability companies (text with EEA relevance) [2005] OJ L310/1.
202. V. Edwards (n. 96), 7.
203. V. Edwards (n. 96), 7. E. Wymeersch (n. 106), 3.

operators in one Member State are unfamiliar with national company law provisions in another (psychological obstacles) – the shareholders and creditors provide capital and credit when they are protected by harmonized laws and, as a result, investment requirements are crystallized and eased, and economic development advances more quickly.[204] Thus, shareholders and third parties feel confident in their transactions and in their decisions when they know that they have broadly the same rights in their dealings with companies.[205]

(2) Differences between national rules demanding compliance with additional terms and conditions with respect to establishment in another Member State.

(3) National rules that (independently from their various specifics from Member State to Member State) obstruct cross-border establishment of legal persons.[206]

The Tenth Company Law Directive on cross-border mergers[207] attempts to eliminate obstacles falling within the second category.[208] It should be noted that, prior to this Directive, only certain Member States allowed cross-border mergers (both inbound and outbound), and some other Member States did not permit cross-border mergers or imposed onerous conditions for their realization (e.g., the dissolution of the acquired companies), making the realization of cross-border mergers very difficult or even de facto impossible. In the explanatory Memorandum of its proposal, the European Commission argued that national diversities in the legal framework regulating cross-border mergers applicable to each of the companies planning to merge are such that the companies have to resort to complex and costly legal arrangements and to follow alternative financial techniques. These arrangements often complicate cross-border merger operations and are not always characterized by transparency and legal certainty. Hence, the costs of cross-border mergers must be rationalized and reduced, and Community legislation has to provide legal certainty and to enable as many companies as possible to benefit.[209] The Tenth Company Law Directive aims to abolish any additional requirements for cross-border establishment by providing a suitable legal instrument enabling companies to carry out cross-border mergers under the most favourable conditions.[210]

Additionally, the Takeover Bid Directive combats barriers belonging to the third category. Such barriers to cross-border establishment are not caused by the different national provisions at the EU level (yet, they could also be the result of

204. R. Buxbaum & K. Hopt (n. 80), 201. E. Stein (n. 21), 429.
205. R. Buxbaum, G. Hertig et al. (eds) (n. 97), 11.
206. D.A. Wyatt & A. Dashwood (n. 46), 865.
207. Directive 2005/56, on cross-border mergers of limited liability companies [2005] OJ L310/1.
208. D.A. Wyatt & A. Dashwood (n. 46), 869.
209. Proposal for a Directive of the European Parliament and of the Council on cross-border mergers of companies with share capital COM (2003) 0703 final.
210. Proposal for a Directive of the European Parliament and of the Council on cross-border mergers of companies with share capital, COM (2003) 0703 final.

these differences). These barriers contained in national rules or in the articles of association of companies result from the fact that the rules in question or practices authorized by such rules are intinsically capable of inhibiting cross-border establishment.[211] Sometimes, the mere existence of those rules or practices could result in a barrier to the cross-border establishment of companies. One example of such a takeover barrier that the Takeover Bid Directive attempts to abolish is the frustration of a tender offer by the company's board. The Directive requires prior authorization of a shareholders' general meeting before the company's board launches any defensive measures against the bidder. This provision of the Takeover Bid Directive is based on the rationale that the issue of corporate control in a takeover contest should be decided by its shareholders.[212] The abolition of this kind of obstacle will assist companies in penetrating foreign markets.

Furthermore, the provisions of the Takeover Bid Directive regulating various aspects of disclosure of information aim to eliminate psychological obstacles, that is, obstacles of the first category. Article 10 of the Takeover Bid Directive obliges a potential target companies to disclose information that could affect the decision of a potential bidder to launch a bid. Article 6 obliges a bidder to disclose information concerning the bid, which is very important for the decision-making of the shareholders (or the board of the company in case of non-implementation of the non-frustration rule) about the bid. The disclosure of information contributes to a great extent to the transparency of the market for corporate control and to the protection of shareholders. The Eighteenth Recital to the Preamble of the Directive states that:

> In order to reinforce the effectiveness of existing provisions concerning the freedom to deal in the securities of companies covered by this Directive and the freedom to exercise voting rights, it is essential that the defensive structures and mechanisms envisaged by such companies be transparent and that they be regularly presented in reports to general meetings of shareholders.

These disclosure provisions of the Directive are mandatory (in comparison with Articles 9, 11, and 12 of the Takeover Bid Directive) and set some specific standards for the disclosure of takeover information at the EU level. Companies wishing to initiate a takeover and to expand their business activities abroad will find that foreign law on the disclosure of various aspects of takeover bids is more familiar as a result of harmonization.[213] Thus, legal certainty is promoted through the abolition of psychological obstacles resulting from the unfamiliarity with foreign legal provisions. Investors seeking a controlling stake in foreign companies would not be discouraged by uncertainty as to the information disclosed by those companies. It should also be noted that disclosure requirements could also fall within the second

211. D.A. Wyatt & A. Dashwood (n. 46), 870.
212. Proposal for a Directive of the European Parliament and of the Council on Takeover Bids, COM (2002) 0534 final [2003] OJ 45E/1.
213. R. Buxbaum & K. Hopt (n. 80), 201.

category of obstacles when offeree or offeror companies have to comply with additional disclosure requirements.[214]

3.3 CATEGORIZING COMPANY LAW DIRECTIVES AND METHODS OF HARMONIZATION

Company law directives can be categorized in four generations. First-generation directives were adopted when there were only six Member States and the drafting process operated under German political and legal influence. These directives have many detailed and precise provisions,[215] leaving little discretion to Member States as to the method of implementation and lead to more uniformity. The First and Second Company Law Directives are first-generation directives.[216] Second-generation directives are prescriptive, but to a lesser extent than are the first-generation directives. They are more flexible, offering options and alternative formulae for their implementation, and thus they accommodate the different approaches of Member States and the needs of enterprises. They do not entail complete freedom, because Member States are bound by certain legislative goals and should adopt one of the formulae laid down in the Directive. Second-generation directives were adopted after the first enlargement, when the German influence in the drafting process became less significant and the legal diversity in the EU increased with the addition of the new Member States. The Third and Sixth Directives, and the Fourth, Seventh, and Eighth Directives (Accounts Directives), fall within the scope of this category (yet the Third and Sixth Directives present many of the characteristics of the first-generation directives).[217] The third-generation directives were introduced by the Commission's White Paper on Completion of the Internal Market[218] and were adopted after the second and third enlargements (when Greece, Spain, and Portugal joined the EEC). This White Paper proposed a 'new approach' for directives, which should be more general, would clarify the essential requirements, and would focus on what is to be achieved rather than how. These Directives were adopted under the cooperation process, and they are relatively short, containing little detail and offering more discretion as to methods of implementation by Member States. The Eleventh and Twelfth Directives belong to this third generation.[219] The fourth-generation directives came into existence after the accession of Austria, Sweden, and Finland and follow the co-decision procedure. These directives could be characterized generally as 'framework' directives. Member States' freedom in choosing the most appropriate method of implementation of these directives is quite wide in comparison with

214. D.A. Wyatt & A. Dashwood (n. 46), 869–871.
215. A critical discussion with comparisons with the rest of the categories: C. Villiers (n. 100), 179.
216. C. Villiers (n. 101), 29 & 31.
217. C. Villiers (n. 101), 29, 36–37 & 224.
218. COM (85) 310 Final.
219. C. Villiers (n. 101), 29, 46.

the other generations of directives. Statements of objectives and general principles dominate the content of these directives, and Member States are responsible for the adoption of specific national legislation in accordance with these general rules. The Tenth and Thirteenth Directives follow this pattern of 'framework directives'.[220] It is easily understood that the harmonization of company law evolves towards a minimum of EU centralized legislation and leaves the details and the technical issues to be decided by the Member States at the national level as long the legislative aims are not infringed upon and the general principles of Article 5 of the EC Treaty are respected.[221]

Various methods of harmonization are used in the regulation of the internal market. When there were only six Member States, it was quite easy for them to adopt a uniform approach to the regulation of the internal market by the means of directives (even if the rationale of directives is not to bring uniformity but rather harmonization). The 1985 White Paper on the Completion of the Internal Market followed the ruling in *Cassis de Dijon*[222] (in the absence of harmonization, a product lawfully produced in a Member State could circulate freely within the internal market and no national restrictions are allowed, apart from cases characterized by mandatory requirements in the general interest) and proclaimed a new approach to harmonization directives, abandoning detail and overregulation.[223] This approach resulted in different harmonization methods being adopted by the European legislature. Total harmonization allows no derogation in the pre-empted (exhausted by the European legislature) area except for safeguarded measures or to the extent permitted in a directive.[224] In this method, the system of the directive and the wording of the directive's provisions are determinative.[225] Optional harmonization allows market participants to apply national norms or Community norms, with some directives allowing the Member States to exercise the option of opting-out.[226] Partial harmonization regulates only one part of the specific area, for example, provisions regulating cross-border activities only.[227] Minimum

220. C. Villiers (n. 101), 29, 48–49, 224.
221. C. Villiers (n. 101) 29, 48–49.
222. Case 120/78 *Rewe-Zentral AG v. Bundesmonopolverwaltung für Branntwein (Cassis de Dijon)* [1979] ECR-649.
223. W. Van Gerven, 'Harmonization of Private Law: Do we need it?', *CML Rev.* 41 (2004): 505, 507.
224. W. Van Gerven (n. 223), 508. A. McGee & S. Weatherill, 'The Evolution of the Single Market-Harmonization or Liberalization', *MLR* 53 (1990): 578, 582.
225. P.J. Slot (n. 192), 383.
226. W. Van Gerven (n. 223), 508. Cl. Lempereur (n. 123), 244. It was argued that optional harmonization in the area of company law could be proved advantageous to small and medium-sized companies, to companies with differential control and ownership structures and to the majority of the stakeholders. G. Hertig & J. McCahery, 'A Legal Options Approach to EC Company Law' (2006) Berkeley Program in Law & Economics Working Paper Series (University of California, Berkeley) No 180. G. Hertig & J. McCahery, 'Legal Options: Towards Better EC Company Law Regulation', in *Better Regulation*, ed. S. Weatherill (Oxford: Hart, 2007), 219.
227. W. Van Gerven (n. 223), 508. A. McGee & S. Weatherill (n. 224), 587.

harmonization sets minimum rules at the EU level, although Member States may individually or jointly provide for more stringent rules.[228] Alternative harmonization provides more than one set of rules and allows Member States to choose among those alternative patterns.[229]

As far as the Takeover Directive is concerned, the European legislature has chosen optional harmonization. The Takeover Directive confers options on Member States and at the individual company level. Article 12 of the Takeover Bid Directive provides the option to Member States not to require companies to apply the non-frustration (Article 9) and/or the breakthrough rule (Article 11). However, where Member States make use of that option, they shall nevertheless grant companies that have their registered offices within their territories the option, which shall be reversible, of applying the non-frustration (Article 9) and/or the breakthrough rule (Article 11). The decision of a company shall be made by a general meeting of shareholders, in accordance with the law of the Member State in which the company has its registered office and in accordance with the rules applicable to amending the articles of association. The decision shall be communicated to the supervisory authority of the Member State in which the company has its registered office and to all the supervisory authorities of Member States in which its securities are admitted to trading on regulated markets or in which such admission has been requested. In addition, the Takeover Directive contains a reciprocity clause. Member States may, under the conditions determined by national law, exempt companies that apply the non-frustration rule (Article 9) and/or breakthrough rule (Article 11) from applying the non-frustration rule and/or breakthrough rule if they become the subject of an offer launched by a company that does not apply the same Articles as they do, or by a company controlled, directly or indirectly, by the latter. It is obvious that the core provisions of the Takeover Directive are subjected to this multilevel regime of optionality and reciprocity because of political compromises in the course of the legislative process. Their harmonizing role has a limited impact on the consolidation of the market for corporate control. Furthermore, the European legislature had chosen partial harmonization in the case of the Cross-Border Mergers Directive because it is obvious that this Directive regulates exclusively cross-border mergers (there is another Directive, the third Company Law Directive, dedicated exclusively to the regulation of domestic mergers). Article 1 of the Cross-Border Mergers Directive states that this Directive shall apply to mergers of limited liability companies formed in accordance with the laws of Member States and having their registered offices, central administration,

228. P.J. Slot (n. 192), 384. P. Rott, 'Minimum Harmonization for the Completion of the Internal Market? The Example of Consumer Sales Law', *CML Rev.* 40 (2003): 1107, M. Dougan, 'Minimum Harmonization and the Internal Market', *CML Rev.* 37 (2000): 853. C.I. Lempereur (n. 123), 243.

229. P.J. Slot (n. 192), 386. W. Van Gerven (n. 223), 508. In the area of company law, the case law of the ECJ had stated that some rules of the Company Law Directives leave room for States to adopt stricter measures and others confer no discretion on Member States (Joined cases C-19/90 and C-20/90. *Karella* [1991] ECR I-02691, Opinion of AG Tesauro *Meilicke* [1992] ECR I-04871 para. 12).

or principal places of business within the Community, provided that at least two of them are governed by the laws of different Member States (hereinafter referred to as cross-border mergers).

3.4 DECISIVE FACTORS IN THE HARMONIZATION PROCESS

The success of the harmonization of European company law depended to a great extent on the area of company law that was planned to be harmonized. As long as Member States tried to harmonize external corporate governance issues (such as protection of third parties, company accounts, and legal capital), it was quite easy to reach an agreement that was supposed to affect cross-border commercial transactions between their companies.[230] Nevertheless, when the European legislature focused on the regulation of internal corporate governance, Member States could not reach an agreement on legislative measures, such as the Fifth Directive on public companies and the Ninth Directive on companies' groups, nor were they able to agree on Directives such as the Tenth Directive on cross-border mergers and the Thirteenth Directive on takeover bids after many years of difficult negotiations and political compromises.[231] It must be noted that, although corporate governance is supposed to regulate listed corporations, it also has a major impact on affairs of and within the entire business associated with that entity for the benefit of investors.[232] All these latter legislative initiatives dealt with the relations between and among shareholders, directors, and other parties in internal corporate governance relations.[233]

Member States were reluctant to accept a possible change of their internal corporate governance legislation because such a change would influence the control structures of their markets and would have opened and made more vulnerable their companies to foreign investors and to global business competition.[234] In the Anglo-Saxon legal systems, it is true that shares of listed corporations are widely held, that no single shareholder (apart from those that are institutional) affects the decisions of the company, that no entrepreneurial shareholder controls

230. E. Wymeersch (n. 106), 15.
231. E. Wymeersch (n. 106), 16.
232. S.M. Bartman, 'Corporate Governance: A Challenge to Company Law', *ECL* 1 (2004): 4.
233. E. Wymeersch (n. 106), 16.
234. E. Wymeersch (n. 106), 16. For empirical research on the relationship between ownership concentration and firm performance, taking into account investor and creditor protection: V. Krivogorsky & G. Grudnitski, 'Country Specific Institutional Effects on Ownership Concentration and Performance of Continental European Firms (2008), SSRN Working Paper <http://ssrn.com/abstract=1115433>, accessed 9 Sep. 2008. S. Mengoli, F. Pazzaglia, & E. Sapienza, 'Is It Still Pizza, Spaghetti and Mandolino? Effect of Governance Reforms on Corporate Ownership in Italy', SSRN Working Paper <http://ssrn.com/abstract=966085>, accessed 9 Sep. 2008. A. J Smith, 'Corporate Ownership Structure and Performance. The Case of Management Buyouts', *J Fin Econ* (1990): 143–164.

the management of the company, and that institutional investors exercise greater influence because of the lack of any countervailing power.[235] Shareholder structures[236] in continental Member States are less dispersed than those in UK and the US and show a smaller market control power; this is connected to internal rather than external control devices. The 2003 Action Plan on Modernizing Company Law and Enhancing Corporate Governance appreciates fully the interrelation between internal corporate governance and capital market regulation. The strongest example is the regulation of the EU market for corporate control by the Takeover Bids Directive (yet, in an unsatisfactory way).[237] Additional factors that have caused numerous difficulties in the harmonization of internal corporate governance structures are primarily German co-determination (employee participation in a company's management through representation on the supervisory board of the company), politically-driven protectionism of Germany against foreign acquisitions, and other peculiarities of German company law and corporate governance.[238] Not only the individual Member States, but also companies, were

235. In the UK, this ownership structure resulted in urging UK companies to seek new finance from shareholders by proceeding to a 'rights issue' contributing to further dilution of the holding. E. Wymeersch (n. 124), 303. M.J.G.C Raaijmakers (n. 124), 235–237. Although the UK and the US regulation of hostile takeover bids are inspired by the same idea of manager accountability and increase of company's performance, there are some differences between them. Managers in a UK offeree company are not allowed to frustrate a public offer, while managers in American corporations have a wider discretion in their actions. The interests of institutional investors had influenced the self-regulatory regime of UK. This is not the case for US companies where shareholders had not affected the takeover rules which were judicially formed. It should not be neglected that US had not followed a self-regulatory model, like the UK, and that federal legislation on takeovers pre-empted self-regulatory solutions and restricted the possibility of institutional investors' coordination and proposals for various legal aspects of takeovers. J. Armour & D.A. Skeel 'Who Writes the Rules for Hostile Takeovers, and Why?: The Peculiar Divergence of US and UK Takeover Regulation', *Georgetown Law Journal* (2007): 1727–1794.

236. O. Lσpez-de-Foronda, F.J. Lσpez-Iturriaga & M. Santamarva-Mariscal, 'Ownership Structure, Sharing of Control and Legal Framework: International Evidence', *CorpGov.* (2007): 1130.

237. COM (2003) 284 (1). P. Leyens supports a more market-based approach to corporate governance at the EU level. P. Leyens, 'Internal Corporate Governance in Europe: Towards a More Market-Based Approach', *Kyoto JLP* 4 (2007): 17, 19–20. The influence of ownership concentration on the returns to shareholders of the offeree company is discussed by H. Donker & S. Zahir, 'Takeovers, Corporate Control and Return to Target Shareholders', *Int J CorpGov* 1 (2008): 106. For a concise analysis of the corporate governance regimes of some Member States, see: C.A. Mallin, *Corporate Governance* (Oxford: Oxford University Press, 2003), 19, 123, 149.

238. E. Wymeersch (n. 106), 16. K. Hopt & P. Leyens, 'Board Models in Europe: Recent Developments of Internal Corporate Governance Structures in Germany, the United Kingdom, France, and Italy', *ECFR* 1 (2004): 135–168, R. Buxbaum & K. Hopt (n. 80), 259, K. Hopt, 'Labor Representation on Corporate Boards: Impacts and Problems for Corporate Governance and Economic Integration in Europe', in *European Economic and Business Law*, ed. R. Buxbaum & others (New York: de Gruyter, 1996), 241, 261. C. Windbichler, 'Cheers and Boos for Employee Involvement: Co-Determination as Corporate Governance Conundrum', *EBOR* (2005): 507, F. Fabricius, 'Co-determination in European Company Law', in

objecting to specific harmonization initiatives. One example is the Ninth Directive on groups of companies: while all Member States were developing group law in practice, both in judicial and administrative case law, the large companies were showing clear unwillingness to let this much-feared subject be governed by statutory provisions, whether imposed by a European regulator or even by their more familiar domestic legislature.[239] Sometimes, the European Commission after conducting careful impact assessments, decided not to proceed to harmonization of new areas of company law. This happened in the cases of the cross-border transfer of the registered office and of proportionality between capital and control in listed companies (commonly referred as to the 'one share, one vote' problem),[240] in which Commissioner C. McCreevy decided that there was no need for action at the EU level on these issues.

3.5 THE FINANCIAL SERVICES ACTION PLAN AND THE COMPANY LAW ACTION PLAN

In 1999, the European Council approved the Commission's Action Plan for a single financial market (the Financial Services Action Plan).[241] A series of policy objectives and specific measures aiming to improve the Single Market for financial services was outlined in this Action Plan, adopted by the European Commission. The Action Plan sets forth three strategic objectives: (1) ensuring the Single Market for wholesale financial services, (2) open and secure retail markets, and (3) state-of-the-art prudential rules and supervision.[242] Among the proposed measures

---

The Harmonization of European Company Law, ed. C.M. Schmitthoff (London: UKNCCL, 1973), 101, L. Fauvera & M.E. Fuersta, 'Does Good Corporate Governance Include Employee Representation? Evidence from German Corporate Boards', *J Fin. Econ.* (2006): 673–710, J. Franks & C. Mayer, 'Ownership and Control of German Corporations', *R Fin St* (2001): 943.

239. E. Wymeersch (n. 106) 15–17. E. Werlauff, 'Group and Community: The European Court's Development of an Independent Community Law Concept of the Group and Its Significance for National Company Law', *ECL* 4 (2007): 201, E. Wymeersch (ed.), *Groups of Companies in the EEC: A Survey Report to the European Commission on the Law Relating to Corporate Groups in Various Member States* (Berlin: Walter de Gruyter, 1993), U. Immenga, 'Groups of Companies: Policy Perspectives', in *Further Perspectives in Financial Integration in Europe*, ed. E. Wymeersch (Berlin-New York: de Gruyter, 1994), 174, S.M. Bartman, 'From Autonomy of Interests to Concurrence of Interests in Dutch Group Company Law', *ECL* 4 (2007): 207.
240. Impact Assessment on the Directive on the Cross-Border Transfer of Registered Office (SEC [2007] 1707) and Impact Assessment on the Proportionality between Capital and Control in Listed Companies (SEC [2007] 1705).
241. Communication of the Commission 'Financial Services: Implementing the Framework for Financial Markets: Action Plan' COM (1999) 232, available at: <http://ec.europa.eu/internal_market/finances/docs/actionplan/index/action_en.pdf>, accessed 16 Sep. 2008.
242. Press Release 'Financial Services: Commission Outlines Action Plan for Single Financial Market' IP/99/327.G. Walker, 'European Financial Programme: Content, Structure and Completion', *EBLR* (2004): 305, 324 A. Sainz de Vicuna, 'The Legal Integration of Financial Markets of the Euro Area', *EBLR* (2001): 223, 228, 232, 236. N. Moloney, 'Law-Making Risks

intending to contribute to the completion of a single wholesale financial market were some company law measures with major significance for financial markets. We should not forget that listed companies are the most important players in these wholesale markets and that their corporate governance matters. These proposed measures focused on the creation of a secure and transparent environment for cross-border restructuring. The Financial Services Action Plan proposed the European Company Statute, the Takeover Bids Directive, the Directive on cross-border mergers, and the Directive on transfers of company headquarters, as well as a Directive imposing a requirement for disclosure of objective and stable criteria for authorization of restructuring in the banking sector.[243] The Financial Services Action Plan envisaged a very important role for cross-border mergers and takeover bids in cross-border industrial restructuring. These legal instruments would contribute significantly to the protection of minority shareholders and to a more rationalized organization of corporate legal structures in the Single Market.[244] The 2001 Proposal of a Takeover Bid Directive (Recital 13 of the Preamble) stated among its main objectives that the proposed Directive would prevent patterns of corporate restructuring within the Community from being distorted by arbitrary differences in governance and management cultures. The framework of cross-border corporate restructuring should be characterized by transparency and security. These characteristics are very important for the application of prudential considerations in the case of mergers and takeovers.[245] When the relevant supervisory authority is called to implement some prudential conditions in a restructuring process of takeovers and mergers, it should take into account the principles of transparency and non-discrimination.[246] The Commission wanted to avoid the possibility of prudential conditions becoming obstacles to cross-border corporate restructuring and required any authorization process to take into account objective, continuous, and publicly disclosed standards.[247] These standards for the application of prudential considerations to corporate restructuring situations should fully respect the Commission's policy on free movement of capital and freedom of investment.[248]

---

in EC Financial Market Regulation after the Financial Services Action Plan', in *Better Regulation*, ed. S. Weatherill (Oxford: Hart, 2007), 321. For an analysis of financial services in the internal market before the Community's Action Plan, see: W. Van Gerven & J. Wouters, 'Free Movement of Financial Services and the European Contracts Convention' and M. Blair, 'Financial Services: the United Kingdom Regulator's Assessment of the 1992 Programme', in *E.C. Financial Market Regulation and Company Law*, ed. S. Kenyon-Slade & M. Andenas (London: Sweet & Maxwell, 1993), 43 & 125.

243. Press Release 'Financial Services: Commission Outlines Action Plan for Single Financial Market', IP/99/327.
244. COM (1999) 232, 9.
245. *Ibid.*
246. *Ibid.*
247. *Ibid.*
248. COM (1999) 232, 9. Communication of the Commission on Certain legal Aspects Concerning Intra-EU Investment. *OJ* C 220 (1997) 15.

In the spring of 2003, the European Commission launched an Action Plan with the title 'Modernizing Company Law and Enhancing Corporate Governance in the European Union', which proposed twenty-four legislative measures. The Action Plan was developed around three pivotal axes: removing national barriers to foster the internal market, avoiding races to the bottom, and promoting a certain degree of uniformity to reduce the informational costs currently borne by investors.[249] The European Commission was convinced that market integration demanded its regulatory intervention in the area of company law. These new legislative proposals were supposed to facilitate freedom of establishment, cross-border restructuring, and cross-border transactions.[250] These initiatives aimed to boost shareholders' confidence that the corporations that they invest in have equivalent corporate governance frameworks. Many voices have demanded a dynamic reaction of the European legislature after the recent financial scandals (e.g., Enron, WorldCom, and Parmalat).[251] The Commission also stressed the role of modern technologies in the framework of modern corporate governance and management. It is true that the accession of new Member States in 2004 and 2007 increased diversity in the EU, which now has twenty-seven different national company laws, and encouraged the European legislature to re-examine the Community's *acquis* in the field of company law, to amend already adopted legal instruments, and to propose new measures if necessary. This highlights the importance of a principles-based approach able to maintain a high level of legal certainty in intra-Community operations.[252] The objectives of the Action Plan are twofold: the first goal is to

249. L. Enriques & M. Gatti, 'The Uneasy Case for Top-Down Corporate Law Harmonization in the European Union', *University of Pennsylvania Journal of International Economic Law* 27 (2006): 939–998, SSRN Working Papers, <http://ssrn.com/abstract=879804>, 55. Communication from the Commission to the Council and the European Parliament, Modernising Company Law and Enhancing Corporate Governance in the European Union: A Plan to Move Forward, COM (2003) 284 final, 6–7, 14.

250. L. Enriques & M. Gatti (n. 249), 51.

251. L. Enriques & M. Gatti (n. 249), 52. J. Armour & J.A. McCahery, 'Introduction: Improving Corporate Law and Modernising Securities Regulation in Europe', *JCLS* 3 (2003): 211. The recent banking scandal of British Northern Rock, its connection with the internal market, and the role of the Bank of England and the European Central Bank are commented on by C. Bamford, 'Northern Rock and the Single Market', *Co Law* 29 (2008): 65–66. The reaction of the public to these scandals was stronger in the US than in the EU. For the justification of these different reactions and for an analysis of the extent the Sarbanes-Oxley Act could be used as a guide for corporate reforms in Europe, see: L. Enriques, 'Bad Apples, Bad Oranges: A Comment from Old Europe on Post-Enron Corporate Governance Reforms', *Wak For LR* 38 (2003): 911, 912–926. Commissioner F. Bolkestein had stated that prompt action is needed to ensure sustainable public confidence in financial markets. 'Company Law and Corporate Governance: Commission Presents Action Plan' (2003) IP/03/716. See also: P. Davies, 'Post-Enron Developments in the United Kingdom' and J. Hill, 'Corporate Scandals Across the Globe: Regulating the Role of the Director', in *Reforming Company and Takeover Law in Europe*, ed. G. Ferrarini, K.Hopt, J. Winter & E.Wymmersch, 1st edn (Oxford: Oxford University Press, 2004), 183, 225.

252. L. Enriques & M. Gatti (n. 249), 52. For principles-based regulatory intervention in the area of business law: J. Black, M. Hopper & C. Band, 'Making Success of the Principles-Based Regulation', *LFMR* (2007) 1. S. Schwarcz, 'The "Principles" Paradox', Duke Law School

strengthen shareholders' rights and the protection of employees, creditors, and other interested parties; and the second goal, which is closely connected with the first one, relates to the fostering of the efficiency and competitiveness of businesses, with special attention to some specific cross-border issues.[253] With respect to the first policy objective, the Commission believes that 'maintaining efficient protection of members and third parties will be even more important in the future, in view of the increasing mobility of companies within the EU', which reveals the Commission's fears that corporate mobility and the liberalization of company law may have some side-effects, like the race to the bottom.[254] As to the second policy objective, in the Commission's view, business efficiency and competitiveness should be promoted (a) through initiatives regulating cross-border business activities (cross-border mergers or transfers of registered offices and the elimination of cross-border impediments to the exercise of shareholder rights) and (b) though a certain degree of harmonization so as to reduce legal uncertainties and to combat psychological obstacles to cross-border business plans of corporations.[255] It seems that these concerns and thoughts of the Commission are depicted in the regulatory goal of the Takeover Directive, which is primarily to foster cross-border takeover bids by eliminating legal uncertainties and psychological obstacles in the area of public offers.

The Commission conducted a consultation from December 2005 to March 2006 on future priorities in company law and corporate governance to check the extent to which the medium- and long-term measures under the 2003 Action Plan and the Lisbon Agenda need to be modified, adapted, or refocused so as to continue to meet the requirements of the market and to ensure its effectiveness and efficiency. While the 2003 Action Plan focused on the restoration of investor confidence after the corporate scandals, the aim of this consultation was to improve the competitiveness of EU companies and to transpose the principles of the EU's better regulation approach. The Commission had shown its intentions to recast the entire company law *acquis* and to cut the red tape in its future regulatory initiatives.[256]

Legal Studies Research Paper Series, Research Paper No. 205 (2008) 1. R. Buxbaum, G. Hertig et al. (eds) (n. 97), 142.

253. K. Hopt, 'European Company Law and Corporate Governance: Where Does the Action Plan of the European Commission Lead?' (2005) ECGI Law Working Paper No. 52/2005, <http://ssrn.com/abstract=863527>, accessed 11 Aug. 2007, 3.

254. L. Enriques & M. Gatti (n. 249), 54. Communication from the Commission to the Council and the European Parliament, Modernising Company Law and Enhancing Corporate Governance in the European Union: A Plan to Move Forward COM (2003) 284 final, 8.

255. L. Enriques & M. Gatti (n. 249), 54.

256. D. Weber-Rey, 'Effects of the Better Regulation Approach on European Company Law and Corporate Governance', *ECFR* 3 (2007): 370, 399–400. European Commission 'Consultation and Hearing on Future Priorities for the Action Plan on Modernising Company Law and Enhancing Corporate Governance in the European Union', <http://ec.europa.eu/internal_market/company/docs/consultation/final_report_en.pdf>, accessed 27 Sep. 2008.

Chapter 4

The Permissible Limits of Harmonization: Subsidiarity Issues

4.1 INTRODUCTION

This chapter deals with subsidiarity, which will help us to see how far the European legislature could go in the regulation of takeovers bids and how it perceives its harmonizing competence in the internal market. The relevant case law will be discussed in detail. This analysis of subsidiarity will attempt to show various regulatory aspects of takeover regulation at the EU level.

4.2 THE PRINCIPLE OF SUBSIDIARITY

Article 5 of the EC Treaty addresses the principle of subsidiarity.[257] The EU

257. The other principles contained in Art. 5 EC Treaty is the principle of attributed competence and the principle of proportionality. For a thorough analysis of the subsidiarity debate at EU level and for some very useful comments and conclusions see: D.A. Wyatt & A. Dashwood (n. 46), 97, 367. P. Craig & G. De Burca (n. 12), 101. S. Weatherill *Cases and Materials on EU Law*, 8th edn (Oxford: Oxford University Press, 2007), 660, D.A. Wyatt (n. 106), S. Douglas-Scott *Constitutional Law of the European Union* (Essex: Longman, 2002), 155, N. Emiliou, 'Subsidiarity: an Effective Barrier against the "Enterprises of Ambition"?', *EL Rev.* 17 (1992): 383, V. Constantinesco, 'Who's Afraid of Subsidiarity?', *YEL* 11 (1991): 33. S. Weatherill, 'Competence Creep and Competence Control', YEL 23 (2004): 1, J. Pelkmans, 'Subsidiarity between Law and Economics' College of Europe Research Papers in Law No. 1/2005, D. Halberstam, 'Subsidiarity in Comparative Perspective' in V. Amar & M. Tushnet, *Comparative Constitutional Law* (Oxford: Oxford University Press, 2008), <http://eu.pravo.hr/fileadmin/Europsko/dokumenti/Dubrovnik_2008/halberstamamaredit_MT_11-15DH1_CLEAN_2.pdf>, accessed 26 Sep. 2008, M. Kumm, 'Constitutionalising Subsidiarity in Integrated Markets: The Case

Glossary[258] states that subsidiarity, introduced by the Maastricht Treaty, is intended to ensure that decisions are made as closely as possible to the needs of citizens and that constant checks are made as to whether action at the Community level is justified in light of the possibilities available at the national, regional, or local level. Specifically, subsidiarity is the principle whereby the EU does not take action (except in the areas that fall within its exclusive competence) unless it is more effective than action taken at the national, regional, or local level. In the case of the Community's non-exclusive competences, the European legislature should intervene only when collective action would have some appreciable advantage as compared to leaving matters to the Member States acting alone.[259] One major problem had been that there was no authoritative list of what falls within the EU's exclusive competence and what falls within the shared competence between the EU and Member States. Article I-13 of the draft Constitutional Treaty introduced such a categorization for the first time.[260] The Edinburgh European Council of December 1992 issued a Declaration on the principle of subsidiarity, which lays down the rules for its application. The Treaty of Amsterdam took up the approach that followed from this Declaration in a Protocol on the application of the principles of subsidiarity and proportionality annexed to the EC Treaty.[261] Two things that this Protocol introduced were the systematic analysis of the impact of

---

of Tobacco Regulation in the European Union', *ELJ* (2006): 503, R. Van den Bergh, 'The Subsidiarity Principle and the EC Competition Rules: The Costs and Benefits of Decentrilization', in *Constitutional Law and Economics of the European Union*, ed. D. Schmidtchen & R. Cooter (Cheltenham: Elgar, 1997), 142, R. Wesseling, 'Subsidiarity in Community Antitrust Law: Setting the Right Agenda', *EL Rev* 22 (1997) 35, N. W Barber, 'The Limited Modesty of Subsidiarity', *ELJ* 11 (2008): 308, U. di Fabio, 'The Allocation of Competences between the European Union and its Member States' and I. Pernice, 'Rethinking the Methods of Dividing and Controlling the Competences of the Union', in *The Treaty of Nice and Beyond*, ed. M Andenas & J. Usher (Oxford: Hart, 2003), 107, 121.

258. Europa EU Glossary, <http://europa.eu/scadplus/glossary/subsidiarity_en.htm>, accessed 11 Feb. 2009.
259. D.A. Wyatt & A. Dashwood (n. 46), 81.
260. D. Chalmers & A. Tomkins, *European Union Public Law* (Cambridge: Cambridge University Press, 2007), 220.
261. Protocols Annexed by the Treaty of Amsterdam to EC Treaty: Subsidiarity and Proportionality (Protocol No. 30 1997). D. Wyatt (ed.), *Rudden & Wyatt's EU Treaties & Legislation*, 9th edn (Oxford: Oxford University Press, 2004), 134. Subsidiarity is a subject matter directly connected to the issue of the quality of Community legislation. Many reports examined quality issues such as the 1992 Sutherland Report, the 1995 Molitor Report, the 1996 SLIM initiative, the UNICE Report, and the Koopmans Report. One of the most important objectives of quality control is the increase of legitimacy of rule-making and acceptance of the rules by citizens, business and society. A rule-making of good quality ensures the realization of the 'bringing the Union closer to its citizens' declaration. C. Timmermans, 'How Can One Improve the Quality of Community Legislation?', *CM LRev* (1997): 1229, 1229–1230, 1238, W. Voermans, The Quality of EU Legislation: What Kind of Problem, by What Kind of Standards? (2008) SSRN Working Paper, <http://ssrn.com/abstract=1272620>, accessed 3 Oct. 2008, E. Xanthaki,

legislative proposals on the principle of subsidiarity and the use, where possible, of less binding European Community measures.[262] Article 9 of the Protocol requires the Commission, in issues of non-exclusive competence, to provide a justification in the accompanying explanatory memorandum. This Protocol also requires the European Commission to consult with the European Council, the Council of the European Union and the European Parliament before any formal proposal is made and affirms that Community action would be appropriate in conditions where the cross-border situations could not be satisfactorily and effectively regulated by the national legislatures. When there has been no Community action or when national action would be incompatible with the Treaty's aims of European integration, Community action and legislative intervention should be considered as being appropriate.[263] Additionally, both Declaration 23 on the Future of the Union attached to the Nice Treaty and the Laeken Summit, which set up the Convention on the Future of Europe, stressed the importance of a better and more transparent division of competences in the EU.[264]

In recent cases, the ECJ was willing to confirm that the Community institutions have taken due account of the requirements of subsidiarity; nonetheless, the ECJ is reluctant to second-guess their choices about the appropriateness or otherwise of exercising supranational rather than purely domestic competences.[265] The ECJ had accepted quite easily that Community legislation would be more efficient than individual national legislation by stating, in *UK v. Council,*[266] that once the Council has found that it is necessary to improve the existing level of protection as regards the health and safety of workers and to harmonize the conditions in this area, achievement of that objective through the imposition of minimum requirements necessarily presupposes Community-wide action. In that case, the ECJ did not pay the required attention to the relevant Treaty Articles also authorizing Member States to take national measures toward the attainment of those goals.[267] The ECJ had minimized the requirement of Community institutions to include thorough subsidiarity considerations into the preambles[268] of

'The Problem of Quality in EU Legislation: What on Earth Is Really Wrong?', *CM L Rev* (2001): 651.

262. Europa EU glossary, <http://europa.eu/scadplus/glossary/subsidiarity_en.htm>, accessed 27 Sep. 2008. For a legal analysis of the historical development of the principle of subsidiarity: D.A. Wyatt, 'Subsidiarity and Judicial Review', in *Judicial Review in European Union Law*, ed. D. O'Keefe (The Hague: Kluwer Law International, 2000), 507–513.
263. N. Foster (n. 157), 113.
264. N. Foster (n. 157), 115.
265. D.A. Wyatt & A. Dashwood (n. 46), 81–82.
266. Case C-84/94, *United Kingdom v. Council* [1996] ECR I-5755 para. 47. For a thorough analysis of this case in light of subsidiarity, see: A. Estella, *The EU Principle of Subsidiarity and its Critique* (Oxford: Oxford University Press, 2002), 142.
267. D.A. Wyatt & A. Dashwood (n. 46), 102.
268. See references to the preambles of various EU Company Law Directives declaring market integration as their aim attainable through harmonization: R. Buxbaum & K. Hopt (n. 80), 196.

Community legislation. As far as the harmonization of company law and securities regulation is concerned, the legislative practice of Community institutions supports the proposition that this harmonization is either already an integral part of the common market or one of the foundations of Community economic policy.[269] If it is shown that a harmonizing instrument of company law is necessary for the development of the common market or that it has a direct impact on the operation of the common market, it is not essential to prove that this legal instrument pursues one or more of the higher objectives of the EC Treaty (Articles 2 and 3 of the EC Treaty).[270] Legal harmonization of company law pursues the goals of Article 2 of the EC Treaty, and Article 2 of the EC Treaty promotes the higher objectives of the EC Treaty; as a matter of fact, no additional justification is required, if this reasoning is adopted.[271] Furthermore, the ECJ seems to accept that if a specific competence for the adoption of internal market measures was attributed to the Community legislature, this also satisfies the compliance with the subsidiarity principle (if there is competence to harmonize, harmonization justifies the exercise of this competence).[272] The conditions of compliance with the principle of subsidiarity became more obscure after the *Deposit Guarantee Directive,*[273] which stated that procedural conditions are fulfilled even where there is no evidence to suppose that the EU legislature actually considered whether proposed legislation complied with subsidiarity and notwithstanding the fact that there is no explicit reference in the proposed legislation to it.[274] Recital 25 of the Preamble of the Takeover Bid Directive discusses compliance with the principle of subsidiarity and states that since the objectives of the action envisaged, namely to establish minimum guidelines for the conduct of takeover bids and ensure an adequate level of protection for holders of securities throughout the Community, cannot be sufficiently achieved by the Member States because of the need for transparency and legal certainty in the case of cross-border takeovers and acquisitions of control, and can therefore, by reason of the scale and effects of the action, be better achieved at the Community level, the Community may adopt measures in accordance with the principle of subsidiarity as set out in Article 5 of the EC Treaty.

---

269. R. Buxbaum & K. Hopt (n. 80), 197.
270. R. Buxbaum & K. Hopt (n. 80), 197.
271. *Ibid.*
272. D.A. Wyatt, 'Subsidiarity', in *Whose Europe? National Models and the Constitution of the European Union*, ed. K. Nicolaidis & S. Weatherill (Oxford: Conference papers, 2003), 91–92, <www.competition-law.ox.ac.uk/iecl/pdfs/whoseeurope.pdf>, accessed 7 Oct. 2008. See also Case C-377/98, *Dutch Biotechnology* [2001] ECR I-7079.
273. Case C-233/94, *Germany v. European Parliament and Council (Deposit Guarantee Directive)* [1997] ECR I-2405 paras 22–28. For very enlightening comments on this case: A. Estella (n. 266), 148.
274. D. Chalmers & A. Tomkins (n. 260), 224–225.

4.3 LIMITS THAT THE PRINCIPLE OF SUBSIDIARITY PLACES ON THE HARMONIZATION EFFORTS OF THE COMMUNITY LEGISLATURE

The ECJ has tried to clarify the substantive issue of compliance with the principle of subsidiarity. In the very important cases of *Dutch Biotechnology,*[275] BAT,[276] and *Alliance for Natural Health*[277] (dealing with Community competence under Article 95 of the EC Treaty), the ECJ affirmed that the Community measure was serving a market-making purpose by eliminating obstacles to trade and distortions of competition within the internal market resulting from the multifarious development of national laws.[278] Community legislative intervention was deemed to be essential because the Member States would not be able to attain individually this objective (the legislative initiatives of Member States so far had resulted only in this multifarious development of national laws that created obstacles and distorted competition).[279] However, this examination of the substantive part of the subsidiarity principle was not a difficult task for the ECJ because the existence of cross-border trade barriers and distortions of competition arising from legal diversity among Member States is a prerequisite for the very existence of Community competence under Article 95 of the EC Treaty.[280] Hence, it is easily understood that the European legislature had to propose Community legislation so as to eliminate those obstacles or distortions.[281]

It would be interesting to examine the limits that the principle of subsidiarity places on the harmonization efforts of the Community. The goals of EU integration are decided by the European legislature, and Member States could question and challenge mainly the attainment and the method of realization of these objects; it could be alleged that these objects can be attained better at the national level, without any EU legislative intervention.[282] The Community institutions enjoy wide discretion, framed in a rather open-ended way, in assessing and determining the objectives that could not be sufficiently achieved by the Member States and could, as a result, be better achieved by the Community on the basis of the scale or

275. Case C-377/98 [2001] ECR I-7079.
276. Case C-491/01 [2002] ECR I-11453.
277. Joined Cases C-154/04 and C-155/04 [2005] ECR I-6451.
278. D.A. Wyatt & A. Dashwood (n. 46), 102–103. In *Alliance for Natural Health*, the ECJ held that when there are obstacles to trade, or it is likely that such obstacles will emerge in the future, because the Member States have taken, or are about to take, divergent measures with respect to a product or a class of products, which bring about different levels of protection and thereby prevent the product or products concerned from moving freely within the Community, Art. 95 EC Treaty authorizes the Community legislature to intervene by adopting appropriate measures. Joined Cases C-154/04 and C-155/04 [2005] ECR I-6451 para. 32(See also C-434/02 *Arnold André* [2004] ECR I-11825 para 34, and Case C-210/03 *Swedish Match* [2004] ECR I-11893 para. 33).
279. D.A. Wyatt & A. Dashwood (n. 46), 103.
280. *Ibid.*
281. Compliance with the principle of attributed competence could possibly be equated with respect to the principle of subsidiarity. D.A. Wyatt & A. Dashwood (n. 46), 103.
282. K. Hopt (n. 253), 10.

effects of the proposed Community action.[283] The ECJ confirmed this inclination toward wide discretion in *Upjohn Ltd*:[284]

> According to the Court's case-law, where a Community authority is called upon, in the performance of its duties, to make complex assessments, it enjoys a wide measure of discretion, the exercise of which is subject to a limited judicial review in the course of which the Community judicature may not substitute its assessment of the facts for the assessment made by the authority concerned. Thus, in such cases, the Community judicature must restrict itself to examining the accuracy of the findings of fact and law made by the authority concerned and to verifying, in particular, that the action taken by that authority is not vitiated by a manifest error or a misuse of powers and that it did not clearly exceed the bounds of its discretion.

The word 'discretion' in this judicial context means the measurement of freedom to make the value-judgments necessary to make the decisions necessary to carry out the task allotted to the institutions instead of the choice of adopting different policy options without totally excluding the latter possibility.[285] It seems that the ECJ considers the substantive aspects of subsidiarity as a subject matter tilting towards politics. The ECJ would uphold a breach of the subsidiarity principle in the case of an EU institution manifestly exceeding the limits of the discretion conferred upon it by Article 5 of the EC Treaty considered in connection with the legal basis for the act in question.[286] If harmonization of national laws in the field of takeover bids is thought by the Commission to be a prerequisite for integration in the market for corporate control (being a fracture of the internal market), then it is difficult to imagine how Member States can possibly achieve this without the necessary

---

283. D.A. Wyatt (n. 262), 513. F. Easterbrook argues that when free movement of economic factors/trade is voluntary the principle of subsidiarity demands national legislation. When free movement is outside the scope of national control or when Member States possess monopoly power being able to export overcharges or taxes, Community institutions should legislate. Demanding 'better law' at the Community level is sometimes the result of lobbying or a political decision. Regulatory competion among the various Member States should not be underestimated because it has equal efficiency and power with the competition in markets. F. Easterbrook, 'Federalism and European Business Law', in *European Economic and Business Law*, ed. R. Buxbaum et al. (New York: de Gruyter, 1996), 11.
284. Case C-120/97 [1999] ECR I-223 para. 34 The ECJ also refers to the following rulings as its well-established case law in this area: Joined Cases 56/64 and 58/64, *Consten and Grundig v. Commission* [1966] ECR 299, Case 55/75, *Balkan-Import Export v. Hauptzollamt Berlin-Packhof* [1976] ECR 19 para. 8, Case 9/82, *Ohrgaard and Delvaux v. Commission* [1983] ECR 2379 para. 14, Case C-225/91, *Matra v. Commission* [1993] ECR I-3203 paras 24 and 25, and Case C-157/96, *National Farmers' Union and Others* [1998] ECR I-2211 para. 39). (cited also by D.A. Wyatt (n. 46), 513–514). Moreover, the ECJ confirmed this discretion of European legislature in Case T-47/02, *Manfred Danzer and Hannelore Danzer v. Council of the European Union* [2006] ECR II-1779.
285. D.A. Wyatt (n. 262), 514.
286. *Ibid.*

coordination of national provisions.[287] A European legal framework for takeover bids is not just another set of rules amounting to more regulation, but this set of Community rules abolishes barriers among Member States, promotes competition, and contributes to the development of a market for corporate control in those Member States with no well-established market for corporate control.[288]

4.4 THE NEW APPROACH TOWARD HARMONIZATION: FLEXIBILITY AND SIMPLIFICATION

The European legislature had adopted a more flexible and simplified approach toward the regulation of the internal market. The EU Glossary[289] states that simplifying legislation means weeding out the superfluous by rigorously applying the principles of necessity and proportionality. The exercise mainly involves the recasting and formal or informal consolidation of legislation. This concept has grown in importance in relation to the internal market since the White Paper on the Completion of the Single Market. It was highlighted by the Edinburgh European Council in 1992. Over the past years, a concentrated effort has been made to establish a market giving priority to the four freedoms, but this has meant a wealth of European legislation, the simplification of which has now become a priority to ensure that Community action is transparent and effective.[290] The pilot programme (Simplification of Legislation for the Internal Market (SLIM)), which covers four specific areas, was launched in May 1996 and has been reinforced by a multi-annual programme on the simplification and updating of Community legislation adopted by the European Commission in February 2003. In response to the declaration on the quality of the drafting of Community legislation appended to the Final Act of the Intergovernmental Conference (1997), an inter-institutional agreement defining the guidelines for improving the quality of the drafting of legislation was adopted in December 1998. A new inter-institutional agreement that goes beyond drafting quality alone and is entitled 'Better Lawmaking' was adopted in December 2003.[291] As has been mentioned, the 2003 Corporate Governance Action Plan guided the European legislature toward a principle-based approach within the framework of Better Lawmaking. The 2003 Corporate Governance Action Plan does not intend to propose a Pan-European corporate governance code and attempts to harmonize a few essential rules with closer coordination between

287. K. Hopt (n. 253), 10.
288. K. Hopt (n. 253), 6.
289. Europa EU Glossary, <http://europa.eu/scadplus/glossary/legislation_simplification_en.htm>, accessed 11 Feb. 2009.
290. Europa EU glossary, <http://europa.eu/scadplus/glossary/legislation_simplification_en.htm>, accessed 27 Sep. 2008.
291. Europa EU glossary, <http://europa.eu/scadplus/glossary/legislation_simplification_en.htm>, accessed 27 Sep. 2008.

and among national codes.[292] Its regulatory approach is far from a 'one-size-fits-all' approach, given the many different national corporate governance models.[293] Moreover, the Lisbon Agenda includes among its eight key actions the improvement and simplification of the regulatory framework of business operations.[294] In this strand of the 'better regulation' approach, the European Commission should not neglect the principle of subsidiarity;[295] the 2003 Corporate Governance Action Plan requires the Commission to fully respect the subsidiarity and proportionality principles of the Treaty and the diversity of many different approaches to the same questions in the Member States, while at the same time pursuing clear ambitions (strengthening the single market and enhancing the rights of shareholders and third parties).[296] It was argued that legal diversity in company laws of Member States and the tools for making it compatible with market integration are just as important an element of the EU policy on company law as harmonization is.[297] Subsidiarity considerations on a case-by-case basis could lead to the conclusion that national

292. D. Weber-Rey, 'Latest Developments in European Corporate Governance in Light of Better Regulation Efforts', in *Better Regulation*, ed. S. Weatherill (Oxford: Hart, 2007), 253. S. Fazio (n. 14), 191–192. Apart from the 2003 Corporate Governance Action Plan, the importance of harmonization of takeover bids was also stressed by the 1999 Financial Services Action Plan. For the implementation of the principle of subsidiarity to financial services, see: D. Mavromati, *The Law of Payment Services in the EU* (The Hague: European Monographs, Kluwer, 2008), 114–116.
293. D. Weber-Rey (n. 292), 253. Legal orders of Member States consist of EU law, harmonized national laws and national laws not under direct influence of harmonization. After the 2004 and 2007 enlargements, when twelve new Member States acceded to the European Union, the range of formally binding EU Law increased together with the variety of interests and national peculiarities. Twenty-seven Member States will add greater ideological, political and socio-economic diversity and more views which would have a wider effect on the company lawmaking process. A. Radwan, '25 Thoughts on European Company Law in the EU of 25', *EBLR* (2006): 1169, 1169, 1171, 1179. This legal diversity at the EU level is enhanced by the limited subject matter of the company law harmonization programme. C. Villiers (n. 101), 226–229. It was also argued that, despite the different national company laws, a common legal pattern with its own distinct features seems to exist. F. Kubler, 'A Shifting Paradigm of European Company Law?', *Col J Eur L* (2005): 219, 219.
294. D. Weber-Rey (n. 292), 253. D.A. Wyatt & A. Dashwood (n. 46), 916–918.
295. Better regulation in the EU is closely connected to the question of vertical distribution of powers and, as a matter of fact, to the subsidiarity debate. Commission Report 'Better Lawmaking 2005' COM (2006) 289. S. Weatherill, 'The Challenge of Better Regulation', in *Better Regulation*, ed. S. Weatherill (Oxford: Hart, 2007), 2.
296. COM (2003) 284, 4–5. D. Weber-Rey (n. 292), 253. K. Hopt argues that a mere recommendation based on 249 EC Treaty, as a soft law legal instrument, would definitely satisfy the subsidiarity objection. However, a recommendation and other voluntary approaches are not always efficient for most areas of company law including the Takeover Bid Directive. This was proved by the fate of the European Code of conduct for security transactions of 1977 with its suggestion that a compulsory takeover bid be introduced, for this was totally ignored by Germany. K. Hopt, 'Company Law in the European Union: Harmonization or Subsidiarity', Working Paper Centro di studi e ricerche di diritto comparator e straniero, Saggi, Conference e Seminari 31 (Roma 1998), 10–11. J.J. Kirton & M. Trebilcock, *Hard Choices, Soft Law* (Aldershot: Ashgate, 2004).
297. S. Grundmann, 'The Structure of European Company Law: From Crisis to Boom', *EBOR* 5 (2004): 602, 602. U. Procaccia & U. Segal, 'Thou Shalt Not Sow Thy Vineyard with Divers

rules are more appropriate in a particular case without producing any obstacles to market integration. The resulting legal diversity, with all these different national rules, operates in one integrated market, which sometimes causes optimal regulatory competition.[298] This legal diversity, originating from the application of the principle of subsidiarity, could possibly allow the satisfaction of different preferences, innovative solutions for corporations, and better regulatory experimentation in the area of company law.[299] G. Hertig and J.A. McCahery support a minimally harmonized takeover regime enhancing transparency and shareholder protection and establishing a limit for the 'race to the bottom', and endorse a default arrangement for takeover bids that would allow firms to choose to be regulated either by the Takeover Bid Directive or by existing Member State law.[300] This approach could lead to regulatory competition between national legislatures, innovation in company law, legal arrangements meeting companies' needs, a solution to the matter of compensation of multiple and dual class shareholders, a selection of better takeover laws, and the development of an active cross-border takeover market in the EU.[301]

4.5 APPLYING THE PRINCIPLE OF SUBSIDIARITY TO THE REGULATION OF TAKEOVER BIDS AT THE EU LEVEL

One area of the company law harmonization programme that involved discussions on subsidiarity was the harmonization of takeover bids. The Commission had chosen a minimum intervention legal instrument for the regulation of takeover bids and securities regulation in general. In 1977, the Commission issued a non-binding recommendation on a code of conduct for securities trading.[302] It is

---

Seeds? The Case Against Harmonization of Private Law', in *Capital Markets and Company Law*, ed. K. Hopt & E. Wymeersch (Oxford: Oxford University Press, 2003), 639.

298. S. Grundmann (n. 297), 608–609. For a US perspective on regulatory competition: R. Romano, *The Advantage of Competitive Federalism for Securities Regulation* (Washington: AEI, 2002). In general, competition within a political system restricts the power of government to attain its regulatory goals or at least to achieve the objectives it sets out to achieve. It could possibly be said that subsidiarity had to do with how markets replace regulation with competition in spite of the best and hard efforts of government. F. Easterbrook, 'Federalism and European Business Law' in *European Economic and Business Law*, ed. R. Buxbaum & others (New York: de Gruyter, 1996), 2–3.
299. S. Grundmann (n. 297), 616.
300. They are also quite critical of the proposed EU Company Law reforms under the Company Law Action Plan. They think that many of these harmonizing measures are excessive regulatory intervention, enhance only costly bureaucratic intervention, and do not help firms and investors. G. Hertig & J. A, McCahery, 'Company and Takeover Law Reforms in Europe: Misguided Harmonization Efforts or Regulatory Competition?', *EBOR* 4 (2003): 179, 179–180, 205–206.
301. G. Hertig & J. A, McCahery (n. 300), 179–180, 205–206.
302. Commission Recommendation 77/534/EEC, concerning a European code of conduct relating to transactions in transferable securities (1977) OJ L212/37. N. Moloney (n. 108), 19. R. Buxbaum & K. Hopt (n. 80), 197.

obvious that this soft law document respected national competences in the field of securities regulation and left plenty of room for Member States to coordinate their capital market laws. This code contained general and supplementary principles; the most important being the third general principle and the seventeenth supplementary principle requiring equal treatment of shareholders through a mandatory bid.[303] This optional legal instrument had limited results. The drafting process of the 1989, 1990, and 1996 proposals for a Thirteenth Directive on Takeovers was concerned with issues of subsidiarity. The Commission proposal of 1989 was withdrawn at the Edinburgh Summit, was assessed under the lens of the subsidiarity principle, and was re-launched again in 1996. The 1996 proposal was a framework directive, much more streamlined than the previous ones, with general principles being used as the guide for proper implementation by the national legislatures, and with the original ideas being considerably modified and greatly watered down in content.[304] The same pattern was followed by the subsequent proposals of 2002 and 2003 and by the final text of the Takeover Bid Directive with the optional provisions, the reciprocity clause and discretion, though narrow, granted to Member States and national authorities.[305] Moreover, the 1996, 2002, and 2003 proposals, as well as the final text of the adopted Directive, imposed only minimum harmonization standards.[306] The Commission preferred

303. J.L. Hansen, 'When Less Would Be More: The EU Takeover Directive in its Latest Apparition', *Col J EL* 9 (2003): 275, 276. In relation to the regulation of companies, transnational law distinguishes between hard law deriving from company law, securities regulation or employment law and the soft law of voluntary codes of conduct, corporate governance codes and corporate social responsibility codes. P. Zumbansen, 'Transnational Law', in *Elgar Encyclopedia of Comparative Law*, ed. J.M Smits (Cheltenham: Elgar, 2008), 742–743.

304. Many were afraid that in the 1989 and 1990 proposals, there would be a retreat like that in the case of the Ninth Directive harmonizing the law on groups of companies; not withstanding this previous experience, there was a new proposal for a Takeover Bid Directive in 1996 taking into account subsidiarity. K. Hopt (n. 296), 9–10, N. Moloney (n. 108), 18.

305. A framework directive sets the framework for the regulation of a particular matter and leaves the determination of details to Member States. Nevertheless, this characteristic is inherent to the nature of the directive as an instrument for harmonization, which is binding only to the legislative goals to be achieved and leaves only discretion to Member States as to the method of implementation into the national legal system. This is understood better if a directive is compared with a regulation. In company law, the result has frequently been much diversity in the harmonized laws of Member States; classic examples are the balance sheet law of the Fourth and Seventh Directives and, more recently, the Twelfth Directive. K. Hopt (n. 296), 9–12. For the implementation process in the UK, see: A. Kennon, 'The Parliamentary Process for Implementation of Community Financial Market and Company Law', in *E.C. Financial Market Regulation and Company Law*, ed. S. Kenyon-Slade & M. Andenas (London: Sweet & Maxwell, 1993), 111.

306. When the European legislature chooses to follow the legislative method of minimum harmonization, only minimum standards are set by the harmonizing directive. Member States may preserve national laws that could be stricter or they may choose to pass stricter ones. Minimum harmonization is expressly provided for in the EC Treaty for the areas of labour law, social law and environmental protection (Arts 138, 174 and 176 EC Treaty), but it is also quite possible in other areas and represents actual practice in company and capital markets law. On the one hand, a directive, such as the Insider Dealing Directive expressly allows stricter national

a more streamlined version, closer to the needs of market operators for flexibility in these subtle financial transactions. The principles-based approach, supporting 'substance over form', and not the rules-based approach, is followed by the European legislature in the field of corporate governance.[307] The 2003 Corporate Governance Action Plan requires harmonization in the area of company law and corporate governance to be flexible in application but to be firm in the principles, and to concentrate on priorities, be transparent, and subject to proper due process and consultation.[308]

The Takeover Bid Directive sets out to establish minimum guidelines for the conduct of takeover bids involving the securities of companies governed by the laws of Member States, where all or some of those securities are admitted to trading on a regulated market; it also seeks to provide an adequate level of protection for holders of securities throughout the Community by establishing a framework of common principles and general requirements that Member States are to implement through more detailed rules in accordance with their national systems and their cultural contexts.[309] The first words of the Directive's Preamble are dedicated to Article 44(1) of the EC Treaty, which aims at the attainment of the freedom of establishment. Preamble (1) of the Directive declares as its legal basis Article 44(2)(g) of the EC Treaty and, as a result, the Directive is classified in the company law harmonization programme (the Thirteenth Company Law Directive). The purpose of the European Company law harmonization programme is manifold: an increase of transparency, the reduction of the cost of cross-border transactions, and the removal of obstacles to establishment and of appreciable distortions of competition.[310] The wording of Article 44(2)(g) of the EC Treaty, 'coordinating to the necessary extent', could be interpretated in different ways. It is argued that only a minimum level of protection throughout the Community is necessary.[311] Others demand a more active and intensive intervention of the

---

provisions (Directive 89/592 [1989] OJ L334/30). For a legal analysis, see: B. Rider & M. Ashe, 'The Insider Dealing Directive', in *E.C. Financial Market Regulation and Company Law*, ed. S. Kenyon-Slade & M. Andenas (London: Sweet & Maxwell, 1993), 209). On the other hand, it does not preclude them, as is the case, according to a contested opinion, with the Second Capital Directive. K. Hopt (n. 295), 12.

307. D. Weber-Rey (n. 292), 250–251 & (n. 256), 384.
308. COM (2003) 284, 4–5. The 'benefit of a company' and other notions surrounding it, together with the pertaining theories, play a decisive role in the legislative choices to be made in the area of company law. J. Dine, 'Companies and Regulations: Theories, Justifications and Policing', in *Regulating Enterprise-Law and Business Organizations in the UK*, ed. D. Milman (Oxford: Hart, 1999), 291. S. Fazio (n. 14), 161.
309. Europa website, 'Activities of the European Union-Internal Market', SCADPLUS: Takeover Bids, <http://europa.eu/scadplus/leg/en/lvb/l26012a.htm>, accessed 21 May 2007.
310. G. Wolff, 'The Commission's Programme for Company Law Harmonisation: The Winding Road to a Uniform European Company Law?', in *E.C. Financial Market Regulation and Company Law*, ed. S. Kenyon-Slade & M. Andenas (London: Sweet & Maxwell, 1993), 19.
311. G. Wolff (n. 310), 21. Reflexive harmonization provides a basis for the evolutionary selection of rules through mutual learning (experimentation and adaptation) between national-level systems. It is true that reflexive harmonization could have positive results at both the national and community levels. At the national level, it allows rules to be matched to local approaches,

European legislature expressed by more uniform provisions through harmonization because all members of companies at the EU level should have the same rights, which calls for uniform laws.[312] Others believe that harmonization is needed to abolish all remaining obstacles to cross-border establishment and that further harmonization would reduce costs and increase efficiency for doing business within the Community.[313] Recent EU company law legislation follows a new minimalist approach to harmonization, which acknowledges diversity in the system and encourages competition among national legal orders.[314] Minimum harmonization in company law promotes diverse, national solutions to regulatory problems by providing the necessary flexibility and discretion to Member States to adopt any necessary measures.[315] One example of this approach is the Takeover Bid Directive, with its multi-layered, opt-in–opt-out/reciprocity system. Following these harmonization rationales and approaches mentioned above, the European Commission in its 2002 proposal for a Directive on Takeover Bids stressed that:

> The new proposal pursues the same objectives as *its predecessor [1996 proposal]*: alongside the *general objectives* of *integrating European markets [i.e., the EU market for corporate control]* in line with the Financial Services Action Plan and undertaking harmonisation conducive to *corporate restructuring*, it sets out to strengthen the *legal certainty [combat psychological obstacles]* of cross-border takeover bids in the interests of all concerned and

and at the community level, it allows innovation by maintaining variety within the 'pool' of legal solutions to common regulatory problems. S. Deakin, 'Two Types of Regulatory Competition: Competitive Federalism versus Reflexive Harmonization: A Law and Economics Perspective on *Centros*', *CYELS* (1999): 231, 232. C. Forstinger argues that reflexive harmonization is the most appropriate method of regulating takeovers because this method uses both centralized legislation of minimum standards to overcome market failures, existing specifically in the area of takeovers, and some degree of self-regulation to obtain discretion for autonomous governance on national level. The aim of reflexive harmonization is to protect legal diversity and to guide the process of evolutionary and participatory adaptation of rules at the national level. C. Forstinger, *Takeover Law in the EU and USA: A Comparative Analysis* (The Hague: Kluwer Law International, 2002), 158, 160, Moreover, P. Zumbansen completes the comment of C. Forstinger by saying that the fact that reflexive law considers the co-evolutionary process of minimum harmonization and ongoing processes of self-regulation and adaptation in the Member States is very positive for market integration because ongoing deliberation and mutual education are facilitated. P. Zumbansen, 'European Corporate Law and National Divergences: The case of Takeover Regulation', (Book Reviews) *Wash U Gl St LR* (2004): 867, 886.

312. G. Wolff (n. 310), 21.
313. *Ibid.*
314. A.S. Reid, 'The Increasing Europeanisation of Company Law', *BLR* 7 (2003): 165, 165. When subsidiarity is reflected in economic terms, it is closely related to regulatory competition, that is, the competition of legislators and rule-makers. When the European legislature decides not to intervene and not to harmonize, this decision does not automatically mean less state and less regulation, because Member States may have even more regulation in this area and regulatory competition may not exist because of persisting barriers such as language, legal culture, history, and politics. K. Hopt (n. 253), 21.
315. C. Forstinger (n. 311), 159.

> to ensure *protection for minority shareholders* in the course of such transactions. It establishes a *framework [framework directive]* for action by Member States by laying down certain *principles* and a limited number of *general requirements* while allowing Member States to adopt the *detailed implementing rules [narrow discretion]* in accordance with their national practices, provided that the differences are not such as to jeopardise implementation of the directive at Community level.[316] (emphasis added)

The EU legislature had to intervene and provide a framework for the conduct of takeover bids at the EU level, considering that takeovers are an effective method of exercising the right of establishment of companies. It was proved in practice that unharmonized (or sometimes non-existent) national safeguards may make this form of establishment too burdensome or even impossible.[317] Each Member State could preserve its competence to regulate takeover bids and its own national safeguards, but harmonization deriving from Article 44(2)(g) of the EC Treaty is essential to guarantee that the fundamental freedom of corporate establishment is not obstructed by the extent of particular national rules.[318] Harmonization also ensures that Member States will not regulate takeover bids in a protectionist way, thereby inhibiting market access to potential investors from other Member States. As a matter of fact, harmonization should enable companies to do what they could not do otherwise and to exercise the fundamental freedom of establishment, given the burden of cumulative and even conflicting national rules.[319]

4.6 CONCLUSION

Article 3 of the Amsterdam Protocol on subsidiarity characterizes the principle of subsidiarity as a dynamic concept that can be expanded, restricted, or discontinued when circumstances so require. Thus, it could be concluded that whichever theoretical or jurisprudential approach and interpretation is followed, the principle of

316. Proposal for a Directive of the European Parliament and of the Council on Takeover Bids COM/2002/0534 (final) [2003] *OJ* 45E/1.
317. G. Wolff (n. 310), 22. Nevertheless, the House of Lords Select Committee and UK Takeover Panel doubted the appropriateness of a directive on takeover bids, argued that it did not solve any problems that could not be addressed by the national laws, and alleged that takeovers should be regulated at the national rather than at the EU level in compliance always with the principle of subsidiarity. N. Moloney (n. 108), 821.
318. G. Wolff (n. 310), 22 U. Bernitz, 'Special Issue Section on Corporate Governance in Europe in the Light of the Takeover Directive', *EBLR* (2004): 1351, 1351.
319. G. Wolff (n. 310), 22. However, it was argued that takeovers are an area that should be left to self-regulation by market forces because of participation of sophisticated financial players in the market for corporate control. The subsidiarity principle would be complied with better if individual Member States exclusively regulated takeovers and then competitive market forces, and regulatory competition provided the best solution. Harmonization should refrain from regulating substantive issues of takeovers, such as the mandatory bid and the breakthrough rule, and should coordinate only the disclosure of information, time-limits and jurisdictional issues. J.L. Hansen (n. 303), 295–298.

subsidiarity will remain as difficult as ever to tie down.[320] The overall stance of the ECJ toward the Community competence to intervene and to regulate the internal market could be characterized by a few inconsistencies. On one hand, the broad interpretation that the ECJ adopted on Treaty Articles guaranteeing the fundamental freedoms in the internal market widened the scope of legal bases available for the regulation of the internal market. On the other hand, those Treaty provisions whose goal was the delimitation of Community competence to regulate the internal market were construed narrowly by the ECJ.[321] This principle should force the Commission to better justify the need for Community action, and especially, for detailed, intrusive European provisions.[322] EU legislative efforts should mainly focus on securing and promoting the coherence of the internal market, which cannot be achieved very effectively by the Member States.[323]

320. N. Foster (n. 157), 113.
321. D.A. Wyatt, 'The Growing Competence of the European Community', *EBLR* (2005): 483, 487.
322. P. Demaret, 'A Short Walk in the Realm of Subsidiarity', in *European Economic and Business Law*, ed. R. Buxbaum et al. (New York: de Gruyter, 1996), 30. Directives characterized by extreme specificity and containing numerous detailed provisions are the subject matter of a very interesting debate. R. Buxbaum & K. Hopt (n. 80), 233–234.
323. P. Demaret (n. 322), 30.

Chapter 5

Weaknesses and Difficulties in Harmonization Efforts in the Field of EU Company Law

5.1 INTRODUCTION

This chapter will analyse a range of drawbacks of company law harmonization and how they already affect or are going to affect the regulation of takeover bids at the EU level. This is a criticism of the harmonization of various company law standards and their efficiency within the internal market framework but not a criticism of the wide discretion that the European legislature enjoys with regard to its legislative evaluations.

5.2 IMPLEMENTATION OF DIRECTIVES

Article 44(1) of the EC Treaty states that the European Council shall act by means of directives so as to attain freedom of establishment. Article 249 of the EC Treaty provides that a directive shall be binding, as to the result to be achieved, upon each Member State to which it is addressed, but that it shall leave to the national authorities the choice of form and methods. A directive must be implemented by a national legislature to be introduced into the national legal order and to form an operative part of it.[324] One problem related to the implementation of directives by Member States is the possibility of misinterpretation of a directive's content or of the amount of discretion conferred by the European legislature upon a

324. M. Horspool & M. Humphreys, *European Union Law,* 4th edn (Oxford: Oxford University Press, 2006), 77.

national legislature.[325] A consequence of this problematic situation is the possibility that a Member State may consider wrongly that its existing national legislation is in conformity with a directive and not proceed to the required implementation of that directive.[326] While regulations are always of general application throughout the EU, directives are addressed explicitly to specific Member States and bind only those Member States but not the rest (however, most directives are in fact addressed to all Member States).[327] According to Article 254 of the EC Treaty, regulations, as well as directives that are addressed to all Member States, shall be published in the Official Journal of the European Union. They shall enter into force on the date specified in them or, in the absence thereof, on the twentieth day following that of their publication. After the ECJ found that directives could have a vertical direct effect in *van Duyn,*[328] it was thought that the difference between regulations and directives could become blurred and perhaps be abandoned.[329] It has also been argued that, to achieve the uniform and consistent application of EU Law, directives should be introduced into domestic law without changes to their wording.[330]

5.3 CRITICIZING THE VARIOUS TECHNIQUES OF HARMONIZATION

There has been much criticism of the efficacy of various techniques of harmonization.[331] Although the European legislature tends to regulate exhaustively or almost exhaustively some areas of the internal market, optional harmonization and minimum harmonization were chosen quite often in the field of company law.

Optional harmonization allows market participants to apply national norms or Community norms, while some directives allow the Member State to opt out.[332] In optional harmonization, there are two sets or rules: one for the domestic market

325. M. Horspool & M. Humphreys (n. 324), 77.
326. M. Horspool & M. Humphreys (n. 324), 77–78.
327. M. Horspool & M. Humphreys (n. 324), 78.
328. Case 41/74, *Yvonne van Duyn v. Home Office*[1974] ECR 1337.
329. M. Horspool & M. Humphreys (n. 324), 78.
330. M. Horspool & M. Humphreys (n. 324), 77–78.
331. C. Villiers (n. 100), 178. For a criticism of the directives regulating sectors of the internal market see: M.B. Kurcz, 'Harmonization by Means of Directives: Never-Ending Story?', *EBLR* (2001): 287. M.B. Kurcz presents various possible scenarios of harmonization of laws in the European Union by means of directives. He discusses the various categories of harmonizing directives (total, partial, optional, alternative, and minimum), criticizes possible trade barriers coming from more stringent rules of minimum harmonization and questions the subsequent diversity that could result. Finally, he alleges that hybrid directives combining more than one legal technique of harmonization could serve better the purposes of market integration.
332. W. Van Gerven (n. 223), 508. P.J. Slot (n. 192), 386. Cl. Lempereur (n. 123), 244.

and one for intra-Community trade.[333] Articles 9 and 11 of the Takeover Bid Directive constitute an example of optional harmonization. The opt-outs of Article 9 and/or 11 of the Takeover Bid Directive and the reciprocity clause of Article 11 are characterized as the main deficiencies of this effort to harmonize the European market for corporate control. Some other examples that contain options are the Fourth and Seventh Directives,[334] the rules on the acquisition by a company of its own shares in the Second Directive[335] and the Sixth Directive,[336] which is wholly optional for Member States that do not already permit division of public companies.[337] These options reveal the defeat of Community initiatives by national idiosyncrasies and interests entrenched by national lobbying. It is also possible that these options create only a superficial equivalence of national standards. Moreover, the possibility that this optional harmonization would affect the content and the scope of the mandatory provision of the harmonizing measure cannot be excluded. This has happened with the mandatory bid rule of the Takeover Bid Directive, which presents many important deficiencies.[338]

Minimum harmonization also results in similar diversity of company and securities laws, yet, at least in this case, a central mandatory core of uniform norms should be implemented (only minimum rules essential for the functioning of the internal market are harmonized[339]).[340] In practice, however, even these directives that most resort to this technique are widely recognized as having made a significant contribution to the establishment of improved equivalent rules in important areas, such as disclosure of information to investors (e.g., accounting

333. M.B. Kurcz (n. 331), 295.
334. Seventh Council Directive 83/349/EEC of 13 Jun. 1983 based on Art. 54(3)(g) of the Treaty on Consolidated Accounts [1983] OJ L193/1. L. Enriques, 'EC Company Law Directives and Regulations: How Trivial Are They?' (2005) ECGI Working Paper Series in Law No. 39/2005, <http://papers.ssrn.com/sol3/papers.cfm?abstract_id=730388>, accessed 17 Mar. 2008, 20 (also published in *UPA J Int'l Econ L* 27 (2006): 1–76).
335. Second Council Directive 77/91/EEC of 13 Dec. 1976, on coordination of safeguards, which, for the protection of the interests of members and others, are required by Member States of companies within the meaning of the second paragraph of Art. 58 of the Treaty, with respect to the formation of public limited liability companies and the maintenance and alteration of their capital, with a view to making such safeguards equivalent [1977] OJ L26. Minimum capital and capital maintenance rules in the Second Directive can be described as optional to certain degree. L. Enriques (n. 334), 21–22. S. Mengoli, F. Pazzaglia, & E. Sapienza, 'Is It Still Pizza, Spaghetti and Mandolino? Effect of Governance Reforms on Corporate Ownership in Italy' SSRN Working Paper, <http://ssrn.com/abstract=966085>, accessed 9 Sep. 2008. A. Engert, 'Life without Legal Capital: Lessons from American Law' (1996) Working Paper Ludwig Maximilians Universitat Munchen, <http://papers.ssrn.com/sol3/papers.cfm?abstract_id=882842>, accessed 3 Oct. 2008. See also the special volume of the European Company and Financial Law Review: M. Lutter (ed.), *Legal Capital in Europe* (Berlin-New York: De Gruyter, 2006).
336. Sixth Council Directive 82/891/EEC of 17 Dec. 1982 based on Art. 54(3)(g) of the EEC Treaty, concerning the division of public limited liability companies [1982] OJ L378/47.
337. V. Edwards (n. 96), 10.
338. R. Buxbaum & K. Hopt (n. 80), 225–226.
339. M.B. Kurcz (n. 331), 296.
340. V. Edwards (n. 96), 10.

and securities directives[341]).[342] It is the case that this minimum harmonization is able to combat psychological obstacles to cross-border establishment of companies by guaranteeing a common framework of minimum protection valid throughout the EU.

The choice of the harmonization techniques of options and minimum standards frequently depicts different national approaches to the regulation of certain parts of company law. Harmonization of these divergently regulated areas of company law is only possible through political compromises, which lead unavoidably to optional harmonization.[343] Optional harmonization satisfies all the Member States independently of their jurisdictional differences. The alternative to a less-than-perfect harmonizing directive preserving to a great extent the previous legal diversity would have been no harmonization in that area.[344] This is particularly true in the case of the Takeover Bid Directive, where the negotiations lasted for almost fifteen years. Even when a compromise had been reached on the terms of the draft Takeover Bid Directive, the 2002 tied vote in European Parliament cancelled the results of all those hard efforts. Finally, the adoption of opt-in and opt-out provisions and a reciprocity clause in the Takeover Bid Directive seemed unavoidable. Apart from the optionality and reciprocity clauses, there were also various substantive deficiencies in core provisions of the Takeover Bid Directive (e.g., the mandatory bid rule).[345] Only this watered-down version of the initial proposed Directive of the European Commission was able to mitigate the concerns of the objecting Member States and the European Parliament.

5.4 PETRIFICATION: A SIDE EFFECT OF HARMONIZATION BY MEANS OF DIRECTIVES

Another negative factor in the evolution of company law harmonization is the so-called danger of petrification that accompanies directives, namely the risk that

341. It is not easy to judge the contribution of the first wave of harmonization measures in the field of mandatory disclosure requirements to the development of European capital markets. Institutional investors were reluctant to receive legislative intervention in their playing field regulating disclosure requirements and preferred a legal development coming directly from market forces. At the framework of retail financial markets, however, better disclosure of information, as imposed by EU Law, has played a crucial role in enhancing investor confidence. Nevertheless, there is little concrete support for any claim about the quality of EU disclosure law being a major factor fuelling investor interest in the securities markets in the 1990s. E. Ferran, *Building an EU Securities Market* (Cambridge: Cambridge University Press, 2004), 38. J. Long, 'Navigating the Maze: Reviewing the Information Disclosure Requirements in the Financial Services *Acquis*', *EBLR* (2008): 485, 500.
342. V. Edwards (n. 96), 10.
343. *Ibid.*
344. *Ibid.*
345. G. Hertig & J. McCahery had developed an opt-in–opt-out default rule approach for EU Company Law within the framework of the European market for corporate control. They

because of the cumbersome legislative process involved, depending on the legal basis chosen, a directive could not be amended and developed easily.[346] The 2002 Report of the High Level Group of Company Law Experts criticized directives as being in practice even more inflexible than primary legislation because it is difficult to change a directive and the specific underlying approach. They proposed that directives should stipulate general principles and should leave the implementation of more detailed provisions to Member States or to market standards.[347] Moreover, the 1986 Single European Act introduced the Commission's flexible 'powers of implementation' under Article 202 of the EC Treaty, enabling the Commission to amend technical details (but not substantive matters) of harmonizing directives by way of secondary legislation, without the need to consult the European Parliament.[348] 'Petrified' directives could also block later national legislation. This results in the significant restriction of any national legal innovation in the field of company law.[349] Article 20 of the Takeover Bid Directive states that five years after the date of transposition of the Takeover Bid Directive (20 May 2006), the Commission shall examine this Directive in light of the experience acquired in applying it and, if necessary, propose its revision. That examination shall include a survey of the control structures[350] and barriers to takeover bids that are not covered by this Directive. To that end, Member States shall provide the Commission annually with information on the takeover bids that have been launched against companies, the securities of which are admitted to trading on their regulated markets. That information shall include the nationalities of the companies involved, the results of the offers, and any other information relevant to the understanding of how takeover bids operate in practice.

---

are critical of mandatory harmonization of company law because there are few incentives for the European legislature to produce optimal regulations, firms have to bear high transactional costs because of inefficient provisions, transactions are being disrupted and benefits for companies are not high enough. G. Hertig & J. McCahery, 'An Agenda for Reform: Company and Takeover Law in Europe', in *Reforming Company and Takeover Law in Europe*, ed. G. Ferrarini et al. (Oxford: Oxford University Press, 2004), 21, 38.

346. V. Edwards (n. 96), 11. M.J.G.C Raaijmakers (n. 124), 238. R. Buxbaum, G. Hertig et al. (eds) (n. 97), 200. S. Fazio (n. 14), 94.
347. P. Burbidge, 'Creating High Performance Boardrooms and Workplaces: European Corporate Governance in the Twenty First Century', *E L Rev.* (2003): 642, 646. Report of the High Level Group of Company Law Experts on a Modern Regulatory Framework for Company Law in Europe (Brussels, 2002), <http://ec.europa.eu/internal_market/company/docs/modern/report_en.pdf>, accessed 11 Aug. 2007, 4 ('the Winter Group').
348. V. Edwards (n. 96), 11. R. Buxbaum, G. Hertig et al. (eds) (n. 97), 15 C. Villiers (n. 100), 179.
349. R. Buxbaum & K. Hopt (n. 80), 241–242. It was suggested that minimum harmonization would leave Member States significant margin to apply their innovative ideas in the area of company law. R. Buxbaum, G. Hertig et al. (eds) (n. 97), 14.
350. E. Wymeersch, 'Investors and Enterprise Structure: A Report: Eddy Wymeersch' and 'Investors and Enterprise Structure: Discussion', in *European Economic and Business Law*, ed. R. Buxbaum et al. (New York: de Gruyter, 1996), 325, 334.

5.5 DIFFERENT LEGAL CONCEPTS AMONG DIFFERENT MEMBER STATES

The European legislature very often confronts another problem in the harmonization of national company laws; different legal concepts originating from the different jurisdictions of EU Member States require a common understanding so as to be included in the harmonizing measure.[351] Some legal notions may appear to be similar to legal notions in other Member States, but in reality, these are only superficial similarities and these notions are completely different in substance. Some legal concepts do not correspond to equivalent legal concepts in other jurisdictions. A directive could seek to regulate an area in which specific concepts are essential to one Member State's application and understanding of the law but alien and obscure in another jurisdiction.[352] An example is the introduction into EU Company Law of the concept of the company organ in the law relating to *ultra vires* transactions: a notion used by Roman-Germanic jurisdictions, which is familiar to Napoleonic jurisdictions but which is incompatible to a great extent with England's analysis of company transactions within the framework of agency.[353] This problem is present in the field of takeover regulation. On the one hand, some Member States, such as the United Kingdom, have long-established regulations in the area of takeover bids (a self-regulatory system in the case of the United Kingdom). Their experience in the development of the relevant legal concepts and in tackling the various regulatory problems is very important. One the

351. V. Edwards (n. 96), 11–12. P. Wood, *Regulation of International Finance*, Law and Practice of International Finance Series, 1st edn (London: Sweet & Maxwell, 2007). P. Wood, *Maps of World Financial Law*, 5th edn (London: Allen & Overy, 2005), 17, 21. D.C. Donald, 'Approaching Comparative Company Law', SSRN Working Paper, <http://ssrn.com/abstract=1092452>, accessed 11 Sep. 2008. M.J.G.C Raaijmakers (n. 124), 239. E. Stein (n. 21), 87–170. This divergence of national company laws at the EU level was attributed to the differences in the general private law (common versus civil law), to the difference in structure between forms of companies (one-tier and two-tier board companies), to national unique regimes of company law (e.g., co-determination), to different groups (managers, workers and financiers) having different positions and enjoying different powers in various Member States, to fragmented harmonization of tax law and to language and cultural differences. M.J. Kroeze & H.M. Vletter-Van Dort, 'History and Future of Uniform Company Law in Europe', *ECL* 5 (2008): 114, 120. C. Villiers asks for a re-evaluation of national company laws. If national company laws were more aligned conceptually and structurally, it might be easier to build a culture of harmony between the company laws of the states. C. Villiers (n. 100), 194.
352. V. Edwards (n. 96), 11–12. Corporate governance issues and notions should not be studied in isolation within only one country. B.R. Cheffins, 'Current Trends in Corporate Governance: Going from London to Milan via Toronto', *Duke J Comp Int'l L* 10 (1999): 5–6. However, harmonization taking into account comparison between existing laws was criticized because it does not satisfy present and future needs of business enterprises. A comparative study beneficial for the harmonization of company law should include an analysis of the actual functioning of the business enterprises, thereby referring to the wider social and 'political' environment and to historical elements. E. Wymeersch (n. 124), 322–323. C.L. Lempereur (n. 123), 246–247.
353. V. Edwards (n. 96), 11–12.

other hand, some other Member States (e.g., Germany) introduced mandatory takeover rules only in the 1990s. This lack of familiarity and lack of experience could cause problems, not so much at the transposition stage, but to a greater extent in the everyday application, interpretation, and compliance with the national takeover rules implementing the Takeover Bid Directive. Such a takeover rule is the concept of equitable compensation in Article 11(5) of the Takeover Bid Directive.[354] This provision states that where rights are removed on the basis of the breakthrough rule, equitable compensation shall be provided for any loss suffered by the holders of those rights. The terms for determining such compensation and the arrangements for its payment shall be set by Member States.

354. In its Takeover Report, the High Level Group of Company Law Experts ('the Winter Group') was against the introduction of this compensation scheme.

Chapter 6
Establishing an Internal Market for Companies: Market Integration in the Area of EU Company Law

6.1 INTRODUCTION

After discussing various facets of the regulation of takeover bids and of the harmonization of company law in general and understanding their structure and their deficiencies, it is appropriate to dedicate a chapter to the ultimate goal of the freedom of establishment: the making of an internal market. This will assist in the understanding of the place where the EU market for corporate control operates, as an element in the internal market. This chapter will seek to show that the market in corporate control forms one indispensable element of the internal market and that the liberalization of takeovers is necessary for the efficient functioning and the completion of the internal market. For this reason, it will be necessary to present concisely the evolution of market integration at the EU level and to explain a few regulatory aspects of this continuing process of market integration.

6.2 BARRIERS TO MARKET INTEGRATION

There are numerous reasons why differences between and among the company laws of the Member States could possibly frustrate the integration of the internal market.[355] The cornerstone of the EC Treaty is the establishment of an internal market.[356] The purpose of the internal market is to abolish obstacles to the free

---

355. Article 14 EC Treaty. V. Edwards (n. 96), 3.
356. V. Edwards (n. 96), 3. For the evolution of the various stages of market integration (Economic Constitution) and the close connection and interdependence of politics and law in this

movement of goods, persons, services, and capital, and to harmonize the laws of Member States to the extent required for the functioning of the internal market.[357] The existence of divergent national company laws could have a negative effect on corporate mobility at the EU level. If national company laws regulating important areas of creditor and shareholder protection and corporate governance are fundamentally different, this may result in a European 'Delaware Effect', urging companies to move into jurisdictions with the laxest laws.[358] When a company plans to penetrate a new business environment or to migrate to a new Member State, its decision will not be based only on economic grounds; the company will also consider the regulatory burdens and the substance of the legislation of the new host Member State.[359] The main advantage of company law harmonization is that it brings equivalent creditor and shareholder protection and that it encourages cross-border credit and investment, without prejudicial treatment of shareholders and creditors of the companies that have decided to cross the borders.[360] Persistent differences in national company laws are responsible for higher transaction costs,

---

process: C. Joerges, 'Law, Economics and Politics in the Constitutionalisation of Europe', *CYELS* 5 (2003): 123.

357. Article 3(h) EC Treaty. V. Edwards (n. 96), 3. In his Opinion in *Alfa Vita Vassilopoulos* (Joined Cases C-158/04 and C-159/04, *Alfa Vita Vassilopoulos AE, formerly Trofo Super-Markets AE and Carrefour Marinopoulos AE v. Elliniko Dimosio, Nomarchiaki Aftodioikisi Ioanninon* [2006] ECR I-08135), Advocate General M. Poiares Maduro proposed a common approach to defining a trade barrier across all the freedoms. There are many papers that examine the possibility of convergence: see, for example, E. Spaventa, 'From Gebhard to Carpenter: Towards a (Non-)economic European Constitution', *CM L Rev* 41 (2004): 743, P. Oliver & W.H. Roth, 'The Internal Market and the Four Freedoms', *CM L Rev* 41 (2004): 407, J. Snell, 'And Then There Were Two: Products and Citizens in Community Law', Ch. 4 in *EU Law for the 21st Century*, ed. T. Tridimas & P. Nebbia (Oxford: Hart Publishing, 2005), J. Meulman & H. de Waele, 'A Retreat from Sager: Servicing or Fine-Tuning the Application of Article 49 EC', *LIEI* 33 (2006): 207, J.L. Hansen, 'Full Circle: Is There Any Difference between the Freedom of Establishment and the Freedom to Provide Services?', in *Services and Free Movement in EU Law*, ed. M. Andenas & W.H. Roth (Oxford: Oxford University Press, 2002), 197, M Poiares Maduro, 'Harmony and Dissonance in Free Movement', *CYELS* 4 (2001): 315, D. O'Keefe & A. Bavasso, 'Four Freedoms, One Market and National Competence: In Search of a Dividing Line', in *Judicial Review in European Union Law*, ed. D. O'Keefe (The Hague: Kluwer Law International, 2000), 541. The Court has not reconsidered the structure of the law and has not answered the question of whether there should be a convergence in the interpretation of the fundamental freedoms under the EC Treaty. S. Weatherill, *Cases and Materials on EU Law*, 8th edn (Oxford: Oxford University Press, 2007), 580. It has also been proposed that there be an introduction of a fifth freedom establishing a competitive market for politics and allowing functional, overlapping and competing jurisdictions (FOCJ). This political approach institutionalizes competition among governmental units at all levels, resulting in a development of welfare. Such competition exist now only for national governments. Competition among newly emerging jurisdictions organized along functions instead of territories should also be promoted. B.S. Frey & R. Eichenberger, 'FOCJ: Creating a Single European Market for Governments', in *Constitutional Law and Economics of the European Union*, ed. D. Schmidtchen & R. Cooter (Cheltenham: Elgar, 1997), 195.
358. V. Edwards (n. 96), 3.
359. *Ibid.*
360. *Ibid.*

because market participants from other Member States have to study carefully the national company law provisions regulating a company before contracting with it or buying its shares. This may hinder cross-border trading and investment.[361]

6.3 THE EU MARKET FOR CORPORATE CONTROL: A SEGMENT OF THE INTERNAL MARKET

The market for corporate control is considered to be a very important part of the internal market, related both to European corporate governance structures and to securities regulation. The market for corporate control leads to the most efficient use of company resources, both on a suppressive basis (the board of directors will try to increase the profits of the corporation; otherwise, they could be replaced by a new board) and on a curative basis (takeovers will happen where the board does not perform satisfactorily, and this change will probably bring better results).[362] The High Level Group of Company Law Experts emphasizes the view that 'actual and potential takeover bids are an important means to discipline' management as part of the basis for the Takeover Bid Directive.[363] Takeovers constitute the most important part of the market for corporate control, but there are more segments of this particular market playing a very important role in EU market integration (such as the establishment of companies, of subsidiaries, and of branches; transactions in company assets and other elements of the business enterprise; mergers and assimilated transactions; the issuing of shares to new shareholders (leading to control change); debt restructuring; and shareholder agreements resulting in changes in control).[364]

6.4 THE ESTABLISHMENT OF A COMMON/ INTERNAL MARKET

The establishment and efficient functioning of a common/internal market[365] is still the most important goal of the European Community. Although the Treaty does not

361. L. Enriques, 'Company Law Harmonization Reconsidered: What Role for the EC?' (November 2005). ECGI Law Working Paper No. 53/2005, SSRN Working Papers, <http://ssrn.com/abstract=850005>, accessed 11 Mar. 2008, 12 (also published in S.M. Bartman (ed.), *European Company Law in Accelerated Progress* (AH Alpen aan den Rijn: European Company Law Series, Kluwer Law International, 2006). L. Enriques characterizes this rationale as 'unconvincing'.
362. B. Sjiafjell, 'The Golden Mean or Dead End? The Takeover Directive in a Shareholder versus Stakeholder Perspective', in *European Company Law in Accelerated Progress*, ed. S. Bartman (Alphen aan den Rijn: Kluwer Law International, 2006), 128.
363. Report of the High Level Group of Company Law Experts on Issues Related to Takeover Bids, 19. B. Sjiafjell (n. 362), 128 ('the Winter Group').
364. E. Wymeersch (n. 124), 301–302.
365. For a very early consideration of the relationship between the common market and English Company Law, see: T. Flanagan, 'The Impact on English Company Law', in *The Law of the Common Market*, ed. B.A. Wortley (Manchester: Manchester University Press-Oceana Publications, 1974), 111.

define the term 'common market' exactly, some treaty articles make reference to it (Article 3(1)(h), Article 32(1)-(4), Article 88(1), Article 119(1), Article 120(1), Article 136, Article 211, Article 267, Article 297, and Article 308).[366] In the beginning, there was a transitional period, which was to prepare progressively for the establishment and the functioning of the common market.[367] The EC Treaty demands the abolition of all categories of national provisions able to obstruct and affect negatively the establishment of this common market. The stages of integration, as proclaimed by Article 2 of the EC Treaty and based on liberal economic thinking, presupposes that the creation of a common market and the gradual approximation of national economic policies will result in a larger market for business operations.[368] Higher revenues would assist companies in reaching optimal sizes and becoming more competitive by increasing their productivity.[369] An increase of output by efficient and healthy companies would force them to diminish their product prices as a result of competition, and this ultimately would increase the purchasing power of consumers.[370] High productivity would also raise workers' wages.[371] This market evolution would increase the social product and would attain the objectives of Article 2 of the EC Treaty.[372] The role of the European Community is very crucial at this stage because of its power of legislative intervention in case of anomalies in this process of market integration.[373] The list of tasks set out in Article 3 of the EC Treaty and the provisions contained in Part Three of the EC Treaty describe the scope of the common market. Problems in achieving the common market have led to the introduction of the concept of the 'internal market' to supplement that of the common market (Article 14 of the EC Treaty).[374]

Article 3(1)(a) of the EC Treaty, aiming at the establishment of the common market, requires the prohibition, as between Member States, of custom duties and quantitative restrictions on the import and export of goods, and of all other measures having an equivalent effect. Moreover, Article 3(1)(c) states that the basic characteristic of the common/internal market is the abolition in the commercial relations among Member States of obstacles to the free movement of goods, persons, services,[375] and capital. In *Schul*,[376] the ECJ attributed to the common market

366. K. Lenaerts & P. Van Nuffel (n. 366), 139.
367. *Ibid.*
368. R. Buxbaum & K. Hopt (n. 80), 199. For the objectives of Art. 2 EC Treaty, see: B. Sjafjell, *Towards a Sustainable European Company Law* (AH Alphen aan den Rijn: Wolters Kluwer, 2009), 175–177.
369. R. Buxbaum & K. Hopt (n. 80), 199.
370. *Ibid.*
371. *Ibid.*
372. *Ibid.*
373. K. Lenaerts & P. Van Nuffel (n. 366), 139.
374. *Ibid.*
375. An early consideration of the market integration of investment services: E. Lomnicka, 'The Internal Financial Market and Investment Services', in *E.C. Financial Market Regulation and Company Law*, ed. S. Kenyon-Slade & M. Andenas (London: Sweet & Maxwell, 1993), 81.
376. Case 15/81, *Gaston Schul Douane Expediteur BV v. Inspecteur der Invoerrechten en Accijnzen, Roosendaal.* [1982] ECR 01409 para. 33.

the aim of the abolition of all obstacles to intra-community trade so as to unify the national markets into a single market, bringing about conditions as close as possible to those of a genuine internal market.[377] This kind of effort would alleviate any drawbacks of the partitioned European markets. In *Polydor*, the ECJ held that its case law on the abolition of trade barriers must be determined on the basis of the European Community's objectives and activities as defined by Articles 2 and 3 of the EC Treaty. The EC Treaty, by establishing a common market and progressively approximating the economic policies and the business environments of the Member States, seeks to integrate national markets into a single market having the characteristics of a domestic market.[378] The aim of these provisions, introducing the four fundamental freedoms (free movement of goods, services/establishment, workers, and capital), is to combat any already existing or future national laws hindering the business activities and the entrepreneurial plans of market participants at the EU level. This will result in an efficient allocation of resources and in the establishment of a level playing field across the Member States, allowing market participants to use in a better way and more efficiently their competitive advantages in this integrated market. As a result, all discrimination on grounds of nationality is also prohibited within the field of application of the Treaty (Article 12 of the EC Treaty).[379] Apart from the promotion of the four fundamental freedoms, the common market emphasizes the importance of free competition. The abolition of trade barriers imposed by the Member States would be useless if undertakings could still frustrate the function of the common market by abusing their dominant position, by forming cartels or by receiving unlawful state aids.[380]

A common market could not be established by a mere deregulatory abolition of national provisions constituting trade barriers, of discriminatory laws, and of appreciable distortions of competition. EC Law can prohibit national rules that constitute obstacles to cross-border trade either because they are discriminatory or

---

377. K. Lenaerts & P. Van Nuffel (n. 366), 139. For an interesting analysis of harmonization methods to abolish obstacles and of market integration approaches to financial services regulation at the EU level, see: E. Lomnicka, 'The Financial Services Single Market and the Interface between Community Law and Domestic Law', in *Continuity and Change in EU Law: Essays in Honour of Sir Francis Jacobs*, ed. A. Arnull et al. (Oxford: Oxford University Press, 2008), 261, 267, 281.

378. Case 270/80 *Polydor Limited and RSO Records Inc. v. Harlequin Records Shops Limited and Simons Records Limited* [1982] ECR 329 para. 16.

379. K. Lenaerts & P. Van Nuffel (n. 366), 140. G. Davies, *Nationality Discrimination in the European Internal Market* (The Hague: European Monographs, Kluwer, 2003).

380. K. Lenaerts & P. Van Nuffel (n. 366), 140–141. A. Jones & B. Surfin, *EC Competition Law, Text, Cases and Materials*, 3rd edn (Oxford: Oxford University Press, 2008), D.G Goyder, *EC Competition Law*, 4th edn (Oxford: Oxford University Press, 2003), G. Monti, *EC Competiton Law* (Cambridge: Cambridge University Press, 2007), M. Furse, *Competition Law of the EC and UK*, 5th edn (Oxford: Oxford University Press, 2006). Company law and capital market law have complementary aims: economic concentration and competition law. As regards national company laws on groups of companies and concentration, takeover bids are regulated early in the formation of a group of companies. Some of these regulations aim at preventing distortion of competition in the market for corporate control and not at blocking concentration. R. Buxbaum & K. Hopt (n. 80), 221–223.

because they restrict market access. Mutual recognition that allows a product lawfully produced in a Member State to circulate freely in the rest of the Member States underpins this approach.[381] Nevertheless, many obstacles to free movement in the common market come from differences between and among national laws, such as in the area of company law.[382] While some of these barriers could be eliminated by mutual recognition, some others (which survive as a result of proper justification according to mandatory requirements of general interest) require legislative intervention by means of directives harmonizing different national standards.[383] These differences should be diminished by introducing new harmonized standards for all the Member States. Hence, positive integration was provided by Article 3(1)(h) of the EC Treaty, which required the approximation of the laws of Member States to the extent required for the functioning of the common market.[384] Positive integration was very important for company and banking law, because many non-tariff barriers were eliminated through harmonization; the negative integration aiming at the abolition of tariffs, quotas, and similar barriers was not enough in these areas of business law.[385] In the internal market, harmonization of company laws is required because harmonization helps companies to exercise their right of freedom of movement and establishment in the internal market and would provide more legal transparency and equivalence; thus, this approximation of conditions would enable companies to move within the internal market in a balanced way without causing appreciable distortions of competition.[386] The Commission's policy in the field of EU Company Law

381. P. Craig & R. De Burca (n. 12), 606. F. Jacobs, 'The Evolution of European Legal Order', *CM L Rev.* (2004): 303, 304–305.
382. K. Lenaerts & P. Van Nuffel (n. 366), 141.
383. P. Craig & R. De Burca (n. 12), 606. It is argued that the judicially created principle of mutual recognition is differentiated from the legislative principle of mutual recognition in the financial services market. The judicially formed principle of mutual recognition is not sufficient in guaranteeing the free provision of financial services. Hence, legislative intervention, based on harmonization and the legislative principle of mutual recognition, are needed for the integration of the EU financial market. M. Ortino, 'The Role and Functioning of Mutual Recognition in the European Market of Financial Services', *ICLQ* 56 (2007): 309, 324.
384. K. Lenaerts & P. Van Nuffel (n. 366), 141. L. Enriques examines empirically the company law directives and case law. He criticizes the fact that negative harmonization (i.e., harmonization removing barriers to the four freedoms) is sometimes followed (in case of justified barriers) with positive harmonization because any profits related to the facilitation of freedom of establishment are usually lost in terms of lower flexibility rules. This argument is based on the alleged rigidity of some EU harmonizing rules, which also diminish the scope of regulatory competition. L. Enriques (n. 361), 2, 9–11.
385. P. Craig, 'The Evolution of the Single Market', in *The Law of the Single European Market*, ed. C. Barnard & J. Scott (Oxford: Hart, 2002), 2.
386. S. Fazio (n. 14), 78. Some academics support the opinion that the internal market has been completed without completion of the harmonization of company law. According to Art. 44(2)(g) EC Treaty, harmonization of company law is only required 'to the necessary extent'. Hence, according to this opinion, there is no need for further company law harmonization because the internal market is complete. C. Timmermans, 'Harmonization in the Future of Company Law in Europe', in *Capital Markets and Company Law*, ed. K. Hopt & E. Wymeersch (Oxford: Oxford University Press, 2003), 627–628. This latter opinion alleging

involves some very difficult decisions, which should be contemplated very carefully. The nature, scope, and focus of national company laws at the EU level were highly fragmented and diversified prior to the introduction of the Commission's harmonization agenda. As far as the protection of shareholders and creditors is concerned, positive harmonization could provide a secure environment for cross-border credit and investment by ensuring that the market access of companies' members and creditors is not prejudiced and impeded.[387] Thus, negative harmonization would not provide an adequate level of legal certainty. Negative harmonization should be accompanied by positive harmonization. Positive harmonization may fill the gaps that negative harmonization does not cover because of duly justified barriers or some residual psychological obstacles to market access. Then, positive harmonizing rules would be definitely required.[388] It should also be stressed that positive harmonization of company law is not an aim in itself, but its ultimate objective is the completion of the internal market.[389] The contribution of positive integration to citizens' realization of the advantages of the internal market project was stipulated in *Paul.*[390] in which the ECJ stated that the population should become more strongly conscious of the reality of the common market and that, to that end, measures should be adopted for the greater liberalization of this specific part of the internal market (this case dealt with tax measures).

The relationship between the harmonization of company law and the establishment of a common market is a very important issue. The harmonization of company law as a method of positive integration aims primarily at the creation and progressive development of a common market. As far as the construction of Article 44(2)(g) of the EC Treaty is concerned, this provision shall be interpreted according not only to Articles 43 and 44(1) of the EC Treaty, which clearly show that the harmonization of national company law systems forms part of the general programme for the abolition of restrictions on freedom of establishment and the facilitation of market access, but also, according to Article 3(h) of the EC Treaty, which provides that the activities of the Community are to include the approximation of national laws to the extent required for the functioning of the

---

that the internal market is completed seems to overestimate the advantages of negative integration through case law. Harmonization of company law is an indispensable part of this market making process whereby legal certainty and equivalent standards are established. It is not easy to see how the various provisions of the Takeover Bid Directive could be established only through case law.

387. S. Fazio (n. 14), 79.

388. A.S. Reid (n. 314), 165.

389. M.J.G.C Raaijmakers (n. 124), 231–232. Positive harmonization could improve the economic efficiency of the internal market in the following ways: doing business under harmonized rules might result in more savings, especially for smaller companies, which have to give up relatively more resources to cope with an international legal environment than do larger ones; the harmonization would probably result in a review of national regulation; harmonization would strengthen entrepreneurs' confidence in their market access; and harmonization would create a level playing field and would prevent the shifts of business and employment. R. Buxbaum, G. Hertig et al. (eds) (n. 97), 54–55.

390. Case 54/84, *Michael Paul v. Hauptzollamt Emmerich* [1985] ECR-915 para. 15.

common market. Therefore, all the proposed company law measures based on Article 44(2) of the EC Treaty should contribute to the effective functioning of the common market. Moreover, the ECJ has talked about the possible limits of the European legislature's competence to facilitate freedom of establishment of companies through harmonization means (directives) seeking to wipe out any national restrictions to cross-border corporate mobility. It has held that the objective of abolishing restrictions on freedom of establishment, which is assigned in very broad terms to the Council and the Commission by Article 44(1) of the EC Treaty, cannot be confined by the list of Article 44(2) of the EC Treaty, which merely sets out a non-exhaustive list of measures to be adopted to attain that goal of revoking barriers to freedom of establishment, as is inferred by the use in that provision of the words 'in particular'.[391] The agenda of the EU institutions cannot be limited by the list of Article 44(2) of the EC Treaty, and they can draw up new legislative measures not included in this non-exhaustive list. Hence, the EU institutions are free to organize their policy and to expand their legislative action into new areas that contain potential barriers to freedom of establishment. However, the requirement of contribution to the effective functioning of the common market as stipulated above should be respected anyway by the European legislature. Of course, it should be recalled that this competence in the field of company law harmonization shall comply with the principles of subsidiarity, of attributed competence, and of proportionality (Article 5 of the EC Treaty), as analysed by the relevant case law.

The Commission adopted in June 1985 the White Paper entitled Completing the Internal Market,[392] which set out an extensive programme with a view to eliminating all the remaining barriers. The White Paper classed the barriers in three categories: physical, technical, and fiscal.[393] The Single European Act added Article 8a, 8b, and 8c to the EEC Treaty (now Article 14(1) of the EC Treaty), which obliged the Community to propose measures 'with the aim of progressively establishing the internal market over a period expiring on 31 December 1992'.[394]

391. Case C-97/96, *Daihatsu* [1997] ECR I-6843 paras 18, 21.

392. Completing the Internal Market: White Paper from the Commission to the European Council (Milan 28–29 Jun. 1985) COM/85/0310 final. D.A. Wyatt & A. Dashwood (n. 46), 914–916. An early consideration of the market integration of investment services: P. Clarotti, 'The Completion of the Internal Financial Market: Current Position and Outlook', in *E.C. Financial Market Regulation and Company Law*, ed. S. Kenyon-Slade & M. Andenas (London: Sweet & Maxwell, 1993), 1.

393. K. Lenaerts & P. Van Nuffel (n. 366), 142.

394. K. Lenaerts & P. Van Nuffel (n. 366), 143. K. Mortelmans 'The Common Market, the Internal Market and the Single Market, What's in a Market?', *CM L Rev.* 38 (1998): 101, 102–108. M. Clough & N. Forwood, 'The Single European Act and Free Movement: Legal Implications of the Provisions for the Completion of the Internal Market', *E L Rev* 11 (1986): 383. T.C. Hartley et al. (eds), *The Legal Foundations of the Single European Market* (Oxford: Oxford University Press, 1991), L.W. Gormley, 'The Internal Market: History and Evolution', in *Regulating the Internal Market*, ed. N.N. Shuibhne (Cheltenham: Elgar, 2006), 19 P. Craig (n. 385), 14. For an evaluation of the progress of market integration since the end of the 1992 deadline and an evaluation of the application of internal market law by Member States: S. Weatherill, *Cases and Materials on EU Law*, 8th edn (Oxford: Oxford University Press,

In the current consolidated version of the EC Treaty, Article 14(2) of the EC Treaty defines the 'internal market' as 'an area without internal frontiers in which the free movement of goods, persons, services and capital is ensured in accordance with the provisions of this Treaty'. Article 14(1) of the EC Treaty refers to potential legal bases for the measures listed in the White Paper.[395] Article 95 of the EC Treaty constitutes a key provision for the harmonization of the internal market, because it provides the basis to adopt, by a qualified majority vote in the Council, the measures for the approximation of the provisions laid down by law, regulation, or administrative action in Member States that have as their goal the establishment and functioning of the internal market.[396]

6.5 DIFFERENCES BETWEEN THE COMMON MARKET AND THE INTERNAL MARKET

The common market and the internal market are different. The main difference between them lies in their respective scopes. The purpose of the internal market is to abolish restrictions to the free movement of goods, persons, services, and capital (Article 3(1)(c) of the EC Treaty) at the EU level and thus has a more limited scope than the common market.[397] The White Paper that launched the internal market does not cover competition, agricultural, or transport policy.[398] As a result, the

---

2007), 299, 304. For a political perspective: C. Hay & A. Menon, *European Politics* (Oxford: Oxford University Press, 2007), 160, R.D. Kelemen & A. Menon, 'The Politics of EC Regulation', in *Better Regulation*, ed. S. Weatherill (Oxford: Hart, 2007), 175.

395. K. Lenaerts & P. Van Nuffel (n. 366), 143. Article 14 did not generate a *stricto sensu* direct effect, as this would be a step too far for the Member States at the time of the adoption of the Single European Act when this provision was inserted in the Treaty. D. Mavromati (n. 292), 17. In *Wijsenbeek* (Case C-378/97 *Wisjsenbeek* [1999] ECR I-6207), the ECJ declared that Art. 14 EC Treaty aims at the creation of new Community rules for the completion of the internal market and that Art. 14 EC Treaty has no independent deregulatory effects. In the absence of harmonization, no obligations for the Member arise based on Art. 14 EC Treaty and Art. 14 EC Treaty could have no direct effect after the expiry of 1992 deadline. In *Echirolles Distribution* (Case C-9/99 [2000] ECR I-8207], the ECJ adopted a similar view on the direct effect of Art. 14 EC Treaty, this time within the framework of free movement of goods. D. Chalmers & others, *European Union Law* (Cambridge: Cambridge University Press, 2006), 467. P. Craig (n. 385), 34.
396. K. Lenaerts & P. Van Nuffel (n. 366), 143.
397. K. Lenaerts & P. Van Nuffel (n. 366), 143. L.W. Gormley stresses that a point of particular concern in the ECJ's reasoning is the continuing failure to distinguish between the concept of a common market and the concept of the internal market and to establish some explicit criteria for this diversification. The limits between the four fundamental freedoms and the elimination of distortions of competition have not been clarified. L.W. Gormley, 'Competition and Free Movement: Is the Internal Market the Same as a Common Market?', *EBLR* (2002): 517.
398. K. Lenaerts & P. Van Nuffel (n. 366), 143. Taking account the ECJ's ruling in *Schul*, where it was held that the common market requires the abolition of all obstacles to trade and intends to bring closer national markets to create a genuine internal market, it could be inferred that the common market lacks in intensivity of its accomplishment compared to the internal market; thus, the internal market is the advanced form of the common market. Case 15/81,

harmonization measures based on Article 95 will cover only a part of the legislative measures required for the establishment of the common market as proclaimed by Article 3(1)(h).[399] With regard to free movement of companies, Article 95(2) of the EC Treaty should not be neglected. According to this latter provision, Article 95 shall not apply to the free movement of persons, including the freedom of establishment of companies. In fact, the internal market realizes the core of the common market within the meaning of Article 2 of the EC Treaty by means of a more flexible harmonization procedure, which reveals an evolution of the regulatory techniques and the intentions of the European legislature.[400]

Gaston Schul Douane Expediteur BV v. Inspecteur der Invoerrechten en Accijnzen, Roosendaal. [1982] ECR 01409. D. Mavromati (n. 292), 14.

399. K. Lenaerts & P. Van Nuffel (n. 366), 143.

400. K. Lenaerts & P. Van Nuffel (n. 366), 143–144. Advocate General Tesauro states that the notion of an internal market is based on that of the common market (Opinion of Advocate General Tesauro, Case C-300/89, *Commission of the European Communities v. Council of the European Communities (Titanium Dioxide)* [1991] ECR I-2867).

Chapter 7

The Relationship between the Treaty Provisions on Freedom of Establishment of Companies and Takeover Bids

7.1 HARMONIZATION OF TAKEOVER BIDS AT EU LEVEL: A FEW REGULATORY CONSIDERATIONS

The foundation of the business regulatory regime is that free markets alone, together with the already established sets of rules of contract law, tort law, and fiduciary duties, will not remedy the various problems and deficiencies of the corporate and financial market, and therefore, detailed legislative intervention is necessary (see also the doctrinal battle between regulatory capitalism versus free market ideology).[401] It could be argued that, for various reasons, there is satisfactory international consensus on business regulation (at least on the central tenets and principles, for example, shareholders' protection rationale).[402] The general

401. P. Wood, *Law and Practice of International Finance* (London: Sweet & Maxwell, 2008), 341. See also G. Visentini & M. Musolino, 'The Financial System and Institutions', in *Financial Services in Europe*, ed. M. van Empel (AH Alpen aan den Rijn: Wolters Kluwer, 2008). See also a very interesting recommendation for the establishment of a World Financial Authority: J. Eatwell, 'New Issues in International Financial Regulation', in *Regulating Financial Services and Markets in the Twenty First Century*, ed. E. Ferran & C. Goodhart (Oxford: Hart. 2001), 235–236.

402. P. Wood (n. 401), 24. M. Siems, *Convergence in Shareholder Law* (Cambridge: Cambridge University Press, 2008). It was argued that, in the EU, convergence of corporate governance regimes is a two-way process. Continental Member States adopt certain features of the Anglo-American model of corporate governance, and the UK incorporates through directives many elements of the continental social model affecting corporate governance structures. P. Burbidge (n. 347), 642. For market-driven approximation of corporate governance and a

assumption of commercial laws and company laws of industrialized countries is to find an organizational form suitable to the economic activity of the types of firms conducting business within that market.[403] Company law should reconcile the various conflicting interests of shareholders, creditors, employees, and the public.[404] Although takeovers are a private law matter, their regulation has generated legal and economic controversies in Europe because it influences general economic policy, the efficient functioning of large companies, stock-exchange financing, and the impact of the shareholders, especially of the institutional investors, on the fate of the company.[405] On one hand, it is argued that takeovers are a very positive market mechanism for the welfare of shareholders, whereby management is submitted to a disciplinary structure[406] and wealth is reallocated in an efficient way; on the other hand, takeover bids are characterized as a new unacceptable face of capitalism.[407] The justification for the launch of defensive measures available to a company's board of directors that plans to frustrate a takeover bid depends on one's point of view. One stance toward takeovers claims that their liberalization supports the protection of shareholders' interests; the other stance claims that the permission of defensive measures gives priority to the interests of the employees, the managers, and the company as a whole.[408] The adoption of defensive tactics could also be determined in accordance with the general interest and the macroeconomic point of view.[409] Disagreements arise regarding the means of achieving and realizing those tenets, goals, and principles. The purposes of business regulation include, among others, the following: protection against systemic risk, protection against insolvency of firms, protection of the public and unsophisticated investors, maintaining a level-playing field, prevention of crime, public confidence and the abolition of various psychological obstacles, awareness and education of the public and market participants, information transparency and disclosure, delegation of monitoring and enforcement, and agency problems.[410]

Among those purposes, the most important purpose constituting one of the basic rationales of the Takeover Bid Directive is the establishment of a level playing field in the EU market for corporate control. The theory of the level playing

critical discussion: K. Hopt, 'Common Principles of Corporate Governance in Europe?' and E. Wymeersch 'Convergence or Divergence in Corporate Governance Patterns in Western Europe?', in *Corporate Governance Regimes*, ed. J. McCahery et al. (Oxford: Oxford University Press, 2002), 176, 230.

403. R. Buxbaum & K. Hopt (n. 80), 174.
404. The differences among various national company laws are not the outcome of an ideological conflict, except for the parts of worker participation in the company's management and the representation of the public interest in the firms. R. Buxbaum & K. Hopt (n. 80), 174.
405. E. Wymeersch (n. 124), 292.
406. J. Coffee, 'Regulating the Market for Corporate Control: A Critical Assessment of the Tender Offer's Role in Corporate Governance', *Col LR* (1984): 1146, 1163.
407. E. Wymeersch (n. 124), 292–293.
408. W.J. Slagter, 'Takeovers and the Draft 13th EC-Directive', in *Further Perspectives in Financial Integration in Europe*, ed. E. Wymeersch (Berlin-New York: de Gruyter, 1994), 174.
409. W.J. Slagter (n. 408), 174.
410. P. Wood (n. 401), 342–343.

field is that companies should bear the same regulatory costs as those in other Member States so that lesser and less-intensive regulation in one Member State does not confer an unfair competitive advantage on that Member State's companies and financial entities to the detriment of the stability and efficiency of the EU and global financial system and of the internal market in general.[411] However, intensive and tough regulation could also result in protectionism rather than equality, because new market players would find difficulties in entering the market and in complying with the strict business regulatory requirements.[412] The Winter Group had stressed the lack of a level playing for takeovers. Moreover, the B. Dauner-Lieb & M. Lamandini Report to the European Parliament on the Commission's new proposal of a Directive on company law concerning takeover bids had also insisted on the establishment of a level playing field.[413] Shareholders from different Member States do not have equivalent opportunities to sell their shares, and takeovers could not be launched with the same expectation of success in different Member States.[414] In the EU market for corporate control, investors must be free to put their money into shares and debentures of EU corporations and thus, first to establish themselves in another Member State and second, to provide the necessary capital for the development and expansion of those companies.[415] The Winter Group proposed that a level playing field must respect the principles of shareholder decision-making and of proportionality between risk-bearing capital and control.[416]

The 2000 Lisbon European Council placed this Directive, which forms part of the Financial Services Action Plan,[417] among the priorities as regards the integration of European financial markets because it would facilitate pan-European restructuring and thus contribute to making Europe the most competitive, knowledge-based economy in the world by 2010.[418] This view is shared by

411. P. Wood, *Regulation of International Finance*, Law and Practice of International Finance Series, 1st edn (London: Sweet & Maxwell, 2007), 30. For an empirical and comparative approach of the role of takeover bid regulation: E. Wymeersch (n. 124), 312–320.
412. P. Wood (n. 411), 30.
413. Dauner-Lieb & M. Lamandini, Report to the European Parliament on the Commission's New Proposal of a Directive on Company Law Concerning Takeover Bids (December 2002), <www.uni-koeln.de/jur-fak/lbrah/pdf_docs/gutachten_daunerlieb_lamandini_en.pdf>, accessed 25 Oct. 2008.
414. J.L. Hansen (n. 303), 280.
415. C.M. Schmitthoff (n. 93), 7.
416. J.L. Hansen (n. 303), 280.
417. COM (1999) 232. The so-called Lisbon Agenda was re-launched by the European Commission in 2005. This 'renewed' endeavour tried to revitalize the EU's economic reform agenda from the 2000 Lisbon Council. There was definitely a need for action as five years after its launch, the Lisbon Agenda was not providing the desired benefits for European integration. Communication of the Spring European Council, 'Working Together for Growth and Jobs: A New Start for the Lisbon Strategy' COM (2005) 24, 2. Communication from the Commission to the Council and the European Parliament, 'Common Actions for Growth and Employment: The Community Lisbon Programme', COM (2005) 330, 2. D. Weber-Rey (n. 292), 249.
418. Proposal for a Directive of the European Parliament and of the Council on Takeover Bids (Explanatory Memorandum, Legislative Financial Statement, Impact Assessment Form)

UNICE,[419] which has repeatedly stressed the need for a common framework for cross-border takeover bids. The European Parliament recognized that the Directive would be useful and important in this field.[420] In these circumstances, the Commission considered it essential to provide a European framework for cross-border takeover bids as part of the Financial Services Action Plan.[421] One important goal of the economic policies of Member States is the assurance of a smooth and efficient flow of capital from savings to investment.[422] A prerequisite of this is easy access to securities markets for the provision of the necessary capital; efforts were launched by the EU in establishing a properly integrated pan-European financial market with numerous benefits for issuers (retail and wholesale) investors, the rest of the market participants, and the national and EU economy as a whole.[423] The Financial Services Action Plan was an attempt by the European Commission to better equip the Community to meet the challenges of a monetary union and to capitalize on the potential benefits of an integrated market in financial services, constituting a major component of the internal market project.[424] We should not forget that the 1985 White Paper on completing the internal market (paragraphs 102–109) places the liberalization of financial services in a key position for the integration of EU capital markets.[425]

The Directive has two main objectives: to give a legal framework for takeovers in Europe and to ensure an adequate level of protection for minority shareholders throughout the EU in the case of a change of company control. Takeover bids and cross-border mergers can contribute to the development and reorganization of European firms, which is a key condition for withstanding international competition and developing a single capital market.[426] Takeover bids, before the adoption of the Takeover Bid Directive, were subject to very divergent national rules and gave rise to numerous problems when they involved two or more Member States (e.g., as to the law applicable and the competent authorities).[427] These uncertainties for market access and the subsequent psychological obstacles to

---

COM (2002) 534 final, *OJ* [2003] 45E/1, 1. M. Maquil, 'The Integration of the Securities Markets in Europe', in *Further Perspectives in Financial Integration in Europe*, ed. E. Wymeersch (Berlin-New York: de Gruyter, 1994), 157. For a critical evaluation of the post-FSAP regulatory landscape: L. Enriques & M. Gatti, 'Is There a Uniform EU Securities Law After the Financial Services Action Plan?' (2007) SSRN Working Paper, <http://ssrn.com/abstract=982282>, accessed 9 Nov. 2008.

419. Union of Industrial and Employers' Confederations of Europe is the expansion for UNICE.
420. COM (2002) 534, 1.
421. Proposal for a Directive of the European Parliament and of the Council on Takeover Bids, Explanatory Memorandum, Legislative Financial Statement, Impact Assessment Form, COM (2002) 534 final, *OJ* [2003] 45E/1, 1.
422. E. Ferran (n. 341), 1.
423. *Ibid.*
424. *Ibid.*
425. R. Buxbaum, G. Hertig et al. (eds) (n. 97), 7.
426. COM (2002) 534, 3.
427. COM (2002) 534, 3. For empirical research about some national takeover bids at the end of 1980s and early 1990s, see: E. Wymeersch (n. 124), 292–293.

cross-border establishment are not acceptable within the European Union.[428] The Takeover Bid Directive, together with the general legislative goals of integrating European financial markets and markets of corporate control according to the Financial Services Action Plan and undertaking harmonization aiming at corporate restructuring, sets out to combat psychological obstacles hindering cross-border takeover bids in the interests of all parties concerned and to ensure protection for minority shareholders[429] in the course of such transactions, as is proclaimed by the legal basis for company law harmonization (Article 44(2)(g) of the EC Treaty: 'members and others').[430] It establishes a framework for action by Member States by laying down certain principles and a limited number of general requirements while allowing Member States to adopt the detailed implementing rules in accordance with their national practices, provided that the differences are not such as to jeopardize implementation of the Directive at the Community level. It is a 'framework' Directive following the structure of the 1996 proposal compared with the 1989 proposal containing many detailed provisions.[431]

7.2 THE CONDUCT OF A TAKEOVER BID INVOLVES AN EXERCISE OF THE RIGHT OF ESTABLISHMENT

Freedom of establishment of legal persons is closely related to cross-border acquisitions. Holding or acquiring shares in a company across national borders can involve the exercise of both of the right of establishment and the right of capital movement, where the shareholding gives the investors definite influence over the company's decisions and allows the investors to determine its activities; where the cross-border investment does not give to the investors such influence that it is known as portfolio investment and falls solely under the Treaty provisions on capital movement.[432] The pertinence of company law harmonization to cross-border acquisitions and corporate establishment is that the Treaty basis for such harmonization is the chapter on establishment (Article 44(2)(g) of the EC Treaty).[433] The rationale of company law harmonization is not to harmonize company law for its own sake, but to remove obstacles to the cross-border activities of individuals and companies.[434] On one hand, mergers and acquisitions fall within the scope of directly applicable Treaty provisions on freedom of establishment and

428. COM (2002) 534, 3.
429. With respect to English law on minority shareholders after the Companies Act 2006: V. Joffe, QC & others, *Minority Shareholders, Law, Practice and Procedure*, 3rd edn (Oxford: Oxford University Press, 2008).
430. COM (2002) 534, 3.
431. COM (2002) 534, 3. An interesting discussion in the period immediately after the release of the 1989 proposal can be found in: R. Buxbaum, G. Hertig et al. (eds) (n. 97), 375.
432. D.A. Wyatt & A. Dashwood (n. 46), 838. See also Case C-251/98, *Baars* [2000] ECR I paras 21–22.
433. D.A. Wyatt & A. Dashwood (n. 46), 838.
434. *Ibid.*

on free movement of capital; on the other hand, the European legislature might harmonize them in compliance with the existing framework of company law harmonization.[435] An individual or company seeking to acquire such a controlling shareholding which confers influence over a target company would also fall within the scope of the right of establishment. This justifies the adoption of a Directive on Takeover Bids removing any restrictions to cross-border takeover bids.[436] The market for corporate control is a part of the internal market, and thus, its integration is a prerequisite for the integration of the other.

435. *Ibid.*

436. *Ibid.*, 850. The differences between the incorporation theory and the real seat theory create problems for European corporate mobility and the exercise of the right of establishment by companies. The significance of this corporate mobility case law will be analysed in the next chapter. For that case law, a recommended analysis can be found in: D.A. Wyatt & A. Dashwood (n. 46), 839–851, R.R. Drury, 'Migrating Companies', *ELR* 24, no. 4 (1999): 354.

Chapter 8

The Significance of the Corporate Mobility Case Law for the Takeover Process

8.1 CORPORATE MOBILITY CASE LAW AND TAKEOVER BIDS: INTRODUCTORY REMARKS

The contribution of the ECJ's case law and of secondary legislation also played an important role in the interpretation of the freedom of establishment and particularly the freedom of establishment of companies. C. Timmermans has commented on EU company law harmonization that 'the internal market has been completed, without completion of the harmonization of company law. That would give the impression that the one does not need the other. So, it seems, the internal market can function without further harmonization of company law'.[437] A company will definitely consider the potential costs that will have to be incurred to expand its activities to another Member State; if this expansion appears attractive, it may well proceed notwithstanding the lack of any harmonization that facilitates access to the market of the other (host) Member State.[438] However, in the EU market for corporate control, harmonization was deemed to be essential because of wide legal diversity and opposing doctrinal approaches. In some Member States, takeovers and subsequent mergers could not be conducted or could only be conducted

437. C. Timmermans (n. 386), 627. S.J. Moran, 'Establishing Establishment: A Modern Chimera: An Investigation into Securing the Right of Establishment for Companies within the Internal Market of the European Community', *Ir S LR* 15 (2007): 149. For an early in-depth overview of the ECJ's case law on companies: T. Tridimas (n. 44), 335.

438. S.J. Moran (n. 437), 150.

very onerously because of the possibility of pre- or post-bid takeover barriers. A company planning to take over a company registered in another Member State and thus to establish itself in this latter Member State would be deprived of this method of establishment. An offeror company could not effectively exercise its fundamental right of establishment by taking over a target company registered in another Member State. Therefore, the European legislature should introduce some minimum standards for the exercise of this aspect of the freedom of establishment, that is, the facilitation of cross-border establishment by means of a takeover. The Takeover Bid Directive (at least in its proposed form) was trying to establish a level playing field by abolishing such distortions in the market of corporate control.

Freedom of establishment aims to remove obstacles to the free circulation of companies at the EU level and thus contributes to the creation of the internal market. Removal of obstacles could ensure that companies are recognized in other national legal orders, could assist companies in having the same freedom to act in all Member States (e.g., by launching takeover bids, by acquiring shares and, in general, by participating in the European market for corporate control), could guarantee the possibility of cross-border mergers, and could facilitate companies' freedom to move from one Member State to another, especially by way of transferring their seat.[439] As far as the role of case law in this market integration process is concerned, the objective of the interpretation of the freedom of establishment by the ECJ and of the harmonizing company law is to ensure that companies can efficiently exercise this fundamental freedom to establish themselves in other Member States. This choice of companies to establish themselves in other Member States should be accompanied by the necessary flexibility required by corporate restructuring, should not be disadvantaged because of the cross-border nature of their establishment, and should not incur excessive high costs or burdensome formalities that could potentially result in obstacles (e.g., Dutch legislation in *Inspire Art*).[440]

Takeover bids are another method of corporate restructuring at the EU level that falls within the scope of these considerations. It is a corporate financial technique that assists one company (the bidder) in becoming established in another Member State by acquiring the control of another company. This consolidation of corporate businesses at the EU level contributes significantly to the creation of economies of scale and to a more efficient allocation of resources. Hence, takeover bids, as a method of cross-border corporate establishment, are closely related to some aspects of corporate mobility jurisprudence. We will discuss here the relationship between the corporate mobility case law of the ECJ and cross-border takeover bids.

439. E. Wymeersch (n. 91), 158, 162.
440. E. Wymeersch (n. 106), 19.

8.2 THE IMPACT OF *SEVIC* ON CROSS-BORDER MERGERS AND TAKEOVER BIDS

A takeover bid is a method for achieving a merger.[441] A merger is the absorption of one company by another, the latter retaining its own name and identity and acquiring assets, liabilities, franchises, and powers of the former, with the absorbed company ceasing to exist as separate business entity. It differs from a consolidation, wherein all the corporations terminate their existence and become parties to a new one.[442] A merger could be the ultimate and desirable result of a takeover; the decision for a merger between an offeror and an offeree company could be taken by the offeror company after a successful takeover bid. Hence, the effect of the *SEVIC* case[443] had the potential to prove to be very important for takeover bids. In this case, a German company (SEVIC) tried to merge with a Luxembourg company (Security Vision SA), with absorption of the latter by the former. As a result, all the assets of Security Vision would be transferred to SEVIC without liquidation and Security Vision would cease to exist. However, the case was brought before the ECJ because German law allowed only domestic mergers and did not permit cross-border mergers. Therefore, SEVIC could not merge with Security Vision SA. Many similarities between mergers and takeovers as means of achieving corporate restructuring and modernization at the EU level could be found in the opinion of Advocate General (AG) Tizzano.[444] AG Tizzano alleged that the instrument of a merger is a particularly effective means of transforming a company insofar as it makes it possible, within the framework of a single operation, to pursue a particular activity in new forms and without interruption, thereby reducing considerably the complications, delay, and costs associated with other forms of company consolidation, such as those that entail, for example, the dissolution of a company with the liquidation of assets and the subsequent formation of a new company, the transfer of individual assets, the exchange of title deeds, and so on. It is well-known that those benefits and advantages are also characteristics of a takeover bid, which aims primarily at corporate restructuring and the enhancement of the performance and competitiveness of European companies. The Takeover Bid Directive (at least in its proposed form by the Commission) offers EU companies greater legal certainty for cross-border takeover bids in the interests of all concerned, including their employees, and the protection of minority shareholders where control of a company changes hands. Internal Market Commissioner F. Bolkestein characterized the Takeover Bid Directive as an essential step towards the objective of fully integrating

441. T. Papadopoulos, 'The Relationship between Takeover Bids and Mergers: Implications for the Internal Market of the European Union', *International and Comparative Corporate Law Journal* 7, no. 2 (2010): 1–19.
442. H.C. Black (n. 82), 891.
443. Case C-411/03, *SEVIC Systems AG*. [2005] ECR I-10805. It should be clarified that seat transfers will be discussed only as far as they are related to takeovers and mergers.
444. [2005] ECR I-10805.

European capital markets by 2005 and as a key element in the drive to make Europe the most competitive economy in the world by 2010.[445]

It is possible to argue that some of the conclusions of the *SEVIC* case on cross-border mergers could be applied to a cross-border takeover bid. The ECJ stated that, as the Advocate General pointed out in point 30 of his Opinion, the right of establishment covers all measures that permit or even merely facilitate access to another Member State and the pursuit of an economic activity in that State by allowing the persons concerned to participate in the economic life of the country effectively and under the same conditions as national operators.[446] It is possible to draw an analogy with takeover bids, which are also characterized by those features of access to the market of another Member State (here, market for corporate control and securities markets in general) and to the participation in the economic life of the country (by investing and bidding for another company and possibly controlling the company). Even if takeover bids are considered to be just means of entering the markets of other Member States and of pursuing economic activities through the acquired companies, they still fall within the protective scope of the freedom of establishment. AG Tizzano, in paragraph 29 of his Opinion, reminds us that the ECJ subjected to freedom of establishment of companies not only the national rules relating directly and specifically to the pursuit of the economic activity in question, but also, all those 'relating to the various general facilities which are of assistance in the pursuit of those activities'.[447] Takeover bids could also constitute such various general facilities (corporate financial methods) contributing to the pursuit of this economic activity and to the participation, on a stable and continuous basis, in the economic life of another Member State (the offeror company establishes itself in the new Member State through the acquisition of the target company). The ECJ also confirmed the direct effect of Treaty provisions on freedom of establishment by stating that while Community harmonization rules are useful for facilitating cross-border mergers, the existence of such harmonization rules cannot be made a pre-condition for the implementation of the freedom of establishment laid down by Articles 43 and 48 of the EC Treaty.[448] The same could be alleged for the takeover process as such, outside the framework of its regulation by the Takeover Bid Directive, which falls directly within the protective scope of freedom of establishment.

In *SEVIC*, the ECJ stated that Articles 43 and 48 of the EC Treaty preclude registration in the national commercial register of the merger by dissolution without liquidation of one company and transfer of the whole of its assets to

445. IP/02/1402.

446. Case C-411/03, *SEVIC Systems AG.* [2005] ECR I-10805 para. 18. It is also notable that the ECJ's approach presents many similarities to the approach followed in *Factortame II* (Case C-221/89 [1991] ECR I-3905], especially the reference to the 'actual pursuit of an economic activity'. S.J. Moran (n. 437), 155.

447. Previous case law: Case C-55/94, *Gebhard* [1995] ECR I-4165 para. 25, Case 63/86, *Commission v. Italy* [1988] ECR 29 para. 14, and Case 305/87, *Commission v. Greece* [1989] ECR 1461 para. 21.

448. See, to that effect, Case C-204/90, *Bachmann* [1992] ECR I-249 para. 11.

another company from being refused in general in a Member State when one of the two companies is established in another Member State, whereas such registration is possible, upon compliance with certain conditions, when the two companies participating in the merger are both established in the territory of the first Member State. AG Tizzano, in his opinion in *SEVIC,* stated that Articles 43 and 48 of the EC Treaty preclude legislation of a Member State, such as the German legislation *(Umwandlungsgesetz)* that does not permit registration in the national register of companies of mergers between companies established in that Member State and companies of other Member States. By permitting cross-border mergers, the ECJ provides an additional incentive for listed companies to become engaged in takeover bids. The companies know that after a successful takeover bid, they will not confront any problems if they plan to merge with the target company that was taken over. The implications of *SEVIC* case law allow offeror companies to realize their strategic plans of merging with offeree companies. This case law broadens the scope of post-takeover choices and adds another possibility for companies that plan to launch a tender offer: the bidder and the target company can merge into a single company and consolidate their respective businesses. In the Takeover Bid Directive and the Cross-Border Mergers Directive, the goal of the European legislature was to promote the combined use of those two corporate financial instruments to result in a more efficient method of corporate restructuring at the EU level. The one complements the other, and the one is essential for the success of the other.

The ECJ, in *SEVIC*, held that national legislation must not discriminate between cross-border and domestic mergers. An extension of this reasoning to takeover bids is inevitable, because mergers and takeovers constitute the two pillars of the mergers and acquisitions market, which is covered by freedom of establishment.[449] Discriminatory national rules of a Member State prohibiting or obstructing a company registered in another Member State from launching a cross-border takeover bid for a company registered in that former Member State are definitely precluded in accordance with *SEVIC*.[450]

8.3 THE CONTRIBUTION OF *UBERSEERING* TO A CROSS-BORDER TAKEOVER PROCESS

The financial transaction from which the facts of the *Uberseering* case[451] originated presented many similarities to a takeover. This case law presents great interest for the examination of some post-takeover situations. *Überseering* was a company incorporated in The Netherlands and having its registered office there. It bought land in Germany and concluded a contract with a company that was supposed to renovate and refurbish its acquired property in Germany. *Überseering*

449. M. Siems, 'SEVIC: Beyond Cross-Border Mergers', *EBOR* 8 (2007): 307, 315.
450. *Ibid.*, 315.
451. Case C-208/00, *Überseering BV v. Nordic Construction Company Baumanagement GmbH (NCC)* [2002] ECR I-9919.

alleged that the refurbishment was defective and brought an action against that company before the German courts. The action was dismissed as inadmissible both at first instance and at second instance because, after the incorporation of the company in the Netherlands, all the shares of *Überseering* had been acquired by two German nationals residing in Germany. As a result, the company that was incorporated and registered in the Netherlands had transferred its centre of management/administration, and thus its real seat, to Germany. According to German rules of private international law, the legal capacity of a company has to be determined by the law at the place of the real seat (in this case German law). As *Überseering* had not implemented German law governing the formation of companies, it had no legal personality and thus no capacity to exercise its right and to appear before a German court. If the company wanted to bring a case before a German court, it would have to re-incorporate in Germany.[452] In *Uberseering,*[453] the ECJ ruled that when a company formed in accordance with the law of a Member State in which it has its registered office is deemed, under the law of another Member State, to have moved its actual centre of administration to the latter Member State, Articles 43 and 48 of the EC Treaty preclude the latter Member State from denying the company legal capacity and, consequently, the capacity to bring legal proceedings before its national courts for the purpose of enforcing rights under a contract with a company established in the latter Member State. As far as the compatibility of German conflict-of-laws rules with freedom of establishment is concerned, the refusal by a host Member State to recognize the legal capacity of a company formed in accordance with the law of another Member State in which it has its registered office on the grounds, in particular, that the company moved its actual centre of administration to the host Member State following the acquisition of all its shares by nationals of that State residing there, with the result that the company cannot, in the host Member State, bring legal proceedings to defend rights under a contract unless it is reincorporated under the law of the host Member State, constitutes a restriction on freedom of establishment, which is, in principle, incompatible with Articles 43 and 48 of the EC Treaty (paragraph 82). Moreover, when a company formed in accordance with the law of a Member State in which it has its registered office exercises its freedom of establishment in another Member State, Articles 43 and 48 of the EC Treaty require the latter Member State to recognize the legal capacity and, consequently, the capacity to be a party to legal proceedings that the company enjoys under the law of its State of incorporation.

Uberseering had the right to invoke freedom of establishment so as to challenge German legislation that did not consider it as a legal person competent to bring a case before a German court.[454] The acquisiton of *Uberseering's* shares

452. P. Dyrberg (n. 14), 531.

453. Case C-208/00, *Überseering BV v. Nordic Construction Company Baumanagement GmbH (NCC)* [2002] ECR I-9919 para. 95.

454. Case C-208/00, *Überseering BV v. Nordic Construction Company Baumanagement GmbH (NCC)* [2002] ECR I-9919 para. 76.

and the subsequent de facto control over this company fall within the protective scope of freedom of establishment of companies. In this judgment, the ECJ confirmed that *Baars* findings also apply here.[455] The ECJ characterized, in *Uberseering*, these conclusions of *Baars* as a 'general rule'. In *Baars*, the ECJ stated that a 100% holding in the capital of a company having its seat in another Member State undoubtedly brings such a shareholder within the scope of application of the Treaty provisions on the right of establishment. It is clear from the second paragraph of Article 43 of the EC Treaty that freedom of establishment includes the right to set up and manage undertakings, in particular, companies or firms, in a Member State by a national of another Member State. Thus, a national of a Member State who has a holding in the capital of a company established in another Member State, which gives him or her definite influence over the company's decisions and allows him or her to determine its activities, is exercising his or her right of establishment.[456] Finally, in *Uberseering*, the ECJ held that the German requirement of re-incorporation before a company could bring legal proceedings to defend rights under a contract was a restriction on freedom of establishment.[457]

What if *Uberseering* had been a listed company?[458] In this case, the acquisition of shares would have been an 'upgraded' capital market transaction, that is, a takeover. The Takeover Bid Directive defines the offeror as 'any *natural* or legal person governed by public or private law making a bid' (emphasis added). Thus, it would be possible for the acquisition of a company's listed shares by natural persons who reside in Member State B (as specified by the ECJ's ruling) to qualify for the definition of a takeover bid. This kind of acquisition of shares therefore falls within the protective scope of the Takeover Bid Directive. However, a takeover bid such as this should comply with all the other requirements imposed by the Takeover Bid Directive. The importance of this case law for takeovers lies in the post-bid period. Without this ruling, natural persons residing in a real-seat jurisdiction would be deterred from launching takeover bids and acquiring the shares of companies registered in jurisdictions that apply the incorporation theory if they knew that the offeree companies would not possess any legal rights in their country of residence. Again, this case law encourages takeover bids and share acquisitions by ensuring that the target company will be recognized in the jurisdiction of the bidder. Additionally, the squeeze-out and sell-out rights (Articles 15 and 16 of

455. Case C-208/00, *Überseering BV v. Nordic Construction Company Baumanagement GmbH (NCC)* [2002] ECR I-9919 para. 77.
456. Case C-251/98, *Baars* [2000] ECR I-2787 paras 21–22.
457. F. Wooldridge, 'Uberseering: Freedom of Establishment of Companies Affirmed', *EBLR* (2003): 227, 233.
458. A recent case that prohibits the discrimination against listed companies that offer services to a host state is the *Placanica* Case: Arts 43 and 49 EC Treaty must be interpreted as precluding national legislation, which excludes – and, moreover, continues to exclude – from the betting and gaming sector operators in the form of companies whose shares are quoted on the regulated markets. Joined cases C-338/04, C-359/04, and C-360/04, *Criminal Proceedings against Massimiliano Placanica* (C-338/04), *Christian Palazzese* (C-359/04) *and Angelo Sorricchio* (C-360/04). [2007] (ECR page not yet specified).

the Takeover Bid Directive) could facilitate 100% shareholdings, which fall clearly within the scope of freedom of establishment.

Article 11(2)(b) of the Takeover Bid Directive provides the possibility to the bidder to amend the articles of association and remove the target company's board of directors after acquiring 75% or more of the capital-carrying voting rights. Article 11(2)(b) states that when, 'following a bid, the offeror holds 75% or more of the capital-carrying voting rights, no restrictions on the transfer of securities or on voting rights, nor any extraordinary rights of shareholders concerning *the appointment or removal of board members* provided for in the articles of association of the offeree shall apply; multiple-vote securities shall carry only one vote each at the first general meeting of shareholders following closure of the bid, called by the offeror to amend the articles of association or *to remove or appoint board members*. To that end, the offeror shall have the right to convene a general meeting of shareholders at short notice, provided that the meeting does not take place within two weeks of notification (emphasis added)'. This appointment or removal of board members could result in a transfer of a company's centre of administration or its real seat. If the new members of the board were residents in a real-seat jurisdiction, it would be necessary to dissolve the company and to re-incorporate in that jurisdiction. *Uberseering* is related to a situation like this. It is easily understood that without the Court's jurisprudence in *Uberseering,* this provision of the Takeover Bid Directive could present many operational problems and deficiencies in its application to situations in which the new members of the board reside in real-seat jurisdictions. The conclusions of *Uberseering* assist not only the company itself in enforcing its rights and in bringing various cases before the national courts, but also, its shareholders who plan to start litigation. This is a clear expression of the protection of 'members' stipulated by Article 44(2)(g) of the EC Treaty. However, the importance of *Uberseering* in this context was diminished after *Cartesio,* a recent ruling of the ECJ.

The latter conclusion mentioned above should be considered in the context of the *Cartesio*[459] ruling, in which the ECJ highlighted that, as Community law now stands, Articles 43 and 48 of the EC Treaty are to be interpreted as not precluding Member State legislation under which a company incorporated under the law of that Member State may not transfer its seat to another Member State while retaining its status as a company governed by the law of the Member State of incorporation.[460] The ECJ held that a Member State has the power to define both the connecting factor required of a company if it is to be regarded as incorporated under the law of that Member State and, as such, capable of enjoying the right of establishment, and that required if the company is to be able subsequently to maintain that status. That power includes the possibility for that Member State not to permit a company governed by its law to retain that status if the company intends to reorganize itself in another Member State by moving its seat to the territory of the latter, thereby breaking the connecting factor required under the

459. Case C-210/06, *CARTESIO Oktató és Szolgáltató bt.* [2008] not yet reported.
460. Case C-210/06, *CARTESIO Oktató és Szolgáltató bt.* [2008] not yet reported para.124.

national law of the Member State of incorporation.[461] Therefore, in a takeover bid, if this appointment or removal of board members could result in a transfer of a company's centre of administration or its real seat, it would be necessary to dissolve the company and to re-incorporate in that jurisdiction.

8.4 APPLICATION OF *CENTROS* AND *INSPIRE ART* CASE LAW TO A POST-TAKEOVER BID SITUATION

Another corporate mobility case that presents an indirect link to takeover bids is *Centros.*[462] This case law widens the available routes of corporate restructuring and consolidation that companies could track after a successful takeover bid. In that case, the ECJ stated that it is contrary to Articles 43 and 48 of the EC Treaty for a Member State to refuse to register a branch of a company formed in accordance with the law of another Member State in which it has its registered office but in which it conducts no business, whereby the branch is intended to enable the company in question to carry on its entire business in the Member State in which that branch is to be created, while avoiding the need to form a company there, thus evading application of the rules governing the formation of companies, which, in that State, are more restrictive as regards the paying of a minimum share capital (this case involved differences between minimum capital requirements established by the Second Company Law Directive). Given that the right to form a company in accordance with the law of a Member State and to set up branches in other Member States is inherent in the exercise, in a single market, of the freedom of establishment guaranteed by the Treaty, the fact that a national of a Member State who wishes to set up a company chooses to form it in the Member State whose rules of company law seem to him or her the least restrictive and to set up branches in other Member States cannot, in itself, constitute an abuse of the right of establishment.[463] Companies have now a right to take advantage of the most business friendly environment in which to establish their companies. The ECJ's decision is quite impressive for its acknowledgement of the rights of natural or legal persons to choose the least-restrictive corporate form of those available in the Member States as the vehicle of their cross-border investments and expansions.[464]

---

461. Case C-210/06, *CARTESIO Oktató és Szolgáltató bt.* [2008] not yet reported para. 110.
462. Case C-212/97, *Centros Ltd v. Erhvervs- og Selskabsstyrelsen* [1999] ECR I-1459.
463. Case C-212/97, *Centros Ltd v. Erhvervs- og Selskabsstyrelsen* [1999] ECR I-1459 paras 27 and 39. See also: P. Cunha & P. Cadral, 'Presumed Innocence': Companies and the Exercise of the Right of Establishment under Community Law', *E L Rev.* (2000): 157, 162, E. Vaccaro, 'Transfer of Seat and Freedom of Establishment in European Company Law', *EBLR* (2005): 1348, 1353, A. Roussos, 'Realising the Free Movement of Companies', *EBLR* (2001): 7, 12, G. Simen Gravir, 'Conflict of Laws Rules for Norwegian Companies after the *Centros* Judgement', *EBLR* (2001): 146, 149, J.L. Hansen, 'A New Look at *Centros* - From a Danish Point of View', *EBLR* (2002): 85, 93.
464. See also: D.A. Wyatt & A. Dashwood (n. 46), 842. The ECJ also clarified that harmonization was not necessary for this exercise of the right of establishment.

This case is very useful for an offeror company that decides to choose the most appropriate legal form for the offeree company after a successful takeover bid. After a successful takeover bid, the acquired target company becomes a subsidiary[465] of the offeror company. The offeror company now controls the newly acquired target company and can decide on the form whereby this latter company will continue its business activities. These two companies could preserve their current corporate forms as separate companies, or they could merge into a single company. In the case of a subsequent merger, the acquired target company could be possibly transformed into a branch[466] of the offeror company. If the offeror company follows the example of *Centros* and decides to carry out almost all of its activities through this branch, the Member State of this branch could not restrict this exercise of the right of secondary establishment by not recognizing this branch and by refusing its registration.[467] Member States should respect the right of EU entrepreneurs to choose the corporate form[468] that they consider most convenient for their conducting of business at a cross-border level and to take all the necessary legal steps for the realization of this choice. This is just a possible scenario that could take place after a successful takeover bid. However, the offeree company would not have these additional managerial choices of corporate restructuring without *Centros*.

In *Inspire Art*,[469] the ECJ held that harmonization of the disclosure to be made by branches, as brought about by Eleventh Company Law Directive 89/666, is

465. N. Moloney (n. 108), 805.
466. A 'branch' is defined as a division, office, or other unit of business located at a different location from the main office or headquarters. H.C. Black (n. 82), 170.
467. In *Inspire Art* (see next paragraph), the ECJ talked about the prohibition of imposition of additional requirements on the exercise of the right of secondary establishment. The ECJ stated that it is contrary to Arts 43 and 48 EC Treaty for national legislation to impose on the exercise of freedom of secondary establishment in that state by a company formed in accordance with the law of another Member State certain conditions provided for in domestic law with respect to company formation relating to minimum capital and directors' liability.
468. Other proposed methods of corporate restructuring and governance that constitute forms of exercising the freedom of establishment are the formulation of a simplified company structure for subsidiaries and joint ventures, which is characterized by greater freedom and flexibility in the agreements among parties while no comparable protective attitudes are needed, and the creation of a horizontal group. These methods are currently confronting many problems in their realization. E. Wymeersch (n. 124), 322–323.
469. Case C-167/01, *Kamer van Koophandel en Fabrieken voor Amsterdam v. Inspire Art Ltd* [2003] ECR I-10155 paras 65, 69–70, 72, 105, 136–139, 143. Interesting annotations: P.S. Ryan, Case Note Case C-167/01, [2005] *Col J EL* 187–201. H. Merkt, 'European Company Law Reform: Struggling for a More Liberal Approach', *ECFR* 1 (2004): 3, 20–21. H-J. De Kluiver, 'Inspiring a New European Company Law?', *ECFR* 1 (2004): 121–134. D. Zimmer, 'Case Annotation', *CM L Rev.* (2004): 1127–1140. A. Looijestijn-Clearie, 'Have the Dikes Collapsed?: Inspire Act a Further Break-through in the Freedom of Establishment of Companies?', *EBOR* (2004): 389–418 H. Hirt, 'Freedom of Establishment, International Company Law and the Comparison of the European Company Law Systems after the ECJ's Decision in *Inspire Art Ltd.*', *EBLR* (2004): 1189–1222. F. Wooldridge, 'The Advocate General's Submissions in Kamer van Koophandel: Further Emphasis on the Right of Establishment', *EBLR* (2003): 497–505. A. Schall, 'The UK Limited Company Abroad: How Foreign Creditors Are

exhaustive. Moreover, the ECJ stated that it is contrary to Articles 43 and 48 of the EC Treaty for national legislation to impose on the exercise of freedom of secondary establishments in that State by a company formed in accordance with the law of another Member State certain conditions provided for in domestic law with respect to a company's formation relating to minimum capital and directors' liability. The reasons for which the company was formed in that other Member State, and the fact that it carries on its activities exclusively or almost exclusively in the Member State of establishment, do not deprive it of the right to invoke the freedom of establishment guaranteed by the Treaty, save where the existence of an abuse is established on a case-by-case basis. A Member State is certainly entitled to take measures designed to prevent certain of its nationals from attempting, under cover of the rights created by the Treaty, to improperly circumvent their national legislation or to prevent individuals from improperly or fraudulently taking advantage of provisions of Community law. However, the provisions of the Treaty on freedom of establishment are intended specifically to enable companies formed in accordance with the law of a Member State and having their registered offices, central administrations, or principal places of business within the Community to pursue activities in other Member States through agencies, branches, or subsidiaries. That being so, the fact that a national of a Member State who wishes to set up a company can choose to do so in the Member State whose company-law rules seem to him or her to be the least restrictive and then set up branches in other Member States is inherent in the exercise, in a single market, of the freedom of establishment guaranteed by the Treaty. In addition, the fact that a company does not conduct any business in the Member State in which it has its registered office and pursues its activities only or principally in the Member State where its branch is established is not sufficient to prove the existence of abuse or fraudulent conduct, which would entitle the latter Member State to deny that company the benefit of the provisions of Community law relating to the right of establishment. This case law confirms that, in the scenario of the previous paragraph, the Member State of the offeree company could not obstruct the offeror company from merging with the offeree company after a successful takeover and, subsequently, from transforming the offeree company into its branch and to carry out almost all of its activities through this branch.

8.5 ADDITIONAL STANDARDS IMPOSED BY CAPITAL MARKET LAW AND THE IMPORTANCE OF CORPORATE MOBILITY CASE LAW

Takeover bids as a financial technique related to both company law and capital market law have an additional significance for the corporate mobility case law of the ECJ. Capital market law could also have a growing regulatory impact on

---

Protected after Inspire Art (Including a Comparison of UK and German Creditor Protection Rules)', *EBLR* (2005): 1534–1554.

subject matters that traditionally have been regulated by company law.[470] National company law in accordance with the corporate mobility case law of the ECJ is responsible for determining the seat of a company incorporated in its jurisdiction. It is possible that capital market law, apart from imposing disclosure requirements, could intervene in the internal corporate governance of companies and could impose additional substantive corporate governance standards for access to capital markets and the conducting of business and investments.[471] These additional requirements imposed by capital market law would not be appropriate for foreign companies that were formed in compliance with foreign company laws. Thus, these foreign companies could find difficulties in accessing some capital markets and benefiting from the flows of such capital. Capital market law should only draft and impose some general principles of corporate governance, which foreign companies could easily follow by adjusting their corporate structures or permitting foreign companies to derogate.[472] By allowing capital market law to impose different corporate governance standards on foreign companies, the importance of the ECJ's case law that deduced that company law of a Member State regulates the substantive corporate governance of companies incorporated in that Member State or having moved their registered office to that State, regardless of the jurisdiction in which they conduct their business or of the jurisdiction to which their real seat was moved, would lose its importance to a great extent.[473]

8.6 CONCLUSION

Both the corporate mobility case law and the Takeover Bid Directive have as their primary aim the promotion of freedom of establishment of companies at the EU level. Their starting point is Article 43 of the EC Treaty. The Takeover Bid Directive is based on Article 44(2)(g) of the EC Treaty, which attempts to attain freedom of establishment (Article 43 of the EC Treaty) as declared by Article 44(1) of the EC Treaty. The corporate mobility case law refers explicitly to the promotion of Article 43 of the EC Treaty. The corporate mobility case law is crucial for post-takeover situations. The facilitation of corporate mobility and the transfer of a corporate seat by the ECJ's case law could also encourage takeover bids, because offeror companies know that they will not find any difficulties in recognizing the transfer of an offeree company's seat after a successful takeover bid. This case law provides an additional incentive for takeover bids and contributes to legal certainty and market integration.

---

470. J. Winter, 'EU Company Law at the Cross-Roads', in *Reforming Company and Takeover Law in Europe*, ed. G. Ferrarini et al. (Oxford: Oxford University Press, 2004), 12–13.
471. *Ibid.*, 12–13.
472. *Ibid.*, 12–13.
473. For an extensive analysis of corporate governance structures imposed by capital market law and their consequences, see the following chapter about 'The EU Takeover Bid Directive: An EU Company Law Instrument with Strong Links to EU Capital Markets Law', J. Winter (n. 470), 12–13.

Chapter 9

The EU Takeover Bid Directive: An EU Company Law Instrument with Strong Links to EU Capital Market Law

The development of the EU capital markets gives many reasons to be optimistic. There is good progress on the ground. Our markets are open and competitive – but there are also reasons to be vigilant. Economic freedom, competition, the free flow of capital are not a given. They have to be defended and promoted every day. Europe has much to gain from more open markets – within and to the outside. That is where the focus of our policies should lie over the coming years.

I have said this before, but I repeat it today. The real challenge we face now is not to draw up framework rules at European level. That to a large extent we have done. No, the real challenge today is to make them right across the spectrum – the best in the world – and to ensure they are enforced and that the basic freedoms in the Treaty are upheld. That is our objective and we are determined to fulfil it.

– Speech by Charlie McCreevy, Former Commissioner for Internal Market and Services

'The Development of the European Capital Market', London School of Economics,

London, 9 March 2006 (SPEECH/06/160).

9.1 COMPANY LAW AND CAPITAL MARKET LAW: AN INTERNAL MARKET INTERACTION REGARDING EU TAKEOVER BIDS

Company law and capital market law[474] are two closely related areas of law. This is clear in the case of takeover bids, which are financial transactions that take place in a regulated capital market and that involve listed companies. Company law harmonization should take into account the needs of the capital markets. It could be argued that the harmonization of company law could strengthen capital markets' security, transparency, and efficiency, because divergent national company law standards (e.g., special classes of publicly traded securities and information asymmetries) have a negative influence on capital markets' transparency.[475]

Nowadays, capital market law regulates more and more matters of company law. There is a capital market regulatory response to perceived deficiencies in the corporate governance system (e.g., the Sarbanes–Oxley Act in the US).[476] Investors in capital markets started to take into account the internal corporate governance structures of listed companies when contemplating investing in them.[477] This was the result of the corporate and financial scandals in the global capital markets, which were partly caused by poor corporate governance, disclosure,[478]

474. This covers the interaction between the law and the securities industry. E. Kitch, 'Regulation of the Securities Market', in *Encyclopedia of Law & Economics*, ed. B. Bouckaert & G. De Geest (London: Elgar and the University of Ghent, 1999), 813. The source of capital market law is found in company law. Capital market law was developed primarily after the 1930s economic crisis. This origin reveals the numerous connections between these two areas of law. R. Buxbaum & K. Hopt (n. 80), 189.

475. E. Wymeersch (n. 91), 158, 173. See also G. Ferrarini, 'Introduction' and R. Dale, 'The Regulation of Investment Firms in the European Union', in *Prudential Regulation of Banks and Securities Firms*, ed. G. Ferrarini (London: Kluwer Law International, 1995), 10, 27.

476. J. Winter (n. 470), 12. For a US perspective on the relationship between company law and capital market law, see: F Cross & R. Prentice, *Law and Corporate Finance* (Cheltenham: Elgar, 2007), 7–21. See also: J. Coffee, 'The Impact of Cross-Listings and Stock Market Competition on International Corporate Governance', in *Global Markets, Domestic Institutions*, ed. C. Milhaupt (New York: Colup, 2003), 437–476.

477. J. Winter (n. 470), 12. According to the 'Opinion of the European Economic and Social Committee on Financial Integration: The Case of European Stock Markets' (own initiative opinion) [2008] *OJ* C 162/96), the EU institutions should inform the citizens of the EU of the benefits that a harmonized legal framework for dealings in securities would offer them to combat the current unwillingness to cross-border capital investments.

478. As far as the disclosure and transparency requirements are concerned, there are different rationales between company law and capital market law underpinning those requirements. In company law, disclosure plays a very important role for the discipline and the accountability of company's board. Disclosure can assist shareholders in deciding if it is necessary to replace company's board because of its low performance. In capital market law, disclosure and transparency assist investors in determining their next investment steps. The harmonization of capital market disclosure and transparency requires implementation of uniform standards because of the high level of standardization of information demanded by the investors and competent authorities in different Member States. This harmonizing technique is quite different from that followed in company law (especially in the fourth-generation directives).

and auditor control standards.[479] This intrusion of capital market law into some areas of company law is very important for encouraging cross-border investments at the EU level and integrating the European market for corporate control. The new reach of securities regulation over corporate matters helps EU investors[480] to make their investment and takeover decisions on a more well-informed basis and to strengthen their trust in EU capital markets. Nevertheless, there is a criticism to be made of this intrusion of capital market law into company law matters when capital market law starts to regulate substantive elements of company law.[481] It is obvious that there is no difference in substance if a corporate governance standard derives from company law or securities regulation. However, from a regulatory perspective, there is a difference, particularly because company law and capital market law make different jurisdictional claims.[482] On one hand, national company law regulates companies that have their real seat or registered office (depending on the adoption of the real-seat theory or of the incorporation theory) in that Member State. The place of the business or investment activities is not important for this determination. On the other hand, the main criterion for the implementation of a certain capital market law of a Member State is the active participation of a company in the capital markets of that Member State.[483] When capital market law of a Member State demands from a foreign company listed in its capital market the adjustment or modification of certain substantive elements of company law, these capital market rules might be incompatible with the foreign company law of that listed company determined by the Member State of its seat.[484] This legislative approach does not contribute to the integration of capital markets, because many companies may be deterred from acceding to capital markets that contradict their 'home-grown' corporate governance structures. Capital market regulators should be very careful when they plan to impose any additional company law standards on foreign companies participating in cross-border takeover bids that take place in their capital market. National legislatures should always have in mind that takeovers lie on the border between capital market law and company law. Excessive zeal on behalf of national capital market regulators could often conflict with foreign company law. If national capital market regulators are aware in advance of the foreign company law provisions (especially those deriving from harmonization), any possible incompatibility between those two laws could be avoided.

The EU market for corporate control is a part of these regulated capital markets. With regard to its regulation, the EU market for corporate control depends heavily on the legislative choices of company law and on the available corporate

---

J. Winter, 'EU Company Law at the Cross-Roads', in *Reforming Company and Takeover Law in Europe*, ed. G. Ferrarini et al. (Oxford: Oxford University Press, 2004), 11–12. C. Villiers (n. 101), 29, 48–49, 224.

479. J. Winter (n. 470), 12.
480. R. Buxbaum & K. Hopt (n. 80), 280.
481. J. Winter (n. 470), 12.
482. *Ibid.*
483. *Ibid.*
484. J. Winter (n. 470), 12–13.

governance structures. If a Member State has a certain doctrine on takeovers, it could structure its company law in a certain way whereby company law promotes or inhibits takeover bids. On one hand, a Member State adopting a positive stance toward takeover bids could use company law to liberalize the field of takeovers. On the other hand, if a national legislature does not support takeover bids, it could pass national company law rules allowing companies to adopt certain corporate governance structures hostile to takeover bids. Additionally, the EU legislature could use company law to establish a level playing field for takeovers at the EU level.[485] Hence, in the company law harmonization programme, there were EU regulatory efforts to establish a level playing field for takeovers at the EU level. These efforts of the EU legislature to establish a level playing field are also mandated by the protection of the 'members and others' rationale of Article 44(2)(g) of the EC Treaty. However, the close relationship between company law and capital market law could sometimes produce a few negative side effects: more uniform regulation of capital market law reduces a company's autonomy and margin of assessment, and hence its flexibility to adjust to the needs of the capital markets. Limiting the use of specific types of financial instruments, for instance, might be prejudicial to financial creativity and appropriate financing conditions.[486]

9.2 EU REGULATORY APPROACHES TO THE HARMONIZATION OF TAKEOVER BIDS: A CONSIDERATION IN LIGHT OF EU COMPANY LAW AND EU CAPITAL MARKET LAW

While, in many national legal orders, securities regulation completes company law, the European legislature has treated company law and capital market law as separate bodies of law. However, the border between those two areas of law is often blurred, as in the case of takeover bids: although takeovers fall within the scope of capital market law in many jurisdictions, the EU deals with them from the perspective of company law under the scope of the Thirteenth Company Law Directive.[487] Formally, this Directive belongs to the EU Company Harmonization Programme, but it regulates a crucial segment of EU capital markets, the EU market for corporate control, and, in many of its provisions, it is inspired more by capital market concepts than by company law notions.[488] The link between the Takeover Bid Directive and capital market law is detected between the interpenetration of capital markets at the EU level and the consequent diversification of shareholder bases across the Member States and the need to guarantee equivalent

485. E. Wymeersch (n. 91), 158, 174.
486. E. Wymeersch (n. 91), 158, 173–174.
487. E. Wymeersch (n. 91), 150. G. Wolff (n. 310), 21. It is argued that the distinction between capital market law and company law is still a valid distinction. J. Garrido-Garcia (n. 85), 762.
488. J. Winter (n. 470), 12. It is also alleged that the Takeover Bid Directive lies more in the area of capital market law than of company law. R. Buxbaum, G. Hertig et al. (eds) (n. 97), 408.

and effective protections for investors as shareholders in the event of a takeover bid.[489] The market integration rationale underpinning EC securities regulation also applies to company law aspects of takeover regulation.[490] A liberalized capital marketplace without legal or structural corporate barriers to takeovers could benefit the competitive position of the EU.[491] From a company law perspective, the Directive is engaged with the external side of corporate governance, that is, the disciplinary function of the threat of takeover bids and the acquisition of control over a company through a takeover bid.[492] The reference in the Financial Services Action Plan[493] to takeover bids makes more indistinct this subtle line between company law and capital market law. Additionally, the fact that the very early 1966 Segré Report, on the development of a European capital market, which called for the removal of the obstacles faced by issuers (among them were many listed companies) of securities wishing to offer or list securities in another Member State, did not distinguish between those two areas of law.[494] Nevertheless, capital market law presents higher regulatory flexibility (because of the use of *Lamfalussy* comitology procedures in the field of securities regulation) and vigour of enforcement (possessing special enforcement instruments and mostly being enforced by a public agencies) than does company law.[495]

At the beginning of the process of harmonization of capital market law, the EU had followed the same approach as with company law harmonization: detailed and almost identical provisions tried to establish equivalence of safeguards for investors and markets to avoid additional onerous controls on access to securities markets and on securities transactions (e.g., prospectus directives).[496] This approach

489. N. Moloney (n. 108), 806–807.

490. N. Moloney (n. 108), 811. See also Commission Communication on Financial Services 'Building a Framework for Action' COM (1998) 625, 7. For the integration of financial and capital markets in European Union, see an excellent collection of essays: M Andenas, 'Who Is Going to Supervise Europe's Financial Markets?', J. Dalhuisen, 'Towards a Single European Capital Market and a Workable System of Regulation', S. Thomadakis, 'Fifteen Regulators for a Single Capital Market: The Project of Regulatory Harmonization in Europe', & R.M. Lastra, 'Regulating European Securities Markets: Beyond the *Lamfalussy* Report', in *Financial Markets in Europe: Towards a Single Regulator?*, ed. M. Andenas & Y. Avgerinos (The Hague: Kluwer, 2003) XV, 35, 75, 211. M. Blair & N. Phipps, 'Regulation of European Markets and Exchanges', in *Financial Markets and Exchanges Law*, ed. M. Blair & G. Walker (Oxford: Oxford University Press, 2007), 381.

491. N. Moloney (n. 108), 811. See also ECOSOC Comments on the 1989 Proposal for a Thirteenth Directive on company law concerning takeover and other general bids [1989] *OJ* C298/56 para. 1(4).

492. J. Winter (n. 470), 12.

493. Communication of the Commission, 'Financial Services: Implementing the Framework for Financial Markets: Action Plan' COM (1999) 232, 9, available at: <http://ec.europa.eu/internal_market/finances/docs/actionplan/index/action_en.pdf>, accessed 16 Sep. 2008.

494. N. Moloney (n. 108), 62–63.

495. E. Wymeersch (n. 91), 150–151.

496. E. Wymeersch (n. 106), 19. It is noticed that all capital market directives (except for the Investment Services and the Market Abuse Directives for secondary markets) are based on Art. 44(2)(g) EC Treaty. Harmonization of capital market law seems also to be more

did not work: authorities in each of the Member States applied their own requirements[497] and submitted the securities transactions to a new, although sometimes simplified, vetting procedure.[498] Then, the European legislature opted for the harmonizing technique of mutual recognition. According to 'mutual recognition', securities could be offered to the public without much in the way of additional administrative procedures. This regulatory model presents many drawbacks in practice, because national authorities retain the power to impose justified and proportionate restrictions (the *Gebhard* test), such as notification, and additional requirements relating to their local marketing and distribution rules.[499] This preserves partly the fragmentation of EU primary capital markets and does not assist in their progressive integration.[500] In the securities field, it is amazing to compare the restrictions that are imposed in the primary market, when securities are offered to the public, and the lack of comparable safeguards in the secondary market, when securities are offered for sale on the stock exchange.[501] Nevertheless, the imposition of those restrictions in the securities transactions of secondary markets could prove to be necessary. This last issue is related directly to the takeover process, as the effective regulation of those transactions dealing with shares is essential for the transfer of corporate control. These regulated transactions should be characterized by efficiency and protection for the parties. The lack of safeguards in the secondary market could prove to be detrimental to the market for

---

'intensive' than harmonization of company law, which does not intervene into the internal structure of companies. S. Grundmann (n. 297), 629–630. R. Buxbaum & K. Hopt (n. 80), 202, 218.

497. That is, legal diversity among national capital market laws. R. Buxbaum & K. Hopt (n. 80), 174.

498. E. Wymeersch (n. 106), 19. It was proposed that priority should be given to capital market law harmonization instead of company law priority because the contribution of the latter to market integration is highly questioned. R. Buxbaum, G. Hertig et al. (eds) (n. 97), 130. R. Buxbaum & K. Hopt (n. 80) 202.

499. E. Wymeersch (n. 106), 19–20. See also E. Ferran & C. Goodhart, 'Regulating Financial Services and Markets in the Twenty First Century: An Overview', E. Wymeersch, 'Regulating European Markets: The Harmonization of Securities Regulation in Europe in the New Trading Environment', and G. Thieffry, 'The Case of European Securities Commission', in *Regulating Financial Services and Markets in the Twenty First Century*, ed. E. Ferran & C. Goodhart (Oxford: Hart, 2001), 13, 190, 211.

500. M. Maquil, 'The Integration of the Securities Markets in Europe', in *Further Perspectives in Financial Integration in Europe*, ed. E. Wymeersch (Berlin-New York: de Gruyter, 1994), 157–169.

501. E. Wymeersch (n. 106), 20. By means of the MiFID (Markets in Financial Instruments) Directive, the European Union has established a comprehensive regulatory regime for the organized execution of investor transactions by stock markets, other trading systems and investment firms. Directive 2004/39/EC of the European Parliament and of the Council of 21 Apr. 2004 on markets in financial instruments amending Council Directives 85/611/EEC and 93/6/EEC and Directive 2000/12/EC of the European Parliament and of the Council and repealing Council Directive 93/22/EEC [2004] OJ L145/1-44. Europa website Markets in Financial Instruments (MiFID) and Investment Services, <http://europa.eu/scadplus/leg/en/lvb/l24036e.htm>, accessed 7 Mar. 2008. See also E. Avgouleas, 'The New EC Financial Markets Legislation and the Emerging Regime for Capital Markets', *YEL* 23 (2004): 321.

corporate control, because it dissuades bidders from participating in risky acquisitions of shares. Even a satisfactory takeover regime (i.e., the Takeover Bid Directive without the opt outs and the reciprocity clause) could be endangered by the lack of safeguards in the secondary securities market.

An indirect enforcement mechanism that is quite common in capital markets and that could prove to be a valuable incentive for implementing the optional provisions (Article 9 and/or 11) of the Takeover Bid Directive is the 'comply or explain' principle. According to this regulatory technique, non-adherents have to declare explicitly whether or not they comply with a stated series of principles or rules and disclose the reasons for not complying.[502] This is well-known in the various corporate governance codes (many of which follow the ideology of the UK's 'Code of Best Practice', the so-called Cadbury Code) whereby companies must provide detailed and well-founded explanations for their decisions not to conform to the requirements of the corporate governance code. The demand from both market organizers (national competent authorities) and listed companies to be able to display a similar instrument of good practice so as to attract investors was driven by the fact that listed companies are being put under pressure to voluntarily adopt rules of good corporate governance, and that, aware of the possible impact – less positive than negative – on investor's interests, they proclaim in their annual accounts the hard efforts they make to comply with these new standards of consistent conduct.[503] It is obvious that this principle allows the corporate governance code to obtain a moderate obligatory character and, simultaneously, permits different corporate strategies as long as they are justified.[504] Companies that do not manage to provide sufficient and convincing reasons for their decisions to diverge from the corporate governance codes have these facts revealed to the other market participants and to the public in general. However, in practice, a usual phenomenon is that the justifications invoked for these differentiations are not always credible and there is no enforcement instrument against those companies that flatly refuse. This potential exposure to market forces (the so-called name and shame) will not deter those companies from adopting different corporate governance standards without concrete justifications.[505]

It can be deduced that similar pressure could be applied to companies that do not voluntarily or involuntarily implement the optional[506] provisions of the

502. E. Wymeersch (n. 91), 156. D. Weber-Rey (n. 256), 382–384.
503. E. Wymeersch, 'Company Law in the 21st Century' Financial Law Institute, University of Gent Working Paper Series WP 1999/14, 9–10.
504. E. Wymeersch (n. 91), 156.
505. *Ibid.*
506. Commissioner F. Bolkenstein expressed his disappointment at the optional provisions and the reciprocity clause, which watered down the impact of this directive on the EU market for corporate control: 'I am not going to pretend that I am pleased with this agreement. Nor am I going to be hypocritical by pretending that the version of the Directive agreed today represents a step forward for EU competitiveness or for the integration of EU capital markets. The Competitiveness Council says that it wants to be seen to be taking decisions. In all sincerity, I have to say that if the Council continues to take decisions like this one, the European Union

Takeover Bid Directive because of their own decisions or because of the Member States' choices. It is possible that this kind of pressure could urge those companies to apply the optional provisions of the Takeover Bid Directive. The Directive contains a similar provision in Article 10, which demands that listed companies publish detailed information on the structure of their capital, including non-listed securities and the different classes of shares; any restrictions on the transfer of securities; any pyramid structures and cross shareholdings; special shareholder rights; any employee share scheme; any restrictions on voting rights; any agreements among shareholders that may result in restrictions on the transfer of securities and/or voting rights, or on the rules governing the appointment and removal of board members; any agreements to which the company is a party and which take effect, alter, or terminate upon a change of control of the company following a takeover bid; and any agreements between the company and its board members and employees providing for compensation. This Article also requires the publication of this information in the company's annual report, as provided for in Article 46 of Directive 78/660/EEC and Article 36 of Directive 83/349/EEC.[507] Additionally, Article 10(3) prescribes that Member States shall ensure, in the case of companies whose securities are admitted to trading on a regulated market in a Member State, that the board of directors presents an explanatory report to the annual general meeting of shareholders on these matters. The Directive tried to follow this 'comply or explain' technique, which derives mainly from the field of securities regulation, so as to put some pressure on the Member States and the individual companies to adopt the optional provisions of the Directive. The Takeover Bid Directive shows that capital market law is very important for corporate governance, because shareholders could affect managers' behaviour by the purchase and sale of their holdings.[508] This incentive, which encourages the application of the optional provisions, contributes to the integration of the European market for corporate control and to the establishment of a more uniform and secure takeover regime at the EU level.

---

will never reach its target of becoming the most competitive economy in the world by 2010. On this issue, we have actually gone a long way in reverse gear since the Council endorsed the previous takeovers Directive in June 2001, with 14 Member States in favour.' Press release MEMO/03/245.

507. Fourth Council Directive 78/660/EEC of 25 Jul. 1978 based on Art. 54(3)(g) of the Treaty on the annual accounts of certain types of companies [1978] OJ L222/11. Seventh Council Directive 83/349/EEC of 13 Jun. 1983 based on the Art. 54(3)(g) of the Treaty on consolidated accounts [1983] OJ L193/1. These directive were amended by the following directives: Directive 2006/46/EC of the European Parliament and of the Council of 14 Jun. 2006 amending Council Directives 78/660/EEC on the annual accounts of certain types of companies, 83/349/EEC on consolidated accounts, 86/635/EEC on the annual accounts and consolidated accounts of banks and other financial institutions, and 91/674/EEC on the annual accounts and consolidated accounts of insurance undertakings [2006] OJ L224/1–7 (This directive applies certain short-term changes proposed by the Company Law Action Plan), Directive 2006/43/EC of the European Parliament and of the Council of 17 May 2006 on statutory audits of annual accounts and consolidated accounts, amending Council Directives 78/660/EEC and 83/349/EEC and repealing Council Directive 84/253/EEC [2006] OJ L157/87-107.

508. S. Grundmann (n. 297), 630.

The Takeover Bid Directive regulates the markets relating to takeover bids for the securities of companies governed by the laws of Member States, where all or some of those securities are admitted to trading on a regulated market within the meaning of Directive 93/22/EEC[509] in one or more Member States. However, the Winter Report also refers to an intermediate class, that is, the 'open companies'.[510] These are 'unlisted' companies that would have qualified for listing, their securities being freely transferable and dispersed among investors.[511] Regulations for listed companies do not cover this category of companies, and their legal position is quite obscure; the Winter Report states that a balance has to be struck, but without giving further details.[512] It was proposed that these companies should ask for listing of their securities immediately after offering their securities to the public, or, if they do not voluntarily ask for listing (as in the case of companies that started as closed companies but whose shares were dispersed over time), to choose either trading on a market or making a bid – or having a shareholder make a bid – for their outstanding shares.[513] Thus, a sufficient degree of liquidity and disclosure is secured for their shareholders.[514] In this way, the protection of 'members and others' proclaimed by Article 44(2)(g) of the EC Treaty is also promoted, because the ambiguous legal status of those companies is not in the best interests of their shareholders. This category of companies should also be regulated by the European legislature so as to diminish legal uncertainties and to ameliorate the status of those companies. It could be alleged that this category of 'open companies' falls within the scope of a wide definition of the European market for corporate control, even if they are not listed in a regulated capital market. Their securities transactions present many similarities to those of a regulated capital market. These companies constitute an additional vehicle for cross-border investments at the EU level, which broadens the already existing options of European investors. As a matter of fact, this additional area of cross-border investment deserves the attention of the European legislature.

A major part of self-regulation and independent supervisory control is delegated in many Member States to bodies set up for this purpose that are closely related to the capital markets, yet the government retains responsibility for the supervision of capital markets. Company law and capital market directives (including the Takeover Bid Directive) refer to the national competent authorities appointed for this purpose, and the decisions of those authorities on capital market

---

509. Council Directive 93/22/EEC of 10 May 1993 on investment services in the securities field (1993) OJ L141/27.
510. Report of the High Level Group of Company Law Experts on a Modern Regulatory Framework for Company Law in Europe (Brussels, 2002), <http://ec.europa.eu/internal_market/company/docs/modern/report_en.pdf>, accessed 11 Aug. 2007.
511. E. Wymeersch (n. 91), 172.
512. E. Wymeersch (n. 91), 172–173.
513. E. Wymeersch (n. 91), 173.
514. E. Wymeersch (n. 91), 173. S. Grundmann categorizes in broad terms modern corporations into private limited companies, public limited companies without capital market orientation, and public limited companies with capital market orientation. The traditional distinction between private and public limited companies is considered to be outdated. S. Grundmann (n. 297), 629.

issues could be reviewed by national (mostly administrative) courts because of their semi-legal status.[515] Sometimes, those semi-legal decisions of the national competent authorities could create problems when they are expanded into the field of company law and corporate governance (especially the harmonized part). These decisions are welcome as long as they help listed companies to adjust to securities regulations. Yet, there are problems when these decisions clash with substantive company law and especially with those national company law standards imposed by harmonization.[516] A potential conflict with a purely national rule could be easily resolved by the Member States, but a potential conflict with harmonized standards could lead to an infringement upon secondary EC law. This possibility of infringement upon secondary Community law increases because of the separate category of rules on exchange listing that are usually enforced by the stock exchange, sometimes even after it has been privatized.[517]

Moreover, the impact of electronic data transmission on corporate governance has been stressed. Electronic data transmission is dominant nowadays in capital markets and is approved by securities regulation. These technological changes already influence company life, law, and practice and are another result of the imposition of those de facto globalized corporate governance standards. The takeover process could benefit from these technological developments. For example, if financial information is made available in electronic form, the general meetings of shareholders and the board of directors' meetings could be organized by videoconferencing, and the easy identification of shareholders would help them to participate in company life thorough proxy voting methods.[518] A very interesting, innovative approach has also been proposed. This proposal would allow directors to initiate defences, as is possible under the optional non-frustration rule (Article 9) of the Takeover Bid Directive, but these would be subject to an ex-post shareholder veto that would, if cast by a majority of record shareholders at any time, probably over the Internet, subject the company's directors to the more restrictive rules of the Thirteenth Directive.[519]

---

515. J.M.M. Maeijer & K.Geens (eds), *Defensive Measures against Hostile Takeovers in the Common Market* (London: Martinus Nijhoff and Graham & Trotman, 1990), 21. A few examples of those national authorities are the Commission on the Operations of the Stock Market in France, the Bank Commission in Belgium, the Panel on Takeovers and Mergers in the United Kingdom, the Association for Trade in Securities in the Netherlands, the Hellenic Capital Market Commission in Greece, and the Securities and Exchange Commission in Cyprus.
516. J.M.M. Maeijer & K.Geens (n. 515), 21.
517. E. Wymeersch (n. 91), 149–151.
518. E. Wymeersch (n. 503), 11.
519. C. Kirchner & R.W.Painter, 'Takeover Defences under Delaware Law, the proposed Thirteenth EU Directive and the New German Takeover Law: Comparison and Recommendations for Reform', *Am. J. Comp. L* 50 (2002): 451, 474–476. However, C. Kirchner & R.W. Painter restrict a generalized application of their proposal with a caveat. Because Internet voting probably would not involve the same disclosure and procedural safeguards as proxy and in-person voting at a formal meeting, the shareholder-veto procedure suggested here should not replace more formal processes, but should rather be used to determine which rule applies until the shareholders at a formal meeting decide upon a different rule.

Chapter 10
Market in Corporate Control: Essential Definitions

A takeover may be defined as a transaction or series of transactions whereby a natural or legal person or group of persons acquires control over the assets of a company, either directly, by becoming the owner of those assets, or indirectly, by obtaining control of the management of the company.[520] When shares are closely held (i.e., by a small number of persons), a takeover will generally be effected by agreement with the holders of the majority of the share capital of the company being acquired. When the shares are held by the public generally, the takeover may be effected by agreement between the acquirer and the controllers of the acquired company, by purchases of shares on the stock exchange, or by means of a takeover bid.[521]

For the takeover bid to be workable as a technique, the applicable company law must make it possible for anyone holding a majority of the voting shares in a company to remove the existing board and appoint new directors to take over its

---

520. M.A. Weinberg, M.V. Blank & A.L. Greystoke, *Takeovers and Mergers*, 4th edn (London: Sweet & Maxwell, 1979), 3.

521. M.A. Weinberg, M.V. Blank & A.L. Greystoke (n. 520), 3. The UK Panel on Takeovers and Mergers, in its statement on *Canary Wharf Group plc* (21 Nov. 2003, [2003/25]), provided a definition so as to determine who can properly be considered to be an offeror (or joint offeror), rather than simply acting in concert with the offeror vehicle (para. 13). It defined the offeror as a person who, acting alone or with others, seeks to obtain control of an offeree company and who, following the acquisition of control, can expect to exert a significant influence over the offeree company, to participate in distributions of profits and surplus capital, and to benefit from any increase in the value of the offeree company, while at the same time bearing the risk of a fall in its value resulting from the poor performance of the company's business or adverse market conditions (para. 14). For more details, see also: J. Mukwiri, *Takeovers and the European Legal Framework, A British Perspective* (London and New York: Routlege-Cavendish, 2009), 5–7.

management; and the law must also be such as to, if not positively encourage, at least not actively obstruct, changes in the control and management of companies in response to market forces.[522] It also helps if, in the case of a company whose shares are listed on the stock exchange, there are no large blocks of shares that are held in private hands and not generally traded, and also if the shares are held in registered form and lists of the current shareholders and their addresses are publicly available.[523]

Takeovers constitute an important external corporate governance mechanism, which facilitates effective corporate restructuring.[524] An aggressive market in corporate control serves as a disciplinary device for management boards of potential target companies, which, because directors are afraid of losing their posts at the hands of a new acquirer if their company were to be taken over, promotes efficient asset structures.[525] However, the separation of ownership and control[526] in the case of public corporations gives rise to a classical principal-agent problem, which can result in the sub-optimal use of capital and a failure to return excess capital to shareholders.[527] This problem creates different approaches to corporate control transactions. There are two models of regulation depicting the relevant approaches: in one model, directors must not frustrate a public offer, while in the other, the directors control access to the shareholders.[528] Under the first model, the board of the company is not permitted to frustrate the efforts of the bidder or to intervene in any other way in the decision – thus making the shareholders the ultimate adjudicators. According to the philosophy of the free enterprise economy, the owners of each party to a takeover or merger are the best judges of their own interests.[529] This first model is implemented in the UK[530] and has

522. L.S. Sealy, 'The Draft Thirteenth Directive on Takeovers', in *E.C. Financial Market Regulation and Company Law*, S. Kenyon-Slade & M. Andenas (London: Sweet & Maxwell, 1993), 136.
523. L.S. Sealy (n. 522), 136.
524. J. Grant, 'Takeovers and the Market for Corporate Control', in *European Takeovers: the Art of Acquisition*, ed. J. Grant 1st edn (London: Euromoney Books, 2005), 4. See also J. Rickford, 'Current Developments in European Law on the Restructuring of Companies: An Introduction', EBLR (2004): 1225–1258. M.C. Jensen, 'Takeovers: Their Causes and Consequences', *J Econ Persp* (1988): 21–48. For an empirical approach to the motives of takeovers: E. Berkovitch & M.P. Narayanan, 'Motives for Takeovers: An Empirical Investigation', *J Fin Quant Analysis* (1993): 347–362.
525. P. Leyens, 'A Framework for Adequate Shareholder Protection', *EBLR* 2 (2001): 42, 43.
526. E. Fama & M.C. Jensen, 'Separation of Ownership and Control', *J Law Econ* (1983): 301.
527. J. Grant, 'Takeovers and the Market for Corporate Control', in *European Takeovers: the Art of Acquisition*, ed. J. Grant, 1st edn (London: Euromoney Books, 2005), 4, M.A. Weinberg, M.V. Blank & A.L. Greystoke (n. 520), 8–13, R. Kraakman et al. (eds), *The Anatomy of Corporate Law* (Oxford: Oxford University Press, 2004), 157–163.
528. R. Kraakman et al. (n. 527), 163–173.
529. M.A. Weinberg, M.V. Blank & A.L. Greystoke (n. 520), 12.
530. See, for an extensive analysis of the UK legal regime, G.Stedman, *Takeovers*, Longman Commercial Series, 1st edn (London: Longman, 1993) and S. Kenyon-Slade, *Mergers and Takeovers in the US and UK: Law and Practice*, 1st edn (Oxford: Oxford University Press, 2004).

constituted the basis for the proposals and harmonization efforts of the European Commission, which have led to Directive 2004/25/EC, on Takeover Bids. Under the second model, the board of the company has the right (under the corporate statute, or as authorized by the general meeting of the shareholders) to frustrate a bid with various defensive measures. This model is encountered in Continental Europe[531] and the US.[532] However, in the US, the shareholders can protect their rights by court action if the board of the company frustrates a potential value-enhancing public offer, or if the target company suffers serious and otherwise unjustified loss as a result of the defensive action of the board (e.g., for serious infringements upon the business judgment rule). Hostile takeover bids[533] in Continental Europe are quite rare (with only sixty-seven hostile bids in the fifteen Member States in the 1990s), because of the historically more permissive attitude towards technical barriers, such as pre- and post-bid defences, and to structural barriers, related to the way in which companies are owned and financed (e.g., concentrated shareholdings and distortion of the distribution of voting rights).[534]

The hostile board of a company can choose from a great variety of defensive measures. The 'poison pill' is a tactic used by a company that fears an unwanted takeover by ensuring that a successful takeover bid will trigger some event that would substantially reduce the value of the company.[535] It is generally a rights plan that entitles existing shareholders to securities or cash if a hostile bidder takes control while being redeemable at the option of the board should a friendly acquirer take control (such as an issue of securities with a conversion option enabling the bidder's shares to be bought at a reduced price if the bid is successful).[536] Other defensive measures that could be deployed by the board of a company and result in the frustration of a bid are 'the sale of crown jewels' or 'spin-offs' (selling valuable assets of the company), 'lock-up options' (granting preferential options over shares or assets to 'white knights' or other persons), 'green mail' (which involves paying the hostile bidder to withdraw its bid), the 'Pac Man' defence (which involves launching a bid for the bidder itself), and 'golden parachutes' (which involve contractually binding the target company to make large severance payments to incumbent managers in the event of a change of control).[537]

531. L. Enriques & P. Volpin, 'Corporate Governance Reforms in Continental Europe', *J Econ Persp.* (2007): 117–140.
532. For a comparative study of these takeover regimes see: C. Forstinger (n. 311).
533. See also: S. Deakin & G. Slinger, 'Hostile Takeovers, Corporate Law, and the Theory of the Firm', *J Law Soc.* (1997): 124–151.
534. J. Grant (n. 527), 10. For a political economy perspective of these models see: A. Nilsen, 'Anglo-American v. Continental-Nordic Models of Corporate Governance: The Political Economy of Takeovers in the European Union', *EBLR* (2004): 1353.
535. J. Pallister & A. Isaacs (eds), *Oxford Dictionary of Business*, 3rd edn (Oxford: Oxford University Press, 2002), 392.
536. D.A. Wyatt & A. Dashwood (n. 46), 881.
537. J. Pallister & A. Isaacs (eds) (n. 535), 393. D.A. Wyatt & A. Dashwood (n. 46), 881 citing the definitions and descriptions from Kirchner & Painter, 'Takeover Defences under Delaware Law, the Proposed Thirteenth EU Directive and the New German Takeover Law: Comparison and Recommendations for reform', *Am.J.Comp.L.* 50 (2002): 452.

Chapter 11

An Overview of the Takeover Bid Directive in the Context of the Internal Market

11.1 INTRODUCTION

The Takeover Bid Directive was the product of long-running legislative efforts by the European Commission. The quite different approaches to the regulation of takeovers existing hitherto in the Member States, as well as the differences between certain aspects of national company and capital market law, made harmonization of takeover bids a very difficult venture. Negotiations and efforts to adopt the Takeover Bid Directive lasted almost fifteen years. The first draft was presented in 1989. The regulation of takeovers at the EC level was considered to be a part of the 1992 internal market project.[538] An amended proposal was brought forward in 1990. After the 1992 Edinburgh European Council, the draft Takeover Bid Directive was examined in light of the principle of subsidiarity.[539] In 1996, the European Commission proposed a more streamlined Takeover Bid Directive, which was revised again in 1997.[540] Meanwhile, the 1999 Financial Services Action Plan called for the adoption of a Directive on Takeover Bids and stressed the benefits thereof for market integration and for the competitiveness of the EU. Although a conciliation procedure between the European Parliament and the European Council was successful and produced a compromise proposal, the European Parliament then rejected the proposal (with a tied vote)

538. J. Wouters, P. Van Hooghten & M. Bruyneel, 'The European Takeover Directive: A Commentary', in *The European Takeover Directive and its Implementation*, ed. P. Van Hooghten (Oxford: Oxford University Press, 2009), 3.
539. *Ibid.*, 3–4.
540. *Ibid.*, 4.

in July 2001.[541] This rejection of the European Commission's proposed Directive by the European Parliament led to the creation of the High-Level Group of Company Law Experts. This Group was formed to propose some viable solutions to the problems encountered in harmonization. A new proposal of the European Commission was presented in 2003; this took into account some of the recommendations of the High-Level Group of Company Law Experts. The Takeover Bid Directive was finally adopted on 21 April 2004.[542]

11.2 THE TAKEOVER REPORT OF THE HIGH-LEVEL GROUP OF COMPANY LAW EXPERTS

As mentioned above, the High-Level Group of Company Law Experts, headed by J. Winter, was established with a mandate to address outstanding issues.[543] The key proposals in its final Report were that (a) when a takeover offer succeeds to the extent of acquiring 75% or more of the risk-bearing share capital in the offeree company, the bidder should be entitled to control the constitution and the board of that company accordingly, notwithstanding any constitutional or structural provisions in the company that prevent the exercise of such control (the breakthrough provisions); (b) when a bidder acquires control, the price to be offered under the mandatory bid for the remaining shares should normally be the highest price paid by the bidder during a period of six to twelve months up to and including that in which control was acquired; and (c) when a bidder has acquired in excess of a threshold (to be set at between 90% and 95%) of the shares in the target, he or she should be entitled to buy out minority holders, and those minority shareholders should be able to require that their shares be bought at a fair price, which will be presumed to be the offer price when there is a 90% or more acceptance of the offer ('squeeze-out' and 'sell-out' rights).[544]

---

541. *Ibid.*. J. Mukwiri, *Takeovers and the European Legal Framework, A British Perspective* (London and New York: Routlege-Cavendish, 2009), 10.
542. J. Wouters, P. Van Hooghten & M. Bruyneel (n. 538), 5. M. Andenas, 'The New European Company Law', in *Liber Amicorum Guido Alpa, Private Law Beyond the National Systems*, ed. M. Andenas et al. (London: BIICL, 2007), 87. For an excellent overview of the Directive's provisions, see: B. Sjafjell, *Towards a Sustainable European Company Law* (AH Alphen aan den Rijn: Wolters Kluwer, 2009), 293–311.
543. J.S. Knudsen, 'Is the Single European Market an Illusion? Obstacles to Reform of EU Takeover Regulation', *ELJ* 11 (2005): 507, 518. The rest of the members were: J. Rickford (UK), J. Simon (France), K. Hopt (Germany), J.M. Garrido Garcia (Spain), J.S. Christensen (Denmark), G. Rossi (Italy).
544. V. Edwards, 'The Directive on Takeover Bids: Not Worth the Paper It's Written on?', *ECFR* 4 (2004): 416, 428. In 2002, after the publication of the Takeover Report by the High-Level Group of Company Law Experts, Internal Market Commissioner F. Bolkestein said: 'I commend the High Level Group of Company Law Experts on their swift, comprehensive and excellent work. We will carefully examine their recommendations with a view to submitting a revised proposal for a Directive on Takeover Bids in the Spring. This Directive is a key element in our drive to make Europe's economy the most competitive in the world by 2010 and

The establishment of a level playing field in the EU market in corporate control has long been vitally necessary, since only this could lead to market integration. The Takeover Report of the High Level Group of Company Law Experts has stressed that it is important that takeover bids be undertaken with a similar expectation of success throughout the EU, and that shareholders in the various Member States have corresponding opportunities to tender their shares in a takeover bid. It advises that any European company law regulation aimed at creating such a level playing-field for takeover bids should be guided by two principles: (1) shareholder decision-making, and (2) proportionality between risk-bearing capital and control.[545] The High Level Group of Company Law Experts proposed full disclosure of information about the capital and control structures of companies; shareholders' authorization to frustrate a bid, with such authorization to be granted on the basis of proportionality; a breakthrough of defensive mechanisms by a bidder acquiring 75% or more of risk-bearing capital; a breakthrough rule also applicable to 'golden shares'; non-transferability provisions of the target company not enforceable against the bidder; and pyramid structures, cross shareholdings, and circular shareholdings to be reviewed. With regard to the last recommendation, the High Level Group of Company Law Experts believes that the Commission should review the issue of whether pyramid structures, cross shareholdings, and circular shareholdings, including several listed companies (which would not be subject to the break-through rule), should be regulated generally, and also what adequate measures of protection for minority shareholders should be enforced in all Member States.[546]

The High Level Group of Company Law Experts also discussed various aspects of the equitable price that must be offered in a mandatory bid. It suggested that an equitable price is the highest price paid by a bidder prior to acquiring a controlling holding, that there should be a few exceptions possible in specific circumstances, and that the mandatory bid shall be made within thirty days.[547] Additionally, the High Level Group of Company Law Experts examined the squeeze-out and sell-out rights. The High Level Group of Company Law Experts recommended that the threshold for a squeeze-out should be set at 90%–95% of capital, that there should be the presumption that the bid price constitutes a fair price when the bid is accepted by shareholders holding 90% or more of the share capital on which the offer was made, and that the thresholds for the sell-out right and for the presumption of a fair price need to be the same, as in the case of the squeeze-out right.[548]

The 2002 proposal of the European Commission that led to the adoption of the Takeover Bid Directive did not completely follow the recommendations of the

the Commission will do its utmost to achieve an early agreement by Council and Parliament on the revised proposal.' IP/02/24.

545. Press release of the High Level Group of Company Law Experts (10 Jan. 2002), 2.
546. Press release of the High Level Group of Company Law Experts (10 Jan. 2002), 2–3.
547. Press release of the High Level Group of Company Law Experts (10 Jan. 2002), 3.
548. Press release of the High Level Group of Company Law Experts (10 Jan. 2002), 3–4.

Report of the High Level Group of Company Law Experts on Takeovers concerning the proposed breakthrough procedure, although it did provide for the un-enforceability of restrictions on the transfer of securities during the period for acceptance of the bid, and for the un-enforceability of restrictions on voting rights when a general meeting of shareholders decides on any defensive measures.[549] The proposal of the High Level Group of Company Law Experts on Takeovers that a bidder should not be required to offer compensation to the holder of shares carrying disproportionate voting rights, when the bidder reaches the breakthrough threshold after a general takeover bid and makes use of the breakthrough right, was not accepted.[550] According to the Winter Report, there should also be definitions of an 'equitable price' and the introduction of squeeze-out and sell-out rights after bidding.[551] The most important feature was that the board neutrality/non-frustration rule was maintained. Finally, the 2002 proposal sought to meet the European Parliament's concerns about employee protection by providing for national measures to govern the provision of information and consultation of representatives of the employees of both the target company and the bidding company.[552]

11.3 THE MANDATORY BID RULE (ARTICLE 5) AND THE SQUEEZE-OUT AND SELL-OUT RIGHTS (ARTICLE 15 AND ARTICLE 16)

Among the few obligatory substantial provisions of the Directive for Takeover Bids are the mandatory bid rule (Article 5), the squeeze-out right (Article 15), and the sell-out right (Article 16). The purpose of these provisions is to protect the minority shareholders according to the legislative base of the Directive (Article 44(2)(g) of the EC Treaty). However, the Directive provides for the possibility of evading the enforcement of these provisions, both when transposing the Directive into national law and, after implementation, when the parties to a bid are obliged to launch a mandatory bid. Additionally, the provisions themselves are characterized by many drawbacks, which reveal their weakness in contributing to the protection of shareholders and, by extension, to the freedom of establishment through takeover bids.

Article 5 contains detailed rules imposing the requirement of making a mandatory bid at an equitable price whenever a natural or legal person gains control of a listed company. The main problem is that this provision gives discretion to the Member States. This discretion does not have to do with adjustments of

549. F. Wooldridge, 'The Recent Directive on Takeover Bids', *EBLR* (2004): 147.
550. Although this proposal aimed at facilitating the bidder in financing his or her offer and encouraging aspiring investors to get engaged with takeovers, it was contrary to the constitutional rights of some Member States (a form of confiscation). There were also concerns about its compatibility with the First Protocol to the European Convention on Human Rights and the 'public interest' justification for restrictions. F. Wooldridge (n. 549), 148.
551. V. Edwards (n. 544), 429.
552. *Ibid.*

the regulation to the Member States' needs and idiosyncrasies, but rather with the waiver or not of the enforcement of the mandatory bid rule in individual cases. Thus, the minimum harmonization technique chosen by the Community legislature (Article 3(2)) is inconsistent with these provisions of the Directive, which allow for derogations even from the minimum safeguards of the Directive. National legislatures are not prompted to adopt further safeguards for minority shareholder protection but are, instead, given the possibility of evading the minimum protection standards of the Directive.

First of all, Article 4(5) states:

> Provided that the general principles laid down in Article 3 (1) are respected, Member States may provide in the rules that they make or introduce pursuant to this Directive for derogations from those rules: (1) by including such derogations in their national rules, in order to take account of circumstances determined at national level and/or (2) by granting their supervisory authorities, where they are competent, powers to waive such national rules, to take account of the circumstances referred to in (1) or in other specific circumstances, in which case a reasoned decision must be required.

Furthermore, Article 5(4), which is the specific provision granting the possibility of derogations to the mandatory bid rule, states:

> Provided that the general principles laid down in Article 3 (1) are respected, Member States may authorize their supervisory authorities to adjust the price referred to in the first subparagraph in circumstances and in accordance with criteria that are clearly determined. To that end, they may draw up a list of circumstances in which the highest price may be adjusted either upwards or downwards, for example where the highest price was set by agreement between the purchaser and a seller, where the market prices of the securities in question have been manipulated, where market prices in general or certain market prices in particular have been affected by exceptional occurrences, or in order to enable a firm in difficulty to be rescued. They may also determine the criteria to be applied in such cases, for example the average market value over a particular period, the break-up value of the company or other objective valuation criteria generally used in financial analysis. Any decision by a supervisory authority to adjust the equitable price shall be substantiated and made public.

In other words, Member States may allow their supervisory authorities to decide, case by case, that the Mandatory bid price should be adjusted, or that the mandatory bid rule does not apply at all in certain special circumstances, whether this is actually specified by the national rules or not ('other special cases').[553] Admittedly, unjustified or overuse of this power may constitute a breach of Article 3(1)(a) (protection of minority shareholders in case of control transfer), unless, of course,

553. L. Enriques, 'The Mandatory Bid Rule in the Takeover Directive: Harmonization without Foundation?', *ECFR* 4 (2004): 440, 443.

some other equivalent form of protection is provided.[554] Although the Directive provides explicitly for one category of derogation[555] (Article 5(2) – when control has been acquired following a 100% voluntary bid to all the holders of securities for all their holdings), there are possibilities for other categories of derogations granted by the Member States at the implementation stage, or by the supervisory authorities and the legislature at the bid stage. These derogations ought, however, to be interpreted narrowly.

This narrow discretion of the Member States and national supervisory authorities to the possible exemption is not only a result of the determination of the price by 'circumstances and in accordance to criteria clearly determined' and the relevant national 'list of circumstances' (Article 5(4) of the Directive). The general principle behind both Article 3(1)(a) of the Directive and Article 43 of the EC Treaty also dictates a narrow national discretion in granting the adjustment. When the national supervisory authority grants a derogation to the mandatory bid rule under Article 5(4) of the Directive ('the highest price paid for the same securities by the offeror, or by persons acting in concert with him/her, over a period, to be determined by Member States, of not less than six months and not more than twelve before the bid referred to paragraph 1 shall be regarded as the equitable price'), it has narrow discretion. A wide discretion would be incompatible with the general principle of Article 3(1)(a) (adjusting the price downwards without adequate justification does not protect 'the other holders of securities') of the Directive and the fundamental freedom of establishment (Article 43 of the EC Treaty (adjusting the price upwards without adequate justification could discourage bidders from exercising their freedom of establishment through a takeover bid). Furthermore, the European Commission, in its 2002 proposal,[556] justified the derogation provision by the need for flexibility in the financial markets and stressed that Member States shall 'authorize their supervisory authorities to adjust that price in circumstances and according to criteria that are clearly determined, by means of a reasoned decision that is made public'.

---

554. *Ibid.*, 443. K. Hopt discusses the issue of 'equivalence'in the framework of the German Company Law (and especially the law relating to groups of companies). He thinks that, within a developed capital market at any rate, a mandatory bid will be functionally superior to a solution based upon the law relating to groups of companies. K. Hopt (n. 296), 18–19. E. Wymeersch (ed.), *Groups of Companies in the EEC: A Survey Report to the European Commission on the Law Relating to Corporate Groups in Various Member States* (Berlin: Walter de Gruyter, 1993).
555. A Council and Commission statement entered in the minutes of the Council on the adoption of the Directive expresses the Council and Commission's agreement that national law may provide that, when control has been obtained following a voluntary bid made in accordance with the Directive, addressed to all holders of securities for at least 60% of their holdings, the obligation to launch a mandatory bid laid down in Art. 5(1) shall not apply, on condition that the offer has been approved by the majority of shareholders with voting rights, excluding from the calculation securities held by the offeror and by any shareholder who, alone or in concert, holds more than 10% of the voting rights. F. Wooldridge (n. 549), 151.
556. Proposal for a Directive of the European Parliament and of the Council on Takeover Bids, COM (2002) 0534 final [2003] *OJ* C45E/7.

Moreover, the mandatory bid rule is not fully comprehensive. This makes its implementation, and its protective function, more difficult. It is possible that the mandatory bid rule's scope will not include some cases of minority shareholder protection. For example, there is no reference to the treatment of acquisitions of control of companies controlling a listed company.[557] The minority shareholders of the listed company need protection from the new acquirers of the controlling company, who are also able to control the listed company. Another example is the possibility of partial bids. The omission of partial bids from the Directive is another negative factor as regards minority shareholder protection. Unfortunately, the Directive does not regulate these situations, not even with a general provision. Instead, it leaves their regulation to the discretion of each Member State.

The definition of 'concerted parties' in the Takeover Bid Directive diminishes still further the contribution of the mandatory bid rule to minority shareholder protection and, subsequently, to freedom of establishment. Article 2(1)(d) of the Directive defines 'concerted parties' as:

> natural or legal persons who cooperate with the offeror or the offeree on the basis of an agreement, either express or tacit, either oral or written aimed either of acquiring control of the offeree company or at frustrating the successful outcome of a bid.

Moreover, the mandatory bid rule (Article 5(1) of the Directive) includes concerted parties[558] in the acquisition of shares and the crossing of the mandatory bid threshold. However, Article 5(3) of the Directive again confers wide discretion upon the Member States:

> The percentage of voting rights which confers control for the purposes of paragraph 1 and the method of its calculation shall be determined by the rules of the Member State in which the company has its registered office.

Thus, the percentage of voting rights that confers control is defined by the Member States. This percentage of shares defines the acquisition of control according to Article 5(1) of the Directive. As a matter of fact, the acquisition of control defines the concerted parties (Article 2(1)(d) of the Directive). It is quite obvious that the definition of 'concerted parties' is based indirectly on the discretion of the Member States. Hence, Member States can influence the definition of 'concerted parties' through their power to define 'acquisition of control'. This discretion might well assist Member States in structuring the definition of 'concerted parties' in accordance with their own national protectionist standards. Again, this wide discretion of Member States is something very dangerous, because of the risk of national protectionism, which is all too common in the field of European takeovers.

---

557. L. Enriques (n. 553), 445. For a critical approach to the mandatory bid rule, see: J. Grant, T. Kirchmaier & A. Kirshner, 'Financial Tunnelling and the Mandatory Bid Rule', *EBOR* (2009): 233.
558. See also for an interesting case study: D. Zetzsche, 'Hidden Ownership in Europe: BAFin's Decision in Schaeffler v. Continental', *EBOR* (2009): 131–132.

The squeeze-out right[559] is described in Article 15 of the Directive, which states:

> Member States shall ensure that an offeror is able to require all the holders of the remaining securities to sell him/her those securities at a fair price.

This rule is aimed at allowing a bidder to gain 100% of the equity so as to simplify accounting and administration by removing the need to deal with minority shareholders (which can incur high costs).[560] The bidder knows in advance that, if he or she reaches the squeeze-out threshold, he or she will be able to exercise the squeeze-out right so as to apply a more efficient management regime. This encourages potential bidders. Hence, freedom of establishment can be promoted, because this measure aims at the protection of investors. Additionally, the protection of shareholders is promoted, because they will have a second chance after the first bid to sell their shares.

The Takeover Bid Directive requires Member States to institute sell-out rights,[561] based on fair pricing provisions[562] similar to those of Article 15 as regards squeeze-outs.[563] More specifically, 'Member States shall ensure that a holder of remaining securities is able to require the offeror to buy his securities at a fair price, under the same circumstances as provided for in Article 15(2).' The aim of this provision is to provide an exit for the remaining shareholders and, as a consequence, to protect them. Otherwise, the remaining shareholders could very easily be abused by the new controller, and the only exit for them would be by selling their depreciated shares at a low price on the market.

Nevertheless, this protection of the sell-out right is again diluted. The sell-out right is granted, according to Article 15(1), only when a bid is made to all the holders of the offeree company's securities, and for all of their securities. This can be either a voluntary or a mandatory bid.[564] Mandatory bids may turn out to be

559. M. Burkart & F. Panunzi, 'Mandatory Bids, Squeeze-out, Sell-out and the Dynamics of the Tender Offer Process', in *Reforming Company and Takeover Law in Europe*, ed. G. Ferrarini, K. Hopt, J. Winter & E. Wymmersch, 1st edn (Oxford: Oxford University Press, 2004), 753.

560. J. Grant, 'Takeover Regulation and the Balancing of Interests', in *European Takeovers: the Art of Acquisition*, ed. J. Grant, 1st edn (London: Euromoney Books, 2005), 48. For an overview of the economic rationale and of the legal framework of the squeeze-out right and the sell-out right: C. Van Der Elst & L. Van Den Steen, 'Opportunities in the M&A Aftermarket: Squeezing Out and Selling Out?' (2006) University of Ghent, Financial Law Institute Working Papers WP 2006-12, and C. Van Der Elst & L. Van Den Steen, 'Squeezing and Selling Out: A Patchwork of Rules in Five European Member States', *ECL* 4 (2007): 19–20, 25.

561. M. Burkart & F. Panunzi, 'Mandatory Bids, Squeeze-Out, Sell-Out and the Dynamics of the Tender Offer Process', in *Reforming Company and Takeover Law in Europe*, ed. G. Ferrarini, K. Hopt, J. Winter & E. Wymmersch, 1st edn (Oxford: Oxford University Press, 2004), 756.

562. See also: T. Kaisanlahti, 'When Is a Tender Price Fair in a Squeeze-Out?', *EBOR* (2007): 497–519.

563. J. Grant (n. 560), 50.

564. L. Enriques, 'The Mandatory Bid Rule and the Sell-out Right in the Takeover Directive: Harmonisation for its Own Sake?', in *European Takeovers: The Art of Acquisition*, ed. J. Grant, 1st edn (London: Euromoney Books, 2005), 123.

easily avoidable, depending on the choices made by Member States and national supervisory authorities.[565] The exercise of the sell-out right depends on the prior launch of a mandatory bid. The mandatory bid depends on the discretion of the Member States and the national supervisory authorities. Hence, the exercise of the sell-out right depends on this discretion, which renders the sell-out right ineffective. The Directive tries to protect the shareholders by conferring this right, but, simultaneously, it cancels this protection by making the mandatory bid rule and, as a consequence, the sell-out right easily avoidable. The exercise of the sell-out right will depend in each case on the national exceptions to the mandatory bid rule. It is obvious that this does not contribute to shareholder protection. This category of remaining shareholders is quite vulnerable, since it has no other effective disengagement possibilities. Furthermore, by setting a sufficiently low price for a voluntary bid for all the shares, the acquirer may succeed in holding securities representing less than 90% of the capital carrying voting rights and 90% of the voting rights in the offeree company, thus preventing minority shareholders from exiting the company by way of the sell-out right.[566] Unfortunately, this circumvention technique is not explicitly banned by the Directive. Undoubtedly, the value of the 'one share, one vote' principle is revealed at this point and could prevent the development of this type of circumvention.

11.4 THE NON-FRUSTRATION/BOARD NEUTRALITY RULE (ARTICLE 9)

The following parts of this chapter will analyse the three key rules of the Takeover Bid Directive: the non-frustration rule (Article 9), the breakthrough rule (Article 11), and the reciprocity rule (Article 12). These three rules constitute the core regulation of the takeover bid process. The first two rules (Articles 9 and 11) regulate the behaviour of the management of the target company during the pre-bid and post-bid period. The intended contribution of these Articles is watered down as a result of a complicated opt-in–opt-out system that renders their application optional. The reciprocity rule adds another component to this optionality regime. The reciprocity rule is nothing more than simply another opportunity to opt out. We will attempt to analyse this intricate system of substantive provisions, with their multi-layered mechanism of opt-ins and opt-outs, by explaining the basic provisions and identifying their defects.

The board neutrality or non-frustration rule characterizes the UK model of the regulation of takeovers at the European level. S. Bartman argues that the term 'non-frustration', rather than the term 'board neutrality' is correct, because the management of the company is not so much required to observe a neutral attitude towards a bid as it is forbidden to frustrate the bid before a general meeting of

565. L. Enriques (n. 564), 124.
566. *Ibid.*

shareholders has had the opportunity to express an opinion on it.[567] Additionally, the board of the bidder, according to Article 9(5) of the Directive, must draw up and make public a document setting out its opinion on the bid. Hence, the word 'neutral' is not suitable if the board of the target expresses its hostility or friendliness in the report – without, of course, taking any of the forbidden frustrating measures.

Article 9(2) of the Directive states that the prior authorization of a general meeting[568] of shareholders is required before any action[569] on behalf of the target's board, which could result in the frustration of the bid. The Directive clarifies that, in two-tier board structures, 'board' should mean both the management and the supervisory boards (Article 9(6)). The Takeover Directive rests on the principle that a takeover bid is made to the shareholders and, consequently, it is up to the shareholders to decide on defensive measures.[570] The Explanatory Memorandum of the Commission's 2002 Proposal states:

> Where control of the offeree company is at stake, it is important to ensure that its fate is decided by its shareholders. The authorization of the general meeting must therefore be given explicitly with a view to responding to a specific bid.[571]

Thus, the non-frustration rule is a way of protecting the interests of shareholders and fulfilling the aims of the legal basis of Article 44(2)(g) of the EC Treaty. The board of a company is permitted to seek alternative bids only to offer a wider and more competitive range of choices to the shareholders of the company.[572] Furthermore, the Directive states that:

> Such authorization shall be mandatory at least from the time the board of the offeree company receives the information referred to in the first sentence of Article 6(1) concerning the bid and until the result of the bid is made public or the bid lapses. Member States may require that such authorization be obtained at an earlier stage, for example as soon as the board of the offeree company becomes aware that the bid is imminent.

567. S. Bartman, 'Analysis and Consequences of the EC Directive on Takeover Bids', *ECL* 1 (2004): 5.
568. The period before the shareholder meetings is of great interest. See also: D. Zetzsche, 'Shareholder Interaction Preceding Shareholder Meetings of Public Corporations: A Six Country Comparison', *ECFR* (2005): 107–157.
569. See also: D. Van Gerven, 'Rules of Community Law Applicable to Takeover Bids', in *Common Legal Framework for Takeover Bids in Europe*, ed. D. Van Gerven (Cambridge: Cambridge University Press, 2008), 27–30, A. Dorresteijn et al., *European Corporate Law*, 2nd edn (The Netherlands: Kluwer Law International, 2009), 236, C. Kirchner & R. Painter, 'European Takeover Law: Towards a European Modified Business Judgment Rule for Takeover Law', *EBOR* (2000): 353, P. Mulbert & M. Birke, 'In Defense of Passivity: On the Proper Role of a Target's Management in Response to a Hostile Tender Offer', *EBOR* (2000): 445.
570. R. Skog, 'The Takeover Directive: An Endless Saga?', *EBLR* 13 (2002): 301, 307.
571. COM (2002) 534 final, 8. D.A. Wyatt & A. Dashwood (n. 46), 870.
572. However, there are strong arguments against the protective scope of the competitive bids. We will focus on this issue below in the part about the problems of the non-frustration rule.

This subparagraph of the Directive attempts to prevent the phenomenon of market manipulation and insider dealing, because, during this period, the circulation of some specific information is quite sensitive. This is also in conformity with the European legislation on market abuse.[573] Furthermore, the general principle of Article 3(d) prohibits the creation of false markets and artificial fluctuations in the market prices of a company's shares. It is obvious that all these provisions aim at protecting the shareholders from reductions in the prices of their shares as a result of unlawful activity.

Additionally, paragraph 2 of Article 9 mentions a particular way of permanently inhibiting a bid for the issuance of new shares. This defensive measure is stated expressly, because it can result in a permanent and irreversible barrier to the attempts of a bidder. The new shares can dilute the stake of the bidder, making it impossible for the bidder to ever reach the desired control level of the company's equity. This restriction also includes securities that confer the pre-emption right to subscribe to such securities, such as convertible bonds and warrants.

According to the Second Company Law Directive,[574] increases in capital are the responsibility of a general meeting of the shareholders. Nevertheless, according to Article 25(1) and (2) of the same Directive, the general meeting can delegate this power for up to five years to the board of the company. It is this delegated right to increase capital that the board of directors is to be deprived of under Article 9 of the Takeover Bid Directive, from the moment that the offeror has publicized his or her intention to make an offer.[575] The general meeting, which will decide on the authorization of defensive measures, is free to authorize the issuance of new shares, since the shareholders are the sole judges of the need for defensive measures. In Member States where the delegation of the right to increase capital deprives the general meeting of its right to do so, it is clear that Article 9 of the Takeover Directive enables the general meeting to regain this power.[576] The shareholders' pre-emption rights should be fully respected.[577] Hence, all the existing

573. Directive 2003/6/EC of the European Parliament and of the Council of 28 Jan. 2003 on insider dealing and market manipulation (market abuse) [2003] OJ L96/16.

574. Second Council Directive 77/91/EEC of 13 Dec. 1976 on coordination of safeguards, which, for the protection of the interests of members and others, are required by Member States of companies within the meaning of the second paragraph of Art. 58 of the EC Treaty, with respect to the formation of public limited liability companies and the maintenance and alteration of their capital with a view to making such safeguards equivalent [1977] OJ L26/1. For an overview of the Second Company Law Directive, see: N. Moloney & T. Papadopoulos, 'EU Company Law', in *Law of the European Union*, ed. D. Vaughan, A. Robertson, & P. Eleftheriadis (Oxford: Oxford University Press, 2009), 115–318.

575. J.M.M. Maeijer & K. Geens (n. 515), 9.

576. J.M.M. Maeijer & K. Geens (n. 515), 9.

577. It is also alleged that the board can withdraw the pre-emption rights. However, this interpretation constitutes a defensive measure, because it can permanently impede the bidder from obtaining control. Only after the bid has been made public can the general meeting authorize a capital increase together with a withdrawal of pre-emption rights. This allegation could be found in J.M.M. Maeijer & K. Geens (eds) (n. 514), 10–11.

shareholders must be allowed to subscribe to the securities issued by the board.[578] The controlling shareholders and the bidder would normally subscribe to the new shares. However, it will not be certain that the minority shareholders will exercise their pre-emption rights, and this is exactly what the board of the company will be hoping.[579] In other words, a hostile board hopes that the minority shareholders will not exercise their pre-emption rights and that this capital increase will function as a potential defensive measure (a watering-down control). The stake of the bidder will be diluted, because it is not certain that all the new-issued shares corresponding to the pre-emption right of the minority shareholders will be bought by the bidder (some of them might be bought by other stakeholders, thus watering down the percentage of the bidder).

What about an issuance of shares that was decided upon before the launch of a bid? Should it be carried out during the bid period? Here we have the safeguard of Article 9(3), pursuant to which a general meeting of shareholders must approve actions that do not form part of the normal course of the company's business. In this way, if the board of the company has confidential information about a future bid, it will not be able to entrench its position by deciding to issue shares and executing the decision later, when the bid is made public. Shareholders' approval will be required. Furthermore, in addition to Article 9(3), Recital 16 of the Preamble is also relevant here:

> In order to prevent operations which could frustrate a bid, the powers of the board of an offeree company to engage in operations of an exceptional nature should be limited, without unduly hindering the offeree company in carrying on its normal business activities.

This provision obliges national authorities to interpret the issue of new shares during the bid period as incontrovertibly a defensive measure. However, the provision is not restricted solely to the issue of new shares. It also covers many other hidden defensive measures, which would be presented by a board as being part of the normal course of business. The underlying idea is to prevent a board from realizing material changes of the position of a target company, such as the sale of substantial assets or the acquisition of a new subsidiary.[580]

The main problem of the non-frustration rule, as aforementioned, lies in Article 12, which leaves the implementation of Articles 9 and 11 to the discretion of the Member States and of individual companies. Hence, the proclaimed aims of facilitating corporate restructuring and corporate mobility at the EU level are not fulfilled, because boards could still retain their power to frustrate bids and discourage investors. Furthermore, there is vagueness about what belongs to the

578. F. Ipekel, 'Defensive Measures under the Directive on Takeover Bids and Their Effect on the UK and French Takeover Regimes', *EBLR* (2005): 341, 347.
579. P. Lambrecht, 'The 13th Directive on Takeover Bids: Formation and Principles', in *Capital Markets in the Age of Euro – Cross Border Transactions, Listed Companies and Regulation*, ed. Ferarrini et al. (London: Kluwer Law International, 2002), 460.
580. V. Edwards (n. 544), 436.

normal course of a company's business. This could create cross-border problems, with each Member State trying to give its own separate definition.[581] Nor does the DD Directive stipulate when exactly the period during which the board is forbidden to act begins. It is possible that this discretion could lead to different periods applying in different Member States.[582] Moreover, there are objections to the argument that a competing bid enhances the position of shareholders and contributes to the protection of their interests.

The only action that a board is allowed to take during the bid period is to seek alternative bids. The potential alternative bidder is called a 'white knight'. This exception from the non-frustration rule is allowed because it enhances shareholders' opportunities by putting their shares up for auction. An alternative bid should definitely not be considered a defensive measure, because it embodies a second choice for shareholders that does not affect the conditions of the first bid at all.[583] Nevertheless, seeking an alternative bid could be detrimental to the shareholders' interests. After the launch of a takeover bid, shareholders face collective action problems, which may tempt them to accept the offer even though this is not in their collective best interest (the so-called pressure to accept the bid).[584] A competing bid could be coercive, compelling shareholders to accept the second bid even though the first bid seems to be more attractive.[585] The collective action problem derives from the fact that shareholders do not know about the decisions of the rest of the shareholders. This unavoidable lack of coordination of decision-making creates in shareholders the fear that they will lose the bid price and be left with under-priced minority shares. The mandatory bid rule mitigates the problem in some cases of two-tier or partial competing bids, but even then, not entirely (e.g., not in 100% public offers, which are exempted from the mandatory bid rule).[586] Shareholders compare the risk of holding minority undervalued shares, in the event of the bid being successful, with the price of the offer; hence the optimal *ex ante* strategy is to sell their shares to the bidder. It is obvious that the pressure to accept the bid does not always lead to the most value-enhancing choice. The shareholders

581. For more details: T. Papadopoulos, 'The European Union Directive on Takeover Bids: Directive 2004/25/EC [2008]', *Int'l Comp've Corp LJ* (2008): 13, 45–52.

582. For more details: *Ibid.*, 45–52.

583. F. Mucciarelli, 'White Knights and Black Knights: Does the Search for Competitive Bids Always Benefit the Shareholders of "target" companies?' (2006) Working Paper 8–9, <http://papers.ssrn.com/sol3/papers.cfm?abstract_id=910220>, accessed 21 Nov. 2006. (For another version of this paper see: F. Mucciarelli, 'White Knights and Black Knights: Does the Search for Competitive Bids Always Benefit the Shareholders of "Target Companies"?', *ECFR* 4 (2006): 408–425.)

584. F. Mucciarelli (n. 583), 3. L. Bebchuk, 'The Pressure to Tender: An Analysis and a Proposed Remedy', *Del J CL* 12 (1987): 911, L. Bebchuk, 'Toward Undistorted Choice and Equal Treatment in Corporate Takeovers', *HLR* 98 (1985): 1693.

585. F. Mucciarelli (n. 583), 3. There is an extensive analysis with numerical examples analysing the different combinations of higher and lower prices in two competing bids in the article of F. Mucciarelli (n. 583), 5–12.

586. See above, the deficiencies of the Mandatory Bid Rule.

cannot assess properly all the available bids, because they only take into account their potential post-bid situation as weak minority shareholders with under-valued shares. This exception of seeking an alternative bid does not distinguish coercive[587] competing bids from non-coercive ones: the Directive does not distinguish white knights from 'black knights'.[588] If the competing bid sought by the board is coercive, it is neither in the best interest of shareholders nor does it represent a simple market alternative. Therefore, a coercive defensive bid does not fit either of the rationales underpinning the white knight exception.[589] A coercive alternative bid therefore should be considered as a defensive measure. The white knight exception includes only non-coercive alternative bids. Each case of an alternative bid should be examined separately. This approach towards the white knight exception should be adopted, because the Directive does not allow only those alternative bids that are higher in price than was the first bid.[590] In the latter case, the shares really are put up for auction, but only as regards 100% voluntary bids to all holders of securities for all their holdings, because in all other cases, the bidder is obliged to launch a mandatory bid when he or she reaches the relevant control threshold (Article 5(2) of the Takeover Bid Directive). Thus, the minority shareholders are protected because of the existence of the mandatory bid provision, as well as because of the fact that the price of the mandatory bid cannot be less than the highest price paid for the same securities by the offeror during a specific period before the mandatory bid. This approach is compatible with the shareholders' protection rationale, because they are protected from this pressure to accept the bid. Otherwise, the board of the company could use this exception to guide the shareholders, through pressure to sell their shares, toward the offer of a bidder that they approve (and of course found) or toward the failure of the takeover in general.

The non-frustration rule (as well as the breakthrough rule) exists only because of the compromise of Article 12. Member States can opt out of Articles 9 and 11.[591] Paragraph 1 of Article 12 states that Member States may reserve the right not to require target companies to apply Article 9(2) and/or Article 11. However,

587. Coercive competing bids are bids that place pressure on the shareholders to accept them. In most cases, coercive competing bids are less attractive (with lower price) than other bids. The 'coerciveness' results from the fact that shareholders are obliged to accept this less profitable 'coercive' bid and reject the other more profitable public offers. The shareholders are led into this value-decreasing choice because they do not want to become minority shareholders with undervalued shares if the less attractive bid is successful. The shareholders prefer to sell their shares at a lower price rather than to find themselves 'trapped' as minority shareholders. Hence, they think that they will be secured from becoming minority shareholders, if they accept the less attractive bid. The less attractive takeover bid is coercive because it leaves no other choice to the shareholders other than accepting this bid and rejecting all others.

588. F. Mucciarelli (n. 583), 13.

589. F. Mucciarelli (n. 583), 13.

590. This 'higher price' solution is proposed by F. Mucciarelli (n. 583), 12.

591. Below, I will refer more extensively to the breakthrough rule and its opt-out.

according to the second paragraph of Article 12, where Member States opt out of Articles 9 and 11:

> they shall nevertheless grant companies which have their registered offices within their territories the option, which shall be reversible, of applying Article 9(2) and (3) and/or Article 11, without prejudice to Article 11(7).

The decision of a company to opt for either or both Articles should be made at the general meeting, and the applicable procedural rules are those for the amendment of the articles of association.

If the Directive had been adopted in its 2001 form, the non-frustration rule would have been obligatory. The optionality system was adopted, mainly in response to German objections, to secure the passage of the Directive through the European Parliament. The non-frustration/board neutrality rule is essential for the promotion of freedom of establishment at the European level. The boards of target companies will not be able to ruin the efforts of a potential investor to gain control of their companies. The fewer barriers that the board of a company can deploy, the more takeover bids that will be successful. The offeror company, by launching a successful bid and establishing itself in another Member State through the target company that it now controls, manages to penetrate new national markets. The market-making function of a non-frustration rule is obvious; this rule assists a company from one Member State in obtaining a controlling stake in a company in another Member State, leading to market integration. This clearly constitutes an exercise of the fundamental freedom of establishment (Article 43 of the EC Treaty). Additionally, reasons of equality would appear to favour the non-frustration rule, as it is unfair for some Member States to protect their companies by allowing defensive measures, while at the same time the companies of other Member States are made more vulnerable to takeovers because of the prohibition of defensive measures. Furthermore, the EC Treaty places corporate mobility among the main objects of European integration (Articles 2, 3(c), 14(2), 43 – especially (2), 44(2)(f), (g), and 48 of the EC Treaty).

The non-frustration rule respects the interests of shareholders by conferring on them the right to decide on the merits of a bid. The counter-argument, to the effect that the board of the company uses defensive measures in favour of the protection of shareholders from value-decreasing takeover bids, is not convincing. This is because of the risk that the board may be trying to entrench its own position by protecting the personal interests of its members and avoiding its replacement in case of a successful bid. It is also argued that, although the non-frustration rule is formulated quite broadly, to prevent all the kinds of conduct that can impede a takeover bid, this does not mean that all conduct incompatible with Article 9 of the Directive will also be incompatible with the right of establishment of a bidder (Article 43 of the EC Treaty).[592] For example, a prior authorization of a general meeting for the board, in advance of any bid being made, to adopt certain defensive

592. D.A. Wyatt & A. Dashwood (n. 46), 883–884.

measures to protect shareholders from inadequate offers infringes upon Article 9(2), but it may in fact serve shareholders' interests, because it increases the ability of the target company to negotiate a higher premium.[593] This kind of measure cannot be regarded as a restriction on the right of establishment (Article 43 of the EC Treaty), because it is a non-discriminatory activity by or on behalf of market operators to improve their market position vis-à-vis their competitors or their suppliers or customers, and it is not discriminatory conduct on the part of market operators and activities that restricts access to other market operators.[594] In the literature, there is a long-standing debate about which system of corporate governance better regulates the conduct of takeovers at the European level.[595] Furthermore, there are arguments about what the stance of a board should be during a takeover from a legal and economic perspective.[596] However, the European Commission has taken all these arguments into account, and it believes that the British model, with a non-frustration rule, should be adopted at the European level. The Council evidently has the same opinion, as it included the regulation of European takeover bids among the priorities of the Lisbon Agenda for the integration of the European Capital Market.

However, the Directive obliges opting-out Member States (Article 12(2)) to allow their companies to implement Articles 9 and/or 11 of the Directive, if they so wish. If a company of an opting-out Member State decides to opt in, it can nonetheless opt out again at a later stage. Only a general meeting of the company can make these decisions 'in accordance with the rules applicable to the amendments of the articles of association'. This implementation possibility for the companies of opting-out Member States mitigates the overall negative effect on European integration of the opt-out system. A Member State that opts out of these articles must enact special legislation that allows the willing companies to implement the rules. Hence, in a Member State that does not implement the non-frustration rule and/or the breakthrough rule, there has to be legislation for the implementation of these rules in voluntary cases. Two categories of listed companies will emerge within opting-out Member States; namely, opted-in companies applying the Directive and opted-out companies that are subject merely to national legislation regarding takeovers.[597] The companies of opting-out Member States could have an incentive to opt in. As was the case with creditworthiness and corporate governance, this arrangement will also give rise to a system of (national and international)

593. *Ibid.*, 884.
594. *Ibid.*
595. See for example: J. Payne (ed.), *Takeovers in English and German Law* (Oxford and Portland, Oregon: Hart Publishing, 2002), M. Gatti, 'Optionality Arrangements and Reciprocity in the Takeover Directive', in *European Takeovers: The Art of Acquisition*, ed. J. Grant, 1st edn (London: Euromoney Books, 2005), 107–108, and R. Kraakman et al. (n. 527), 157–191.
596. G. Bittlingmayer, 'The Market for Corporate Control (Including Takeovers)' *Online Encyclopedia of Law and Economics,* 725–771, <http://encyclo.findlaw.com/5640book.pdf>, accessed 21 Feb. 2007.
597. S.M. Bartman (n. 567), 6.

comparison and rating on the market.[598] The opted-in and opted-out status may, subsequently, lead to a certain ranking on the securities market, similar to the degree of creditworthiness.[599] Many companies that need liquidity will try to present themselves as open to potential investors on the European and global capital markets. The disclosure obligation under the Directive with regard to the internal control structure (Article 10) and the current protection regime (Article 11(4)) are of great importance here.[600] If any significant differences in prices occur between opted-in and opted-out companies, which are in other respects very similar companies, the latter will sooner or later find themselves under pressure to apply the voluntary regime as well.[601] This will lead to a boost in the market for corporate control, because listed companies will be discouraged from applying defensive measures. This element meets the need for empiricism in the field of European company law.[602] Takeover legislation will be harmonized from the bottom up.[603]

11.5 THE BREAKTHROUGH RULE (ARTICLE 11)

The High Level Group of Company Law Experts set out two basic principles. The first principle was that of shareholder decision-making, which is reflected in the general principle of Article 3(1)(c), and in the non-frustration rule of Article 9 of the Directive. This principle is directly related to the shareholder protection rationale. The second principle is the proportionality principle.[604] According to this principle, the degree of risk/reward that the shareholders are prepared to accept should determine the degree of control to be exercised by shareholders. Thus, the greater a shareholder's stake in the company in terms of his or her exposure to the company's success or failure through his or her holding in the risk-capital or general cash-flow rights, the greater his or her voice should be in determining the

598. S.M. Bartman (n. 567), 6. The Rating Agencies play an important role in providing an incentive for companies to implement these optional provisions. The Rating Agencies assess the creditworthiness of governments and corporations, as well as particular issues of securities as a guide to investors, for example, AAA for the best risks and D for firms that have either defaulted or are expected to default. The most important rating agencies are in the US (Standard and Poor's, Moody's Investor Service, Fitch Investor Service, Dominion). See P. Wood, 'Handout: Introduction to the Course of Global Comparative Financial Law', Degree of Magister Juris, University of Oxford, Acad. Year 2005–2006, 9.
599. S. Bartman, 'Crack the OOC Code!', *ECL* 3 (2006): 162, 163.
600. S.M. Bartman (n. 567), 6.
601. S.M. Bartman (n. 567), 7.
602. D.A. Wyatt & A. Dashwood et al. (n. 46), 874–875.
603. S. Bartman (n. 599), 163.
604. P. Mulbert, 'Make It or Break It: The Break-Through Rule as a Break-Through for the European Takeover Directive?', in *Reforming Company and Takeover Law in Europe*, ed. G. Ferrarini, K. Hopt, J. Winter & E. Wymmersch, 1st edn (Oxford: Oxford University Press, 2004), 717.

manner of its control.[605] This principle is expressed in the breakthrough rule. It aims at the facilitation of takeover activity and requires that when contractual and property rights are exercised in ways that inhibit takeover bids, these rights should be overridden.[606] Thus, the breakthrough provision embodies an enhanced, idealized, and even paternalistically imposed freedom of shareholders based on a defined optimal redistribution of rights.[607] This could also be called a 'one share, one vote' principle. Here we come again to the necessary balancing of partially conflicting rationales: the shareholders' protection rationale and the takeover promotion rationale. Article 11 of the Directive lays down that any restrictions on the transfer of securities or voting rights provided for in the articles of association of the offeree company, in contractual agreements between the offeree company and the holders of its securities, or in contractual agreements between holders of the offeree company's securities shall not apply vis-à-vis the offeror during the time allowed for acceptance of the bid (paragraphs 2 and 3). The Directive covers only contractual agreements entered into after the adoption of the Directive. The Directive expressly states that 'Multiple-vote securities shall carry only one vote each at the general meeting of shareholders which decides on any defensive measures in accordance with the Article 9.' Restrictions on the transfer of securities or on voting rights and any extraordinary rights of shareholders concerning the appointment or removal of board members are prohibited if the bidder obtains 75% or more of the voting capital of the target company (paragraph 4). The 'one share, one vote' principle is implemented, and multiple voting rights are declared inactive 'at the first general meeting of shareholders following closure of the bid, called by the offeror in order to amend the articles of association or to remove or appoint board members' (paragraph 4). The bidder has the right to convene a special post-breakthrough meeting so as to strengthen his or her controlling position in the target company (paragraph 4).[608] However, the Directive itself provides for two exceptions to the breakthrough rule. First, the breakthrough rule does not apply when restrictions on voting rights are compensated for by 'specific pecuniary advantages' (paragraph 6). Neither does it apply to legal 'golden shares' held by Member States.[609]

605. J. Rickford, 'The Emerging European Takeover Law from a British Perspective', *EBLR* (2004): 1379, 1385.
606. J. Rickford, 'Takeovers in Europe: Shareholders Decisions and Open Markets: A UK Perspective', in *European Takeovers: The Art of Acquisition*, ed. J. Grant, 1st edn (London: Euromoney Books, 2005), 67.
607. J. Rickford (n. 605), 67. See also: J. Coates IV, 'Ownership, Takeovers and EU Law: How Contestable Should EU Corporations Be?', in *Reforming Company and Takeover Law in Europe*, ed. G. Ferrarini, K. Hopt, J. Winter & E. Wymmersch, 1st edn (Oxford: Oxford University Press, 2004), 677–709.
608. See also: D. Van Gerven, 'Rules of Community Law Applicable to Takeover Bids', in *Common Legal Framework for Takeover Bids in Europe*, ed. D. Van Gerven (Cambridge: Cambridge University Press, 2008), 32. See also: L.A. Bebchuk, 'Reply. Letting Shareholders Set the Rules', *Harv L Rev* (2006): 1784.
609. See para. 7, 'where Member States hold securities in the offeree company which confer special rights on the Member States which are compatible with the Treaty, or to special rights provided for in national law which are compatible with the Treaty or to cooperatives'.

After objections from the European Parliament, and contrary to the suggestions of the High Level Group of Company Law Experts, a provision was included in the Directive concerning equitable compensation. This compensation is to be given when loss is suffered by the holders of special rights that are overridden (paragraph 5).

The breakthrough rule is deficient in two respects: as regards the substance of the rule and as regards the optional character of Article 11.[610] Both deficiencies are results of the political compromise to which the Directive owes its existence. The objectives of the proportionality principle are not fulfilled, and, as a result, takeover activity in Europe is not encouraged. Hence, obstacles to the freedom of establishment of legal persons still remain. As was already mentioned above, the breakthrough rule facilitates the activities of bidders by overriding disproportionate corporate structures. It prohibits any pre-bid defensive structures that might be deployed by a board so as to make it impossible for a bidder to finally obtain control. This facilitation of the activities of bidders should mean that takeover activity in Europe will increase, and cross-border mobility and the establishment of companies will be promoted. However, the deficiencies referred to above will frustrate the accomplishment of this aim to a great extent.

The breakthrough rule is called a 'mini-breakthrough' because it allows the breakthrough of some, but not all, of the restrictions that infringe upon the proportionality principle.[611] I contend that it is necessary to examine which categories of securities have survived the implementation of the breakthrough rule. It is obvious that there are many exceptions to the rule because of its narrow scope. The categories of securities that are outside the scope of the rule constitute obstacles to any potential bidder. These categories of securities that fall outside the scope of the breakthrough rule could inhibit the integration of the EU market in the realm of corporate control. Only a fully comprehensive breakthrough rule that covers all the securities constituting barriers to takeover activity will ever be able to contribute to an effective exercise of the freedom of establishment (Article 43 of the EC Treaty).

The first problem is created because of the text of the Directive itself. Article 2(1)(g) defines' multiple-voting securities' as 'securities included in a distinct and separate class and carrying more than one vote each'. Ceiling or time-lapse voting securities are not covered by the breakthrough rule. These shares are fully enfranchised after a specific holding period and are not covered because, while the voting rights will vary from time to time, according to the contingency of the duration of a holding, they remain of the same class.[612] This kind of share is

610. J. Rickford (n. 6054), 1389–1390. For more details: T. Papadopoulos (n. 581), 54–68.

611. J. Rickford (n. 605), 1389. However, there are questions as to whether certain categories of securities or types of company fall within the scope of the breakthrough rule. One example is the partnerships limited by shares. It seems that the corporate structure of partnerships limited by shares is covered by the Directive (this is particularly common in France, Italy, and Germany).

612. J. Rickford (n. 606), 69.

very common in France. The defensive aim of this kind of share is to discourage any potential bidder by ensuring that the offeror acquiring such a share obtains a diluted control right unless he or she is able to wait for up to four years for the shares to be fully enfranchised.[613] The requirement that shares comprise part of a distinct and separate class excludes an important category of shares from the scope of the breakthrough rule. The scope of this rule should be determined by the aim of negating the potential of certain shares to inhibit the takeover process, and not by formalities such as the requirement for different classes of shares. The breakthrough rule aims at preventing recourse to any pre-bid system of shares, which violates the proportionality principle, regardless of the class of the shares. It is unfortunate that the European Commission, the defender of freedom of establishment and corporate mobility, confirms this exception from the breakthrough rule.[614] Nevertheless, multiple-voting shares in separate classes are undoubtedly covered by the breakthrough rule. These kinds of shares are often found in Scandinavian Member States and sometimes in the UK. Thus, we have the side-effect that multiple-voting shares, which have exactly the same result of obstructing the course of the bid, are treated differently only because they belong to different classes. Furthermore, this creates inequality and does not level the playing field among the EU countries. France[615] has managed to exclude its own structures from the breakthrough rule without even opting out of the relevant provision. The argument that the harmonization of European company law should respect the idiosyncrasies of national company law and provide flexibility at the implementation stage is not convincing in this case. It is clear that the Directive tolerates the defensive structures available in some Member States (e.g., French ceiling shares) while prohibiting defences available in other Member States (e.g., Scandinavian dual-class shares).[616] Such states have not been able to effectively advocate their national interests in the Council. This exception also provides the incentive for companies, where national company law allows such changes, to move from dual- to single-class share structures while retaining disproportionate voting rights. The market for corporate control and the freedom of establishment cannot benefit from this diversified approach of the breakthrough rule to pre-bid defences.

Another category of shares that evades the application of the breakthrough rule is that of non-voting shares. Furthermore, in those Member States where the issuing of non-voting shares is prohibited, alternatives with the same effect are inevitably sought.[617] One alternative technique that has the same result as non-voting shares involves certificates for shares or non-voting depository receipts for shares. The shares are transferred to an independent administration office, which

613. *Ibid.*
614. Commission Proposal of 2 Oct. 2002 and Explanatory Memorandum [2003] *OJ* C45E/9.
615. For the implementation of the Takeover Bid Directive by France, see: F. Carle, 'Are French Listed Companies Takeover-Proof?', *ECL* (2007): 154.
616. U. Bernitz, 'The Attack on the Nordic Multiple Voting Rights Model: The Legal Limits under EU Law', *EBLR* (2004): 1423.
617. J.M.M. Maeijer & K. Geens (eds) (n. 515), 15.

manages the shares and exercises the voting rights in the interests of the company. The shareholders receive certificates in return for their shares and retain the proprietary rights arising from the shares.[618] This financial technique is the norm in the Netherlands, France, and Belgium.[619]

Another alternative to non-voting shares is securities that are not shares but nonetheless carry equity risk through a right to participate in profits (such 'enjoyment rights' are common in Germany).[620] The breakthrough rule undoubtedly does not cover these corporate instruments, which are not even shares. From these examples, it appears that there exist numerous means of avoiding or circumventing a national prohibition on non-voting shares. Boards can still entrench their positions even in cases in which a Member State tries to limit the exceptions to the breakthrough rule by prohibiting non-voting shares. I believe that these loopholes exist because the Directive does not designate the scope of the breakthrough rule by the effect of certain types of shares (i.e., the frustration of the bid), but by a specific requirement (i.e., to which category of shares it belongs). The Takeover Bid Directive gives emphasis to a formality (the category of shares) and does not take into account the substantive effects on the EU market in corporate control (the frustration of the bid). As mentioned above, this is probably a result of political opportunism in the legislative process, whereby some Member States have managed to exempt their national company share structures but others have not.

Another deficiency of the breakthrough rule is that it does not cover some categories of very effective pre-bid defences. Pyramid structures are not covered by the breakthrough rule. Pyramids are a form of corporate control structure whereby a company holds shares in another company, which in turn holds shares in another one.[621] Control of the corporation at the top of the pyramid combines with the stakes all the way down to achieve outright control of the chain.[622] Collectively, these are 'tunnelling' devices, inter-company dealings whose terms benefit the controlling shareholder at the top of the pyramid, often at the expense of minority shareholders.[623] Thus, the voting rights of the shareholders of the company at the bottom of the pyramid are diluted. The proportionality principle is distorted, because the controlling shareholder at the top of the pyramid can gain voting control of the company at the bottom of the pyramid by having disproportionately low cash-flow rights. The High Level Group of Company Law Experts recommended dealing with pyramids separately by not allowing stock exchange listing for holding companies whose sole activity was to hold shares in other listed companies.[624] This measure was not adopted by the Takeover Bid Directive, but it

618. J.M.M. Maeijer & K. Geens (eds) (n. 515), 15.
619. See an analysis of the national legislation at this point in J.M.M. Maeijer & K. Geens (eds) (n. 515), 15.
620. J. Rickford (n. 605), 1379.
621. J. Grant (n. 527), 15.
622. *Ibid.*
623. *Ibid.*
624. J. Winter, 'The Good, the Bad and Ugly of the European Takeover Directive', in *European Takeovers: The Art of Acquisition*, ed. J. Grant, 1st edn (London: Euromoney Books, 2005), 27.

is possible that it will be adopted in future legislation relating to securities and stock market regulation.

Furthermore, the breakthrough rule does not apply to cross-shareholdings. Cross-shareholdings are defensive arrangements whereby two companies buy stakes in each other and senior managers/owners sit on each other's boards and vote their shares together defensively.[625] 'Double-headed' companies constitute an advanced form of cross-shareholding. These corporate associations adopt a double corporate form but ensure that takeovers must be of both companies. This may be done by linking shareholdings in one company to shareholdings in the other, or coordinated, and sometimes entrenched, control may be assured by conferring cross-rights of board nomination and special, often preferential, share structures.[626] I propose that there should be a provision in the Directive stating that cross-shareholdings are in fact covered by the breakthrough rule. This is because cross-shareholdings infringe upon both of the principles (proportionality and shareholder decision-making) advocated by the High Level Group of Company Law Experts. The fact that one company interferes so extensively in the takeover of another company is negative for the shareholders of the target company, because a third party weakens their voting rights. It is also obviously negative for the bidder, who must bid for both companies rather than for only one of them because of these sophisticated corporate links. This aids neither the integration of the market for corporate control nor the creation of economies of scale. Bidders should be able to bid for their companies of preference and should not be pressed to bid for additional corporate bodies. This pressure can lead to unsatisfactory results: failure of a bid because of this defensive structure, withdrawal of a bid because of the incapability of financing a bid for both connected companies, or a value-decreasing situation because of the takeover of two companies, one of which the bidder does not really want. As a result, the freedom of establishment through a vibrant market for corporate control is not promoted, and there remain ways available for avoiding the minimum shareholder protection safeguards of the Directive. However, the possible cross-rights of board nomination in 'double-headed companies' are probably covered by the current form of the breakthrough rule, because they can be regarded as extraordinary rights within the meaning of Article 11(4). The only obligation is that, according to Article 10(1)(c)), pyramid structures and cross-shareholdings must be included in the information that is to be disclosed pursuant to this Article. This disclosure of information concerning the defensive structures of pyramids and cross-shareholdings could be crucial for the creditworthiness and ranking of the companies.

Additionally, Article 11(4) prohibits the exercise of extraordinary rights of shareholders at a general meeting for the amendment of the articles of association or for the removal or appointment of members of the board, following the

625. J. Grant (n. 527), 15.
626. J. Rickford (n. 605), 1392.

acquisition of 75% or more of the capital carrying voting rights.[627] These private 'golden shares' involve distortions of the proportionality principle, which are not related to direct restrictions on voting rights. The voting rights of the rest of the shareholders are distorted indirectly. Although the shareholders do not lose their rights to cast their votes, these are watered down as a result of the decisive role of these extraordinary rights in the appointment or removal of board members. Hence, it is obvious that the application of the proportionality principle is also undermined. It is useful to make reference to these extraordinary, priority shares. In companies with this category of shares, the exercise of some rights by a general meeting remains valid only if approved by the priority shareholders. Moreover, the general meeting may only exercise its rights upon the proposal of the priority shareholders.[628] This kind of extraordinary share is found in several continental European countries, and it is provided for by the articles of association of a target company. Article 11(4) does not state the appointment or removal of board members as the sole category of shares having extraordinary rights. Thus, we may conclude that all privileges conferred by the articles of association that distort the proportionality principle are undermined. This interpretation facilitates the exercise of the freedom of establishment (Article 43 of the EC Treaty) through a successful takeover bid.

The most important deficiency of the breakthrough rule is an 'external' one and derives from Article 12. The potential beneficial effects of the breakthrough rule have been tempered by the fact that Member States are allowed to opt out of the rule.[629] Between a defective breakthrough rule, with the deficiencies and weaknesses mentioned above, and an optional defective breakthrough rule, I suggest that the former be chosen. An optional breakthrough rule permits the deployment of pre-bid defences, which will probably permanently impede the takeover of a company. This does not really protect the interests of shareholders, who should, according to the principles of the Takeover Report, be the ultimate decision-makers on takeover issues. A non-optional breakthrough rule is genuinely able to protect the interests of shareholders by giving them the power to decide on the merits of a bid and to facilitate the bidder in his or her acquisition efforts by prohibiting pre-bid defensive tactics. One might also argue that a non-optional breakthrough rule could perform these tasks, even allowing for the fact that the breakthrough rule, in its current form, is not comprehensive, allowing many defensive structures to evade the application of the rule, even if it is watered down in practice by inconsistencies and ambiguities. It is quite obvious that a mandatory defective breakthrough rule is better than an optional defective breakthrough rule, because at least it constitutes a rule of some sort! The effects of the optionality

---

627. This provision states that the extraordinary rights shall concern 'the appointment or removal of board Members provided for in the articles of association of the offeree company' (delegation rights).
628. J.M.M. Maeijer & K. Geens (eds) (n. 515), 18.
629. F. Ipekel (n. 578), 345.

regime, analysed above in the non-frustration rule context,[630] apply to the breakthrough rule context too.

The breakthrough rule does not establish a level playing field for takeover bids at the European level for two reasons. The first is that the rule is optional both for Member States and companies (Article 12). The second is that, whether the rule is implemented on a mandatory or voluntary basis, there remain many share and corporate structures that evade its application, and there are also many ways of interpreting certain facets of Article 11[631] that can lead to inconsistencies. Thus, the breakthrough rule, in addition to its many deficiencies, is optional. Both of the reasons for the lack of a level playing field have to do with the political nature of this area of European company law, which is characterized by protectionist and mercantilist ideas. S. Bartman alleges that courts should interpret the scope of application of the Directive as widely as possible when judging protection devices that may not be covered by the Directive when it is read literally.[632] However, we should not neglect the fact that the Takeover Bid Directive is a political compromise, which tries to balance completely different mentalities of takeover regulation. The deficiencies and the opt-in–opt-out system of the Directive create a faulty incentive. It is a fact that many Member States will implement the breakthrough rule not because they intend to promote the freedom of establishment, but because they know in advance that their national corporate and financial structures infringing upon the proportionality principle are not covered by the breakthrough rule.

11.6 THE RECIPROCITY RULE (ARTICLE 12)

The reciprocity rule is found in Article 12(3):

> Member States may, under the conditions determined by national law, exempt companies which apply 9(2) and (3) and/or Article 11 from applying Article 9(2) and (3) and/or Article 11 if they become the subject of an offer launched by a company which does not apply the same Articles as they do, or by a company controlled, directly or indirectly, by the latter, pursuant to Article 1 of Directive 83/349/EEC.

Hence, the reciprocity rule is nothing more than a possibility granted to the companies by their Member States. Paragraph 5 of the same Article gives the

630. See above, on the deficiencies of the non-frustration rule.
631. Substantive deficiencies of Art. 11. Some of these issues are: syndical agreements, ceiling or time lapse voting shares, non-voting shares, pyramid share structures, cross-shareholdings, preference shares, proxies, extraordinary rights, multi-jurisdictional cases, equitable compensation.
632. S. Bartman, 'The EC Directive on Takeover Bids: Opting in as a Token of Good Corporate Governance', in *European Company Law in Accelerated Progress*, ed. S. Bartman (The Hague: Kluwer Law International, 2006), 3.

procedural conditions for the application of the reciprocity rule when it is granted by a Member State:

> Any measure applied in accordance with paragraph 3 shall be subject to the authorization of the general meeting of shareholders of the offeree company, which must be granted no earlier than 18 months before the bid was made public in accordance with Article 6(1).

Hence, the decision-making process for the application of the reciprocity rule has two levels: a legislative application by Member States and, subsequently, an individual application by the relevant companies.

However, the reciprocity rule[633] of the Takeover Bid Directive is very unclear because of its lack of a fixed and invariable basis. The provisions with respect to which the company is allowed to reciprocate are not always the same, as these depend on the method of application of the first two paragraphs of Article 12 by the offeree and the offeror company. The multiple levels of the reciprocity rule and the opt-in–opt-out provisions can create some quite complicated situations and subsequent interpretative dilemmas, which are closely related to the promotion, or not, of freedom of establishment.

In a Member State that has opted out of Articles 9 and/or 11, the board of a target company that has opted into either or both of these Articles may frustrate a bid by another company registered in that same Member State that has not opted in, but it may not frustrate a bid by a company registered in that same Member State that has opted in or by a company registered in any other Member State that is subject to the relevant Articles, either because the relevant Member State has not opted out, or because, although the relevant Member State has opted out, the bidder has opted in.[634] This appears to be a quite complicated outcome, which does not contribute to legal certainty. This reciprocity regime may lead to a bid from a company in the same Member State being subject to Articles 9 and/or 11 while a bid from a company registered in another Member State is not, which might seem to amount to indirect discrimination on grounds of nationality, contrary to Article 43 of the EC Treaty.[635] Yet any such difference in treatment is not, in truth, by reference to the Member State of registration of the company, but by reference instead to differences in the legal regimes that may be applicable in different Member States and, indeed, within the same Member State – differences, moreover, which reflect not only Member State choices, but also the choices of individual companies.[636] Therefore, a potential bidder could evaluate the full effects of the takeover bid if he or she knows in advance the legal framework to which the target company is subject, based on the exercise of the optional

633. For an interesting analysis, see: M. Becht, 'Reciprocity in Takeovers', in *Reforming Company and Takeover Law in Europe*, ed. G. Ferrarini, K. Hopt, J. Winter & E. Wymmersch, 1st edn (Oxford: Oxford University Press, 2004), 647–675.
634. D.A. Wyatt & A. Dashwood (n. 46), 882–883.
635. *Ibid.*
636. *Ibid.*

rights.[637] This evaluation on behalf of the bidder seems to be difficult because of the complex outcome of the optionality and reciprocity regime.

Nevertheless, the reciprocity rule presents one positive aspect with regard to the promotion of the freedom of establishment (Article 43 of the EC Treaty). The reciprocity rule creates an unintended incentive for those EU listed companies that want to be players (offerors) in consolidating markets rather than targets (offerees) to apply Articles 9 and 11 voluntarily.[638] Only then will the companies obtain immunity when they bid for other companies, which will not be able to opt out of these two ground rules (provided, of course, that the reciprocity rule is available in their jurisdiction). Thus, companies that want to be bidders on the takeover market rather than targets must first accept the takeover facilitating rules as being applicable to them.[639] Since every target company may be a (potential) acquirer in the various phases of its existence, it may be wise, for the sake of desirable or even necessary expansion, to assume the status of an opted-in company.[640] This helps the promotion of freedom of establishment by liberalization of the market for corporate control through the removal of post-bid and pre-bid takeover defences.

11.7 A FEW COMMENTS ON THE NON-FRUSTRATION/BOARD NEUTRALITY RULE (ARTICLE 9), THE BREAKTHROUGH RULE (ARTICLE 11), AND THE RECIPROCITY RULE (ARTICLE 12)

Takeovers are a means for investors to create synergies between existing businesses and target companies, because many European companies will need to grow to an optimal size (and, therefore, invest by means of takeover bids), while the financial markets should benefit as well from more liquidity.[641] It is well-known

637. S. Maul, D. Muffat-Jeandet & J. Simon, 'Introduction, Cross-Border Transactions', in *Takeover Bids in Europe*, ed. S. Maul, D. Muffat-Jeandet & J. Simon (Freiburg: Memento Verlag, 2008), 1.
638. J. Winter, 'The Good, the Bad and Ugly of the European Takeover Directive', in *European Takeovers: The Art of Acquisition*, ed. J. Grant, 1st edn (London: Euromoney Books, 2005), 28. Firms that subsequently become takeover targets make acquisitions that significantly reduce their equity value, and firms that do not become takeover targets make acquisitions that raise their equity value. M.L. Mitchell & K. Lehn, 'Do Bad Bidders Become Good Targets?', *J Pol Econ* (1990): 372–398. Moreover, very large companies aere not often the target of takeover bids and would therefore be relatively unrestrained by the market in corporate control. This will give them the possibility of not applying the optional provisions of the Takeover Bid Directive, because they can play only the role of the offeror company. Nevertheless, some financial techniques have enabled companies to overcome traditional barriers in the financial markets and to acquire very large offeree companies. R.A. Chatterjee, 'The Financial Performance of Companies Acquiring Very Large Takeover Targets', *Appl Fin Econ.* (2000): 185–191.
639. J. Winter, 'We All Want to Go to Heaven but Nobody Wants to Die', *ECL* 1 (2004): 4, 4.
640. S.M. Bartman (n. 567), 7.
641. COM (2002) 534, 35.

that takeover bids are a very important source of external growth, which is vital for EU corporations that are seeking to penetrate new markets and to become more competitive at the global level against non-EU corporations.[642] Although the Takeover Bid Directive does not promote takeover bids as such, the minimum harmonization of some of the rules that govern takeover bids (e.g., the mandatory bid rule) will contribute to the improvement, to a certain extent, of the competitive position of companies in Europe.[643] The mere possibility that companies could be taken over even against the will of their boards is something positive for the private enterprise system, because takeovers eliminate inefficient companies or exercise pre-emptive pressure on boards to ameliorate their performance.[644] The proclaimed aim of the Takeover Bid Directive was to promote cross-border takeovers by providing minimum harmonized conditions for conducting successful cross-border takeover bids and by establishing a level-playing field in the European market for corporate control. Thus, cross-border corporate mobility and corporate restructuring were also to be promoted, with the intention being to facilitate the fundamental freedom of establishment of companies (liberalization of the market for corporate control). Harmonization was necessary because there were legal, economic, and structural differences among the Member States with respect to defensive measures that could be put into operation to fight hostile takeover bids, so that companies in some Member States were better protected than were companies in other Member States.[645] This legal diversity was the ideal environment for national protectionism to flourish within the market for corporate control. The Takeover Bid Directive was supposed to reduce these differences in several ways, without compromising the competitiveness of EU companies in relation to companies of third countries.[646] However, the reduction of legal diversity in the EU market in corporate control is by no means an indisputable fact, because of the optionality and the reciprocity regimes.

---

642. S. Grundmann, *European Company Law, Organization, Finance and Capital Markets* (Antwerpen: Intersentia, 2007), 492–493, 573, 592.
643. COM (2002) 534, 35. It is quite interesting to refer here to the argument against harmonization of takeovers, which maintains that harmonization on corporate governance matters does not enhance the economic system and in fact disrupts the equilibria that constitute the basis of our economic welfare. This is so because harmonization, apart from the level-playing field rationale, does not always take into account essential elements of social consensus, such as the defensive mechanisms in a takeover. A level playing field could not be established for those societal issues. Harmonization does not consider thoroughly essential elements of social consensus (sometimes shown by the co-determination model) which justify the social role of private business enterprises. Hence, regulatory competition is the optimal method of regulating takeovers and of promoting competition among enterprise structures. E. Wymeersch, 'The Regulation of Takeover Bids in a Comparative Perspective', in *European Economic and Business Law*, ed. R. Buxbaum et al. (New York: de Gruyter, 1996), 321.
644. E. Wymeersch (n. 643), 306–307.
645. COM (2002) 534, 35. K. Byttebier, 'Protective and Defensive Measures Against Hostile Takeovers', in *Further Perspectives in Financial Integration in Europe*, ed. E. Wymeersch (Berlin-New York: de Gruyter, 1994), 181–192.
646. COM (2002) 534, 35.

Although the primary objective of these Articles is to protect shareholders by conferring on them the possibility of deciding on the merits of a bid, neither this multi-layered opt-in–opt-out system nor the reciprocity rule contributes to this aim. It amounts to 'harmonized' legal diversity and multi-formity. Hence, there are three levels of regulatory competition available in the market for corporate control: competition among national company laws, competition among the individual legal regimes of domestic companies, and competition among the individual legal regimes of domestic and other EU registered companies. The choices that the opt-in–opt-out system, combined with the reciprocity rule, offer to Member States and to companies can result in numerous combinations. Hence, the Takeover Bid Directive makes sixteen different legal regimes available to Member States. The available legal regimes can be dramatically increased through decisions at the company level.[647,648] The significance of multiple options in a harmonization measure is that they place in doubt the extent to which the harmonization in question is worthy of the name, and they might be said to imply that the objective of achieving solutions at the European level has overshadowed the aim of promoting cross-border business activity.[649] This is not to question the area of harmonization as regards takeover bids or European company law, but rather the method of harmonization, which provides so many totally different options. Moreover, the argument that different standards should co-exist and compete is more convincing in the case of tradeable goods and services than it is in that of company law

647. Pursuant to Art. 12 of the Takeover Bid Directive, each Member State must make four choices in connection with the non-frustration and breakthrough rules. Each Member State must decide: (1) whether or not to implement the non-frustration rule, (2) whether or not to implement the reciprocity clause in relation to the non-frustration rule (which, if not opted into by the Member State, can always be opted into at the company level), (3) whether or not to implement the breakthrough rule, and (4) whether or not to implement the reciprocity clause in relation to the breakthrough rule (given that, like the non-frustration rule, if the breakthrough rule is not implemented by a Member State, it can always be opted into at the company level). Given these four binary choices, and all the possible combinations thereof, theoretically the Takeover Directive gives Member States the possibility of choosing from among sixteen different regimes. The actual number of possible combinations increases dramatically if two more possibilities are added: (1) where a Member State has opted out, making opt-ins at the company level with regard to choices about the non-frustration rule and/or the breakthrough rule (Art. 12(2)); and (2) where a Member State has adopted the reciprocity clause, deciding, again at the company level, whether or not to exploit reciprocity (Art. 12(5)) M. Gatti, 'Optionality Arrangements and Reciprocity in the Takeover Directive', in *European Takeovers: The Art of Acquisition*, ed. J. Grant, 1st edn (London: Euromoney Books, 2005), 104.
648. M. Gatti questions whether the opt-in–opt-out system of the Directive is superior to an easier and functionally equivalent one in which a Member State that does not impose the board neutrality rule as mandatory would be required to set such a regime as the default rule but with the possibility for companies to opt out of it. This proposed system, if compared with the opt-out–opt-in mechanism of Art. 21(1) and (2), is more pro-freedom of establishment, and has the virtue of clearly signaling to the market which issuers intend to depart from the pro-shareholders standard provided for by the board neutrality rule. M. Gatti (n. 647), 110.
649. D.A. Wyatt & A. Dashwood (n. 46), 871–872.

legislation, because it comprises package deals.[650] The only positive thing is that, because of the Directive, at least now we know in advance the content of these regimes and do not have twenty-seven national takeover regimes, which can be completely unpredictable and perhaps arbitrary. However, the number of available legal regimes is still quite high and does not provide legal certainty, nor does it combat the psychological obstacles to cross-border corporate establishment. Furthermore, the biggest problem is that the degree of flexibility resulting from the optionality and reciprocity regimes has provided Member States with several ways to evade imposing strict regulation on takeover defences.[651] This is definitely not compatible with the general principles of the Directive and especially with the general principle of Article 3(1)(c). However, opting out of Article 9(2) does not suspend or create an exception to the application of the general principle laid down in Article 3(1)(c) of the Directive, and this general principle might be read as aiming in part to ensure that opting out of Article 9(2) remains compatible with Article 43 of the EC Treaty.[652] This general principle in Article 3(1)(c) provides protection of the shareholders' rights in cases of opt-outs from Article 9(2). Otherwise, without the guarantee and the overarching protection of this general principle, the conduct of a board might well run the risk of infringing upon the freedom of establishment. An example of this kind of infringing behaviour, according to D.A. Wyatt, would be the break-up of a company by the board, without the authorization of a general meeting, when the acceptance of a bid by the shareholders and the success of the takeover are considered imminent.[653] The general principles might be characterized as a corrective to the deficiencies of the opt-in–opt-out and reciprocity arrangements.

11.8 SUPERVISORY AUTHORITY AND APPLICABLE LAW

Article 4 determines the authority that is to supervise the conduct of takeover bids, as well as the applicable law that will regulate the several aspects of a takeover bid. Each Member State must designate an authority or authorities to supervise those aspects of bids that are governed by the Takeover Bid Directive and to ensure that parties to takeover bids comply with the rules made pursuant to this Directive.[654] All those authorities should cooperate[655] with one another (Recital 5 of the

650. G. Wolff (n. 310), 20.
651. M. Gatti (n. 647), 104.
652. Article 3(1)(c) of the Takeover Bid Directive states that 'the board of an offeree company must act in the interests of the company as a whole and must not deny the holders of securities the opportunity to decide on the merits of the bid'. D.A. Wyatt, A. Dashwood et al. (n. 46), 884.
653. D.A. Wyatt, A. Dashwood et al. (n. 46), 884.
654. See also: D. Van Gerven, 'Rules of Community Law Applicable to Takeover Bids', in *Common Legal Framework for Takeover Bids in Europe*, ed. D. Van Gerven (Cambridge: Cambridge University Press, 2008), 10–14.
655. Article 4(4) states that the supervisory authorities of the Member States for the purposes of this Directive and other authorities supervising capital markets, in particular, in accordance with

Preamble). In accordance with Article 4(1), Member States are to designate the authority or authorities competent to supervise bids for the purposes of the rules that they make or introduce pursuant to this Directive. The authorities thus designated must be public authorities, associations or private bodies recognized by national law, or public authorities expressly empowered for that purpose by national law. Member States shall inform the Commission of those designations, specifying any divisions of functions that have been made. They shall ensure that those authorities exercise their functions impartially and independently of all parties to a bid.

The possibility that, in addition to public authorities, associations or private bodies recognized by national law could supervise takeover bids was inserted into this Article of the Takeover Bid Directive because of some UK concerns about the preservation of the special status of the self-regulatory body, the Takeover Panel.[656] It was in the UK that national takeover regulation first emerged, and the UK was also the most shareholder-protective state in Europe, as a result of several highly publicized takeovers that provoked demands for improvement of the situation for target company shareholders. The UK market players (the Bank of England, the British Bankers Association, the Institute of Chartered Accountants, the London Investment Banking Association, the Confederation of British Industry, the Association of British Insurers, and the National Association of Pension Funds) agreed to regulate themselves, and this led to the adoption of the UK Takeover Code in 1968 and the creation of a self-regulatory body, the Takeover Panel.[657] These UK organizations and their members decided to develop this self-regulatory regime so as to impose discipline on the market in corporate control, by which they are significantly affected. The UK feared that the shift towards a harmonized legislative system would create problems for its active self-regulated takeover market with the creation of obstructive litigation and delays.[658] The main

Directive 93/22/EEC, Directive 2001/34/EC, Directive 2003/6/EC, and Directive 2003/71/EC of the European Parliament and of the Council of 4 Nov. 2003 on the prospectus to be published when securities are offered to the public or admitted to trading, shall cooperate and supply each other with information wherever necessary for the application of the rules drawn up in accordance with this Directive and in particular in cases covered by para. 2(b), (c) and (e). Information thus exchanged shall be covered by the obligation of professional secrecy to which persons employed or formerly employed by the supervisory authorities receiving the information are subject. Cooperation shall include the ability to serve the legal documents necessary to enforce measures taken by the competent authorities in connection with bids, as well as such other assistance as may reasonably be requested by the supervisory authorities concerned for the purpose of investigating any actual or alleged breaches of the rules made or introduced pursuant to this Directive.

656. R. Skog (n. 570), 301. The examination of the UK Takeover Code falls outside the scope of this book. I will refer to the UK Takeover Code only where it has inspired the European legislature. For an extensive analysis of the UK Takeover Code see: G. Stedman, *Takeovers*, Longman Commercial Series, 1st edn (London: Longman, 1993) and S. Kenyon-Slade, *Mergers and Takeovers in the US and UK: Law and Practice*, 1st edn (Oxford: Oxford University Press, 2004).

657. R. Skog (n. 570), 301.

658. J.S.Knudsen, 'Is the single European Market an Illusion? Obstacles to Reform of EU Takeover Regulation', *ELJ* 11 (2005): 507, 509. See also for a more extensive and well-founded

objections of the UK concerned the fact that the takeover rules would be given the force of law, and that there would be more delays as a result of more frequent litigation, which could put an end to particular takeover bids (the English courts, under the then-current City Code regime, practised self-restraint and discouraged tactical litigation). Moreover, the UK government alleged that the Takeover Panel would also lose its flexibility to adjust the takeover rules and to give rulings on issues arising in the course of a bid.[659] The British criticism was especially troublesome for the Commission, since the UK Takeover Code had served as a model for the Commission's proposal, and also for the various takeover regulations that by then had gradually begun to be promulgated across Continental Europe.[660]

Finally, the European Commission took into account the UK concerns and formed the Directive's provision on the supervisory authorities in such a way that the special status and powers of the Takeover Panel could be preserved.[661] Recital 8 of the Takeover Bid Directive's Preamble stresses that, in accordance with general

---

analysis: S. Kenyon-Slade & M. Andenas, 'The Proposed Thirteenth Directive on Takeovers: Unravelling the United Kingdom's Self-Regulatory Success?', in *E.C. Financial Market Regulation and Company Law*, ed. S. Kenyon-Slade & M. Andenas (London: Sweet & Maxwell, 1993), 149–188. M. O'Neill, 'When European Integration Meets Corporate Harmonization', *Comp. Law.* 21 (2000): 173, 175–176. For an early consideration of the Code: A. Johnston, *The City Take-Over Code* (Oxford: Oxford University Press, 1980) and N.S. Poser, *International Securities Regulation* (Toronto: Little Brown & Company, 1991). Furthermore, see for a comparison between the two systems of regulation, self-regulatory/private regulation and statutory/public regulation, and their analysis (arguments in favour and against each system of regulation): B. Pettet, 'Private versus Public Regulation in the Field of Takeovers: The Future under the Directive', *EBLR* 5 (2000): 381. For an extensive critical analysis of the self-regulatory takeover regime of England, one of the most advanced in the world, see: G. De Minico, 'A Hard Look at Self-Regulation in the UK', *EBLR* (2006): 183, P.L. Davies, *Gower and Davies' Principles of Modern Company Law*, 7th edn (London: Sweet & Maxwell, 2003), 704, D. Kershaw, 'The Illusion of Importance: Reconsidering the UK's Takeover Defence Prohibition', *ICLQ* 56 (2007): 267. For an interesting comparison between England's self-regulatory, standards-based system and the US's more formal, rules-based system see: B.E. Rosenzweig, 'Private versus Public Regulation: A Comparative Analysis of British and American Takeover Controls', *Duk. J. Comp. Int. L.* 18 (2007): 213. See also a very interesting article on disputes and litigation in takeover bids: T.I. Ogowewo, 'Tactical Litigation in Takeover Contests', *JBL* (2007): 589–619. For a critical approach to General Principle No. 7 of the UK Takeover Code (shareholders should decide the outcome of a takeover bid), which was the basis of the non-frustration rule of the Takeover Bid Directive, see: A. Dignam, 'The Globalisation of General Principle 7: Transforming the Market for Corporate Control in Australia and Europe?', *Legal Studies* 28 (2008): 96–118.

659. V. Edwards (n. 544), 420. Securities arbitration is another very flexible method of alternative dispute resolution: S. Ware, 'What Makes Securities Arbitration Different from Other Consumer and Employment Arbitration?', *U Cinc LR* 76 (2008): 447, J.Gross & B. Black, 'When Perception Changes Reality: An Empirical Study of Investors' Views of the Fairness of Securities Arbitration', *J Disp Res* (2008): 349., B. Black & J. Gross, 'Making It Up as They Go Along: The Role of Law in Securities Arbitration', *Card LR* 23 (2002): 991, J. Johnson & E. Brunet, 'Substantive Fairness in Securities Arbitration', *U Cinc L.*76 (2007).

660. R. Skog (n. 570). 303.

661. See also Recital 7 of the Directive's Preamble, which states that self-regulatory bodies (such as the UK Takeover Panel) should be able to exercise supervision.

principles of Community law, and in particular the right to a fair hearing, decisions of a supervisory authority should, in appropriate circumstances, be subject to review by an independent court or tribunal. However, Member States should be left to determine whether rights are to be made available for assertion in administrative or judicial proceedings, either in proceedings against a supervisory authority or in proceedings between parties to a bid. This latter part of Recital 8 was deemed to satisfy the UK concerns with regard to judicial intervention into the Takeover Panel's proceedings. In addition, Article 4(6) states that this Directive does not affect either the power of the Member States to designate judicial or other authorities responsible for dealing with disputes and for deciding on irregularities committed in the course of bids, or the power of Member States to regulate whether and under which circumstances parties to a bid are entitled to bring administrative or judicial proceedings. In particular, this Directive does not affect the power which courts may have in a Member State to decline to hear legal proceedings and to decide whether or not such proceedings affect the outcome of a bid. The Directive also does not affect the power of the Member States to determine the legal position concerning the liability of supervisory authorities or concerning litigation between the parties to a bid (Article 4(6)). Therefore, litigation before UK courts, which causes delays and could be responsible for irreversible damage to the takeover process, will continue to be infrequent.

Article 4(2) circumscribes the national authorities that are competent to supervise the conduct of takeover bids within the framework of the internal market. The authority competent to supervise a bid is to be that of the Member State in which the offeree company has its registered office, if that company's securities are admitted to trading on a regulated market in that Member State (Article 4(2)(a)). If the offeree company's securities are not admitted to trading on a regulated market in the Member State in which the company has its registered office, the authority competent to supervise the bid shall be that of the Member State containing the regulated market where the company's securities are admitted to trading. Moreover, if the offeree company's securities are admitted to trading on regulated markets in more than one Member State, the authority competent to supervise the bid shall be that of the Member State containing the regulated market to which the securities were first admitted to trading (Article 4(2)(b)). Additionally, if the offeree company's securities were first admitted to trading on regulated markets in more than one Member State simultaneously, the offeree company is to determine which of the supervisory authorities of those Member States shall be the authority competent to supervise the bid by notifying those regulated markets and their supervisory authorities on the first day of trading. If the offeree company's securities have already been admitted to trading on regulated markets in more than one Member State and were admitted simultaneously, the supervisory authorities of those Member States shall agree which one of them shall be the authority competent to supervise the bid. Otherwise, the offeree company shall determine which of those authorities shall be the competent authority (Article 4(2)(c)). Member States shall ensure that the decisions on the national competent authorities responsible for the supervision of cross-border bids are made public (Article 4(2)(d)).

The Takeover Bid Directive also contains a provision on the role of the national competent authorities during the takeover process. Article 4(5) states that the supervisory authorities shall be vested with all the powers necessary for the purpose of carrying out their duties, including that of ensuring that the parties to a bid comply with the rules made or introduced pursuant to this Directive. Provided that the general principles laid down in Article 3(1) are respected, Member States may provide, in the rules that they make or introduce pursuant to this Directive, for derogations from those rules: (1) by including such derogations in their national rules, so as to take account of circumstances determined at the national level, and/or (2) by granting their supervisory authorities, where they are competent, powers to waive such national rules to take account of the circumstances referred to in (1) or in other specific circumstances, in which case a reasoned decision is required. Furthermore, Recital 6 of the Preamble states that, to be effective, takeover regulations should be flexible and capable of dealing with new circumstances as they arise and should, accordingly, provide for the possibility of exceptions and derogations. However, in applying any rules or exceptions laid down or in granting any derogations, supervisory authorities should respect certain general principles. These principles are found in Article 3 of the Takeover Bid Directive and contain certain very important safeguards. These principles play an overarching role. They cover all the provisions of the Takeover Bid Directive, and all the implementing measures of the Member States must comply with them. As a matter of fact, the national competent authorities are also bound by these general principles when they are exercising their supervisory duties.

As regards the applicable law, Article 4(2)(e) states that in the cases referred to in Article 4(2)(b) and Article 4(2)(c) mentioned above, matters relating to the consideration offered in the case of a bid (in particular, the price), and matters relating to the bid procedure (in particular, the information on the offeror's decision to make a bid), the contents of the offer document and the disclosure of the bid shall be dealt with in accordance with the rules of the Member State of the competent authority. In matters relating to the information to be provided to the employees of the offeree company and in matters relating to company law, in particular, the percentage of voting rights that confers control and any derogation from the obligation to launch a bid, as well as the conditions under which the board of the offeree company may undertake any action that might result in the frustration of the bid, the applicable rules and the competent authority shall be those of the Member State in which the offeree company has its registered office.

11.9 INFORMATION FOR AND CONSULTATION OF EMPLOYEES' REPRESENTATIVES

The European Parliament asked for better protection of employees working for companies involved in takeover bids. The Takeover Bid Directive sought to meet the European Parliament's concerns about employee protection by providing for national measures to govern the provision of information and consultation of representatives of the employees of both the target company and the bidder.[662] The Takeover Bid Directive does not introduce new consultation rights for employees. It does, however, specifically refer to the various Community measures that have already been adopted in this area.[663] The Preamble of the Takeover Bid Directive emphasizes this requirement for information and consultation of employees' representatives. Recital 13 of the Preamble demands that the holders of securities be properly informed of the terms of a bid by means of an offer document. Appropriate information should also be given to the representatives of the company's employees or, failing that, to the employees directly. Recital 17 of the Preamble calls on the board of an offeree company to make public a document setting out its opinion of the bid and the reasons on which that opinion is based, including its views on the effects of implementation on all the company's interests, and specifically on employment.

The Takeover Bid Directive refers explicitly to the already existing Community legal framework of employees' information and consultation. As far as the information for and the consultation of employees' representatives is concerned, Article 14 stipulates that the Takeover Bid Directive shall be without prejudice to the EU rules relating to information and to consultation of representatives, and that, if Member States so provide, co-determination with the employees of the offeror and the offeree company shall be governed by the relevant national provisions, in particular, those adopted pursuant to Directives 94/45/EC, 98/59/EC, 2001/86/EC, and 2002/14/EC.[664] Moreover, Recital 23 of the Preamble mentions all these Community legal instruments on the information and consultation of employees that also apply to the area of takeover bids: the disclosure of information to and the consultation of representatives of the employees of the offeror and the offeree company should be governed by the relevant national provisions, in particular, those adopted pursuant to Council Directive 94/45/EC, on the establishment of a European Works Council, or a procedure in Community-scale undertakings and Community-scale groups of undertakings for the purposes of informing and consulting employees;[665] Council Directive 98/59/EC, on the approximation of the laws of the Member States relating to collective redundancies;[666] Council Directive 2001/86/EC, supplementing the statute for a European Company with regard to the involvement of employees;[667] and Directive 2002/14/EC of the European Parliament and of the Council, establishing a general framework for informing and

662. V. Edwards (n. 544), 429.
663. Proposal for a Directive of the European Parliament and of the Council on Takeover Bids (Explanatory Memorandum, Legislative Financial Statement, Impact Assessment Form) COM (2002) 534 final, *OJ* [2003] 45E/1-17.
664. See also: C. Barnard, *EC Employment Law*, 3rd edn (Oxford: Oxford University Press, 2006), 743.
665. [1994] OJ L254/64. Directive as amended by Directive 97/74/EC ([1998] OJ L10/22).
666. [1998] OJ L225/16.
667. [2001] OJ L294/22.

consulting employees in the European Community[668] – a joint declaration of the European Parliament, the Council, and the Commission on employee representation. In addition to these Community legal instruments applying to takeover bids, Recital 23 of the Takeover Bid Directive's Preamble explicitly gives the opportunity to employees or to their representatives to express their opinions on the impact of a takeover bid. It states that the employees of the companies concerned, or their representatives, should be given an opportunity to state their views on the foreseeable effects of the bid on employment. Additionally, Recital 23 of the Preamble also refers to an EC securities regulation legal instrument connected to the information and consultation framework. Without prejudice to the rules of Directive 2003/6/EC of the European Parliament and of the Council, on insider dealing and market manipulation (market abuse),[669] Member States may always apply or introduce national provisions concerning the disclosure of information to, and the consultation of representatives of, the employees of the offeror before an offer is launched (Recital 23).

The obligation for information for employees is also included among the general principles of Article 3. Article 3(1)(b) states that, when it advises the holders of securities, the board of the offeree company must give its views on the effects of implementation of the bid on employment, the conditions of employment, and the locations of the company's places of business. Taking into account the overarching role of the general principles, the inclusion of this information requirement among the general principles shows the interest of the European legislature. The European legislature took into account the concerns of the European Parliament and decided to confer the status of a general principle of the Directive on the requirement for information for employees. Furthermore, according to Article 6(1), as soon as the bid has been made public, the boards of the offeree company and of the offeror shall inform the representatives of their respective employees or, when there are no such representatives, the employees themselves. When the bidder drafts the offer document, he or she is also obliged to inform the employees about the various aspects of the takeover bids. Article 6(2) states that Member States shall ensure that an offeror is required to draw up and make public in good time an offer document[670] containing the information necessary to enable the holders of the offeree company's securities to reach a properly informed decision on the bid. Before the offer document is made public, the offeror shall communicate it to the supervisory authority. When it is made public, the boards of the offeree company and of the offeror shall communicate it to the representatives

668. [2002] OJ L80/29.
669. [2003] OJ L96/16.
670. The Takeover Bid Directive allows a European passport to be granted for the offer document of a takeover bid. When a bidder possesses a European passport, the offer document can be circulated freely in the internal market and without re-approval being required in other Member States where the offeree company's shares are accepted. D. Van Gerven, 'Rules of Community Law Applicable to Takeover Bids', in *Common Legal Framework for Takeover Bids in Europe*, ed. D. Van Gerven (Cambridge: Cambridge University Press, 2008), 4.

of their respective employees or, when there are no such representatives, to the employees themselves. The Takeover Bid Directive also determines the minimum content of this offer document and includes explicitly the provision of information on the business plans of the offeror as regards the offeree company and the offeror company. It shall state, at the very minimum, the offeror's intentions with regard to the future business of the offeree company and, insofar as it is affected by the bid, the offeror company, and with regard to the safeguarding of the jobs of their employees and management, including any material changes in the conditions of employment, and, in particular, the offeror's strategic plans for the two companies and the likely repercussions on employment and the locations of the companies' places of business (Article 6(3)(i)). The Takeover Bid Directive also stresses the importance of the effective disclosure of these documents required by Article 6. Article 8(2) states that Member States shall provide for the disclosure of all information and documents required by Article 6 in such a manner as to ensure that they are both readily and promptly available to the holders of securities at least in those Member States containing the regulated markets to which the offeree company's securities are admitted for trading. The disclosure must be made to the representatives of the employees of the offeree company and the offeror or, when there are no such representatives, to the employees themselves.

Not only must the board of the offeror company disclose its intentions on the future of employment in the target company, but also, the board of the offeree company can express its point of view on the bid and its various terms concerning employment. According to Article 9(5), the board of the offeree company must draw up and make public a document setting out its opinion of the bid and the reasons on which it is based, including its views on the effects of implementation of the bid on all the company's interests and, specifically, employment, as well as its views on the offeror's strategic plans for the offeree company and their likely repercussions on employment and the locations of the company's places of business as set out in the offer document. The board of the offeree company must at the same time communicate that opinion to the representatives of its employees or, when there are no such representatives, to the employees themselves. When the board of the offeree company receives in good time a separate opinion from the representatives of its employees on the effects of the bid on employment, that opinion shall be appended to the document (Article 9(5)). While the board neutrality/non-frustration rule of Article 9 does allow the board of the target company to take any defensive measures against the bid without the prior authorization of a general meeting, it gives the board an opportunity to influence the decision of the shareholders to reject the bid or to get the necessary permission from the general meeting to frustrate the bid through this document expressing its opinion. If the arguments of the company's board against the bid are well-founded and substantiated, the shareholders will probably be convinced, provided that they trust the board of their company. Then, the bid can be probably rejected or frustrated.

11.10 TRANSPOSITION OF THE DIRECTIVE

In 2007, the European Commission published a report on the implementation of the Takeover Bid Directive by the Member States.[671] Internal Market and Services Commissioner C. McCreevy, commenting on this Report, declared that:

> Too many Member States are reluctant to lift existing barriers, and some are even giving companies yet more power to thwart bids. The protectionist attitude of a few seems to have had a knock-on effect on others. If this trend continues, then there is a real risk that companies launching a takeover bid will face more barriers, not fewer. That goes completely against the whole idea of the Directive.[672]

As far as the mandatory bid is concerned, Member States enjoy discretion and could determine the length of the pre-acquisition period (six or twelve months), the threshold triggering the takeover bid, how the price for the securities to be bought is reached, and whether the consideration could be a cash offer or a transfer of securities (which can influence the total sum of the bid and the consideration to be acquired).[673] The threshold above which control is deemed to have been acquired is defined at the national level. If the threshold is set lower than it was before the implementation of the Directive, the protection of minority shareholders will be strengthened. The introduction of the mandatory bid rule in Member States that did not have such a provision previously constitutes a huge step toward effective protection of minority shareholders.[674] Nevertheless, the European Commission's Report found that the Member States had taken advantage of the various deficiencies of the mandatory bid rule at the implementation stage. It states that Member States had widely used the flexibility provided by the Directive to derogate from the Directive's provisions so as to maintain their exceptions from the mandatory bid rule. Some of these exceptions are necessary to ensure that this obligation applies only when the holding actually confers control, while others are more far-reaching. Furthermore, in some Member States, supervisory authorities seem to have extensive powers to grant exceptions to the rule. Exceptions and wide-ranging discretionary power can undermine the effectiveness of the protection provided by such a rule.[675]

According to this Report, most of the Member States decided to apply the board neutrality/non-frustration rule: eighteen Member States in total now impose the board neutrality rule. However, the board neutrality obligation is not new in any of these Member States, except one. Five of these Member States have introduced

---

671. Commission Staff Working Document, Report on the Implementation of the Directive on Takeover Bids, SEC (2007) 268.
672. IP/07/251.
673. S. Maul, D. Muffat-Jeandet & J. Simon (n. 637), 3.
674. Commission Staff Working Document, Report on the Implementation of the Directive on Takeover Bids, SEC (2007) 268, 9.
675. Commission Staff Working Document, Report on the Implementation of the Directive on Takeover Bids, SEC (2007) 268, 9.

the reciprocity exception, which may inhibit the emergence of an active EU market in corporate control, contrary to the original objective of the Directive.[676] No Member State has decided to implement the board neutrality rule where it was not (fully) applied before implementation, except for Malta.[677] Some Member States had no strict board neutrality obligation before the implementation of the Directive. All these Member States have decided to introduce the rule only on a voluntary basis, in conformity with the optionality system of Article 12, again, except for Malta. The rules on board neutrality/non-frustration, compared to previous or existing rules, will therefore remain almost the same. Although these Member States do not impose a strict board neutrality rule, the discretion of management as regards the use of post-bid defences is quite restricted.[678]

Most of the Member States have not adopted the breakthrough rule on a mandatory basis. They have made it optional for companies. Therefore, its impact on the EU market in corporate control will be quite restricted. Only the Baltic countries (Estonia, Latvia, and Lithuania)[679] have implemented the breakthrough rule on an obligatory basis. None of the other countries oblige their companies to apply this provision in full. Consequently, a mere 1% of listed companies in the EU will apply this rule on a mandatory basis.[680]

The reciprocity rule of Article 12 has certainly been implemented by the majority of Member States, most of which have allowed companies to reciprocate against a bidder not subject to the board neutrality and/or breakthrough rules.[681] Reciprocity in general does not contribute to the integration of the EU market in corporate control, however, and does not facilitate the exercise of the freedom of establishment by the offeror company, because it allows the target company to opt out of the two key provisions of the Directive, Articles 9 and/or 11. This decision of the Member States to implement the reciprocity rule was made as a result of certain level-playing-field considerations. Those Member States that implemented the non-frustration and/or the breakthrough rule were afraid that, without reciprocity, there would be no level playing field between themselves and those countries that do not apply these rules. It is not hard to grasp that Member States were afraid of regulatory competition and of seat transfers to jurisdictions opting out of the non-frustration and/or the breakthrough rule.[682] The European Commission's Report

676. Commission Staff Working Document, Report on the Implementation of the Directive on Takeover Bids, SEC (2007) 268, 6.
677. Commission Staff Working Document, Report on the Implementation of the Directive on Takeover Bids, SEC (2007) 268, 7.
678. Commission Staff Working Document, Report on the Implementation of the Directive on Takeover Bids, SEC (2007) 268, 7.
679. See: G. Lisauskas & E. Lauraityte, 'Baltic Takeover Practices Already in Line with EC', *I FL Rev.* (2004): 43, T. Klauberg, 'Rules on Takeover Bids in Latvia', *EBL Rev.* (2005): 1474.
680. Commission Staff Working Document, Report on the Implementation of the Directive on Takeover Bids, SEC (2007) 268, 7.
681. Commission Staff Working Document, Report on the Implementation of the Directive on Takeover Bids, SEC (2007) 268, 8.
682. *Ibid.*

also found that reciprocity is considered to be an incentive for companies that have acquisition plans to apply the rules of the Directive voluntarily so as to be able to benefit from the liberal regime abroad. However, the Report admits that this argument is undermined by the fact that any company's decision to voluntarily apply the board neutrality or breakthrough rule remains reversible.[683]

683. Commission Staff Working Document, Report on the Implementation of the Directive on Takeover Bids, SEC (2007) 268, 8–9.

Chapter 12

The Direct Effect of the Fundamental Freedoms in EU Law

12.1 THE DOCTRINE OF DIRECT EFFECT IN EU LAW

The founding Treaties did dot make express provisions for the effect of EC law in the national legal orders of Member States, the possibility of conferral of rights and obligations on individuals, and the possible enforcement of such rights. The original Member States had the impression that EC law would have the same domestic effects as international law, which would have meant that the impact of EC law on domestic law would be determined by each Member State's own constitutional law (following either a monist or dualist approach).[684] However, the ECJ had a different view and adopted the doctrine of direct effect.

In general, direct effect concerns the way in which a provision of one legal system is applied to another and encompasses the transfer of a provision between two legal systems.[685] There is academic and judicial uncertainty about the exact

684. K. Davies, *Understanding European Union Law*, 3rd edn (Abingdon: Routledge-Cavendish, 2007), 63–64. P.-J. Kuijper, 'Epilogue: Symbiosis?', in *Direct Effect-Rethinking a Classic of EC Legal Doctrine*, ed. J. Prinssen & A. Schrauwen (Groningen/Amsterdam: Europa, 2002), 255, 260.

685. This transfer depends on the relationship between the two legal systems. When one system derives its validity from the other, the terms of this transfer are provided by the primary system. If neither legal system is dependent on the other, each legal system decides for itself whether provisions of the other can be transferred to it. T.C. Hartley, 'The Constitutional Foundations of the European Union', *LQR* (2001): 225, 237. M. Dougan, 'When Worlds Collide! Competing Visions of the Relationship between Direct Effect and Supremacy', *CM L Rev.* (2007): 931, 932. For an interesting study on the common constitutional principles governing the relationship between national and international law, see S. Prechal, 'Direct Effect, Indirect Effect, Supremacy and the Evolving Constitution of the European Union', in *The Fundamentals of EU Law Revisited: Assessing the Impact of the Constitution Debate*, ed. C. Barnard

meaning of the term 'direct effect', and two definitions, a broad one and a narrow one, have been introduced. According to the broad definition, 'direct effect' is the capacity of a provision of EC law to be invoked before a national court (objective direct effect).[686] In a narrower sense, 'direct effect' is the capacity of a provision of EC law to confer rights on individuals, which they may enforce before national courts (subjective direct effect).[687] The definition of a 'right' being used determines the degree of difference between these two definitions. If a 'right' is defined as the freedom to invoke EC law in a national court to assist one's case and to ameliorate its position, then the difference between these two definitions is not very significant.[688] Nevertheless, if the conferral of 'rights' on individuals includes the conferral of a substantive right (e.g., prohibition of discrimination on grounds of nationality) or of a particular remedy or the imposition of a corresponding duty on a third party, then the difference between these two definitions is more significant.[689]

Direct effect is further divided into vertical and horizontal. On one hand, vertical direct effect refers to a situation in which an individual can rely on a Treaty article in judicial proceedings against a Member State or its emanations.[690] On the other hand, horizontal direct effect refers to a situation in which an individual can rely on a Treaty article in judicial proceedings against another individual.[691] These two categories of direct effect will be approached through an analysis of the relevant case law. The ECJ's case law played a very important role in the evolution of the direct effect of the EC Treaty's provisions.

12.2 ESTABLISHMENT OF VERTICAL DIRECT EFFECT

Van Gend & Loos[692] was the ground-breaking ruling that introduced the doctrine of direct effect into the Community legal order. In that case, the ECJ examined

---

(Oxford: Oxford University Press, 2007), 35–69. See also: R. Barents, *The Autonomy of Community Law* (The Hague: Kluwer Law International, 2003), 167, 193, 299. For an EEA view, see: M. Johansson & L. Sevon, 'The Protection of the Rights of Individuals under the EEA Agreement', *E L Rev.* (1999): 373. Direct effect is often characterized as a general principle of EC law by some academics. This is based on the rationale that direct effect is founded on a general principle of effectiveness being a typical feature of EC law. J. Bengoetxea, 'Is Direct Effect a General Principle of European Law?', in *General Principles of EC Law in a Process of Development*, ed. U. Bernitz et al. (AH Alpen aan den Rijn: Kluwer Law International, 2008), 4.

686. P. Craig & G. De Burca (n. 12), 269–270. See also: S. Prechal (n. 685), 37, 44.
687. P. Craig & G. De Burca (n. 12), 270.
688. *Ibid.*
689. P. Craig & G. De Burca (n. 12), 270. See also: T.A. Downes & C. Hilson, 'Making Sense of Rights: Community Rights in EC Law', *E L Rev.* (1999): 121–138.
690. A. Kaczorowska, *European Union Law* (Abingdon: Routledge Cavendish, 2009), 303.
691. *Ibid.*, 304. B. Bercusson, 'Economic Policy: State and Private Ordering', in *Law as an Instrument of Economic Policy: Comparative and Critical Approaches*, ed. T. Daintith (Berlin/New York: de Gruyter, 1988), 363–365, 369, 376, 386–390, 414.
692. Case 26/62, *Van Gend & Loos* [1963] ECR English special edition 1.

whether a Dutch importer could argue before a Dutch national court that Article 25 of the EC Treaty was infringed upon and, more specifically, whether the importer could claim the protection of rights conferred on it by EC law.[693] Three out of the six original Member States intervened in the proceedings. The Dutch and Belgian governments argued that the ECJ lacked jurisdiction and that the process of Articles 226 and 227 of the EC Treaty should have been followed. Additionally, the Dutch and Belgian governments did not exclude the possibility of an additional remedy and added that a national remedy could also be invoked. This national remedy would be determined by the Member States and not by the ECJ. The two governments believed that the influence of EC law on national legal proceedings is a matter of pure national law and must be determined only by the Member States.[694]

AG Roemer argued that Community law does not consist of contractual relations between certain States, as does international law. Community rules create rights in favour of and impose duties on Member States, as well as their authorities and citizens. He accepted that some EC Treaty provisions were intended to apply directly in the national systems (e.g., Articles 81 and 82 of the EC Treaty). Finally, he concluded that Article 25 of the EC Treaty did not have direct effect because it did not refer explicitly to individual rights and contained an obligation on the part of the Member States.[695]

The ECJ rejected the arguments of the Dutch and Belgian governments that only the procedure of Articles 226 and 227 of the EC Treaty should be followed and held that the existence of Articles 226 and 227 of the EC Treaty does not mean that individuals cannot plead a breach of Member State obligations before a national court.[696] In *Van Gend & Loos*, the action was against the Dutch State; hence, in that case, the ECJ examined a vertical relationship between the State and the citizens. In general, vertical direct effect concerns the relationship between EC law and national law. Some Treaty articles create obligations on the State to ensure their observance. If a Member State does not comply with these obligations, then the European Commission could pursue the process of Articles 226 and 227 of the EC Treaty. Although the process of Articles 226 and 227 of the EC Treaty is always open, vertical direct effect empowers an individual to invoke Treaty provisions in an action against a state.[697] The doctrine of direct effect was based on the premise that the EC Treaty created rights for citizens, which, if invoked by them in the domestic courts, would provide an additional supervisory function to that already contained in Articles 226 and 227 of the EC Treaty.[698] Despite the fact that the EC Treaty does not contain an explicit provision on the direct effect of Treaty articles,

---

693. D. Chalmers et al. (n. 395), 366.
694. D. Chalmers et al. (n. 395), 366–367.
695. For a brief discussion of the Advocate General's Opinion, see: A. Arnull, *The European Union and Its Court of Justice*, Oxford EC Law Library, 2nd edn (Oxford: Oxford University Press, 2006), 164–165.
696. D. Chalmers et al. (n. 395), 367.
697. T. Storey & C. Turner, *Unlocking EU Law*, 2nd edn (London: Hodder Education, 2008), 169.
698. J. Fairhurst, *Law of the European Union,* 6th edn (Essex: Pearson Longman, 2007), 265.

the ECJ found that 'the spirit, the general scheme and the wording of the Treaty' produce direct effects and create individual rights which national courts must protect'.[699]

Another strong argument of the ECJ is contained in its reference to the preliminary reference process (Article 234 of the EC Treaty). The existence of this article in the Treaty shows that the Member States have understood that EC law possesses an authority that can be invoked by their nationals before the domestic courts. The preliminary reference process reveals that, at the very least, Treaty articles may have some legal consequences when invoked before domestic courts.[700]

In *Van Gend & Loos*, the ECJ also set certain conditions that needed to be fulfilled before a Treaty article could obtain direct effect. The conditions that were satisfied by Article 25 of the EC Treaty and that, subsequently, conferred direct effect on it were that it was clear, negative, unconditional, contained no reservation on the part of the Member State, and not dependent on any national implementing measure.[701] These conditions seemed to be quite strict, but, in its subsequent case law, the ECJ loosened these initial conditions.[702]

The conditions that a Treaty article should be clear, unconditional, and contain no reservation on the part of the Member State were loosened. The ECJ did not consider that Member States' discretion could exclude the direct effect of a Treaty article. Direct effect could apply even where the Member States possessed discretion, on the grounds that the exercise thereof could be controlled by the courts.[703] Even when Treaty articles require the appreciation of complex issues, they are not precluded from being directly effective, as long as the requisite conditions are fulfilled.[704]

Furthermore, the condition that a Treaty article should not be dependent upon any national implementing measure was amended. The ECJ found that Article 43 of the EC Treaty was sufficiently certain and conferred direct effect on it, and the Court disregarded the absence of implementing measures at the national and EC levels (as of the end of the transitional period for the realization of Community's general programme on freedom of establishment).[705] The pivotal point in *Reyners,*[706] which was about the freedom of establishment of Member

699. D. Chalmers et al. (n. 395), 367.
700. D.A. Wyatt & A. Dashwood (n. 46), 149.
701. P. Craig & G. De Burca (n. 12), 275.
702. P. Craig & G. De Burca (n. 12), 275. J.H. Jans, R. de Lange, S. Prechal & R. Widdershoven, *Europeanisation of Public Law* (Groningen/Amsterdam: Europa, 2007), 65.
703. P. Craig & G. De Burca (n. 12), 275. Case 13-68, *SpA Salgoil v. Italian Ministry of Foreign Trade, Rome* [1968] ECR 453 English special edition.
704. In *Fink-Frucht,* the ECJ discussed the direct effect of Art. 90(1) EC Treaty, which entails complex evaluations of economic factors. D.A. Wyatt & A. Dashwood (n. 46), 151–152. Case 27/67, *Firma Fink-Frucht GmbH v. Hauptzollamt München-Landsbergerstrasse* [1968] ECR 223 English special edition.
705. P. Craig & G. De Burca (n. 12), 275.
706. Case 2/74, *Jean Reyners v. Belgian State* [1974] ECR 631.

State nationals (Article 43 of the EC Treaty) was the realization of the Community's general programme on freedom of establishment. The general programme on freedom of establishment was aimed at the abolition of trade barriers in this part of the common market and required the adoption of the essential directives for market integration.[707] The ECJ found that the basic principle of non-discrimination is directly effective and could be invoked before the national courts, although the freedom of establishment has not yet reached a satisfactory level of integration because of the slow realization of the Community's general programme on freedom of establishment.[708] Article 43 of the EC Treaty seeks to facilitate the realization of the Community's general programme on freedom of establishment but does not depend on it.[709]

The ECJ has moved from the strict conditions on direct effect introduced by *Van Gend & Loos* to a more relaxed test.[710] This test could be characterized as a test of feasibility: if a provision is open to judicial application, it is capable of direct effect. It could be argued that the ECJ does not regard direct effect as an exceptional phenomenon but rather as the norm.[711]

12.3 ESTABLISHMENT OF HORIZONTAL DIRECT EFFECT

Horizontal direct effect deals with the relationship between individuals and other individuals; this could include any private body, including companies.[712] With regard to the substance of horizontal direct effect, it creates rights between persons and is therefore enforceable by them in national courts.[713] It concerns a situation in which an individual (i.e., a natural or legal person) is allowed to invoke a provision of EU law in national proceedings against another individual before a domestic court.[714] It is possible that the actions of one individual obstruct another individual from exercising effectively the fundamental freedoms within the framework of the internal market. The significance of the horizontal effect of fundamental freedoms is raised because of the privatization programmes in many Member States and because of the increasing importance of private conduct for the organization and operation of the internal market.[715] With regard to horizontal direct effect, the ECJ has adopted different approaches toward free movement of goods and free movement of persons.

707. General Programme for the Abolition of Restrictions on Freedom of Establishment [1962] OJ 2/36–45 and English special edition: Series II Vol. IX/7–15].
708. P. Craig & G. De Burca (n. 12), 275–276.
709. D.A. Wyatt & A. Dashwood (n. 46), 766.
710. T.C. Hartley, *The Foundations of European Community Law*, 6th edn (Oxford: Oxford University Press, 2007), 197.
711. *Ibid.*, 197.
712. T. Storey & C. Turner (n. 697), 169. B. Bercusson (n. 837), 365.
713. T. Storey & C. Turner (n. 697), 170.
714. A. Kaczorowska (n. 691), 304.
715. J. Baquero Cruz, 'Free Movement and Private Autonomy', *E L Rev.* (1999): 603, 604.

The ECJ discussed the vertical effect of Treaty articles in *Van Gend & Loos,* but, in *SABAM,*[716] it had the opportunity for the first time to examine the horizontal effect of Treaty articles. In this case, the ECJ found that Articles 81 and 82 of the EC Treaty are capable of horizontal direct effect, which is derived by 'their very nature' as competition law provisions. The ECJ started to endorse the proposition that Treaty articles could affect the rights of private parties (natural or legal persons) per se.[717] While, in *Dansk Supermarked,*[718] the ECJ considered that private parties are also bound by the obligations imposed by Article 28 of the EC Treaty, this approach was abandoned in later cases handed down by the ECJ (*van de Haar,*[719] *Vlaamse Reisbureaus,*[720] *Süllhöfer,*[721] and *Sapod Audic*[722]). Therefore, Articles 28 and 26 of the EC Treaty bind only Member States and not private parties.[723] This kind of anti-competitive behaviour of private persons (undertakings) falls within the scope of Articles 81 and 82 of the EC Treaty, as long as it distorts competition in an appreciable manner. An application of the free movement of goods provision to these actions would undermine the effectiveness of Articles 81 and 82 of the EC Treaty.[724]

Even within the sphere of free movement of goods and within other areas of the internal market that were related to commercial activities and were closely linked to the free movement of goods, the ECJ has not adopted a uniform approach toward horizontal direct effect. Some Treaty articles enjoyed both horizontal and vertical direct effect, while others were declared to have only vertical direct effect. The ECJ conferred both horizontal and vertical direct effect on many different Treaty articles, for example, Article 25 of the EC Treaty, which prohibits impositions by the Member States of customs duties on imports and exports and charges having equivalent effect (*Van Gend & Loos* and *Dubois & Fils*[725]), Article 31(1) of the EC Treaty, regarding state monopolies (*Hansen*[726]), and Article 90 of the EC treaty, disallowing the imposition of discriminatory taxes on imported goods

716. Case 127/73, *Belgische Radio en Televisie v. SV SABAM and NV Fonior* [1974] ECR 51.
717. D.A. Wyatt & A. Dashwood (n. 46), 152.
718. Case 58/80, *Dansk Supermarked A/S v. A/S Imerco* [1981] ECR 181 para. 17.
719. Cases 177 and 178/82, *Van de Haar* [1984] ECR 1787 paras 11–12.
720. Case 311/85, *Vlaamse Reisbureaus* [1987] ECR 3801 para. 30.
721. Case 65/86, *Bayer AG and Maschinenfabrik Hennecke GmbH v. Heinz Süllhöfer* [1988] ECR 5249 para. 11.
722. Case C-159/00, *Sapod Audic* [2002] ECR I-5031 para. 74.
723. P. Oliver & W.-H. Roth, 'The Internal Market and the Four Freedoms', *CM L Rev.* (2004): 407, 422. *Dansk Supermarked* is not considered anymore to be good law, since its findings were never confirmed by subsequent rulings. J. Baquero Cruz (n. 861), 608.
724. P. Oliver & W.-H. Roth (n. 723), 422. The fundamental freedoms and the competition rules constitute the basis of an efficient functioning of the internal market. Both sets of rules aim at the protection of the internal market, yet their respective emphasis is different. D. Vaughan, 'Free Movement and Competition Pillars of the Single Market', *CLI* 4 (2003): 8. For the notion of appreciable distortion of competition (Art. 81 EC Treaty) see: Case 56/65, *Maschinenbau Ulm* [1966] ECR 235 and Case 5/69, *Volk* [1969] ECR 295.
725. Case C-16/94, *Édouard Dubois & Fils SA and Général Cargo Services SA v. Garonor Exploitation SA* [1995] ECR I-2421.
726. Case 91/78, *Hansen* [1979] ECR 935.

(*Lütticke*[727]).[728] Other Treaty articles that have only vertical direct effect are Article 23 of the EC Treaty, requiring the establishment of a customs union (*Denkavit*[729]), Article 31(2), prohibiting the introduction of new discriminatory measures in relation to state monopolies (*Costa*[730]), and Article 88(3), prohibiting state aids not notified to the Commission (*Capolongo* and *Lorenz*[731]).[732]

Commission v. France concerned the destructive actions of French farmers against Spanish agricultural products imported into France. In this case, the French government had infringed upon Article 28 of the EC Treaty in combination with Article 10 of the EC Treaty by failing to adopt all necessary and proportionate measures to prevent the free movement of goods from being obstructed by actions of private individuals.[733] Trade barriers do not necessarily derive only from State measures, but also include situations in which a Member State fails to adopt the rules or to take the measures that aim to abolish trade barriers not caused by the state.[734] Moreover, the ECJ held that the fact that a Member State abstains from taking action or, as the case may be, fails to adopt adequate measures to prevent obstacles to the free movement of goods that are created, in particular, by actions of private individuals on its territory aimed at products originating in other Member States is just as likely to obstruct intra-Community trade as is a positive act.[735] This positive obligation (preventing individuals from obstructing the free movement of goods) of a Member State must always be read in accordance with Article 10 of the EC Treaty.[736] The argument that Article 28 of the EC Treaty imposes both a positive and a negative obligation on Member States was referred to implicitly in *de Peijper*, but the ECJ had not had the opportunity to specifically address this issue.[737]

Another case that involved the failure of a Member State to take measures against trade barriers imposed by individuals was *Schmidberger*.[738] Austria decided not to prohibit an environmental demonstration, which resulted in the temporary closure of a central motorway passing through Austria.[739] This restriction on the free movement of goods was found to be justified on the basis of

727. Case 57/65, *Lütticke GmbH v. Hauptzollamt Sarrelouis* [1966] ECR 205 English special edition.
728. A. Kaczorowska (n. 691), 305–306.
729. Case 251/78, *Denkavit* [1979] ECR 3369.
730. Case 6/64, *Costa* [1964] ECR 585.
731. Case 77/72, *Capolongo* [1973] ECR 611, Case 120/73, *Lorenz* [1973] ECR 1471.
732. A. Kaczorowska (n. 691), 306.
733. Case C-265/95 *Commission v. French Republic*. [1997] ECR I-6959 para. 66. J. Snell, *Goods and Services in EC Law* (Oxford: Oxford University Press, 2002), 153.
734. Case C-265/95, *Commission v. French Republic*. [1997] ECR I-6959 para. 30.
735. Case C-265/95, *Commission v. French Republic*. [1997] ECR I-6959 para. 31.
736. Case C-265/95, *Commission v. French Republic*. [1997] ECR I-6959 para. 32. See also E.F. Hinton, 'Case Note, *Commission v. France*', *Col J Eur L* (1999): 477, 483.
737. Case 104/75, *de Peijper* [1976] ECR 613. J. Baquero Cruz (n. 861), 610.
738. Case C-112/00, *Eugen Schmidberger, Internationale Transporte und Planzüge v. Republik Österreich* [2003] ECR I-5659.
739. J. Shaw, J. Hunt & C. Wallace (n. 30), 131.

the overriding interest in respecting citizens' fundamental rights of freedom of expression and assembly.[740] Apart from the very important issue of the place of fundamental rights in the Community legal order, it is quite interesting that the ECJ acknowledged that individuals could frustrate intra-community trade and that the state is responsible for securing the free movement of goods by taking all necessary measures against such actions.

One of the fundamental cases in the area of horizontal effect that concerned a Treaty article specifically addressed to Member States was *Defrenne*.[741] *Defrenne* concerned Article 141 of the EC Treaty, which demanded that 'Each Member State shall ensure that the principle of equal pay for male and female workers for equal work or work of equal value is applied.' This Article appeared not to be sufficiently precise in accordance with the *Van Gend & Loos* conditions.[742] However, the ECJ declared the direct effect of the principle that men and women should receive equal pay, which is provided by Article 141 of the EC Treaty. More precisely, it was held that this principle could be relied on before the national courts, which must ensure the protection of the rights conferred on individuals, in particular, in the case of those forms of discrimination that have their origin directly in legislative provisions or collective labour agreements, as well as when men and women receive unequal pay for equal work that is carried out in the same establishment or service, whether private or public.[743] The horizontal direct effect of this provision could possibly result in amendments of independent agreements concluded privately or in the sphere of industrial relations, such as individual contracts and collective labour agreements. The ECJ does not consider national legislatures to be the exclusive recipients of this provision's mandate and explains that this Article must be interpreted as including the intervention of the domestic courts so as to establish its direct applicability.[744]

As far as the free movement of persons is concerned, there was a very interesting series of cases concerning the collective regulation of professional activities, mostly in sports, by sports federations or other non-state regulatory bodies. In *Walrave and Koch*,[745] two professional pacesetters for motorcyclists claimed

740. *Ibid.*

741. Case 43/75, *Gabrielle Defrenne v. Société anonyme belge de navigation aérienne Sabena.* [1976] ECR 455. While *Van Gend & Loos* was about a negative obligation, this case was about a positive obligation imposed on Member States. F.G. Jacobs, 'The Evolution of the European Legal Order', *CM L Rev.* (2004): 303, 307.

742. P. Craig & G. De Burca (n. 12), 277. The contribution of *Defrenne* to the liberalization of the direct effect of Treaty articles as endorsed by *Van Gend & Loos* is significant. Treaty articles that were less clear and unconditional could also have direct effect. D. Chalmers & A. Tomkins (n. 260), 369.

743. Case 43/75, *Gabrielle Defrenne v. Société anonyme belge de navigation aérienne Sabena.* [1976] ECR 455. para. 40.

744. Case 43/75, *Gabrielle Defrenne v. Société anonyme belge de navigation aérienne Sabena.* [1976] ECR 455. para. 37–38.

745. Case 36/74, *B.N.O Walrave and L.J.N. Koch v. Association Union cycliste internationale, Koninklijke Nederlandsche Wielren Unie et Federación Española Ciclismo.* [1974] ECR 1405 para. 16–17.

that a specific rule of the relevant sporting association requiring that a pacesetter must be of the same nationality as the stayer breaches the EC Treaty's prohibition of discrimination on grounds of nationality. It was stated that Articles 12, 39, and 49 of the EC Treaty have in common the prohibition, in their respective spheres of application, of any discrimination on grounds of nationality. The ECJ upheld that the prohibition of such discrimination does not only apply to the action of state bodies but includes rules seeking to regulate, in a collective manner, gainful employment and the provision of services. These private bodies act in a quasi-legislative role when they regulate collectively some professional activities. In a subsequent case, *Dona,*[746] the ECJ stated that Articles 39 and 49[747] enjoy horizontal effect and the domestic courts must ensure that the rules of sporting associations are not discriminatory on grounds of nationality.

In *Bosman,*[748] the ECJ confirmed its previous approach in *Walrave,* regarding horizontality, and stated that Article 39 of the EC Treaty not only applies to the actions of public authorities but also extends to the rules of any other nature aimed at regulating gainful employment and the provision of services in a collective manner. The underpinning grounds, that the abolition, as between Member States, of obstacles to freedom of movement for persons and to freedom to provide services would be compromised if the abolition of state barriers could be neutralized by obstacles resulting from the exercise of their legal autonomy by associations or organizations not governed by public law, was also repeated in *Bosman*. Exactly the same findings were affirmed once more in *Deliège*[749] and *Lehtonen.*[750] It seems that this rationale was crystallized in the case law: if rules of private bodies regulating business activities in a collective manner compromise fundamental objectives of the internal market and neutralize the abolition of public obstacles to trade, then they fall within the scope of the fundamental freedoms.[751] A further

---

746. Case 13/76, *Gaetano Donà v. Mario Mantero*. [1976] ECR 1333. E. Stein, 'Lawyers, Judges and the Making of a Transnational Constitution', *Am J Int'l L* (1981): 1, 17–20.

747. The ECJ's decision, in *Van Ameyde*, started from the assumption that private parties can infringe upon Art. 49 EC Treaty. It was stated that in principle it was irrelevant whether the barrier came from measures of public authority or from rules produced by the national insurers' bureaux. However, in this case, the ECJ decided that there was no restriction to Art. 49 EC Treaty as there was no discrimination. J. Snell, 'Private Parties and the Free Movement of Goods and Services', in *Services and Free Movement in EU Law*, ed. M. Andenas & W.-H. Roth (Oxford: Oxford University Press, 2002), 224. Case 90/76, *Van Ameyde v. S.r.l. Ufficio centrale italiano di assistenza assicurativa automobilisti in circolazione internazionale (UCI)* ECR 1091 paras 28–30.

748. Case C-415/93, *Union royale belge des sociétés de football association ASBL v. Jean-Marc Bosman, Royal club liégeois SA v. Jean-Marc Bosman and others, and Union des associations Européennes de football (UEFA) v. Jean-Marc Bosman*. [1995] ECR I-4921 paras 82–83.

749. C-51/96 and C-191/97, *Deliège v. Ligue francophone de judo et disciplines associées ASBL, Ligue belge de judo ASBL, Union Européenne de judo (C-51/96) and François Pacquée (C-191/97)* [2000] ECR I-2549 para. 47.

750. Case C-176/96, *Lehtonen and Castors Canada Dry Namur-Braine ASBL v. Fédération royale belge des sociétés de basket-ball ASBL (FRBSB)* [2000] ECR I-2681 para. 35.

751. J. Baquero Cruz (n. 715), 607. See interesting research on the available remedies for compensation in case of 'horizontal liability' of private bodies regulating collectively economic

contribution of *Bosman* was that non-discriminatory measures, and not only discriminatory measures, of private regulatory bodies could constitute restrictions to free movement.[752]

In *Haug-Adrion*,[753] the ECJ scrutinized the refusal to grant a bonus to insured persons in Germany who had vehicles registered under customs plates and that mainly concerned nationals of Member States other than Germany or persons not residing in Germany. The application of these tariff conditions in (private) insurance contracts was found not to constitute an infringement of Articles 39, 49, and 54 of the EC Treaty because they were not discriminatory. Although the ECJ did not refer at all to rules regulating the market in a collective manner, it was argued that the standardized contract terms in the insurance plan could be considered comparable to collective agreements.[754]

The next important case that concerned private rules regulating collectively professional activities was *Wouters*.[755] The ECJ stipulated that Articles 43 and 49 of the EC Treaty also apply to rules that are not public in nature but that are designed to regulate, collectively, self-employment and the provision of services. It also stated that the abolition, as between Member States, of obstacles to freedom of movement for persons would be compromised if the abolition of state barriers could be neutralized by obstacles resulting from the exercise of their legal autonomy by associations or organizations not governed by public law.[756]

The horizontal effect of the Treaty Articles on free movement of persons was extended in *Angonese*.[757] Article 39 of the EC Treaty is binding on private parties (e.g., employers) with regard to employment contracts and other conditions.[758] It was acknowledged that the principle of equality provided by Article 39 covers the actions of private persons, and not only in situations concerning collective regulation of the relevant sphere of employment or services.[759] The ECJ examined Article 39 by reference to *Defrenne*. It held that the fact that certain provisions of the Treaty are formally addressed to the Member States does not prevent rights from being conferred at the same time on any individual who has an interest in compliance with the obligations thus laid down and that, in relation to a provision of the Treaty that was mandatory in nature, the prohibition of discrimination applied equally to all agreements intended to regulate paid labour collectively,

---

activities (these private bodies could breach EC law and could cause damage to individuals): N. Reich, 'Horizontal Liability in EC Law: Hybridization of Remedies for Compensation in Case of Braches of EC Rights', *CM L Rev.* (2007): 705.

752. S. Van Den Bogaert, 'Horizontality: The Court Attacks?', in *The Law of the Single European Market*, ed. C. Barnard & J. Scott (Oxford: Hart, 2002), 127.
753. Case 251/83, *Haug-Adrion v. Frankfurter Versicherungs-AG* [1984] ECR 4277 paras 14–18.
754. S. Van Den Bogaert (n. 751), 126.
755. Case C-309/99, *J. C. J. Wouters* [2002] ECR I-1577.
756. Case C-309/99, *J. C. J. Wouters* [2002] ECR I-1577 para. 120.
757. Case C-281/98, *Roman Angonese v. Cassa di Risparmio di Bolzano SpA* [2000] ECR I-4139.
758. P. Oliver & W.-H. Roth (n. 723), 423.
759. D.A. Wyatt & A. Dashwood (n. 46), 153.

as well as to contracts between individuals.[760] Article 39[761] is a specific application of the general prohibition of nationality discrimination of Article 12[762] of the EC Treaty and, together with Article 141 of the EC Treaty, seeks to ensure that there is no discrimination in the labour market.[763] It is quite odd that the ECJ based its reasoning on *Walrave and Koch* and on *Bosman,* because the case did not concern rules aimed at regulating gainful employment in a collective manner.[764]

Nevertheless, the ECJ restricted the horizontal effect of Article 39 of the EC Treaty to discriminatory situations on the basis of nationality and did not include non-discriminatory barriers (*Bosman*). If horizontality were extended into non-discriminatory situations, the contractual freedom of private parties would be unduly restricted.[765] It should be kept in mind that *Bosman* and *Lehtonen* dealt with non-discriminatory rules of private regulatory bodies that constituted non-discriminatory restrictions on the free movement of workers. This could potentially result in differentiated treatment of private persons, undertakings, associations, and organizations. If regulatory measures of a collective character coming from private regulatory bodies were non-discriminatory, they would be prohibited. Terms and conditions of agreements, contracts, and other regulatory actions of individuals would be prohibited only as long as they were discriminatory on grounds of nationality.[766]

Another development that took place in *Angonese* was that the terms and conditions of a contract[767] could constitute barriers to the free movement of workers. The prohibition of discrimination applied equally to all agreements intended to regulate paid labour collectively, as well as to contracts between individuals.

760. Case 43/75, *Gabrielle Defrenne v. Société anonyme belge de navigation aérienne Sabena.* [1976] ECR 455 paras 31, 39; Case C-281/98, *Roman Angonese v. Cassa di Risparmio di Bolzano SpA* [2000] ECR I-4139. para. 34.
761. Case 167/73, *Commission v. France.* [1974] ECR 359 paras 43–48.
762. In *Ferlini*, the ECJ moved a little bit forward by declaring that Art. 12 EC Treaty binds private organizations exercising 'a certain power' over individuals. It stated that Art. 12 EC Treaty applies in situations where a private group or organization exercises a certain power over individuals and is in a position to impose on them conditions which adversely affect the exercise of the fundamental freedoms guaranteed under the Treaty (see, to that effect, Case 36/74, *Walrave* [1974] ECR 1405; Case 43/75, *Defrenne* [1976] ECR 455; and Case C-415/93, *Bosman* [1995] ECR I-4921). Case C-411/98, *Ferlini v. Centre hospitalier de Luxembourg* [2000] ECR I-8081 para. 50. P. Oliver & W.-H. Roth (n. 723), 422.
763. Case C-281/98, *Roman Angonese v. Cassa di Risparmio di Bolzano SpA* [2000] ECR I-4139. para. 35.
764. A. Dashwood, 'Viking and Laval: Issues of Horizontal Direct Effect', *CYELS* (2008) (Oxford: Hart, 2008), 530.
765. D.A. Wyatt & A. Dashwood (n. 46), 709.
766. P. Oliver & W.-H. Roth (n. 723), 423, 426.
767. This expansion of the horizontal direct effect also grants the extension of the scope of party autonomy and private initiative at cross-border level. The autonomy of forming contracts and shaping their contents are now protected against discrimination. P.M. Muller-Graff, 'Basic Freedoms-Extending Party Autonomy across Borders', in *Party Autonomy and the Role of Information in the Internal Market*, ed. S. Grundmann, W. Kerber & S. Weatherill (Berlin: de Gruyter, 2001), 137.

A condition in a contract that is not of a collective nature could also inhibit free movement of workers; this was a significant evolution. Nevertheless, the significance of collective agreements in the area of industrial relations should not be underestimated. A collective agreement could also have a more general application and be binding, or produce effects, on third parties that, for example, are not members of the participating trade unions. AG Fennelly argued that, when a collective agreement is attended by such consequences, whether by operation of law or through its approval by a public body, it should be deemed to be a law, regulation, or administrative provision capable of regulating a professional activity. The fact that the state may not control the exact content of such agreements, in the absence of an overriding legislative measure, does not reduce their public and normative character.[768]

Another case that was based on the conclusions of *Angonese* is *Raccannelli.*[769] It was confirmed that Article 39 of the EC Treaty is a specific application of Article 12 of the EC Treaty and applies equally to all agreements intended to regulate paid labour collectively, as well as to contracts between individuals. Additionally, a private-law association, such as the research institute in question, must observe the principle of non-discrimination on grounds of nationality in relation to workers within the meaning of Article 39 of the EC Treaty.[770] As in *Angonese* and *Ferlini*, this private body enjoys a certain degree of dominance in a horizontal relation, exercises a certain power over individuals, and is capable of imposing certain conditions affecting their right to exercise the fundamental freedoms.[771] If a private body concentrates these characteristics, it could definitely breach Article 39.

As far as the justification of these restrictions is concerned, individuals could invoke the exceptions of Article 39(3) of the EC Treaty and the judicially developed mandatory requirements in the general interest. The ECJ had clearly stated, in *Bosman*, that there is nothing to preclude individuals from relying on justifications on grounds of public policy, public security, or public health and that neither the scope nor the content of those grounds of justification is in any way affected by the public or private nature of the rules in question.[772] This might be possible when a private body regulates conditions of employment or of a professional activity and conducts a quasi-public function.[773] However, the judicially developed mandatory requirements are public in their nature and might not fit well into every

768. Opinion of Mr Advocate General Fennelly, Case C-234/97, *Teresa Fernández de Bobadilla v. Museo Nacional del Prado.* [1999] ECR I-4773 paras 23–24.
769. Case C-94/07, *Andrea Raccanelli v. Max-Planck-Gesellschaft zur Förderung der Wissenschaften eV,* nry.
770. Case C-94/07, *Andrea Raccanelli v. Max-Planck-Gesellschaft zur Förderung der Wissenschaften eV,* nry. paras 45, 48.
771. S. Prechal & S. De Vries, 'Seamless Web of Judicial Protection in the Internal Market?', *E L Rev* (2009): 5, 15–16.
772. Case C-415/93, *Bosman* [1995] ECR I-4921 paras 85–86.
773. J. Snell (n. 747), 231.

horizontal relationship. For example, it would be difficult to imagine how a private party could serve the cohesion of a national tax system. The mandatory requirements should definitely be adjusted to the nature and the role of individuals. For example, it could be assumed that a private party could possibly serve the interests of consumer protection.[774] The same considerations apply to the exceptions of Articles 30 and 46 of the EC Treaty. The allegation of an individual that it serves these objectives is certainly not convincing. Individuals have neither the power nor the duty to protect the public interest because they are deemed to act in their self-interest.[775]

Nevertheless, the ECJ's approach toward certain Treaty articles does not mean that every Treaty article has both horizontal and vertical direct effect. The specific objective and the broader context of the Treaty article play a decisive role in this conferral of horizontal and vertical direct effect. With regard to Treaty articles capable of direct effect, Member States have a legal obligation to give direct effect to provisions that are suitable for direct effect. The assessment of whether a specific Treaty article is suitable is an EC law matter that must be decided by the ECJ.[776] If it is reasonably feasible for a national court to apply a certain Treaty article to a specific case, then this Treaty article is capable of direct effect.[777] A Treaty article that has met the conditions of direct effect is capable of judicial adjudication, but the court has to decide whether it is applicable to the pending case. The application of the provision to a certain relationship is crucial. Legal effects are not derived from inherent qualities of EU law but are the result of the interpretation and application of a rule to a concrete situation.[778] Additionally, AG Van Gerven suggested that the ECJ should examine whether the Treaty articles are sufficiently operational in themselves to be applied by a national court in a specific situation.[779]

The different approaches of the ECJ's case law to the horizontal effect of the free movement of goods and to the horizontal effect of the free movement of persons reflects the difference in balancing these fields. Whereas the free movement of persons covers private individual restrictions, the free movement of goods

774. J. Snell (n. 747), 232.

775. R. Lane, 'The Internal Market and the Individual', in *Regulating the Internal Market*, ed. N.N. Shuibhne (Cheltenham: Elgar, 2006), 273.

776. T.C, Hartley, *European Union Law in a Global Context* (Cambridge: Cambridge University Press, 2004), 156.

777. For the stance of some Member States' courts towards direct effect and supremacy, see: *Ibid.*, 156, 157–165.

778. P. Eleftheriadis, 'The Direct Effect of Community Law: Conceptual Issues', *YEL* (1996): 205, 212. J. Baquero Cruz, *Between Competition and Free Movement, The Economic Constitutional Law of the European Community* (Oxford-Portland: Hart, 2002), 107.

779. Opinion of Mr Advocate General Van Gerven, Case C-128/92, *H. J. Banks & Co. Ltd v. British Coal Corporation* [1994] ECR I-1209. J. Lever, 'Mutual Permeation of Community and National Tort Rules', in *Principles of Proper Conduct for Supranational, State and Private Actors in the European Union: Towards Ius Commune*, ed. J. Wouters, J. Stuyck & T. Kruger (Groningen: Intersentia, 2001), 106–107.

does not (*Dansk Supermarked* was an exception).[780] This enhanced protection granted to persons is justified not only by the wording of Article 39 of the EC Treaty, but also, by the importance of employment and persons as societal values bearing more weight in Member States' legislation. The relationship between an employer and an employee is not considered to be a fully private matter, as is the relationship between a buyer and seller of goods, and in many Member States, employment is regulated by public law rules.[781] This special interest of Member States in the relationship between an employer and an employee is based on the potential imbalance of power.[782]

The spillover of horizontality from workers to services is founded on their common connection with persons.[783] This expansion has also taken place in the area of freedom of establishment. The analogy between Articles 39 and 141 of the EC Treaty[784] can be transposed to Article 43 of the EC Treaty, as Article 43 is also mandatory in nature, provides a fundamental freedom, and applies the general prohibition of discrimination contained in Article 12 of the EC Treaty. AG Mayras suggested, in *van Binsbergen*, that the principle of equal treatment on grounds of nationality in Article 12 is the basis of the Treaty articles on workers, establishment, and services alike.[785] Article 43 is open to adopt the analogy between Articles 39 and 141 because the social objectives of Article 141 are also met in the freedom of establishment (yet, in the area of self-employed activities).[786]

780. G. Davies, *Nationality Discrimination in the European Internal Market* (The Hague: Kluwer Law International, 2003), 168.
781. *Ibid.*
782. *Ibid.*
783. *Ibid.*
784. See *Angonese*.
785. S. Van Den Bogaert (n. 752), 148–149. Opinion of Mr Advocate General Mayras, Case 33/74, *Van Binsbergen v. Bestuur van de Bedrijfsvereniging voor de Metaalnijverheid* [1974] ECR 1299.
786. S. Van Den Bogaert (n. 752) 149.

Chapter 13
Horizontality after *Viking* and *Mangold*

13.1 HORIZONTALITY AFTER *VIKING*

The ECJ's ruling in *Viking*[787] confirmed the ECJ's previous case law on the horizontal effect of Articles 39, 43, and 49 of the EC Treaty. Its major contribution is that the horizontal effect of Articles 43 and 49 was expanded and covers collective action of trade unions (e.g., strikes, boycotts, etc.).[788] With regard to the factual background of *Viking*, Viking was a Finish maritime firm that owned a ferry, the *Rosella*, which operated between Helsinki and Tallin. The *Rosella* sailed under the Finish flag (was registered in Finland), and most of its employees were Finnish.[789] The Finnish firm planned to re-register the *Rosella* in Estonia because of economic considerations. If its vessel were registered in Estonia, it could employ workers at much lower wages. The International Transport Workers' Federation (ITF) has a long-standing and well-known campaign against the use of flags of convenience.[790] The ITF and the Finnish Seamen's Union, which is affiliated with the ITF, took industrial action against Viking with a view to prevent the imminent re-flagging.

The ECJ decided that Article 43 of the EC Treaty is to be interpreted as meaning that, in principle, collective action initiated by a trade union or a group

---

787. Case C-438/05, *International Transport Workers' Federation and Finnish Seamen's Union v. Viking Line ABP and OÜ Viking Line Eesti* [2007] ECR I-10779.
788. D.A. Wyatt, 'Horizontal Effect of Fundamental Freedoms and the Right to Equality after *Viking* and *Mangold*, and the Implications for Community Competence', *CYELP* (2008): 1.
789. A.C.L. Davies, 'The Right to Strike versus Freedom of Establishment in EC Law: The Battle Commences', *ILJ* (2006): 75.
790. A flag of convenience means the use of the flag of one country (typically with lower labour standards) by a beneficial owner situated in another country. A.C.L. Davies (n. 789), 75.

of trade unions against a private undertaking so as to induce that undertaking to enter into a collective agreement, the terms of which are liable to deter it from exercising its freedom of establishment, is not excluded from the scope of that article.[791] Moreover, Article 43 is capable of conferring rights on a private undertaking that may be relied on against a trade union or an association of trade unions.[792] As a matter of fact, Article 43 is to be interpreted to the effect that collective action, such as that at issue in the main proceedings, which seeks to induce a private undertaking whose registered office is in a given Member State to enter into a collective work agreement with a trade union established in that State and to apply the terms set out in that agreement to the employees of a subsidiary of that undertaking established in another Member State, constitutes a restriction within the meaning of that Article.[793] The collective action in question made less attractive, or even pointless, as the national court had pointed out, Viking's exercise of its right to freedom of establishment, inasmuch as such action would prevent both Viking and its subsidiary from enjoying the same treatment in the host Member State as other economic operators established in that State.[794] That restriction may, in principle, have been justified by an overriding reason of public interest, such as the protection of workers, provided that it were established that the restriction was suitable for ensuring the attainment of the legitimate objective pursued and did not go beyond what was necessary to achieve that objective.[795]

The ECJ held that the collective action in question, which tried to induce an undertaking to accept the demands of trade unions and which was liable to deter this undertaking from exercising its freedom of establishment, fell within the scope of freedom of establishment.[796] This conclusion was based on the fact that Articles 39, 43, and 49 of the EC Treaty do not apply only to the regulations of public bodies but include also rules of any other nature aimed at regulating in a collective manner gainful employment, self-employment, and the provision of services. The ECJ referred to its previous case law on the regulation of professional activities by private bodies in a collective manner.[797] It was stated that the organization of collective action by trade unions must be regarded as being covered by the legal autonomy that those organizations, which are not public law entities,

791. Case C-438/05, *Viking* [2007] ECR I-10779 para. 55.
792. Case C-438/05, *Viking* [2007] ECR I-10779 para. 66.
793. Case C-438/05, *Viking* [2007] ECR I-10779 para. 90. See also: N. Reich, 'Free Movement v. Social Rights in an Enlarged Union: The *Laval* and *Viking* Cases before the ECJ', *Ger L J* (2008): 125, 136, S. Sciara, 'Viking and Laval: Collective Labour Rights and Market Freedoms in the Enlarged EU' (2008) *CYELS* (Oxford: Hart, 2008), 563.
794. Case C-438/05, *Viking* [2007] ECR I-10779 para. 72.
795. Case C-438/05, *Viking* [2007] ECR I-10779 para. 90.
796. Case C-438/05, *Viking* [2007] ECR I-10779 para. 55. The Commission in its submission argues that Art. 43 EC Treaty does not have horizontal direct effect, so as to grant rights on a private undertaking that may be invoked against a trade union. B. Bercusson, 'The Trade Union Movement and the European Union: Judgement Day', *ELJ* (2007): 279, 288.
797. Case C-438/05, *Viking* para. 33, Case 36/74, *Walrave and Koch* para. 17, Case 13/76, *Donà* para. 17, *Bosman* para. 82; Joined Cases C-51/96 and C-191/97, *Deliège* para. 47, Case C-281/98, *Angonese* para. 31, and Case C-309/99, *Wouters* para. 120.

enjoy pursuant to the trade union rights accorded to them, *inter alia*, by national law.[798] The collective action taken by the trade unions against Viking could be characterized as integral to a process of collective regulation of an economic activity.[799] Trade unions could participate in the regulation of the labour market by way of collective agreements. Their negotiating position would be strengthened by the possibility of collective action.[800] The ECJ found that the regulatory role of trade unions is broadly analogous to that of private bodies regulating professional activities in a collective way, because the collective action taken by the trade unions could inhibit establishment or the provision of services to another Member State.[801] Nevertheless, the ECJ did not comment on the fact that this case concerned a phase before the introduction of those collective rules; trade unions were taking industrial action against Viking to convince it to accept a certain collective agreement.[802]

Additionally, the argument that the same subject matters are often regulated by rules of different natures in the various Member States was reiterated. For example, working conditions in the various Member States are regulated either by provisions laid down by law or regulation or by collective agreements and other acts concluded or adopted by private persons. If these regulations concluded or adopted by private persons fell outside the scope of the freedom of establishment, it would probably result in unequal situations.[803] The analogy with collective action is easily drawn. If collective action did not fall within the scope of the fundamental freedoms, the power to invoke fundamental freedoms would differ from one Member State to another, depending on the regulatory choices and the intensity of national laws. Member States could evade the application of the fundamental freedoms by adjusting their laws accordingly.[804]

Finally, the arguments of the ITF and of the Finnish Seamen's Union that the approach in *Albany*[805] must be applied by analogy to *Viking* because certain

798. Case C-438/05, *Viking* para. 35.
799. A. Dashwood (n. 764), 536.
800. A. Dashwood (n. 764), 539. See also: B. Bercusson, 'Trade Union Rights in EU Law', in *The Europeanisation of Law: The Legal Effects of European Integration*, ed. F. Snyder (Oxford: Hart, 2000), 202–205.
801. A. Dashwood (n. 764), 539.
802. S. Prechal & S. De Vries (n. 771), 14.
803. Case C-438/05, *Viking* para. 33, *Walrave and Koch* para. 19; *Bosman* para. 84, *Angonese* para. 33.
804. T. Blanke, 'Three Steps of Reflections Regarding the Viking and Laval Case: Towards an Effective European Right to Strike', in *Social Responsibility in Labour Relations*, ed. F. Pennings et al. (AH Alpen aan den Rijn: Kluwer, 2008), 504.
805. In *Albany*, the ECJ stated that it is beyond question that certain restrictions of competition are inherent in collective agreements between organizations representing employers and workers. However, the social policy objectives pursued by such agreements would be seriously undermined if management and labour were subject to Art. 85(1) EC Treaty when seeking jointly to adopt measures to improve conditions of work and employment. It therefore follows from an interpretation of the provisions of the Treaty as a whole that is both effective and consistent that agreements concluded in the context of collective negotiations between management and labour in pursuit of such objectives must, by virtue of their nature and purpose, be regarded as

obstacles to freedom of establishment and freedom to provide services are inherent in collective action taken in the context of collective negotiations, was not endorsed by the ECJ.[806] This analogy was rejected because of the lack of the inherent effect of the collective action on the fundamental freedoms.[807] The exclusion of an analogy with *Albany* and the application of the fundamental freedoms mean that whenever there appears to be an intra-Community aspect to an industrial dispute, the collective action taken by the trade unions could be challenged before the courts. This is certainly an important change for established domestic systems of industrial relations.[808] Future litigation will show its impact on these industrial relations systems.

The horizontal direct effect of Article 43 of the EC Treaty was also examined. Article 43 was found to be capable of conferring rights on a private undertaking that may be relied on against a trade union or an association of trade unions. The first argument of the ECJ referred to the sources of possible trade barriers and could be characterized as a policy consideration.[809] A dichotomy between obstacles deriving from public law bodies or from private law bodies would weaken significantly the effective exercise of the fundamental freedoms. In accordance with the previous case law, it was decided that the abolition of obstacles to freedom of movement for persons and freedom to provide services would be compromised if the abolition of state barriers could be neutralized by barriers resulting from the exercise, by associations or organizations not governed by public law, of their legal autonomy.[810] This approach does not allow Member States to circumvent the application of the scope of Treaty articles by determining the private or public character of the regulatory body.

The next proposition was based on *Defrenne*.[811] Rights could still be conferred on individuals having an interest in compliance with the obligations thus laid down, even if these specific Treaty articles are addressed to the Member States. It was also stated that the prohibition on prejudicing a fundamental freedom laid down in a provision of the Treaty that is mandatory in nature applies, in particular, to all agreements intended to regulate paid labour collectively.[812] It was finally

---

falling outside the scope of Art. 85(1) EC Treaty. Case C-67/96, *Albany International* [1999] ECR I-05751 para. 59–60. See also: T. Novitz, 'Labour Rights as Human Rights: Implications for Employers' Free Movement in an Enlarged European Union', *CYELS* (2007): 377.

806. Case C-438/05, *Viking* paras 48–49. N. Reich, ' "Widening" vs. "Deepening" The European Union: Free Movement vs. Social Rights in the Laval Case before the ECJ', in *Reconciling the Deepening and Widening of the European Union*, ed. S. Blockmans & S. Prechal (The Hague: Asser, 2007), 33. B. Bercusson (n. 796), 282.
807. Case C-438/05, *Viking* paras 49–52.
808. T. Novitz, 'A Clash in EC Treaty Priorities', *CLI* 6 (2007): 13, 14.
809. D.A. Wyatt (n. 788), 5.
810. Case C-438/05, *Viking* para. 57. It was argued that applying horizontal direct effect of the fundamental freedoms to restrictions and not only to discriminatory behaviour on grounds of nationality constitutes a disproportionate interference with the exercise of the private autonomy of individuals. S. Prechal & S. De Vries (n. 771), 18.
811. Case 43/75, *Defrenne* paras 31, 39.
812. Case C-438/05, *Viking* para. 58.

concluded that these considerations must also apply to Article 43 of the EC Treaty, which lays down a fundamental freedom.[813] The ECJ also found that, in the case in question, the collective action taken by the two trade unions tried to induce Viking to conclude an agreement which was meant to regulate the work of Viking's employees collectively and that those two trade unions are organizations that are not public law entities but exercise the legal autonomy conferred on them, *inter alia*, by national law.[814] Nevertheless, the ECJ omitted to mention a very important aspect of *Defrenne*; the reference to 'Member States' in Article 141 of the EC Treaty encompasses the judicial as well as the legislative authorities of the Member States. AG Maduro noted that this aspect of *Defrenne* could support the horizontal effect of Treaty articles.[815]

An additional basis underpinning this conclusion on horizontality of freedom of establishment was the reference to the ECJ's previous case law on free movement of goods. According to *Commission v. France* and *Schmidberger*, the Member States were responsible for the trade barriers caused by individuals because they failed to take all the necessary measures to prevent the actions of these individuals. Restrictions could also derive from actions of individuals or groups of such individuals, rather than actions caused by the state.[816] The ECJ invoked its previous case law on free movement of goods[817] so as to strengthen the conclusion that Article 43 of the EC Treaty is capable of conferring rights on a private undertaking that may be relied on against a trade union or an association of trade unions. This reference to its previous case law was quite odd, because the factual background of these cases had to do with state inaction.[818]

AG Maduro pondered over this point and adopted a much broader view. He suggested that constitutional rights should be given binding force for the judiciary when a case is adjudicated between private parties. Thus, constitutional rights could enjoy normative force in horizontal relations. Moreover, it was stated that constitutional rules that are addressed to the state translate into legal rules that apply between private parties, illustrating that the government is the third party to every private suit and is so in the very form of the law and the judge who administers it.[819] AG Maduro also discussed the potential differences between indirect horizontal effect and direct horizontal effect, and he found that there were not any

813. Case C-438/05 *Viking* para. 59.
814. Case C-438/05, *Viking* para. 60.
815. Case C-438/05, Opinion of Mr Advocate General Poiares Maduro, *International Transport Workers' Federation and Finnish Seamen's Union v. Viking Line ABP and OÜ Viking Line Eesti* [2007] ECR 2007 I-10779 para. 40. D.A. Wyatt (n. 788), 6.
816. Case C-438/05, *Viking* para. 62, Case C-265/95, *Commission v. France* para. 30, and Case C-112/00, *Schmidberger* paras 57, 62. See also T. Blanke (n. 804), 501.
817. While according to *Commission v. France* and *Schmidberger*, the traders cannot exercise at all the relevant fundamental freedom, Viking can always run its ferry under the new flag with reduced profits. Viking continued to run its ferry for more than four years following protracted negotiations with the trade unions. N. Reich (n. 793), 154.
818. A. Dashwood (n. 764), 532.
819. Case C-438/05, Opinion *Viking* para. 39.

substantial differences. He contended that the fact that there were no differences explained why the ruling in *Defrenne* is considered as having recognized the 'direct horizontal effect' of Article 141 of the EC Treaty, even though the Court construed the horizontal effect of that provision as a duty on the national courts.[820] The suggestion that there is no difference between indirect horizontal effect and direct horizontal effect was founded on the alleged equivalence between granting a right by way of an action against public authorities for their inaction and giving the same right to be directly invoked against the individuals responsible for the interference.[821] This equivalence seems to indicate that a private action alleging an infringement of a fundamental freedom could be brought against individual protesters or the organizers of a strike.[822] It is very difficult to accept this suggestion. In general, this approach of AG Maduro constitutes a rather broad interpretation, which was not followed by the ECJ, yet the ECJ does cite *Defrenne*.[823] The ECJ had used its previous case law on free movement of goods to boost its reasoning in the area of freedom of establishment. However, broader approaches should be avoided, as the factual backgrounds in the free movement of goods cases and *Viking* are different. Any generalizations should be adopted carefully.

The ECJ also addressed the issue of the bodies producing the regulations. It did not accept that the horizontal direct effect applies only to quasi-public organizations or to associations exercising a regulatory task and having quasi-legislative powers.[824] It stated that there is no indication in thecase law that could validly support the view that it applies only to associations or to organizations exercising a regulatory task or having quasi-legislative powers.[825] Furthermore, it was held that, in exercising their autonomous power, pursuant to their trade union rights, to negotiate with employers or professional organizations the conditions of employment and pay of workers, trade unions participate in the drawing up of agreements seeking to regulate paid work collectively.[826] Therefore, it is clear that the intention of the ECJ was not to restrict horizontal effect to regulations coming from 'formal' private regulators, such as sports federations or professional supervisory bodies.[827]

---

820. Case C-438/05, Opinion *Viking* para. 40. N. Reich does not agree that indirect horizontal effect and direct horizontal effect present any similarities. N. Reich (n. 793), 153. See also: G. Orlandini, 'Right to Strike, Transnational Collective Action and European Law: Time to Move on?' (2007) The Jean Monnet Working Paper Series No. 8/07, 15–18.
821. A. Dashwood (n. 764), 532–533.
822. A. Dashwood (n. 764), 532–533. For an interesting perspective on damages claims raised against trade unions for breach of Arts 43 and 49 EC Treaty, see: K. Apps, 'Damages Claims against Trade Unions after Viking and Laval', *E L Rev.* (2009): 141.
823. D.A. Wyatt (n. 788), 7–8. The ECJ might have adopted deliberately such an ambiguous stance on this matter.
824. Case C-438/05, *Viking* para. 64. A. Dashwood (n. 764), 536.
825. *Ibid.*, para. 65.
826. *Ibid.*
827. D.A. Wyatt (n. 788), 8. Private law making constitutes a central and expanding feature of EU law. Some types of norms are introduced by private parties. This results in a 'privatization' of the legislative process. The Community institutions play indirect roles in this private law

Pure private bodies could also breach the fundamental freedoms if they substitute the state as a regulator in the relevant parts of the market. Even if the public element is missing completely from a regulatory body, it could still be covered by the horizontal effect of Treaty articles. If private parties were treated differently from the state, this would create an anomaly in the market and would allow the possibility of evasion of the application of the fundamental freedoms; Member States could simply delegate their legislative powers to private bodies or organizations. Other market participants who are not formally regulators could also interfere and inhibit the effective exercise of fundamental freedoms (e.g., the protesters in *Commission v. France*).

It is relevant to mention here that AG Maduro discussed the private action that falls within the scope of fundamental freedoms: the horizontal effect would follow logically from the Treaty when it would be necessary to enable market participants throughout the Community to have equal opportunities to gain access to any part of the common market.[828] He argued that the rules on freedom of movement cannot always be brought into play in proceedings against a private individual. He analysed the inherent characteristics of state actions; these characteristics add more potential to the state to impede market integration than do individuals.[829] The weakness of individuals to regulate market access in comparison with the state was further discussed by AG Maduro. In his opinion, it was stated that, in contrast, in many circumstances, private actors simply do not wield enough influence to successfully prevent others from enjoying their rights to freedom of movement.[830] He gave an example to clarify his view: the case of an individual shopkeeper who refuses to purchase goods from other Member States would not be liable to obstruct the functioning of the common market.[831] This individual shopkeeper would not possess sufficient power to influence the market access of foreign suppliers. Alternative marketing channels would always be available to foreign suppliers, and the competitive behaviour of other shopkeepers would ‘punish’ this shopkeeper. In this example, this kind of action does not fall within the horizontal effect of the Treaty articles. Hence, AG Maduro asserted that the rules on freedom of movement apply directly to any private action that is capable of effectively restricting others from exercising their right to freedom of movement.[832] Nevertheless, he was not absolutely sure of how one should determine whether or not that is the

making (review, mandate, monitoring, organization, recognition, reference in legal statutes, legal benefits) to make this private legislative process more effective and beneficial. D. Chalmers, ‘Private Power and Public Authority in European Union Law’ *CYELS* (Oxford: Hart, 2006), 59–60.

828. Case C-438/05, Opinion *Viking* para. 35.
829. Case C-438/05, Opinion *Viking* para. 41.
830. Case C-438/05, Opinion *Viking* para. 42.
831. Case C-438/05, Opinion *Viking* para. 42.
832. Case C-438/05, Opinion *Viking* para. 43. C. Barnard, ‘Viking and Laval: An Introduction’, (2008) *CYELS* (Oxford: Hart, 2008), 470–471. A Dashwood criticizes the ambiguousness of this ‘action’/‘conduct’ restricting the exercise of fundamental freedoms through an obstacle that cannot be reasonably circumvented. A. Dashwood (n. 764), 534.

situation. He admitted that the ECJ had proceeded very carefully, on a case-by-case basis, in recognition of the horizontal direct effect of the fundamental freedoms.[833] Finally, he concluded that the provisions on freedom of movement apply to a private action that, by virtue of its general effect on the holders of rights to freedom of movement, is capable of restricting them from exercising those rights by raising an obstacle that they cannot reasonably circumvent.

The opinion of AG Maduro urges us to contemplate the characteristics of a 'situation' in which actions of an individual restrict other individuals from exercising their right to freedom of movement. If the basic elements of this 'situation' would be tracked down, the case-by-case recognition of the horizontal effect of Treaty articles by the ECJ would be better understood. The notion of normal market behaviour is crucial in understanding the basic elements of this 'situation'. A first remark is that the EC fundamental freedoms ensure the right of market operators to pursue cross-border economic and business activities and to compete with other market operators.[834] Therefore, normal market behaviour of an individual market operator that is intended to improve the market position or the economic benefits of this market operator should not in principle constitute a restriction on the fundamental freedom of another market operator.[835]

The previous case law shows clearly that both state and private regulation of the market fall within the scope of the fundamental freedoms. This is justified by the fact that both categories of regulation could control market access and could potentially result in trade barriers. With regard to private regulatory action, discriminatory behaviour by market participants or behaviour that is not normal in market conditions (when the conduct involves an element of regulation of the market) would be covered by the horizontal effect of a fundamental freedom. This kind of behaviour restricts market access of other market participants or consumers and does not allow them to effectively exercise their fundamental freedoms.[836]

In these cases, a private party plays the role of the state and regulates the conditions of market access. It is easily understood that this regulatory power exercised by private parties could potentially restrict the market access of other market participants and consumers, and it could frustrate market integration.

833. Case C-438/05, Opinion *Viking* para. 43.
834. D.A. Wyatt (n. 788), 11.
835. *Ibid.*
836. D.A. Wyatt (n. 788), 12. A market access model results in closer scrutiny of national laws, including national employment laws, by the ECJ. In case of a conflict between national law and EC law, this market access test provides an additional solution; the ECJ had found in some cases that this market access model goes too far and that there is no substantial hindrance of market access (Case C-285/01, *Burbaud* [2003] ECR I-8219 and *Deliege*). M. Ronnmar, 'Introduction: EU Industrial Relations v. National Industrial Relations-Conflict, Interplay or Harmony?', in *EU Industrial Relations v. National Industrial Relations,* ed. M. Ronnmar (AH Alpen aan den Rijn: Kluwer, 2008), 30–31. C. Barnard, 'Employment Rights, Free Movement under the EC Treaty and the Services Directive', in *EU Industrial Relations v. National Industrial Relations*, ed. M. Ronnmar (AH Alpen aan den Rijn: Kluwer, 2008), 141–142, 145–146.

Individuals could abuse their power to regulate market access, and this would exclude or deter other market operators or consumers from exercising their fundamental freedoms.

However, certain restrictions on competitors are inherent in normal competitive behaviour by market operators. Discriminatory conduct or conduct that is inconsistent with normal market behaviour might be justified on commercial grounds.[837] Market behaviour, such as the behaviour of the trade unions in *Viking*, that seeks to preserve the market position of members, could fall within the scope of normal market behaviour.[838] If collective action seeks to develop or to impose additional conditions and not only to preserve the market position of their present members or seeks to protect their future members, this market behaviour might be equivalent to the role of the regulator and might constitute an infringement of the freedom of establishment.

A further consideration to this market access model that was declared by the ECJ is that private actors may often still do things that public authorities may not. Workers are not in the superior position of power, which is characteristic of state authorities.[839] The ECJ stated that the finding that certain private actors are subject to the rules on freedom of movement does not automatically mean the end of their private autonomy and does not necessarily mean that they must be held to exactly the same standards as state authorities. The Court may apply different levels of scrutiny, depending on the source and seriousness of the impediment to the exercise of the right to freedom of movement, and on the force and validity of competing claims of private autonomy.[840] Private autonomy should always be taken into account when actions of individuals are scrutinized as potential trade barriers. In accordance with the principle of subsidiarity, the national legislature and the domestic courts are responsible for determining the framework of private autonomy.[841] However, when adjudicating on the disputes thus brought before it, the national court is invited to apply its domestic law in a manner that is consistent with the Treaty rules on freedom of movement. If that is not possible, and domestic law conflicts with the rules on freedom of movement, then the latter will prevail.[842]

837. D.A. Wyatt (n. 788), 12.
838. *Ibid.*, 18. It is argued that while the Services Directive does not seek to regulate national employment laws, in cases falling outside the scope of the Services Directive, the fundamental freedoms apply. The interpretation of freedom of establishment in *Viking* shows that there is very little room for legitimate industrial action to interfere with the exercise of the four freedoms. M. Ronnmar (n. 836), 31. C. Barnard (n. 836), 168.
839. T. Blanke (n. 804), 504.
840. Case C-438/05, Opinion *Viking* para. 49. It was argued that the extension of the fundamental right to the demand side of the market blurs the difference between barriers to market access and the autonomy of the individual. Private parties may suffer limitations to their liberty, but exceptionally only and always in the framework of the EC Treaty. The ECJ had shown this approach in *Angonese*, in which it fettered the freedom of an individual (employer) only when it inhibits a worker from exercising his or her right to free movement. R. Lane (n. 775), 271–272.
841. T. Blanke (n. 804), 504.
842. Case C-438/05, Opinion *Viking* para. 53.

An additional consideration is related to the substance of the market behaviour. It was argued that the fundamental freedoms apply to private parties and to trade unions in particular when they exercise regulatory tasks that would otherwise be exercised by the state itself (e.g., setting a minimum wage).[843] However, when trade unions perform a function that the state cannot perform (e.g., collective bargaining over wages above the minimum laid down by law), this would not normally constitute a barrier to the fundamental freedoms.[844] With regard to the latter functions, it could be said that they amount to normal market behaviour and that they seek to ameliorate the position of the trade union members in the labour market.

The element of 'influence' that AG Maduro mentioned does not contribute to legal certainty in this field: 'Private actors simply do not wield enough *influence* successfully to prevent others from enjoying their rights to freedom of movement' (emphasis added).[845] It is not quite clear when a certain action of a private party was great or influential enough for free movement provisions to apply.[846] This suggestion could also have wider effects outside the area of collective action. For example, a distribution agreement between private parties that is lawful under EC competition law should also be examined under the fundamental freedoms to see whether this agreement is capable of effectively restricting others from exercising their freedom of movement.[847] This approach is definitely against the aims of EC competition law.

Another issue that was not touched by the ECJ in *Viking* was the position of individual employees who proceed to collective action.[848] If collective action is not supported by the trade unions and is organized by individual employees, will it still be covered by freedom of establishment? The ECJ's reference to *Commission v. France* and to *Schmidberger* seems to indicate that the actions of individuals not necessarily guided or coordinated by a union or an association fall within the scope of freedom of establishment and are capable of obstructing this fundamental freedom. The position of individual workers having recourse to autonomous collective action is connected to the position of shareholders in a company who decide to take protectionist defensive measures against an imminent takeover bid. This issue will be discussed in Chapter 14.

843. P. Syrpis & T. Novitz, 'Economic and Social Rights in Conflict: Political and Judicial Approaches to Their Reconciliation', *E L Rev.* (2008): 411. C. Barnard (n. 832) (2008) 472–473.
844. P. Syrpis & T. Novitz (n. 843), 411. C. Barnard (n. 832), 472–473.
845. Case C-438/05, Opinion *Viking* para. 42.
846. T. Novitz (n. 808), 15.
847. T. Novitz (n. 808), 15.
848. C. Barnard (n. 832), 472.

13.2 HORIZONTALITY AFTER *MANGOLD*

Additionally, the horizontal effect of the fundamental principle of equality as structured by *Mangold*[849] is very important. The ECJ, in *Mangold,*[850] held that the general principle of equality (the case was about discrimination on grounds of age) is capable of having horizontal effect. This conclusion could enhance the horizontal effect of the fundamental freedoms. More specifically, it was held that it is the responsibility of the national court, hearing a dispute involving the principle of non-discrimination with respect to age, which is a general principle of Community law, to provide, in a case within its jurisdiction, the legal protection that individuals derive from the rules of Community law and to ensure that those rules are fully effective, setting aside any provision of national law that may conflict with that law, even when the period prescribed for transposition of a directive based on that general principle, such as Directive 2000/78, establishing a general framework for equal treatment in employment and occupation, has not yet expired.[851]

The general principle of equality[852] encompasses Article 12 of the EC Treaty, which prohibits discrimination on grounds of nationality. Article 12 applies within the scope of application of this Treaty, and without prejudice to any special provisions contained therein.[853] These special provisions include the application of the

849. Case C-144/04, *Mangold v. Helm* [2005] ECR I-09981. In *Barber*, AG Van Gerven argued that a provision of international law (the prohibition of gender discrimination included in the relevant UN covenants) could possibly of its own accord apply in a horizontal relationship between private parties. Opinion of Mr Advocate General Van Gerven Case C-262/88, *Barber* [1990] ECR I-1889 para. 53.
850. Case C-144/04, *Mangold v. Helm* [2005] ECR I-09981. S. Prechal, 'Enforcement of EC Labour Law: Some Less Felicitous Consequences?', in *Social Responsibility in Labour Relations*, ed. F. Pennings et al. (AH Alpen aan den Rijn: Kluwer, 2008), 17.
851. Case C-144/04, *Mangold* para. 75–77. See also: C. Barnard, 'Social Policy Revisited in the Light of the Constitutional Debate', in *The Fundamentals of EU Law Revisited: Assessing the Impact of the Constitution Debate*, ed. C. Barnard (Oxford: Oxford University Press, 2007), 138.
852. In *Deutsche Post*, the ECJ recognized that equality was also a fundamental right. Joined Cases C-270/97 and C-271/97, *Deutsche Post* [2000] ECR I-929 para. 57. C. Barnard (n. 851), 138. Some old but very interesting papers on the position of equality in EU law are the following: G. de Burca, 'The Role of Equality in European Community Law', E. Szyszczak, 'Building a European Constitutional Order: Prospects for a General Non-discrimination Standard', S. O'Leary, 'The Principle of Equal Treatment on Grounds of Nationality in Art. 6 EC: A Lucrative Source of Rights for Member State Nationals', in *The Principle of Equal Treatment in EC Law*, ed. A. Dashwood & S. O'Leary (London: Sweet & Maxwell, 1997), 13, 35, 105.
853. Case C-309/89, *Codorniu* [1994] ECR I-1853 para. 26. D.A. Wyatt (n. 788), 12. In *Hayes v. Kronenberger Gmbh*, the principle of non-discrimination on grounds of nationality was confirmed once more. A rule of civil procedure of one Member State, such as one requiring nationals and legal persons of another Member State to provide security for costs when they wish to sue a resident of the former state or a company established there, falls within the scope of the Treaty within the meaning of Art. 12 EC Treaty and is subject to the general principle of non-discrimination laid down by that Article insofar as it has an effect, even though indirect, on trade in goods and services between Member States. Such an effect is liable to arise in

general principle of non-discrimination on grounds of nationality to specific internal market situations in other Treaty articles, for example, free movement of workers, freedom of establishment, and freedom to provide services. With regard to the relationship between this general prohibition and the more specific ones, the ECJ held that the general prohibition of discrimination on grounds of nationality applies independently only to a case for which the EC Treaty does not contain a specific prohibition of discrimination.[854] This means that Article 12 of the EC Treaty applies independently where the fundamental freedom in question does not cover the discriminatory behaviour on grounds of nationality. Hence, Article 12 supplements the scope of fundamental freedoms in certain situations not covered by them and contributes to a more complete and stronger protection against discrimination on grounds on nationality.[855] *Mangold* seems to imply that Article 12 of the EC Treaty could be applied horizontally because it embodies an aspect of the general principle of equality, which the ECJ in this case treated as having horizontal direct effect.[856]

Mangold was criticized by many Advocate Generals in their opinions.[857] This case was considered to be inconsistent with the legal framework of horizontality. The opinion of AG Sharpston in *Bartsch*[858] reveals the substantial extent of this criticism. She refers to the opinion of AG Geelhoed in Case C-13/05, *Chacon Navas*; herself in Case C-227/04 P, *Lindorfer*; AG Mazak in Case C-411/05,

---

particular where security for costs is required where proceedings are brought to recover payment for the supply of goods. Art. 12 EC Treaty must be interpreted as precluding a Member State from requiring security for costs to be furnished by a national of another Member State that has brought an action in one of its civil courts against one of its nationals where that requirement may not be imposed on its own nationals who have neither assets nor a residence in that country, in a situation where the action is connected with the exercise of fundamental freedoms guaranteed by Community law. Case C-323/95, *David Charles Hayes and Jeannette Karen Hayes v. Kronenberger GmbH.* [1997] ECR I-01711. J. Steiner, L. Woods & C. Twigg-Flesner (n. 21), 458.

854. Case 305/87, *Commission v. Greece* [1989] ECR 1461 para. 13. D.A. Wyatt (n. 788), 13.
855. D.A. Wyatt (n. 788), 13.
856. *Ibid.* S. Prechal & S. De Vries use a fundamental rights model. They think that the horizontal direct effect of Art. 12 EC Treaty as well as the horizontal direct effect of the more specific prohibitions of discrimination on grounds of nationality contained in the fundamental freedoms are based on this fundamental rights approach. However, this fundamental rights approach does not underpin the prohibition of restriction but applies only to discrimination on grounds of nationality. S. Prechal & S. De Vries (n. 771), 17–18.
857. Nevertheless, some authors welcome this ruling by analysing it in the light of the hierarchy of norms. They did not consider as something surprising that the general principles of EU law can have direct effect and can apply to a horizontal relationship. J. Jans, 'The Effect in National Legal Systems of the Prohibition of Discrimination on Grounds of Age as a General Principle of Community Law', *LIEI* (2007): 53, 59, 66, 62. X. Groussot & H.H. Lidgard, 'Are There General Principles of Community Law Affecting Private Law?', in *General Principles of EC Law in a Process of Development*, ed. U. Bernitz et al. (AH Alpen aan den Rijn: Kluwer, 2008) 173.
858. Opinion of Advocate General Sharpston, Case C-427/06, *Bartsch v. Bosch und Siemens Hausgeräte (BSH) Altersfürsorge GmbH* [2008] ECR I-07245 paras 33–41.

Palacios de la Villa; and AG Ruiz-Jarabo Colomer in Case C-267/06, *Maruko.*[859] AG Sharpston scrutinized the general theme of the criticism in *Mangold*. She stated that the Court (of its own volition, without good reason and against the wishes of the legislature) conferred horizontal direct effect on a directive before the end of its transitional period by making an innovative reference to a general principle of Community law. She added that the ruling is criticized for having produced a situation of considerable legal uncertainty.[860] However, AG Sharpston suggested that it is not wise to exclude at the outset the possibility that a general principle of EU law could have horizontal direct effect. This latter comment should not be overestimated. It is argued that this does not mean that the *Mangold* approach should be accepted and that the general principle of equality enjoys horizontal direct effect in every possible situation. It seems that a narrower reading of the case was needed: the general principle of equality and, in particular, the prohibition of discrimination on grounds of nationality of Article 12 of the EC Treaty should be granted horizontal direct effect only when it supplements and enhances the protective scope of fundamental freedoms.[861] This narrower interpretation would be more consistent with the purpose of market integration.

The proposition that Article 12 could apply to horizontal relationships is supported by *Walrave and Koch*. It was stipulated that the ECJ has recognized that the general principle of equal treatment, as regards nationality, can be applied horizontally when it is incorporated in a substantive Treaty article. Thus, in *Walrave and Koch,* the ECJ held that the prohibition of discrimination on grounds of nationality contained in what are now Articles 12, 39, and 49 of the EC Treaty apply not only to the action of public authorities, but also, to rules of private organizations that aim to regulate in a collective manner gainful employment and services. The Court also held that the rule on non-discrimination applies in judging all legal relationships located within the Community. The Court developed this idea in *Angonese*, which concerned access to employment in a private bank, and ruled that 'the prohibition of discrimination on grounds of nationality laid down in [Article 39 of the EC Treaty] must be regarded as applying to private persons'.[862] An additional argument that was invoked in other cases[863] and that underpins the horizontality of Article 12 of the EC Treaty is that it does not refer explicitly to the issue of the sources of the discriminatory rules (public or private).[864]

A very important condition for the application of the general principle of equality was not explained sufficiently in *Mangold*. The requirement that the

---

859. Case C-13/05, *Chacon Navas* [2006] ECR I-6467, Case C-227/04, P *Lindorfer* [2007] ECR I-6767, Case C-411/05, *Palacios de la Villa* [2007] ECR I-8531, and Case C-267/06, *Maruko*, nyr. D.A. Wyatt (n. 933), 14. For interesting comments, see: A. Dashwood, 'From *Van Duyn* to *Mangold* via *Marshall:* Reducing Direct Effect to Absurdity?' (2007) *CYELS* (Oxford: Hart, 2007), 107.
860. Opinion of Advocate General Sharpston, Case C-427/06, *Bartsch* para. 31.
861. D.A. Wyatt (n. 788), 15.
862. Opinion of Advocate General Sharpston, Case C-427/06, *Bartsch* para. 84.
863. *Angonese* para. 30, *Walrave and Koch* para. 20.
864. D.A. Wyatt (n. 788), 15–16.

application of general principles demands that a situation falling within the scope of the EC Treaty needs to be clarified further by the ECJ. In *Mangold*, the national provisions in question satisfied this condition because they were implementing EC rules on fixed-term contracts of employment.[865] A scenario in which an autonomous national provision was adopted on a Member State's own initiative seems to be quite problematic. In *Bartsch*,[866] the ECJ held that the application, which the courts of Member States must ensure, of the prohibition under Community law of discrimination on the grounds of age is not mandatory when the allegedly discriminatory treatment contains no link with Community law. No such link arises from Article 13 of the EC Treaty or from Directive 2000/78, establishing a general framework for equal treatment in employment and occupation, before the time limit allowed to the Member State concerned for its transposition has expired. It remains to be seen whether the ECJ will confirm, in future cases, its approach with regard to the examination of whether Directive 2000/78 could provide this link with EC law. Only if a link with EC law is established could the general principle of equality be invoked before the Court.

A short reference to Article 13 of the EC Treaty should also be made. When Article 13 of the EC Treaty was introduced, the authors of the Amsterdam Treaty did not want to impose a directly effective prohibition of non-discrimination, as Article 12 of the EC Treaty does.[867] The Community legislature was given competence to implement the principle of non-discrimination as regards sex, racial or ethnic origin, religion or belief, disability, age, or sexual orientation by legislation. With regard to the disability and age discrimination aspects of Directive 2000/78/EC, Member States enjoy broad discretion in relation to its implementation.[868] The judicial intervention of the ECJ in *Mangold* was thought to undermine the system underlying the EC Treaty and the institutional balance, as stated in the opinion of AG Geelhoed in *Chacon Navas* and in the opinion of AG Mazak in *Palacios de la Villa*.[869]

---

865. A. Dashwood (n. 859), 107.
866. Case C-427/06, *Bartsch v. Bosch und Siemens Hausgeräte (BSH) Altersfürsorge GmbH* [2008] ECR I-07245 para. 25.
867. S. Prechal (n. 996), 19. See also: L. Waddington, 'Editorial: Throwing Some Light on Article 13 EC Treaty', *MJ* (1999): 1, M. Bell, 'The New Article 13 EC Treaty: A Sound Basis for European Anti-discrimination Law?', *MJ* (1999): 5, R. Allen, 'Article 13 EC, Evolution and Current Contexts', in *Equality Law in an Enlarged European Union*, ed. H. Meenan (Cambridge: Cambridge University Press, 2007), 38.
868. S. Prechal (n. 850), 19.
869. Case C-13/05, *Chacon Navas* [2006] ECR I-6467, Case C-411/05, *Palacios de la Villa* [2007] ECR I-8531. S. Prechal (n. 850), 19.

Chapter 14

The Extent to Which Conduct of the Board and Articles in the Corporate Constitution Might be Said to Constitute Restrictions on the Freedom of Establishment and on the Free Movement of Capital

14.1 THE SCOPE OF THIS CHAPTER

This chapter will first of all discuss the notions of direct investment and portfolio investment. This discussion will assist in the understanding of the link between takeover bids and the fundamental freedoms, because these financial techniques constitute an exercise of takeover bids. After this link is shown, there will be an examination of the horizontal effect of the free movement of capital. It should be noted that the horizontal effect of the freedom of establishment was analysed in the previous chapter. The horizontal effect of the free movement of capital has not been examined up to now by the ECJ. Policy considerations and other arguments tend to support the view that this fundamental freedom does not have horizontal direct effect. After analysing horizontality, we will then focus on a horizontal relationship within the framework of the market in corporate control. This is the relationship between the shareholders and the board of the offeree company and the offeror company. We will scrutinize whether discriminatory and non-discriminatory provisions in the corporate constitution and defensive conduct of an offeree company's board against a takeover bid constitute restrictions on the internal market.

14.2 DIRECT INVESTMENTS AND PORTFOLIO INVESTMENTS: THE LINK BETWEEN TAKEOVER BIDS AND THE FUNDAMENTAL FREEDOMS

Free movement of capital is one of the four fundamental freedoms. It constitutes a precondition for the effective exercise of the other fundamental freedoms and, in particular, the right of establishment (*Casati*).[870] Article 56 of the EC Treaty states that all restrictions on the movement of capital and on payments between Member States and between Member States and third countries shall be prohibited. Article 58 of the EC Treaty contains some derogations from the liberalization of capital and payment movements, and it stipulates that:

> The provisions of Article 56 shall be without prejudice to the right of Member States:
>
> (a) to apply the relevant provisions of their tax law which distinguish between taxpayers who are not in the same situation with regard to their place of residence or with regard to the place where their capital is invested;
>
> (b) to take all requisite measures to prevent infringements of national law and regulations, in particular in the field of taxation and the prudential supervision of financial institutions, or to lay down procedures for the declaration of capital movements for purposes of administrative or statistical information, or to take measures which are justified on grounds of public policy or public security.

The text of Article 56 of the EC Treaty shows that the deciding factor is the movement of capital/payments between given geographical areas and not the residence or nationality of the person making or receiving a transfer.[871] This could possibly lead to the application of this freedom to residents of the same Member State conducting movement of capital between different Member States, while this freedom will not apply to residents of different Member States participating in movement of capital within the area of one Member State.[872] Nevertheless, this presumption was not confirmed by the ECJ yet and is based only on the text of Article 56 of the EC Treaty.

The EC Treaty does not provide a definition for 'movement of capital', but the ECJ referred to Directive 88/361[873] and to its annexed nomenclature so as to find such a definition.[874]

---

870. Case 203/80, *Criminal Proceedings against Guerrino Casati* [1981] ECR 2595. A.G. Toth, *The Oxford Encyclopaedia of European Community Law,* vol. 2, *The Law of the Internal Market* (Oxford: Oxford Clarendon Press, 2005), 354.
871. J. Handoll, *Capital, Payments and Money Laundering in the EU* (Oxford: Richmond, 2007), 40.
872. *Ibid.*
873. Council Directive 88/361/EEC of 24 Jun. 1988 for the implementation of Art. 67 of the Treaty [1988] OJ L178/5.
874. Case C-222/97, *Trummer and Mayer* [1999] ECR I-1661.

Apart from an exercise of the freedom of establishment, a takeover bid also constitutes an exercise of the right to free movement of capital. This takes place mainly through direct investments. In *Commission v. Belgium*, the ECJ provided a definition for 'direct investment' by reference to Directive 88/361 and to its annexed nomenclature. Points I and III in the nomenclature set out in Annex I to Directive 88/361,[875] and the explanatory notes appearing in that Annex, indicate that direct investment in the form of participation in an undertaking by means of a shareholding or the acquisition of securities on the capital market constitute capital movements within the meaning of Article 56 of the EC Treaty. Investments of all kinds by natural persons or by commercial, industrial, or financial undertakings, which serve to establish or to maintain lasting and direct links between the person providing the capital and the entrepreneur to whom or the undertaking to which the capital is made available so as to carry on an economic activity, fall within the scope of direct investments.[876] This concept must therefore be understood in its widest sense.[877] The explanatory notes state that direct investment is characterized, in particular, by the possibility of participating effectively in the management of a company or in its control.[878]

Moreover, the Commission referred to Directive 88/361 to define 'portfolio investments'. In its 1997 Communication on certain legal aspects concerning intra-EU investment, it stated that in the Directive, the heading 'Acquisition . . . of domestic securities' includes, among others, transaction 'acquisition by non-residents' of shares and bonds in domestic companies on pure financial investment grounds, that is, without the aim of exerting any influence in the management of the company. Thus, this type of transaction is considered to be a form of capital movement.[879] Usually, venture capitalists participating in portfolio companies choose to exit their investments through an initial public offering, through transferring their shares gradually or in a block transfer, or through a takeover bid.[880]

---

875. Council Directive 88/361/EEC of 24 Jun. 1988 for the implementation of Art. 67 of the Treaty [1988] OJ L178/5. The explanatory notes of this Directive also clarify that direct investments encompass investments of all kinds by natural persons or commercial, industrial or financial undertakings, and that serve to establish or to maintain lasting and direct links between the person providing the capital and the entrepreneur to whom or the undertaking to which the capital is made available to carry on an economic activity. This concept must therefore be understood in its widest sense.
876. Council Directive 88/361/EEC of 24 Jun. 1988 for the implementation of Art. 67 of the Treaty [1988] OJ L178/5.
877. Council Directive 88/361/EEC of 24 Jun. 1988 for the implementation of Art. 67 of the Treaty [1988] OJ L178/5.
878. Case C-503/99, *Commission v. Belgium* [2002] ECR I-4809 para. 38.
879. Communication of the Commission on certain legal aspects concerning intra-EU investment [1997] OJ C 220/15. As far as the position of portfolio companies in the internal market is concerned, the European venture capital market is characterized by regulatory hurdles obstructing early stage investments, and capital market structures that do not permit portfolio companies to liquidate their positions. E. Vermeulen, 'Towards a New "Company" Structure for High-Tech Start-ups in Europe', *MJ* (2001): 233.
880. E. Vermeulen (n. 879), 235.

Therefore, portfolio investments are also connected with the market in corporate control. These definitions differentiating between direct effect and portfolio investments were reiterated in some subsequent cases.[881]

The scope of the free movement of capital is considered to be quite broad. While the free movement of capital protects both the potential investor and the shareholder, the freedom of establishment, apart from including the right to set up a company in another Member State, also includes direct investments into a company as far as they are regarded as entrepreneurial investments. Such investments must confer corporate control on the investor, or at least a blocking minority.[882] Additionally, the Directive's nomenclature states that the free movement of capital includes all the financial techniques available on the market approached for the purpose of carrying out this capital movement. As an example, transactions in securities are mentioned. Thus, the concept of acquisition of securities and other financial instruments covers not only spot transactions, but also, all the dealing techniques available: forward transactions, transactions carrying an option or warrant, trades against other assets, and so on.[883] This implies that any of these techniques attached to a takeover bid also fall within the scope of the free movement of capital. In a takeover, the free movement of capital covers not only the acquisition of shares and the change of control, but also, all the other financial instruments used in this tender offer process.

Different parts of securities transactions that result in a corporate control change fall within the scope of the free movement of capital and of the freedom of establishment. In *Baars*, it was stipulated that a national of a Member State who has a holding in the capital of a company established in another Member State that gives him or her a definite influence over the company's decisions and allows him or her to determine its activities is exercising his or her right of establishment.[884] Therefore, an individual and a company seeking to acquire such a shareholding also fall within the scope of the freedom of establishment.[885] Hence, there is a difference between the conduct of a direct investment in a company incorporated in a Member State and the subsequent exercise of rights granted by that shareholding

---

881. The ECJ stated that movements of capital for the purposes of Art. 56(1) EC Treaty include in particular direct investments in the form of participation in an undertaking through the holding of shares, which confers the possibility of effectively participating in its management and control ('direct' investments), and the acquisition of shares on the capital market solely with the intention of making a financial investment without any intention to influence the management and control of the undertaking ('portfolio' investments) (Joined Cases C-282/04 and C-283/04, *Commission v. Netherlands* [2006] ECR I-9141 para. 19, Case C-222/97, *Trummer and Mayer* [1999] ECR I-1661 para. 21, *Commission v. France* [2002] ECR I-4781 paras 36–37, *Commission v. United Kingdom* [2003] ECR I-4641 paras 39 and 40).
882. M. Andenas, T. Gutt & M. Pannier, 'Free Movement of Capital and National Company Law', *EBLR* (2005): 757, 766.
883. Council Directive 88/361/EEC of 24 Jun. 1988 for the implementation of Art. 67 of the Treaty [1988] OJ L178/5.
884. Case C-251/98, *C. Baars* [2000] ECR I-02787 para. 22.
885. D.A. Wyatt (n. 788), 41. This seems consistent with the choice of the Commission to insist on the adoption of a Takeover Bid Directive.

to exert a definite influence over the management and control of that EU company. The former falls within the scope of the free movement of capital, but the latter falls within the scope of the freedom of establishment and entails the exercise of actual control or decisive influence over the investment.[886] The first stage of this process is the acquisition of shares, which falls within the scope of the free movement of capital and which confers control on the new shareholders. The second stage is the exercise of control over the company, which falls within the freedom of establishment and which derives from the acquisition of a controlling shareholding. In *Uberseering*, the ECJ had confirmed this differentiation. It stated that the acquisition by one or more natural persons residing in a Member State of shares in a company incorporated and established in another Member State is covered by the Treaty provisions on the free movement of capital, provided that the shareholding does not confer on those natural persons definite influence over the company's decisions and does not allow them to determine its activities. In contrast, where the acquisition involves all the shares in a company having its registered office in another Member State and the shareholding confers a definite influence over the company's decisions and allows the shareholders to determine its activities, it is the Treaty provisions on freedom of establishment that apply.[887] Although transactions in shares are such capital movements (in particular, direct investments), they fall within the scope of freedom of establishment when they are aimed at the acquisition of control over the offeree company.[888] It could be deduced that the conduct of a takeover bid is covered by the freedom of establishment, because the investor aims at the acquisition of control. Thus, the constituent actions of a takeover bid (e.g., a mandatory bid, squeeze-out, sell-out, determination of the bid price, etc.) fall within the freedom of establishment. However, the direct investment as such, aimed at the acquisition of shares, which would subsequently grant participation in the company's management, falls within the protective scope of the free movement of capital. The same considerations also apply to mergers as a possible outcome of a takeover bid within the framework of EU corporate restructuring.

It is interesting to mention here that neither the Takeover Bid Directive nor its explanatory Memorandum refers to Article 294 of the EC Treaty. Article 294 states

886. T. O'Shea, '*Thin Cap GLO* and Third-Country Rights: Which Freedom Applies?', *Tax N Int'l* (2007): 371, 373, Case C-208/00, *Überseering BV* [2002] ECR I-9919 paras 74–75.

887. Case C-208/00, *Überseering BV* [2002] ECR I-9919 para. 77.

888. G. Kemperink & J. Stuyck, 'The Thirteenth Company Law Directive and Competing Bids', *CM L Rev.* (2008): 93, 100. In *Commission v. Germany (Volkswagen)*, it was confirmed by previous case law that national provisions that apply to holdings by nationals of the Member State concerned in the capital of a company established in another Member State, giving them definite influence on the company's decisions and allowing them to determine its activities, come within the substantive scope of the provisions of the EC Treaty on freedom of establishment (Case C-251/98, *Baars* [2000] ECR I-2787 para. 22; Case C-196/04, *Cadbury Schweppes and Cadbury Schweppes Overseas* [2006] ECR I-7995 para. 31; Case C-524/04, *Test Claimants in the Thin Cap Group Litigation* [2007] ECR I-0000 para. 27; and Case C-112/05, *Commission v. Germany (Volkswagen)* [2007] ECR I-8995 para. 13.

that Member States shall accord nationals of the other Member States the same treatment as their own nationals as regards participation in the capital of companies or firms within the meaning of Article 48 of the EC Treaty, without prejudice to the application of the other provisions of this Treaty. As far as the 'without prejudice' clause is concerned, this Article, dealing with portfolio investments, presents some differences from Article 43 of the EC Treaty. The freedom to acquire an absolute majority of shares (or even a controlling interest[889]) is covered by Article 43 as an exercise of this fundamental freedom.[890] The acquisition of shares below the control level is covered by Article 294 of the EC Treaty.[891] It is interesting to mention here that the Commission was really concerned with this issue of cross-border acquisition of shares since the early days of market integration. In the 1960s, there were deliberations between the Commission and Belgium for the abolition of discriminatory company legislation requiring an authorization by the Belgian Ministry of Justice as a prerequisite for a takeover of a Belgian company by a company of another Member State, as well as a Commission's reasoned opinion addressed to France for restrictions on direct investment transactions.[892]

Furthermore, with regard to the relationship between the free movement of capital and the freedom of establishment, the ECJ held, in its 'golden shares' case law, that to the extent that the legislation at issue involves restrictions on freedom of establishment, such restrictions are a direct consequence of the obstacles to the free movement of capital considered above, to which they are inextricably linked. Consequently, since a violation of Article 56 of the EC Treaty has been established, there is no need for a separate examination of the measures at issue in light of the Treaty rules concerning freedom of establishment.[893]

14.3 HORIZONTAL EFFECT OF THE FREE MOVEMENT OF CAPITAL

In *Sanz de Lera*, the ECJ conferred vertical direct effect on the free movement of capital.[894] Article 56 of the EC Treaty was found to have vertical direct effect, unlike the original Article 67 of the EEC Treaty,[895] on free movement of capital, which did not have direct effect. Only after the expiration of the time for

889. A controlling interest such as that acquired in a mandatory bid.
890. While Art. 43 EC Treaty had to be implemented progressively over the transitional period, Art. 294 EC Treaty had full effect since 1960. E. Stein (n. 21), 47–48.
891. E. Stein (n. 21), 47–48.
892. *Ibid.*
893. Case C-367/98, *Commission v. Portugal* [2002] ECR I-4731 para. 56, Case C-483/99, *Commission v. France* [2002] ECR I-4781 para. 56, Case C-463/00, *Commission v. Spain* [2003] ECR I-4581 para. 86.
894. Joined cases C-163/94, C-165/94, and C-250/94, *Criminal Proceedings against Lucas Emilio Sanz de Lera and Others* [1995] ECR I-4821.
895. A.G. Toth, *The Oxford Encyclopaedia of European Community Law*, vol.2, *The Law of the Internal Market* (Oxford: Oxford Clarendon Press, 2005), 359.

transposing Directive 88/361/EEC (1 July 1990) into national law, was direct effect established for the first time (*Bordessa*[896]). On that account, Article 56 of the EC Treaty grants rights to individuals, which they can invoke before national courts if these individuals consider that this article is breached by certain national provisions. The vertical direct effect of this article was not affected by the words 'within the framework of the provisions laid down in this chapter' or by the exceptions of Article 58 of the EC Treaty.[897] Although Article 56 of the EC Treaty definitely has vertical direct effect, it is not clear whether or not it has also horizontal direct effect. There is no case law that could clarify this issue.[898]

Article 56 does not specify the source of the restrictions (public/private bodies) that must be abolished. This was invoked as an argument in favour of the horizontal direct effect of this article. This approach was reinforced by previous case law on Articles 39 and 49 of the EC Treaty, which used this lack of specificity in the sources of restriction as grounds for the establishment of horizontal direct effect for these two fundamental freedoms.[899] When private bodies play the same regulatory role on capital movements as the state does, then private action could inhibit the free movement of capital (as state action could).[900] While this lack of precision in the sources of the restrictions was used as an argument in favour of the horizontal effect of Article 56 of the EC Treaty, Article 58 of the EC Treaty suggests that the addressees of Article 56 are the Member States and that this freedom does not apply to individuals.[901]

The ECJ, in *Commission v. Belgium*,[902] missed the opportunity to clarify the conditions of the horizontal effect of the free movement of capital. The case was about a Eurobond issue. The terms and conditions of this issue of the Eurobond prohibited any sale to Belgian residents, apart from the sophisticated investors. The Commission alleged that this term infringed upon the free movement of capital and brought the case before the ECJ. The first argument of the Belgian government was

896. Joined Cases C-358 and 416/93, *Bordessa* [1995] ECR I-361.

897. J. Handoll (n. 871), 42. This seems to refer implicitly to the ECJ's decision in *Van Duyn*, where limited discretionary vested to Member States was found not to inhibit the direct effect of Treaty articles. S. Mohamed, *European Community Law on the Free Movement of Capital and the EMU* (Stockholm: Kluwer, 1999), 45.

898. A.G. Toth, *The Oxford Encyclopaedia of European Community Law*, vol.2, *The Law of the Internal Market* (Oxford: Oxford Clarendon Press, 2005), 359. A few counter-arguments against the vertical direct effect of the freedom of establishment had been put forward. However, after *FII*, the direct effect of Art. 56 EC Treaty should not be contested anymore. Case C-446/04, *Test Claimants in the FII Group Litigation* [2006] I-11753 para. 196. D. Smit & B. Kiekebeld, *EC Free Movement of Capital, Corporate Income Taxation and Third Countries: Four Selected Issues* (AH Alphen aan den Rijn: Kluwer, 2008), 77–78.

899. Case 36/74, *Walrave and Koch* para. 20, Case C-281/98, *Angonese* para. 30. D.A. Wyatt (n. 788), 37.

900. D.A. Wyatt (n. 788), 40–41.

901. M. Andenas, T. Gutt & M. Pannier (n. 882), 777. Moreover, it was argued that this lack of specificity on the sources of restriction might imply that this situation could be analogous to the free movement of goods situation. G. Davies (n. 780), 154, 160.

902. Case C-478/98, *Commission v. Belgium* [2000] ECR I-7587.

that the prohibition in question did not constitute a state measure of general application but was a simple commercial term. The second argument of the Belgian government was that its actions would not be covered by Article 56 of the EC Treaty because it had acted in its capacity as a private operator and not in its capacity as a public authority.[903] This distinction between actions of the state as a private operator and actions of the state as a public authority was established in Directive 80/723/EEC, on the transparency of financial relations between Member States and public undertakings[904] and in the ECJ's previous case law (*Ufficio Distrettuale* and *LTU v. Eurocontrol*[905]). The ECJ finally found that the Belgian government exercised its power as a public authority because it had introduced tax waiver provisions. Moreover, the argument that the state did no more, as a borrower, than agree with the financial intermediaries on a contractual term to be included in the conditions of the loan, in the same way as with contracts concluded by private borrowers, was not accepted.[906] Neither the ECJ nor AG Jacobs examined the 'private operator' allegation of Belgium.[907] The ECJ could have explained whether the free movement of capital has horizontal direct effect and, subsequently, whether a private operator is covered by this freedom in its relationships with other market operators. The finding that Belgium was acting as a public authority could not have curbed the ECJ from clarifying this issue.

Notwithstanding the ECJ's silence on this matter, some policy considerations do not support the establishment of horizontal direct effect of the free movement of capital.[908] One of the major differences between the free movement of capital and the other fundamental freedoms is that the free movement of capital also covers movements of capital between Member States and third countries, and not only movements of capital among the Member States. If free movement of capital applied horizontally to relationships between market participants situated in a Member State and market participants situated in a third country, this would definitely improve the legal position of a third country market participant but would worsen the legal position of a Community-based market participant. A market participant located in a Member State could be the target of actions by third-country market participants on the basis of free movement of capital, but it is uncertain whether the former market participant is also granted this right against

903. T. Van Byck, 'Case Note: Case C-478/98 *Commission v. Belgium*', *Col J EL* (2002): 311, 313.
904. [1980] OJ L195/35.
905. Joined Cases 231/87 and 129/88, *Ufficio Distrettuale delle Imposte Dirette di Fiorenzuola d'Arda and Others v. Comune di Carpaneto Piacentino and Others* [1989] ECR 3233 and Case 29/76, *LTU v. Eurocontrol* [1976] ECR 1541.
906. Case C-478/98, *Commission v. Belgium* [2000] ECR I-7587 paras 22–26. S. Mohamed, 'Recent Case Law in the Field of Free Movement of Capital', *EBLR* (2001): 263, 268–270.
907. T. Van Byck (n. 903), 320.
908. D.A. Wyatt (n. 788), 38. Additionally, the Commission seems to be cautious in expanding the scope of free movement of capital into new parts of the financial sector. In some Commission decisions, banks were found to breach the competition rules and more specifically Art. 81 EC Treaty. There was no extension to the free movement of capital. Decision 2003/25, *German Banks,* OJ [2003] L15/1 and Decision 2004/138, *Austrian Banks-Lombard Club,* OJ [2004] L56/1. R. Lane (n. 775), 270–271.

the latter market participant on the basis of mutuality.[909] The legal rights of the market participant located in a Member State against another third-country market participant depends solely on the laws of the third country, and mutuality could not be taken for granted.

It could be contended that the general principle of equality, in conjunction with Article 56 of the EC Treaty, would prohibit provisions of the articles of association of a company incorporated in a Member State that does not allow nationals or companies of other Member States to acquire shares in that company.[910] Although Article 56 of the EC Treaty covers capital movements between Member States as well as capital movements between Member States and third countries, it cannot be maintained that the general principle of equality and, in particular, the prohibition of discrimination on grounds of nationality in Article 12 of the EC Treaty[911] will apply to nationals of third countries as regards shareholding of a company incorporated in a Member State.[912] Policy grounds argue for this approach.[913] A company incorporated in a Member State and the rest of its shareholders who are nationals of Member States become quite vulnerable to third-country nationals acquiring shares in that company, especially when the third country does not provide sufficient laws for the protection of the interests of the company and its shareholders who are EU nationals. A situation like this could create many inequalities; free movement of capital provisions could be invoked by the third-country nationals against the company and the other shareholders, but the company and the rest of the shareholders could not invoke these provisions in the courts of this third country against its nationals. In the sphere of shareholding and of the financial transactions attached to it, the conferral of horizontal direct effect to the free movement of capital would create many problems in cases of litigation between Member State nationals and third-country nationals.[914]

Apart from the policy reasoning, an additional argument[915] against the horizontal direct effect of free movement of capital derives from Article 57(1). This article states that the provisions of Article 56 of the EC Treaty shall be without prejudice to the application to third countries of any restrictions that exist on 31 December 1993 under national or Community law adopted with respect to the movement of capital to or from third countries involving direct

909. D.A. Wyatt (n. 788), 38.
910. *Ibid.*
911. It was mentioned above that Art. 12 EC Treaty supplements the scope of fundamental freedoms in certain situations not covered by them and contributes to a more complete and stronger protection against discrimination on grounds of nationality. D.A. Wyatt (n. 788), 13.
912. D.A. Wyatt (n. 788), 37–38.
913. *Ibid.*
914. In recent case law, the ECJ has seemed to be aware of the rights that third-country nationals could derive from the free movement of capital and has been quite willing to accept that a cross-border commercial activity between a Member State and a third country falls within the scope of the free movement of services instead of the scope of the free movement of capital. Case C-452/04, *Fidium Finanz AG* [2006] ECR I-9521.
915. D.A. Wyatt (n. 788), 39.

investment – including in real estate – establishment, the provision of financial services, or the admission of securities to capital markets.

Some recent judgments of the ECJ on restrictions on the movement of capital between the Member States and third countries seem to imply this lack of horizontality in the field of free movement of capital. In *Skatteverket*, the ECJ held that ECJ case law that relates to restrictions on the exercise of freedom of movement within the Community cannot be transposed in its entirety to movements of capital between Member States and third countries, since such movements take place in a different legal context from that of the cases that gave rise to some other judgments (*Bachmann*, *Commission v. Denmark*, *ELISA*, *Baxter and Others*, *Laboratoires Fournier*).[916] This approach seems to be in agreement with the ECJ's earlier reluctance to equate internal market relations and relations between Member States and third countries.[917] The ECJ did not transpose the interpretation of EC Treaty concepts to agreements between the EC and third-countries (*Polydor*[918]). An internal market concept should not be construed in the same way in the framework of relations between Member States and third countries as in the relations between Member States because there is no intention to create an internal market under the free trade agreements.[919] Furthermore, AG Geelhoed, in his opinion in *Test Claimants in the FII Group Litigation*, distinguished an intra-EU capital movement from an exercise of the free movement of capital by a third country national. He held that, in analysing whether such restrictions are justified (whether under Article 58(1) of the EC Treaty or under the discrimination analysis of Article 56 of the EC Treaty), different considerations may apply from those in cases with purely intra-Community restrictions. He justified this proposal by referring to his previous opinion in *Ospelt:*[920] The particular context of intra-Community freedom of capital is that it must be regarded as a constituent element of an economic and monetary union, and the fact that monetary policy is, following completion of an economic and monetary union, set by the European Central Bank, presupposes complete unity in terms of the movement of money and capital. AG Geelhoed deduced that this context does not apply to cases of movement of capital between Member States and third countries, although the movement of capital has been to a large extent liberalized worldwide. The conclusion was that a Member State may be able to prove that a restriction of capital movements with third countries is justified on given grounds, in circumstances in which such grounds

916. Case C-101/05, *Skatteverket v. A* [2008] nyr para. 60. Case C-204/90 *Bachmann* [1992] ECR I-249 para. 20; Case C-150/04 *Commission v. Denmark* [2007] ECR I-1163 para. 54; and Case C-451/05 *ELISA* [2007] ECR I-08251 paras 94 and 95, Case C-254/97 *Baxter and Others* [1999] ECR I-4809 paras 19 and 20; Case C-39/04 *Laboratoires Fournier* [2005] ECR I-2057 para. 25.
917. J. Usher, 'EMU and Financial Services', in *European Union Law for the Twenty-First Century, Rethinking the New Legal Order,* vol. 2, ed. T. Tridimas & P. Nebbia (Oxford: Hart, 2004), 75.
918. Case 270/80, *Polydor Limited and RSO Records Inc. v. Harlequin Records Shops Limited and Simons Records Limited* [1982] ECR 329.
919. J. Usher (n. 917), 75.
920. Opinion of AG Geelhoed, Case C-452/01, *Ospelt* [2003] ECR I-9743 paras 35–42.

would not amount to a valid justification of a restriction on purely intra-Community capital movements.[921] The ECJ endorsed the latter conclusion and the reasoning of AG Geelhoed.[922]

Hence, Article 56 of the EC Treaty should have only vertical direct effect. However, the acquisition of shares in a company incorporated in a Member State is covered by Article 56, and any restrictions on such an acquisition are prohibited.[923] Any provisions of a corporate constitution excluding non-residents from acquiring shares in the company would constitute indirect discrimination on the grounds of nationality contrary to Article 12 of the EC Treaty,[924] which seems to be horizontally applicable to such situations.[925] Nationals of Member States could invoke Article 12 against such discriminatory provisions, but third country nationals could not.[926] Only if a third-country national resides in a Member State could he or she invoke the general principle of equality, a part of which is embodied by Article 12.[927] This approach seeks to rationalize the financial relationships between nationals of Member States and third-country nationals. On one hand, unfair situations will be avoided. These situations are caused by conferral of full horizontal effect on third-country nationals, while EU citizens are deprived of the protection of free movement of capital outside the EU. On the other hand, Article 56 of the EC Treaty, liberalizing capital movements between Member States and between Member States and third countries, would not be misinterpreted, because a third-country national could be protected against discriminatory provisions as long as he or she resides in a Member State.

A third-country national must be established in a Member State to be covered by the freedom of establishment; only then could he or she be protected in a horizontal relationship by the freedom of establishment. This establishment provides an economic link with the Community. As long as this link is real and continuous, going beyond a mere registered office, third-country nationals can

921. Opinion of AG Geelhoed, Case C-446/04, *Test Claimants in the FII Group Litigation v. Commissioners of Inland Revenue* [2006] ECR I-11753 para. 121.

922. Case C-446/04, *Test Claimants in the FII Group Litigation v. Commissioners of Inland Revenue* [2006] ECR I-11753 para. 171.

923. D.A. Wyatt (n. 788), 40. It was also argued that obligations of Member States should be read in conjunction with Art. 10 EC Treaty and that they should take all the necessary measures to ensure that individuals respect the fundamental freedoms (Case C-265/95, *Commission v. France* para. 32). Member States as legislators are responsible for private law legislation and therefore determine the limits of the acting of individuals. In this way, private autonomy of market operators is not limited by the EC treaty. It is limited by state measures and is protected by the fundamental freedoms. Individuals could also invoke the protection of the fundamental freedoms but are also bound by them. This proposition preserves the structure of the EC Treaty. It could be assumed that AG Maduro inclined towards this proposition when he found that there were not any substantial differences between indirect horizontal effect and direct horizontal effect (Case C-438/05, Opinion, *Viking* para. 40). M. Andenas, T. Gutt & M. Pannier (n. 882), 777–778.

924. D.A. Wyatt (n. 788), 41.

925. *Ibid.*

926. *Ibid.*

927. *Ibid.*

invoke the freedom of establishment.[928] The freedom of establishment applies to EU companies or subsidiaries set up by a third-country national but does not apply to a third-country national directly. This can be illustrated by *Halliburton,*[929] in which the US parent company's establishment of German and Dutch subsidiaries triggered the application of the freedom of establishment to this intra-EU corporate group. It should be stressed, though, that the formation of those subsidiaries by the foreign parent company entails an exercise of the free movement of capital.[930] However, it is this secondary establishment of the foreign company that enjoys the freedom of establishment, and not the foreign company. The free movement of capital permits third-country nationals to invest in EU businesses, but the freedom of establishment does not protect the control or managerial rights of these third-country investors over their businesses.[931] The secondary establishment of the foreign company enjoys these managerial rights over any further secondary establishments in the Community.

14.4 DISCRIMINATORY AND NON-DISCRIMINATORY PROVISIONS IN A CORPORATE CONSTITUTION

A provision of a corporate constitution prohibiting non-nationals or non-residents of Member States from acquiring shares in a target company would breach the general principle of equality, especially the prohibition of discrimination on the grounds of nationality in Article 12 of the EC Treaty, and the freedom of establishment, either alone or in conjunction with the general principle of equality and Article 12 of the EC Treaty.[932] It should be noted that the corporate constitution regulates in a collective way the terms and conditions of the acquisition and the selling of a company's shares.[933]

Article 43 of the EC Treaty prohibits provisions of corporate constitutions that discriminate on grounds of nationality and inhibit nationals of other Member States from acquiring shares and from participating in the management of these companies.[934] An analogy with the previous case law in *Walrave & Koch* underpins this argument. Such a discriminatory provision in a corporate constitution regulates in a collective way access to the self-employed activity of management of a corporate undertaking, because this discrimination encompasses all potential EU bidders seeking to acquire a shareholding granting decisive control over the management of the company. In *Walrave & Koch,* the ECJ refers to Article 7(4) of

928. T. O'Shea (n. 886), 373.
929. Case C-1/93, *Halliburton Services BV* [1994] ECR I-1137.
930. T. O'Shea (n. 886), 373.
931. T. O'Shea (n. 886), 375.
932. D.A. Wyatt (n. 788), 40.
933. *Ibid.*
934. *Ibid.*, 42.

Regulation 1612/68/EEC[935] to enhance its proposition that Article 39 of the EC Treaty extends likewise to agreements and rules that have not been adopted by public bodies.[936] Article 7(4) of Regulation 1612/68/EEC declares that any clause of a collective or individual agreement or of any other collective regulation concerning eligibility for employment, employment, remuneration, and other conditions of work or dismissal shall be null and void insofar as it lays down or authorizes discriminatory conditions with respect to workers who are nationals of other Member States. In *Walrave & Koch*, the ECJ clarified that the activities referred to in Article 49 of the EC Treaty are not to be distinguished by their nature from those in Article 39 of the EC Treaty, but only by the fact that they are performed outside the ties of an employment contract.[937] This consideration could also apply by analogy to Article 43 of the EC Treaty. The horizontal direct effect of Article 39 applying to agreements and rules that do not derive from public bodies and that impose discriminatory rules on access to employed activities applies the horizontal direct effect of Article 43 with regard to rules in a corporate constitution excluding nationals of other Member States from the self-employed activity of managing a company.[938]

This analogy is also upheld by Article 8 of Regulation 1612/68/EEC, which pronounces that a worker who is a national of a Member State and who is employed in the territory of another Member State shall enjoy equality of treatment as regards membership of trade unions and the exercise of rights attaching thereto, including the right to vote. Therefore, Article 39 of the EC Treaty protects the participation of workers in trade unions that are private bodies: their members enjoy equality of treatment as regards the right to membership and the right to vote (i.e., the right to take part effectively in the decision-making process and the governance of such private associations). It could be inferred that Article 43 of the EC Treaty should also confer equality and should protect the rights of persons willing to become members and subsequently to exercise their voting rights in private bodies, such as companies.[939]

---

935. Regulation (EEC) No. 1612/68 of the Council of 15 Oct. 1968 on freedom of movement for workers within the Community [1968] OJ L257/2.
936. Regulation 1612/68/EEC was found not to create any new rights but to determine the scope and detailed rules for the exercise of rights conferred directly by the EC Treaty, Case 48/75, *Royer* [1976] ECR 497 para. 28. Case 36/74, *Walrave* paras 21–22. D.A. Wyatt (n. 788), 41–42.
937. *Walrave* para. 23. D.A. Wyatt (n. 788), 42.
938. D.A. Wyatt (n. 788), 42. Article 44(2)(f) EC Treaty states that 'the Council and the Commission shall carry out the duties devolving upon them under the preceding provisions, in particular, by effecting the progressive abolition of restrictions on freedom of establishment in every branch of activity under consideration, both as regards the conditions for setting up agencies, branches or subsidiaries in the territory of a Member State and as regards the subsidiaries in the territory of a Member State and as regards the conditions governing the entry of personnel belonging to the main establishment into managerial or supervisory posts in such agencies, branches or subsidiaries'. Along this line, see also Case 79/85 *Segers* [1986] ECR 2375 para. 15.
939. D.A. Wyatt (n. 788), 42.

Even if this analogy could not be based upon Article 43, the prohibition of provisions of corporate constitutions that discriminate on the grounds of nationality and inhibit nationals of other Member States from acquiring shares and from participating in the management of these companies could be founded on Article 12 of the EC Treaty. This Article supplements the protection of Article 43 of the EC Treaty. In *Commission v. France*, the ECJ held the general prohibition of discrimination on the grounds of nationality laid down in Article 12 of the EC Treaty has been implemented by Article 43 of the EC Treaty in the specific domain that it governs and that, consequently, any rules incompatible with the latter provision are also incompatible with Article 12.[940] Since the acquisition of shares aiming at the acquisition of control over the management of a company falls within the protective scope of the freedom of establishment, Article 12 could be invoked against such provisions of a corporate constitution that discriminates on the grounds of nationality.[941] Additionally, when an investor does not seek acquisition of corporate control but plans to proceed to a portfolio investment, any discriminatory provisions of a corporate constitution frustrating such an investment would be incompatible with Article 12.

With regard to free movement of capital, the ECJ ruled that Article 56 of the EC Treaty lays down a general prohibition on restrictions on the movement of capital between Member States. That prohibition goes beyond the mere elimination of unequal treatment, on the grounds of nationality, as between operators on the financial markets.[942] Not only discriminatory behaviour against nationals of other Member States, but also, every restriction of cross-border transfer of capital is prohibited.[943] In many cases[944] before it, the ECJ has characterized as restrictions national measures that could dissuade or deter residents from investing capital, from conducting a financial transaction, or from participating in capital movements in general. This seems to constitute a quite wide[945] approach toward the definition of 'restriction'. Even though the national provisions may not result in unequal treatment, they could still inhibit the acquisition of shares in the relevant undertakings and to dissuade investors in other Member States from investing in the capital of those undertakings.[946] For example, in *Weidert*, it was held that

940. Case C-334/94, *Commission v. France* [1996] ECR 1996 I-1307 para. 13.
941. D.A. Wyatt (n. 788), 42.
942. Case C-483/99, *Commission v. France* [2002] ECR I-4781 para. 40. S.M. Seyad, 'Contribution of General Principles to EC Financial Market Integration', in *General Principles of EC Law in a Process of Development*, ed. U. Bernitz et al. (AH Alpen aan den Rijn: Kluwer, 2008), 184–185.
943. M. Andenas, T. Gutt & M. Pannier (n. 882), 769.
944. Case C-484/93, *Svensson et Gustavsson* [1995] ECR I-03955, C-439/97, *Sandoz GmbH* [1999] ECR I-07041, Joined cases C-163/94, C-165/94 and C-250/94, *Criminal Proceedings against Lucas Emilio Sanz de Lera and Others* [1995] ECR I-4821 para. 25, Case C-222/97, *Trummer and Mayer* [1999] ECR I-1661, Case C-302/97, *Konle* [1999] ECR I-3099 para. 44.
945. This wide approach was criticized and various solutions were proposed: S. Peers, 'Free Movement of Capital: Learning Lessons or Slipping on Spilt Milk?', in *The Law of the Single European Market*, ed. C. Barnard & J. Scott (Oxford: Hart, 2002).
946. M. Andenas, T. Gutt & M. Pannier (n. 882), 770.

Articles 56(1) and 58(1)(a) of the EC Treaty preclude a legal provision of a Member State that denies the availability of income tax relief to natural persons for the acquisition of shares representing cash contributions in capital companies established in other Member States.[947] Additionally, the series of cases known as the 'golden shares' cases[948] confirms this approach towards restrictions. In all these cases, the ECJ ruled not only that discriminatory conduct on the grounds of nationality constitutes a restriction, but also, that every national measure that may possibly impede an investment or dissuade an investor from investing constitutes a restriction.[949] A possible refusal by the relevant national authorities of the Member States to approve an important decision, proposed by the organs of the company concerned as being in the company's interests, or an exercise of other defensive measures against a profitable bid would be capable of depressing the (stock market) value of the shares of that company and thus reduce the attractiveness of an investment in such shares.[950] This is considered to be sufficient to discourage investors from other Member States to proceed to a takeover bid.

As far as non-discriminatory provisions in a corporate constitution are concerned, it should be examined whether they constitute obstacles to freedom of establishment and to free movement of capital. It should be borne in mind that normal market behaviour on behalf of one market operator does not in itself restrict the exercise of fundamental freedoms by another market operator. Therefore, if any such provision of a corporate constitution constitutes an expression of normal market behaviour, this provision would not restrict the exercise of fundamental freedoms.[951] The so-called golden shares case law will assist in an analysis of this. Golden shares represent a category of state-imposed restrictions on takeovers, and they may give clues to the kind of restrictions on takeovers that could infringe upon freedom of establishment and free movement of capital if they are carried out by the board of a company. It should also be mentioned that the European Commission had emphasized this case law in its 2002 proposal. The Commission claimed indirect links between the 'golden shares' case law and restrictions stemming from corporate constitutions. Although these decisions concerned only rules adopted by Member States, the Court recalled, generally, that any restriction on investments or on the exercise of control in European companies is in breach of the principle of the free movement of capital: the free movement of capital, as a fundamental principle of the EC Treaty, may lawfully be restricted only by national rules that are justified

947. Case C-242/03, *Weidert* [2004] nry.

948. Case C-367/98, *Commission v. Portugal* [2002] ECR I-4731, Case C-483/99, *Commission v. France* [2002] ECR I-4781, Case C-503/99, *Commission v. Belgium* [2002] ECR I-04809, Case C-463/00, *Commission v. Spain* [2003] ECR I-04581, Case C-98/01, *Commission v. United Kingdom* [2003] ECR I-464, Joined Cases C-282/04 and C-283/04, *Commission v. Netherlands* [2006] ECR I-9141, Case C-112/05, *Commission v. Germany (Volkswagen)* [2007] ECR I-8995.

949. M. Andenas, T. Gutt & M. Pannier (n. 882), 770.

950. Joined Cases C-282/04 and C-283/04, *Commission of the European Communities v. Kingdom of the Netherlands* [2006] ECR I-9141 para. 27.

951. D.A. Wyatt (n. 788), 42–43.

by reasons referred to in Article 58 of the EC Treaty or by overriding requirements of the general interest and that are applicable to all persons and undertakings pursuing an activity in the territory of the host Member State. Furthermore, to be so justified, the national legislation must be suitable for securing the objective that it pursues and must not go beyond what is necessary to attain it, so as to accord with the principle of proportionality (the *Gebhard* test).[952] The Commission then contended that the breakthrough rule of Article 11 of the Takeover Bid Directive is founded on this rationale: Article 11 is concerned specifically with private-law restrictions on the transfer of securities and the exercise of voting rights, and it renders them unenforceable or ineffective in the event of a takeover bid.[953] Hence, some conclusions of the 'golden shares' case law could prove to be very useful f the examination of restrictions arising from corporate constitutions.

The ECJ accepted the possibility of the existence of non-discriminato restrictions on capital movements deriving from the provisions of a corpora constitution. In *Commission v. United Kingdom(BAA)*, the ECJ declared that, b maintaining in force the provisions limiting the possibility of acquiring voting shares (a maximum of 15% of the share capital) in British Airports Authority (BAA) as well as the procedure requiring ministerial consent to the disposal of the company's assets, to the control of its subsidiaries, and to its dissolution on the basis of a unique one United Kingdom Pound 'special share' owned by the relevant Minister, the United Kingdom had breached Article 56 of the EC Treaty. Although the relevant restrictions on investment operations apply without distinction to both residents and non-residents, it must nonetheless be held that they affect the position of a person acquiring a shareholding as such and are thus liable to deter investors from other Member States from making such investments and, consequently, affect access to the market.[954] National company laws inhibit market integration not only when they have an adverse impact on the market as a whole (i.e., rules with structural effects on company law and/or ownership structure), but also, when they restrict specific investment possibilities under the fundamental freedoms.[955]

It is worth mentioning here that Article 56 of the EC Treaty covers not only golden shares created by legislation, but also, golden shares created by domestic

---

952. Proposal for a Directive of the European Parliament and of the Council on Takeover Bids [2002] COM 534 final [2003] OJ 45E/4.
953. Proposal for a Directive of the European Parliament and of the Council on Takeover Bids [2002] COM 534 final [2003] OJ 45E/4.
954. Case C-463/00, *Commission v. Spain* [2003] ECR I-4579 para. 61, Case C-98/01, *Commission v. United Kingdom* [2003] ECR I-4641 para. 47. This shrinks the distinction between purely internal situations and cross-border situations. These non-discriminatory provisions were held to infringe upon the free movement of capital, although they had no special propensity to hinder cross-border activity. D.A. Wyatt, 'Trade, Tax and Takeovers: Can the European Court De-regulate Europe Despite Resistance from the Council and Parliament?', *CYELP* (2005): 95, 102.
955. S. Grundmann & F. Moslein, 'Golden Shares. State Control in Privatised Companies: Comparative Law, European Law and Policy Aspects' SSRN Working Paper Series 24, <http://papers.ssrn.com/sol3/papers.cfm?abstract_id=410580>, accessed 27 Jan. 2009.

company law. The free movement of capital does not permit general company law to confer on the state special rights over companies. Apart from *Commission v. United Kingdom(BAA)*, the ECJ, in *Commission v. Netherlands,* scrutinized the articles of association of two Dutch companies that granted a special share to the Dutch authorities conferring on it special rights to approve major decisions of the representatives of these companies and found that they infringed upon the free movement of capital.[956] The fact that special rights are granted to the state by mechanisms of general company law does not prevent them from falling within the scope of the free movement of capital. In *Commission v. Netherlands*, AG Maduro analysed the case in terms of a state acting as a normal market participant. He stated that the Treaty rules on the free movement of persons, services, and capital impose obligations on the Member States' national authorities, regardless of whether those authorities act in their capacity as public authorities or as entities under private law. Member States are subject to the rules on free movement, of which they are clearly addressees, not on account of their functional capacity as public authorities, but on account of their organic capacity as signatories of the Treaty. To the extent to which those rules do not create obligations for individuals, Member States, when operating as market participants, may be subject to constraints that do not apply to other market participants.[957] AG Maduro did not consider the means and the forms used for the introduction of such special rights as being important. Both general company law and special legislation could constitute sources of special rights infringing upon the free movement of capital.[958] Moreover, with regard to horizontality, AG Maduro contended that even if it were the case that the Dutch public authorities were exempt from Article 56 of the EC Treaty when acting, like any other shareholder, under general company law, the question should be raised as to whether legislation that enables some shareholders to obtain certain special rights to shield them from the market process may itself constitute a restriction on the free movement of capital.[959] Legislation of this type may restrict access to capital in the national market by protecting the position of certain operators who have acquired a stronghold in that market. Such operators, moreover, are likely to be domestic shareholders. Legislation of this kind may therefore hinder access to the national

956. A. Looijestijn-Clearie, 'All That Glitters Is Not Gold: European Court of Justice Strikes Down Golden Shares in Two Dutch Companies', *EBOR* (2007): 429, 430–431. Joined Cases C-282/04 and C-283/04, *Commission of the European Communities v. Kingdom of the Netherlands* [2006] ECR I-9141.

957. Opinion of Mr Advocate General Poiares Maduro, Joined Cases C-282/04 and C-283/04, *Commission of the European Communities v. Kingdom of the Netherlands* [2006] ECR I-9141 para. 22.

958. Opinion of Mr Advocate General Poiares Maduro, Joined Cases C-282/04 and C-283/04, *Commission of the European Communities v. Kingdom of the Netherlands* [2006] ECR I-9141 para. 23.

959. Opinion of Mr Advocate General Poiares Maduro, Joined Cases C-282/04 and C-283/04, *Commission of the European Communities v. Kingdom of the Netherlands* [2006] ECR I-9141 para. 24.

market for investors established in other Member States.[960] It should be stressed that the latter suggestion of AG Maduro was restricted to legislation (state measures). It is legislation that authorizes certain shareholders to entrench their position and to obstruct market access. He did not discuss whether special rights included autonomously in the articles of association of a company and being exercised by shareholders infringe upon the free movement of capital.[961] Nevertheless, the ECJ did not respond to the proposal of AG Maduro to clarify the limits that the fundamental freedoms place on Member States acting as market participants.[962]

In spite of the public source of measures in *Commission v. United Kingdom,* which were adopted by the UK government, this proposition could partly apply to a horizontal situation between private parties. If the provisions requiring consent to the disposal of a company's assets, to control of its subsidiaries, and to its dissolution were adopted by private shareholders through a normal corporate resolution, it could be contended that these provisions would not have inhibited unlawfully a potential offeror company from launching its public offers because they would not constitute trade barriers.[963] Nonetheless, an equity limitation (such as the maximum shareholding of 15% of a company's capital in *Commission v. United Kingdom*) introduced in a corporate constitution by private shareholders could definitely deter potential bidders from launching a public offer and from taking over the company. This limitation of the possibility of acquiring voting shares is a permanent barrier to takeover bids and inhibits any investment aiming at participating decisively in the management of the company. The element of the single 'special share' to which these barriers are attached is purely procedural. It makes no difference whether this share is being held by the state or by a private shareholder. Even if this single 'special share' did not exist at all in a horizontal relation and the equity limitation were just inserted into a corporate constitution by private parties, the freedom of establishment and the free movement of capital would be breached. It should be noted here that while the horizontal direct effect of the free movement of capital is dubious, the horizontal effect of the freedom of establishment is well-established.[964]

As was mentioned, in a horizontal relationship, normal market behaviour could not result in a trade barrier. The fundamental freedoms apply to private action only when it is similar to public action. This presupposes that private action does not simply follow market rules so as to compete with other market participants but constitutes some sort of private regulation that restricts unduly the exercise of the fundamental freedoms by other market participants.[965] A crucial

960. Opinion of Mr Advocate General Poiares Maduro, Joined Cases C-282/04 and C-283/04, *Commission of the European Communities v. Kingdom of the Netherlands* [2006] ECR I-9141 para. 24.
961. A. Looijestijn-Clearie (n. 956), 430–444.
962. A. Looijestijn-Clearie (n. 956), 430–443.
963. D.A. Wyatt (n. 934), 43.
964. *Ibid.*, 43–44.
965. J. Baquero Cruz (n. 715), 618.

point is the position of the individual vis-à-vis the other individual; if the individual is in the same position vis-à-vis the other individual as in its position vis-à-vis the state, then it would be possible to have a restriction on the exercise of this fundamental freedom by the individual. This would depend on the binding nature of the private rules imposed on individuals. If an individual could not avoid the application of private rules, barriers could be created. This situation assimilates the regulatory role of the state and the possibility that such state regulation could infringe upon the fundamental freedoms.[966] In his opinion in *Viking*, AG Maduro had also talked about the mandatory nature of private rules and the fact that the other market participants could not avoid the effects of any possible barriers. He declared that the provisions on freedom of movement apply to private action that, by virtue of its general effect on the holders of rights to freedom of movement, is capable of restricting them from exercising those rights by raising an obstacle that they cannot reasonably circumvent.[967]

In the EU market for corporate control, an equity limitation inserted into a corporate constitution by private parties could not be considered to be normal market behaviour.[968] An equity limitation does not enable shareholders or the company itself to maintain or improve its position in the market but rather entrenches the position of the company's board and does not permit shareholders to benefit from the market of corporate control.[969] Actually, an equity limitation could not allow the market in corporate control to operate at all or could allow it to operate only until the prescribed percentage of shares is reached. This is clearly against the goals of market integration. Takeovers could be proved to be beneficial for shareholders, who could sell their shares to the bidder at a premium. In addition to that, the mandatory bid rule, the squeeze-out rule, and the sell-out rule do not allow inequalities in the prices at which the shares are being sold and, in general, contribute to the shareholders' protection. The fact that the European Commission considered shareholding and voting caps as incompatible with the internal market and decided that they should be abolished is the strongest argument against the allegation that an equity limitation is an outcome of normal market behaviour. Additionally, the fact that an equity limitation inhibits access to the market in corporate control is compatible with the ECJ's approach toward restrictions on the free movement of capital.

Yet, this equity limitation could be preserved in a corporate constitution if it is justified in accordance with mandatory requirements in the general interest. The ECJ, in *Bosman,*[970] accepted that individuals could justify their actions that infringe upon fundamental freedoms by reference to mandatory requirements in the general interest. For example, a company engaged with business in the media sector could invoke the public interest in press diversity to justify such an equity

966. *Ibid.*
967. Case C-438/05, Opinion, *Viking* para. 43.
968. D.A. Wyatt (n. 788), 44.
969. *Ibid.*
970. Case C-415/93, *Bosman* [1995] ECR I-4921 paras 85–86.

limitation.[971] With regard to available justifications, in *Viking*, the ECJ stated that Article 43 of the EC Treaty is to be interpreted to the effect that collective action, which seeks to induce an undertaking whose registered office is in a given Member State to enter into a collective work agreement with a trade union established in that State and to apply the terms set out in that agreement to the employees of a subsidiary of that undertaking established in another Member State, constitutes a restriction within the meaning of that Article. The Court held that this restriction may, in principle, be justified by an overriding reason of public interest, such as the protection of workers, provided that it is established that the restriction is suitable for ensuring the attainment of the legitimate objective pursued and does not go beyond what is necessary to achieve that objective.[972] Judging from the ECJ's stance in *Viking* toward the justifications invoked, the ECJ seems hesitant to accept such justifications and to allow private parties to protect mandatory requirements by their actions.

14.5 DEFENSIVE CONDUCT OF AN OFFEREE COMPANY'S BOARD AGAINST A TAKEOVER BID

In addition to the provisions of a corporate constitution, action taken by the board of a company could also deter a potential bidder from launching a takeover bid and, thus, from investing in the company.[973] The measures described in Article 9(2) of the Takeover Bid Directive seem to constitute such an action. According to this provision, the board of the offeree company must not adopt any measures, apart from seeking alternative bids, that could frustrate a takeover bid; such defensive measures are permitted only if they are authorized by a general meeting of shareholders after the launch of the bid. It is interesting to mention here that Article 9(3) states that, as regards decisions made before the beginning of the crucial period of Article 9(2) and not yet partly or fully implemented, a general meeting of shareholders shall approve or confirm any decision that does not form part of the normal course of the company's business and whose implementation may result in the

971. Reuters contains a similar provision in its corporate constitution. Case C-368/95, *Familiapress* [1997] ECR I-3689. D.A. Wyatt (n. 788), 44. In *Mikhaniki A.E.*, the ECJ held among other things that the role of manager or shareholder of an undertaking active in the media sector is not incompatible with the role of a shareholder or management of an undertaking that contracts with the state. It stated that Community law must be interpreted as precluding a national provision, which, while pursuing the legitimate objectives of equal treatment of tenderers and of transparency in procedures for the award of public contracts, establishes an irrebuttable presumption that the status of owner, partner, main shareholder, or management executive of an undertaking active in the media sector is incompatible with that of owner, partner, main shareholder, or management executive of an undertaking that contracts with the state or a legal person in the public sector in the broad sense to perform a work, supply, or services contract. Case C-213/07, *Mikhaniki A.E. v. Ethniko Simvoulio Radiotileorasis, Ipourgos Epikpatias; Interveners: Pantekhniki A.E., Sindesmos Epikhiriseon Periodikou Typou*, nry.
972. Case C-438/05, *Viking* [2007] ECR I-10779 para. 90.
973. D.A. Wyatt (n. 788), 44.

frustration of the bid. Thus, Article 9(3) introduces an exception from Article 9(2). The term 'not yet partly or fully implemented' is quite ambiguous. Whether a decision is not partly or fully implemented is a very subtle point. Further details were required here.[974]

In the 2002 Commission's proposal for a Takeover Bid Directive,[975] it was stressed that in corporate control transactions, only the target company's shareholders are entitled to decide on the acceptance or the rejection of a bid. The board of the offeree company can only take measures that ameliorate the position of shareholders, for example, by seeking alternative bids that would boost the premium offered. If shareholders consider a specific public offer to be unsatisfactory, their general meeting could authorize the board of the company to adopt the necessary defensive measures against this inadequate bid. Only a general meeting resolution could authorize the adoption of these defensive measures by the ECJ. This might be interpreted as 'shareholders' consent' for the restriction of their rights to sell their shares to the bidder. However, there are special safeguards attached to this process of granting 'consent' for any restrictions introduced by the board: Article 11(3) of the Takeover Bid Directive does not permit any restrictions on voting rights or any multiple voting shares that could distort the decision-making process.

Moreover, the Takeover Bid Directive does not define the measures that can frustrate a bid. In general, such measures may all be operations that are not carried out in the normal course of a company's business or not in conformity with normal market practices.[976] The European Commission's view on this point fits with my prior approach to normal market behaviour. A market behaviour of one market operator that is not normal could inhibit the exercise of a fundamental freedom of another market operator.[977] It is clear that the Commission, in its 2002 proposal, considered defensive measures within the framework of Article 9(2) as not being carried out in the normal course of a company's business and as not being in conformity with normal market practices.[978] This indicates that unauthorized defensive measures aimed at the frustration of a bid constitute market behaviour that is not normal. However, the broad definition of 'defensive measures' contained in Article 9(2) of the Takeover Bid Directive does not necessarily mean that all defensive measures incompatible with Article 9(2) would also infringe upon the freedom of establishment.[979] In its proposal, the Commission stated that the proposed Directive did not define the measures that can frustrate a bid, that is, that can infringe upon the freedom of establishment. This implies that the Commission did not envisage a definition for unauthorized defensive measures

974. B. Clarke, 'Takeover Regulation: Through the Regulatory Looking Glass', *Germ L J* (2007): 381, 395.
975. Proposal for a Directive of the European Parliament and of the Council on Takeover Bids (COM/2002/0534 final) [2003] OJ 45E/1, 8.
976. *Ibid.*
977. D.A. Wyatt (n. 798), 46.
978. D.A. Wyatt (n. 788), 46.
979. *Ibid.*

encompassing these defensive measures in total. Only measures capable of frustrating a bid and subsequently of breaching the freedom of establishment could fall within this definition.

One example of a defensive measure that breaches Article 9(2) but that does not infringe upon the freedom of establishment is the case of a company whose general meeting authorizes the board in advance of any bid being launched to adopt certain defensive measures against inadequate bids.[980] This conduct clearly violates Article 9(2) of the Takeover Bid Directive, because this provision allows authorization only after the launch of the bid when its terms and conditions are published. Nonetheless, this conduct seeks to protect shareholders of the offeree company from inadequate public offers and to enhance the positions of the offeree company in the negotiations on the level of the premium. This defensive measure strengthens the position of the potential target company in the EU market for corporate control. The board of the company would frustrate inadequate bids but would welcome any bids satisfying the standards set by the shareholders. By authorizing the board in advance of any bid being launched to adopt certain defensive measures against inadequate bids, the shareholders improve their market position vis-à-vis a bidder who plans to buy a shareholding in the company through a takeover bid. It was argued that non-discriminatory actions of a market participant aiming at improving his or her market position vis-à-vis his or her competitors, suppliers, or customers does not constitute restrictions on the fundamental rights of others.[981] When the shareholders of a company protect their interests and seek to secure better conditions for the tender offer process (e.g., by receiving a higher premium), then the exercise of the freedom of establishment by the bidder is not infringed upon. The shareholders of the offeree company might not want to consider bids that do not fulfil certain minimum standards.

It should be assumed that this prior authorization is not discriminatory and is addressed to all inadequate bids. The prior authorization should not exclude bids launched by certain categories of shareholders (e.g., non-nationals), because then it would restrict access to the market in corporate control of other bidders. The prior authorization should focus only on economic criteria of which bid is adequate and which is not. It should be stressed that the prior authorization to adopt defensive measures against insufficient bids should be detailed and should specify which bids are considered to be insufficient and which are not. Only then would the risk of an

980. *Ibid.* Despite the fact that shareholders benefit from the frustration of certain inadequate bids, another approach stresses the importance of the disclosure of the bid before the launch of defensive measures. Defensive measures that that have been authorized by the general meeting being fully informed on the conditions of the bid do not constitute barriers on the market in corporate control. Any defensive measures that are not authorized by the general meeting or that are authorized by the general meeting before being informed on the exact terms and conditions of the bid must be scrutinized in light of the fundamental freedoms. The latter defensive measures do not necessarily infringe upon freedom of establishment, if they have a wealth-enhancing impact on shareholders. G. Kemperink & J. Stuyck (n. 888) 118.

981. D.A. Wyatt (n. 788), 46.

abusive use[982] of this prior authorization be avoided. In this same line of argument, Article 10(1)(i) of the Takeover Bid Directive demands all listed companies, even if there are no indications of an imminent takeover bid, to disclose information on the powers of board members, and, in particular, the power to issue or buy back shares. This disclosure duty would increase transparency by revealing whether certain powers of board member constitute normal market behaviour or not.

Even though the Takeover Bid Directive allows certain opt outs, national law has to be in conformity with EU law. When the EU legislature adopts full harmonization, national measures must be examined in light of the provisions of the harmonizing instrument and not of the fundamental freedoms.[983] Notwithstanding this rule, exceptions apply to cases in which a directive determines only a minimum standard and Member States can adopt stricter provisions. In these latter cases, the implementing provisions are scrutinized on the basis of the Treaty provisions on the fundamental freedoms.[984] The opt-out provisions of the Takeover Bid Directive seem to allow Member States to preserve or to introduce national laws that are incompatible with the aims of the Directive and with market integration. Nevertheless, it could be argued that, as in the case of minimum harmonization, implementing national provisions in the case of optional harmonization must also be examined in light of the fundamental freedoms, most specifically, in light of the freedom of establishment and of the free movement of capital.[985]

The fact that Article 9(2) of the Takeover Bid Directive is optional at both the national and company levels hints that at least some defensive measures taken by the board of a target company are against market integration. However, this situation is mitigated by the fact that the opt-out of Articles 9 and/or 11 of the EC Treaty is still covered by the general principle[986] of Article 3(1)(c) of the Takeover Bid Directive and by Article 43 of the EC Treaty; otherwise, there would be infringement of a general principle of the Directive and consequently of a fundamental freedom.[987] All defensive measures must comply with the general principle of Article 3(1)(c) of the Takeover Bid Directive and, as a result, of Article 43 of the EC Treaty. This means that, in the case of a national or corporate opt-out, the board of the company should obstruct only inadequate offers and should not frustrate adequate bids. Even in the case of an opt-out, the board of the company should not deprive shareholders of the opportunity to decide on the merits of an adequate bid that would be beneficial to them; otherwise, the board of the company is not acting in the interests of the company as a whole.[988] An opt-out

982. Abusive conduct such as this would also infringe upon the general principle of Art. 3(1)(c) of the Takeover Bid Directive: 'The board of an offeree company must act in the interests of the company as a whole and must not deny the holders of securities the opportunity to decide on the merits of the bid.'
983. Case C-37/92, *Vanacker and Lesage* [1993] ECR I-4947 para. 9, Case C-324/99, *DaimlerChrysler* [2001] ECR I-9897 para. 32. M. Andenas, T. Gutt & M. Pannier (n. 882), 783.
984. M. Andenas, T. Gutt & M. Pannier (n. 882),783.
985. *Ibid.*, 785.
986. N. Moloney (n. 108), 823.
987. D. Wyatt & A. Dashwood (n. 46), 884. N. Moloney (n. 108), 823.
988. D.A. Wyatt (n. 788), 47.

of Articles 9 and/or 11 does not entail an opt-out of the general principles of Article 3 or a derogation from the fundamental freedom of establishment.[989] Whatever limitations may exist in this context on the horizontal effect of the Treaty provisions on freedom of establishment, it is argued that Member States are obliged to take all appropriate measures, that is, having company law provisions that prevent the board from frustrating an advantageous public offer by the bidder and the shareholders' decision-making to ensure that private individuals do not interfere with the effective exercise of fundamental freedoms.[990] Member States should definitely take into account the liberalizing effects of the freedom of establishment and the free movement of capital when they implement the Takeover Bid Directive.

Furthermore, the indirect effect of directives could also prove to be useful here. The ECJ has ruled that, since Member States have to take all appropriate measures to ensure fulfilment of the obligations arising out of the EC Treaty, in accordance with Article 10 of the EC Treaty, then the domestic courts are also obliged to interpret national provisions so that they would give full effect to EC law, irrespective of whether or not they are directly effective (*Von Colson, Harz,* and *Marleasing*).[991] Domestic courts must interpret national law and, in particular, national provisions that have been adopted for compliance with the requirement of a directive, as far as possible, in light of the directive concerned.[992] This strengthens the argument that a national or corporate opt-out must be interpreted in conformity with the general principles of Article 3 of the Takeover Bid Directive. The indirect horizontal effect could assist natural or legal persons in relying on national legislation when their rights are violated as a result of defensive measures allowed under the opt-out provisions. Such national legislation should be interpreted in conformity with the general principles of Article 3 of the Takeover Bid Directive.[993] Therefore, the judicially developed doctrine of indirect effect could contribute to the protection of shareholders from defensive actions that breach Article 3(1)(c) of the Takeover Bid Directive.

As far as justifications are concerned, the ECJ adopted a quite restrictive approach toward the justifications that could be proposed by state-controlled companies. With regard to the available justifications, we should distinguish between discriminatory and non-discriminatory provisions. Discriminatory measures violating the free movement of capital can be justified only on the basis of Articles 58 and 59 of the EC Treaty. The mandatory requirements of the general interest could be invoked as justifications of (indistinctly applicable) restrictions. The latter justification requires compliance with the *Gebhard* formula. The ECJ demanded

989. *Ibid.*
990. Case C-265/95, *Commision v. France* [1997] E.C.R. I-6959 and Case C-112/00, *Schmidberger* [2003] ECR I -5659. D. Wyatt & A. Dashwood (n. 46), 863.
991. T. Storey & C. Turner (n. 697), 179. Case 14/83, *Von Colson* [1984] ECR 1891, Case 79/83, *Harz* [1984] ECR 1921, Case C-106/89, *Marleasing* [1990] ECR I-4135.
992. G. Kemperink & J. Stuyck (n. 888), 127.
993. G. Kemperink & J. Stuyck (n. 888), 128.

the application of this formula and stressed the legal certainty requirement. In an examination of whether the least restrictive measure has been chosen, three conditions must be fulfilled: (1) the limits of the control power, (2) the design of administrative proceedings, and (3) the possibility of judicial review.[994] In a possible horizontal relationship brought before the ECJ, one could deduce that the ECJ probably would not be less stringent toward the validity of the mandatory requirements invoked by purely private companies. A private company might not easily invoke the protection of the general interest to legitimize its actions, which would restrict a fundamental freedom. Moreover, the allegations of the board of a company seeking to protect the interests of all the company's stakeholders and not only the interests of its shareholders could not be easily accepted by the ECJ.[995] Additionally, the approach that the ECJ took to the available justifications in its golden shares case law is quite important for the breakthrough provision of the Takeover Bid Directive. Article 11(7) of the Takeover Bid Directive states that the breakthrough rule shall not apply either where Member States hold securities in the offeree company that confer special rights on the Member States that are compatible with the Treaty, or to special rights provided for in national law that are compatible with the Treaty or to cooperatives.

994. C-483/99, *Commission v. France* and paras 47–48, 50–53. Case C-503/99, *Commission v. Belgium* para. 28. S. Grundmann & F. Moslein, 'Golden Shares: State Control in Privatised Companies: Comparative Law, European Law and Policy Aspects' SSRN Working Paper Series, 29, <http://papers.ssrn.com/sol3/papers.cfm?abstract_id=410580>, accessed 27 Jan. 2009.

995. G. Kemperink & J. Stuyck (n. 888), 118.

Chapter 15
Conclusion

Protectionism denies everyone in Europe the economic benefits of market integration – higher growth, and more jobs. This is why I have made defending the common market freedoms my credo in Brussels.

European companies must be able to adjust quickly to the new global business realities. Those realities include securing the economies of scale that come with takeovers: Scale for best-in-class marketing. Scale for best-in-class technology. Scale for best-in-class research and development. Scale for best-in-class procurement and supply chain management. Scale for best-in-class innovation.

To build these scale economies companies must be allowed to acquire, merge, and restructure – be it nationally or on a cross-border basis in a fair and openly competitive environment. This is essential for competitiveness and economic efficiency, for keeping management dynamic and alert, and for the rational allocation of capital.

My job is to promote and defend the principles that underpin the internal market and the free flow of capital, goods, services and workers.

– Speech by Charlie McCreevy, Former Commissioner
for Internal Market and Services

'The Development of the European Capital Market',
London School of Economics,

London, 9 March 2006 (SPEECH/06/160)

Another former Commissioner for Internal Market and Services, F. Bolkenstein, has stated that the Takeover Bid Directive is not worth the paper that it is written on.[996] He was not satisfied with the final text of the Directive, which was the result of a political compromise. The Takeover Bid Directive did not achieve the aim of harmonization of the European market in corporate control, which was envisaged by the European Commission. The Commission was hoping that after all those years of efforts and negotiations, there would finally be enacted a Directive that would establish a level playing field for takeovers at the EU level. The meaning of the statement above by C. McCreevy is that the Commission did not simply have objections to minor issues but that it disagreed with the key provisions of the Directive.

The Takeover Directive was one of the ten priorities outlined in the Financial Services Action Plan for the creation of a fully integrated market in financial services, which is one of the last remaining areas in the process of completing the internal market. The EU wishes to offer European businesses greater legal certainty with regard to takeover bids while protecting the interests of shareholders (particularly, minority shareholders), employees, and any other interested parties.[997] The European Commission was aware of the differences among the capital markets of the various Member States that influence national takeover regulations. These differences concern terms of ownership patterns, the structures and stages of development of the capital markets, the availability of finance, the role of the banking sector and of the various institutional investors, socio-economic factors, and political dimensions.[998] In response to these differences, the European Commission envisaged the creation of an EU market for corporate control that would promote the internal market procedure of consolidating the internal financial market – not only financial services and investments, but also, with implications for the integration of EU industry.[999] The European Commission intended to introduce transparent rules that would apply throughout the EU to cross-border takeover bids and be in the interests of all parties.[1000] In this way, according to the Lisbon Agenda and to the Financial Services Action Plan, the EU sought to promote European corporate re-structuring to help boost the competitiveness of the internal market.[1001]

It is quite interesting to refer here to the argument against harmonization of takeovers, which states that harmonization of corporate governance matters does not enhance the economic system and disrupts equilibria constituting the basis of economic welfare. This happens because harmonization, apart from the level-playing-field rationale, does not always take into account essential elements of

996. *Bulletin Quotidien Europe*, 26 Nov. 2003.
997. Europa, SCADPlus, Summaries of Legislation <http://europa.eu/scadplus/leg/en/lvb/l26012a.htm>, accessed on 7 Jul. 2007.
998. B. Clarke (n. 974), 382.
999. M. Andenas, 'European Takeover Directive and the City', *Comp. Law* (1997): 101, 103.
1000. Europa, SCADPlus, Summaries of Legislation, <http://europa.eu/scadplus/leg/en/lvb/l26012a.htm>, accessed on 7 Jul. 2007.
1001. Europa, SCADPlus, Summaries of Legislation, <http://europa.eu/scadplus/leg/en/lvb/l26012a.htm>, accessed on 7 Jul. 2007.

social consensus, such as the defensive mechanisms in a takeover.[1002] A level playing field could not be established for those societal issues. Harmonization does not consider thoroughly the essential elements of social consensus (sometimes shown by the co-determination model) that justify the social role of private business enterprises. Hence, regulatory competition is argued to be the optimal method of regulating takeovers and promoting competition among enterprise structures.[1003]

Therefore, apart from the optionality and the reciprocity regimes, the non-frustration and breakthrough rules are also characterized by substantive deficiencies. For example, French double-vote shares are not covered by these provisions. It is also not clear whether restrictions on the transfer of securities or of voting rights do not apply vis-à-vis the bidder or whether they are suspended. If they do not apply vis-à-vis the offeror, it means that they still apply to the contractual parties. If the restrictions are suspended, they do not produce any legal effects.[1004] Furthermore, the reciprocity rule does not specify what happens in case of simultaneous bids, when one offeror applies Articles 9 and/or 11 and another offeror does not;[1005] practical difficulties may arise from such a situation if each offeror is treated differently. The reciprocity rule also does not explain the position of non-listed offerors.[1006] Do they fall within the scope of this rule or not? The optional character of these provisions combined with the reciprocity rule confirm the statement of former Commissioner Bolkenstein that the Takeover Bid Directive is not worth the paper that it is written on. It is obvious that the optionality and the reciprocity rules are a blow to the efficacy of the Directive and to its practical effects on the market in corporate control. However, these deficiencies are not related only to the optional character of these provisions. There are many substantive deficiencies in these key provisions, the majority of which have to do with the fact that some defensive measures are not covered by the Directive. The fact that these defensive measures are outside the scope of the Directive is the result, in some cases, of political compromise (e.g., cross-shareholdings and pyramid structures) and in others of negligence and lack of careful policy considerations (e.g., competing bids and proxy voting). This opt-in–opt-out reciprocity system, together with the deficient substance of the relevant key provisions, does not contribute to legal certainty. Opted-in Member States or companies give the impression that

1002. E. Wymeersch (n. 124), 321.

1003. E. Wymeersch (n. 124), 321. The drafting process of the Takeover Bid Directive revealed the different political dynamics in this area. In general, British and German employer federations did not agree with an EU codetermination model, while trade unions supported this initiative. Nevertheless, in the area of takeover bids, different coalitions were formed. The German employer federations together with the German trade unions fought against an EU takeover regulation inspired by the UK regulatory approach. For an interesting political analysis see: H.J. Callaghan, 'Battle of the Systems or Multi-level Game? Domestic Sources of Anglo-German Quarrels over EU Takeover Law and Worker Consultation', Northwestern University Working Paper,(2003), 1–28.

1004. M. Menjucq, 'The European Regime on Takeovers', *ECFR* (2006): 222, 231.

1005. *Ibid.*, 233.

1006. *Ibid.*

they are subject to the regime of the Directive, but they can opt out or can use the financial and share structures that are not covered by the Directive to avoid the application of the Directive. Moreover, the mandatory bid rule, the squeeze-out right, and the sell-out right, some of the few obligatory provisions of the Directive, present many disadvantages. For example, the quantification of an equitable price is a very difficult and subtle process, and the Directive does not provide the essential details for it. Member States and national supervisory authorities should be very careful when they quantify an equitable price, and when they grant an exception to it. These deficiencies of both the optional and the mandatory provisions of the Directive constitute a serious disadvantage.

Member States have to decide on a number of important issues when they transpose the Directive into their national legal systems. The transposition should follow the general principles of Article 3 of the Directive and be in accordance with the market-making objective of the harmonization initiative. National protectionism is hostile to the creation of an internal market. The national legislatures and national supervisory authorities should always have in mind that the aim of this Directive is the protection of shareholders and the creation of a vibrant market in corporate control at the EU level. The fact that the Member States could not agree and reached only a political compromise does not mean that the initial aims of the harmonization should be forgotten.

The opt-in–opt-out system coupled with a reciprocity rule decreases significantly the potential contribution of the Takeover Bid Directive to freedom of establishment. The Commission's proposal for an EU-wide takeover regime that would have made for a more competitive Europe was modified into a regime that allows Member States to adopt protectionist opt-outs and target companies to invoke reciprocity against bidders, both of which seem difficult to reconcile with the aims of the EC Treaty Chapter on Establishment.[1007] The fact that Article 12 of the Takeover Bid Directive authorizes at least some defensive conduct by the board of a target company, which would seem to amount to an infringement of the right of establishment of a bidder, constitutes a possible objection against the optionality and the reciprocity rules of the Takeover Bid Directive.[1008] The optionality and the reciprocity regimes raise doubts about their effectiveness of coordinating the national provisions aimed at protecting shareholders of an offeree company.[1009] Moreover, it might be difficult to discern how they might be reconciled with the recognized need to combat distortions of EU corporate restructuring, which derive from arbitrary differences in corporate governance and management cultures.[1010] Definitely, there are some more effective and less dynamic national 'adaptive mechanisms' than optionality and reciprocity. It is probably national 'adaptive mechanisms', such as stock options and shorter service

1007. D.A. Wyatt & A. Dashwood (n. 46), 882–883.
1008. D.A. Wyatt (n. 788), 46.
1009. B. Clarke, 'Articles 9 and 11 of the Takeover Directive (2004/25) and the Market for Corporate Control', *JBL* (2006): 355, 374.
1010. *Ibid.*, 374.

contracts, and not the optional Articles 9 and 11, which could possibly force managers to get after the maximization of shareholder value.[1011]

Nevertheless, apart from these national mechanisms seeking to restrict the negative effects of the optionality and reciprocity regimes, the Takeover Bid Directive contains certain safeguards that prohibit a wide interpretation of the optionality and the reciprocity rules. One important effect of the Directive is that takeovers at the European level will no longer be left to the complete discretion of Member States. Member States will be bound by the (few) mandatory provisions of the Directive and, more importantly, by the general principles of Article 3. These general principles constitute an overarching guarantee, which requires the respect of certain safeguards during the conduct of a takeover bid and with which (harmonized and non-harmonized) national provisions should comply. The introduction of the general principles of Article 3 follows the ideas of the Lamfalussy Report[1012] on the regulation of securities markets at the EU level. However, the general principles set only minimum standards for the conduct of takeover bids, and Member States may lay down additional conditions and provisions more stringent than the general principles of this Directive for the regulation of bids (Article 3(2)).[1013] Potentially, better and more comprehensive protection for shareholders could arise from more stringent rules.

The fundamental freedoms constitute the cornerstone of EU company law, which is a very important part of the internal market. In particular, Article 43 of the EU Treaty was found to embody one of the fundamental principles of the Community legal order and has been directly applicable in the Member States since the end of the transitional period.[1014] It should be stressed that national company law cannot be applied without considering the case law of the ECJ[1015] on the fundamental freedoms, especially on the freedom of establishment and on the free movement of capital. Neither can EU company law directives, such as the Takeover Bid Directive, be applied without regard to the fundamental freedoms

1011. A. Johnston, 'The European Takeover Directive: Ruined by Protectionism or Respecting Diversity?', *Comp. Law* (2004): 270.

1012. The Committee of Wise Men Report on the Regulation of European Securities Markets [2001].

1013. Minimum harmonization of some basic principles entails different regulation of takeovers in every Member State. B. Clarke (n. 974), 386.

1014. Case C-270/83, *Commission v. France* [1986] ECR 273 para. 13. Although the Treaty provisions were claimed to have direct effect, this has not resulted in the integration of an internal market in corporate restructuring and in financial services. S.M. Seyad, 'Contribution of General Principles to EC Financial Market Integration', in *General Principles of EC Law in a Process of Development*, ed. U. Bernitz et al. (AH Alpen aan den Rijn: Kluwer Law International, 2008), 188–189. Additionally, it should be mentioned that the legal consequences of an applicant's successful reliance on the direct effect of a Treaty article are two-fold: EC law must be applied in its entirety and the provision of a national law that infringes upon EC law must be set aside. Case 106/77, *Simmenthal* [1978] ECR 629. J.H. Jans, R. de Lange, S. Prechal, R. Widdershoven (n. 702), 84.

1015. M. Andenas, 'Free Movement of Companies', *LQR* (2003): 221–225.

and the case law of the ECJ.[1016] The fundamental freedoms shall constitute a guide for the Member States when they implement EU legislation. This overarching role of the fundamental freedoms over national legislation is more crucial in the case of optional EU legislation, such as the Takeover Bid Directive, according to which Member States are granted discretionary powers. Respect for fundamental freedoms by Member States entails compliance with certain common rules regulating the internal market, as those common rules are interpreted by the ECJ. Thus, in case of optional harmonizing measures, the fundamental freedoms will prevent widely divergent or even conflicting implementing measures from frustrating the smooth functioning of the internal market.

Some of these EU law considerations could be questioned if they are scrutinized in light of a legal and economics perspective. The European Commission's legislative goal of harmonizing takeover bids at the EU level was accused of lacking empirical evidence. The Directive's rationales (managerial discipline and cross-border restructuring of EU industry) were criticized for not being based on generally accepted economic theories underpinned by strong empirical evidence.[1017] The economic foundations of the harmonization of takeovers at the EU level were undermined by the political compromises reached during the drafting process. The adoption of a Takeover Bid Directive became an end in itself[1018] without consideration for the economic effectiveness of the Directive's substantive provisions. For example, the Takeover Bid Directive does not take into account the fact that defensive measures sometimes increase the premiums paid for an offeree company.[1019] The Takeover Bid Directive does not allow directors to protect shareholders from inadequate bids or from coercive bids.[1020]

It might also follow that certain activities of the board of a target company that have the aim of frustrating a takeover bid might amount to restrictions on the freedom of establishment of the bidding company.[1021] To be characterized as restrictions of freedom of establishment, the activities of the board must comply with the *Bosman* and *Walrave* test,[1022] which results in considering private

1016. M. Andenas, 'EU Company Law and the Company Laws of Europe', *ICCLJ* (2008): 7, 8.
1017. B. Sjafjell, 'Political Path Dependency in Practice: The Takeover Directive', *YEL* (2008): 395, 396. For an economic analysis of the Takeover Bid Directive, see: J. McCahery & L. Renneboog, *The Economics of the Proposed European Takeover Directive* (Brussels: CEPS, 2003).
1018. B. Sjafjell (n. 1017), 401.
1019. C. Bergstrom et al., 'The Regulation of Corporate Acquisitions: A Law and Economics Analysis of European Proposals for Reform', *Col. B L Rev.* (1995): 495, 510. C. Kirchner & R.W. Painter (n. 519), 458.
1020. C. Kirchner & R.W. Painter (n. 519), 458.
1021. D.A. Wyatt & A. Dashwood (n. 46), 850.
1022. The collective regulation of economic activities by private operators under private law may amount to a restriction on fundamental freedoms, including non-discriminatory restrictions on access to the market. Mandatory requirements in the general interest may be invoked to justify these restrictions. Case C-415/93, *Jean Marc Bosman* [1995] ECR I-4921 and Case 36/74, *B.N.O. Walrave and L.J.N. Koch v. Association Union Cycliste Internationale, Koninklijke Nederlandsche Wielren Unie et Federación Española Ciclismo.* [1974] ECR 01405.

operators as regulators.[1023] Discriminatory conduct on the part of market operators or action that restricts access to the market of other market operators would seem capable of amounting to a restriction of a fundamental freedom.[1024] Hence, the hostile behaviour of the board (especially defensive measures) and the stance of certain activist shareholders of the target company toward the takeover bid could be characterized as restrictions of the freedom of establishment because they inhibit the bidder from exercising this fundamental freedom through the acquisition of shares (and potentially, control of the company). When the European Commission decided to propose the harmonization of takeover bids at the European level, it thought that the conduct of a board in general might impede the exercise of the freedom of establishment by the bidder, and it did not mention all the specific impeding practices that might occur. The explanatory Memorandum of the Commission's 2002 proposal[1025] states: 'The Directive does not define the measures which can frustrate a bid. In general, such measures may be all operations which are not carried out in the normal course of the company's business or not in conformity with normal market practices.' Furthermore, defensive measures embedded in the articles of association (such as restrictions on the transfer of shares or multiple voting rights,[1026] or special rights for the appointment of members of the management that are combated by the breakthrough rule of Article 11 of the Directive) of the target company could also be characterized as barriers to freedom of establishment, because they entrench the position of the target company's board or certain shareholders without improving their position in the market and restrict access to the market in corporate control by preventing that market from operating. Hence, national legislation and rules of the company's articles of association constitute restrictions in the exercise of the right of establishment by companies that do not result from the disparities between national rules in one or more Member States, but from the fact that the rules in question, or practices authorized by such rules, are intrinsically capable of inhibiting cross-border establishment.[1027] Nevertheless, not all the activities of the board of a company result in a barrier to freedom of establishment. Non-discriminatory activities by or on behalf of market operators to improve their market position vis-à-vis their competitors, suppliers, or customers do not infringe upon this fundamental freedom,[1028] for example, actions that form part of the 'normal course of a company's business' (Article 9(3) of the Takeover Bid Directive).

However, the optionality regime of Article 12 of the Takeover Bid Directive seems to be inconsistent with the previous approach. An opt-out from Articles 9 and/or 11 of the Takeover Bid Directive permits types of defensive behaviour that constitute restrictions on freedom of establishment. Therefore, it is implied

1023. D.A. Wyatt & A. Dashwood (n. 46), 861.
1024. *Ibid.*
1025. COM (2002) 534 final, 8. D.A. Wyatt & A. Dashwood (n. 46), 870.
1026. It refers to the principle of proportionality between ownership and control.
1027. D.A. Wyatt & A. Dashwood (n. 46), 870.
1028. *Ibid.*, 861.

that these restrictions of a fundamental freedom are allowed, again, by the European legislature. By proposing the non-frustration rule (Article 9) and the breakthrough rule (Article 11), the Commission strongly believed that these defensive behaviours obstruct the exercise of a fundamental freedom.[1029] However, this negative situation could be alleviated by the fact that the opt-out of Articles 9 and/or 11 is still covered by the general principle[1030] of Article 3(1)(c) of the Takeover Bid Directive and Article 43 of the EC Treaty; otherwise, there would be an infringement of a general principle of the Directive and consequently of a fundamental freedom.[1031] Hence, the defensive behaviour should respect the meaning of the general principle of Article 3(1)(c) of the Takeover Bid Directive and, as a result, of Article 43 of the EC Treaty. Whatever limitations may exist in this context on the horizontal effect of the Treaty provisions on freedom of establishment (and on the free movement of capital), it is argued that Member States are obliged to take all appropriate measures, that is, having company law provisions that prevent a board from frustrating the public offer of a bidder and the shareholders' decision-making, to ensure that private individuals do not interfere with the effective exercise of fundamental freedoms.[1032]

Of course, optionality and reciprocity do not diminish totally the importance of the Takeover Bid Directive for Member States not possessing a sophisticated regulatory framework for takeover bids and its significance as an internal market measure. Many Member States had introduced new takeover legislation before the adoption of the Directive,[1033] but the Takeover Bid Directive guides them towards a common direction and limits totally divergent regulatory approaches. While it was argued that a directive without Articles 9, 11, and 12 would have been simpler and clearer,[1034] the slow movement toward a common regulatory approach would have never started without these Articles. More specifically, the reciprocity rule might contribute to an indirect harmonization, because it could urge companies to

1029. *Ibid.*, 883.

1030. N. Moloney (n. 108), 823. S. Schwarcz declares that although principles-based regulation is thought to more closely achieve normative goals than rules, the extent to which that occurs can depend on the enforcement regime. A person who is subject to unpredictable liability is likely to attach to the most conservative interpretation of the principle, especially when that person would be a potential 'deep pocket' in litigation. This creates a paradox: Unless protected by a regime enabling one in good faith to exercise judgment without fear of liability, such a person will effectively act as if he or she is subject to a rule and, even worse, an unintended rule. S. Schwarcz, 'The "Principles" Paradox', Duke Law School Legal Studies Research Paper Series, Research Paper No. 205, March 2008, 1. This view could have significant influence on the interpretative approach of the Takeover Directive's general principles that could follow both the Member States, which should implement the Directive, and the company's board, which could frustrate a bid.

1031. D.A. Wyatt & A. Dashwood (n. 46), 884. N. Moloney (n. 108), 823.

1032. Case C-265/95, *Commission v. France* [1997] ECR I-6959 and Case C-112/00, *Schmidberger* [2003] ECR I-5659. D.A. Wyatt & A. Dashwood (n. 46), 863.

1033. B. Clarke (n. 974), 386.

1034. J. Simon, 'OPA: Divine Surprise ou faux Semblant?', *Euredia* (2003): 229. M. Menjucq (n. 1149), 223.

opt in voluntarily since an offeree company could also be an offeror under other circumstances.[1035] Thus, this may result in a trend toward the convergence of national laws on takeover bids or toward the convergence of rules applied voluntarily by listed companies.[1036] Although the non-frustration and the breakthrough rules are diluted because of the optionality and reciprocity regimes, they constitute a common legal framework for the EU. The Directive provides certain minimum safeguards for minority shareholders. Additionally, without Articles 9, 11, and 12, the general principles of Article 3 would not be so important. The importance of the mandatory provisions of the Takeover Bid Directive, such as the general principles of Article 3, the mandatory bid rule, the equitable price rule, the determination of the competent authority, the mutual recognition of offer documents,[1037] the disclosure and transparency provisions, the endorsement of the information and consultation rights of employees, and the possibility for individual companies to opt in Articles 9 and/or 11 should not be underestimated. Even if these mandatory provisions are characterized by various deficiencies, they impose some minimum harmonized standards at the EU level. Nobody could exclude the possibility of a removal of the opt-out and reciprocity regimes and of the various substantive deficiencies in a future amendment of the Directive. However, the Directive, in its current form, is not capable of altering decisively cultural or institutional obstacles to the creation of a market for corporate control, but it can contribute to a movement in this direction.[1038]

1035. M. Menjucq (n. 1004), 235.
1036. *Ibid.*
1037. J. Wouters, P. Van Hooghten & M. Bruyneel (n. 538), 75.
1038. M. Andenas, 'European Takeover Directive and the City', *Comp Law* (1997): 101, 102.

Bibliography

1. BOOKS

Andenas, M. & W.H. Roth (eds). *Services and free movement in the EU.* Oxford: Oxford University Press, 2002.

Andenas, M. & S. Kenyon-Slade (eds). *E.C. Financial Market Regulation and Company Law.* London: Sweet & Maxwell, 1993.

Andenas, M. & J. Usher (eds). *The Treaty of Nice and Beyond.* Oxford: Hart, 2003.

Andenas, M. & Y. Avgerinos (eds). *Financial Markets in Europe: Towards a Single Regulator?* The Hague: Kluwer, 2003.

Aretz, E. *European Company Law.* ICSA Publishing Limited, Cambridge, 1993.

Arner, D.W. *Financial Stability, Economic Growth and the Role of Law.* Cambridge: Cambridge University Press, 2007.

Arnull, A., et al. (eds). *Continuity and Change in EU Law: Essays in Honour of Sir Francis Jacobs.* Oxford: Oxford University Press, 2008.

Baquero Cruz, J. *Between Competition and Free Movement, The Economic Constitutional Law of the European Community.* Oxford – Portland, Oregon: Hart, 2002.

Barents, R. *The Autonomy of Community Law.* The Hague: Kluwer, 2003.

Barnard, C. *The Substantive Law of the EU.* 2nd edn. Oxford: Oxford University Press, 2007.

Barnard, C. *The Fundamentals of EU Law Revisited: Assessing the Impact of the Constitution Debate.* Oxford: Oxford University Press, 2007.

C. Barnard & J. Scott. *The Law of the Single European Market.* Oxford – Portland, Oregon: Hart, 2002.

Bartman, S. (ed.). *European Company Law in Accelerated Progress.* Kluwer, Aspen Publishers: Alphen aan den Rijn, 2006.

Bernitz, U., et al. (eds). *General Principles of EC Law in a Process of Development.* AH Alpen aan den Rijn: Kluwer, 2008.
Black, H.C. *Black's Law Dictionary.* 5th edn. St. Paul, Minnesota: West Publishing Co, 1979.
Blair, M. & G. Walker (eds). *Financial Markets and Exchanges Law.* Oxford: Oxford University Press, 2007.
Blockmans, S. & S. Prechal (eds). *Reconciling the Deepening and Widening of the European Union.* The Hague: Asser, 2007.
Bouckaert, B. & G. De Geest (eds). *Encyclopedia of Law & Economics.* London: Elgar and the University of Ghent, 1999.
Buxbaum, R. & K. Hopt. *Legal Harmonization and the Business Enterprise.* de Gruyter, Berlin: Integration through Law Series, 1988.
Buxbaum, R., et al. (eds). *European Economic and Business Law.* New York: de Gruyter, 1996.
Buxbaum, R. & G. Hertig et al. (eds). *European Business Law.* Berlin – New York: de Gruyter, 1991.
Chalmers, D., et al. *European Union Law.* Cambridge: Cambridge University Press, 2006.
Chalmers, D. & A. Tomkins. *European Union Public Law.* Cambridge: Cambridge University Press, 2007.
Chiu, I.H.Y. *Regulatory Convergence in EU Securities Regulation.* Alphen aan den Rijn: Kluwer Law International, 2008.
Clarke, M. *Policies and Perceptions of Insurance Law in the Twenty-First Century.* Oxford: Oxford University Press, 2007.
Craig, P. & G. De Burca. *EU Law, Text, Cases and Materials.* 4th edn. Oxford: Oxford University Press, 2008.
Coleman, M. & M. Jones, edited by M. Button & S. Bolton. *The Acquisition of Private Companies in the European Union (A Practitioner's Guide).* 1999/2000 edn. London: City and Financial Publishing.
Cross, F. & R. Prentice. *Law and Corporate Finance.* Cheltenham: Elgar, 2007.
Daintith, T. (ed.). *Law as an Instrument of Economic Policy: Comparative and Critical Approaches.* Berlin – New York: de Gruyter, 1988.
Dashwood, A. & S. O'Leary (eds). *The Principle of Equal Treatment in EC Law.* London: Sweet & Maxwell, 1997.
B. Dauner-Lieb & M. Lamandini, Report to the European Parliament on the Commission's New Proposal of a Directive on Company Law Concerning Takeover Bids (December 2002).
Davies, K. *Understanding European Union Law.* 3rd edn. Abingdon: Routledge-Cavendish, 2007.
Davies, G. *Nationality Discrimination in the European Internal Market.* The Hague: European Monographs, Kluwer, 2003.
Davies, P.L. *Gower and Davies' Principles of Modern Company Law.* 7th edn. London: Sweet & Maxwell, 2003.
de Vries, S.A. *Tensions within the Internal Market.* Groningen: Europa, 2006.

Dorresteijn, A., et al. *European Corporate Law.* 2nd edn. The Alphen aan den Rijn, Netherlands: Kluwer, 2009.

Douglas-Scott, S. *Constitutional Law of the European Union.* Essex: Longman, 2002.

Edwards, V. *EC Company Law.* Oxford: Oxford EC Law Library, Oxford Clarendon Press, 1999.

Estella, A. *The EU Principle of Subsidiarity and Its Critique.* Oxford: Oxford University Press, 2003.

Fairhurst, J. *Law of the European Union.* 6th edn. Essex: Pearson Longman, 2007.

Fazio, S. *The Harmonization of International Commercial Law.* AH Alpen aa den Rijn: Kluwer, 2007.

Ferran, E. *Building an EU Securities Market.* 1st edn. Cambridge: Cambridge University Press, 2004.

Ferran, E. & C. Goodhart (eds). *Regulating Financial Services and Markets in the Twenty First Century.* Oxford: Hart, 2001.

Ferrarini, G., K. Hopt, J. Winter & E. Wymmersch (eds). *Reforming Company and Takeover Law in Europe.* 1st edn. Oxford: Oxford University Press, 2004.

Ferarrini, G., et al. (eds). *Capital Markets in the Age of the Euro – Cross Border Transactions, Listed Companies and Regulation.* London: Kluwer Law International, 2002.

Ferrarini, G. (ed.). *Prudential Regulation of Banks and Securities Firms.* London: Kluwer Law International, 1995.

Forstinger, C. *Takeover Law in the EU and USA, A Comparative Analysis.* The Hague: Kluwer Law International, 2002.

Foster, N. *EU Law Directions.* Oxford: Oxford University Press, 2008.

Furse, M. *Competition Law of the EC and UK.* 5th edn. Oxford: Oxford University Press, 2006.

Gavalda, C. & G. Parleani. *Droit des Affaires del' Union Europeenne.* 5th edn. Paris: Litec LexisNexis, 2006.

Gevurtz, F.A. *Global Issues in Corporate Law.* Thomson West: American Casebook Series, 2006.

Gkizari, A. *New Mechanisms of Environmental Policy in the European Union.* Athens – Thessaloniki: Sakkoulas, 2003. (in Greek)

Goyder, D.G. *EC Competition Law.* 4th edn. Oxford: Oxford University Press, 2003.

Grant, J. (ed.). *European Takeovers: The Art of Acquisition.* 1st edn London: Euromoney Books, 2005.

Grundmann, S., W. Kerber & S. Weatherill (eds). *Party Autonomy and the Role of Information in the Internal Market.* Berlin: de Gruyter, 2001.

Handoll, J. *Capital, Payments and Money Laundering in the EU.* Oxford: Richmond, 2007.

Hartley, T.C. *The Foundations of European Community Law.* 6th edn. Oxford: Oxford University Press, 2007.

Hartley, T.C. *European Union Law in a Global Context.* Cambridge: Cambridge University Press, 2004.
Hartley, T.C., et al. (eds). *The Legal Foundations of the Single European Market.* Oxford: Oxford University Press, 1991.
Harvey, N., G. Norman & A. Nourry (eds). *A Practitioner's Guide to Takeovers and Mergers in the European Union.* 4th edn. London: City & Financial Publishing, 2005.
Hay, C. & A. Menon. *European Politics.* Oxford: Oxford University Press, 2007.
Hopt, K. & E. Wymeersch (eds). *European Takeovers.* 1st edn. London: Butterworths, 1992.
Hopt, K. & E. Wymeersch (eds). *Comparative Corporate Governance: Essays and Materials.* Berlin – NY: Walter de Gruyter, 1997.
Hopt, K., et al. *Comparative Corporate Governance: The State of the Art and Emerging Research.* Oxford – NY: Oxford University Press, 1998.
Hopt, K., E. Wymeersch, H. Kanda & H. Baum. *Corporate Governance in Context.* Oxford: Oxford University Press, 2005.
Hopt, K. & E. Wymeersch (eds). *Capital Markets and Company Law.* Oxford: Oxford University Press, 2003.
Hopt, K. & E. Wymeersch (eds). *European Company and Financial Law, Texts and Leading Cases.* 3rd edn. Oxford: Oxford University Press, 2004.
Horn, N. (ed.). *Cross-Border Mergers and Acquisitions and the Law.* Studies in Transnational Economic Law, vol. 15. The Hague: Kluwer Law International, 2001.
Horspool, M. & M. Humphreys. *European Union Law.* 4th edn. Oxford: Oxford University Press, 2006.
Howells, G. *European Business Law.* Dartmouth: Dartmouth Publishing Company, 1996.
Jans, J.H., R. de Lange, S. Prechal & R. Widdershoven. *Europeanisation of Public Law.* Groningen – Amsterdam: Europa, 2007.
Joffe, V., Q.C., et al. *Minority Shareholders, Law, Practice and Procedure.* 3rd edn. Oxford: Oxford University Press, 2008.
Johnston, A. *The City Take-Over Code.* Oxford: Oxford University Press, 1980.
Jones, A. & B. Surfin. *EC Competition Law, Text, Cases and Materials.* 3rd edn. Oxford: Oxford University Press, 2008.
Kaczorowska, A. *European Union Law.* Abingdon: Routledge Cavendish, 2009.
Kalavros, G. (ed.). *The Influence of Enlargement on Law and Policies of the European Union, Conference Proceedings.* Thursday 28 March 2002. Athens: Ant. N. Sakkoulas Publications, 2003. (in Greek)
Kanellopoulos, P. *Law of the European Union.* Athens: Ant. N. Sakkoulas Publications, 2004. (in Greek)
Kent, P. *Law of the European Union.* 4th edn. Essex: Pearson Longman, 2008.
Kenyon-Slade, S. *Mergers and Takeovers in the US and UK: Law and Practice.* 1st edn. Oxford: Oxford University Press, 2004.
Kirton, J.J. & M. Trebilcock. *Hard Choices, Soft Law.* Aldershot: Ashgate, 2004.

Kotsiri, L. *European Commercial Law I.* Athens – Thessaloniki: Sakkoulas, 2003. (in Greek)

Kraakman, R., et al. *The Anatomy of Corporate Law.* 1st edn. Oxford: Oxford University Press, 2004.

Ktenidis, J. *Measures against Unfair Commercial Practices.* Athens – Thessaloniki: Sakkoulas, 1996. (in Greek)

Lenaerts, K., P. Van Nuffel & R. Bray. *Constitutional Law of the European Union.* 2nd edn. London: Sweet and Maxwell, 2005.

Lombardo, S. *Regulatory Competition in Company Law in the European Community. Prerequisites and Limits.* New York: P. Lang, 2002.

Lutter, M. (ed.). *Legal Capital in Europe.* Berlin: De Gruyter, 2006.

Maeijer, J.M.M. & K. Geens (eds). *Defensive Measures against Hostile Takeovers in the Common Market.* London: Martinus Nijhoff Publishers and Graham & Trotman, 1990.

Mallin, C.A. *Corporate Governance.* Oxford: Oxford University Press, 2003.

Martin, E.A. (ed.). *Oxford Dictionary of Law.* 5th edn. Oxford: Oxford University Press, 2003.

Maul, S., D. Muffat-Jeandet & J. Simon. *Takeover Bids in Europe.* Freiburg: Memento Verlag, 2008.

Mavromati, D. *The Law of Payment Services in the EU.* The Hague: European Monographs, Kluwer, 2008.

McCahery, J., P. Moerland, T. Raaijmakers & L. Renneboog. *Corporate Governance Regimes, Convergence and Diversity.* Oxford: Oxford University Press, 2006.

McCahery, J., et al. (eds). *Corporate Governance Regimes.* Oxford: Oxford University Press, 2002.

McCahery, J., et al. *The Economics of the Proposed European Takeover Directive.* Brussels: Research Report, Center for European Policy Studies, 2003.

McCahery, J. & L. Renneboog. *The Economics of the Proposed European Takeover Directive.* Brussels: CEPS, 2003.

Meenan, H. (ed.). *Equality Law in an Enlarged European Union.* Cambridge: Cambridge University Press, 2007.

Milhaupt, C. *Global Markets, Domestic Institutions.* New York: ColUp, 2003.

Milman, D. (ed.). *Regulating Enterprise-Law and Business Organizations in the UK.* Oxford: Hart, 1999.

Mohamed, S. *European Community Law on the Free Movement of Capital and the EMU.* Stockholm: Kluwer, 1999.

Moloney, N. *EC Securities Regulation.* Oxford EC Law Library. 1st edn. Oxford: Oxford University Press, 2002.

Monti, G. *EC Competiton Law.* Cambridge: Cambridge University Press, 2007.

Mukwiri, J. *Takeovers and the European Legal Framework, A British Perspective.* London – New York: Routlege-Cavendish, 2009.

Murphy, D.D. *The Structure of Regulatory Competition, Corporations and Public Policies in a Global Economy.* Oxford: Oxford University Press, 2004.

Nicolaidis, K. & S. Weatherill (eds). *Whose Europe? National Models and the Constitution of the European Union.* Oxford: Conference Papers, 2003.
Oesterle, D.A. *The Law of Mergers and Acquisitions.* 3rd edn. American Casebook Series. St Paul, Minn West Group, 2005.
O'.Keefe, D. (ed.). *Judicial Review in European Union Law.* The Hague: Kluwer Law International, 2000.
Pallister, J. & A. Isaacs (eds). *Oxford Dictionary of Business.* 3rd edn. Oxford: Oxford University Press, 2002.
Paync, J. (ed.). *Takeovers in English and German Law.* Oxford – Portland, Oregon: Hart, 2002.
Pennings, F., et al. (eds). *Social Responsibility in Labour Relations.* AH Alpen aan den Rijn: Kluwer, 2008.
Perrakis, S. & M. Chrisomallis. *The Court of First Instance of the European Communities.* Athens: Ant. N. Sakkoulas Publications, 1990 (in Greek).
Poser, N.S. *International Securities Regulation.* Toronto: Little Brown & Company, 1991.
Prechal, S. *Directives in EC Law.* 2nd edn. Oxford: Oxford University Press, 2004.
Prinssen, J. & A. Schrauwen (eds). *Direct Effect: Rethinking a Classic of EC Legal Doctrine.* Groningen – Amsterdam: Europa, 2002.
Rammeloo, S. *Corporation on Private International Law: A European Perspective.* Oxford: Oxford University Press, 2001.
Rickford, J. (ed.). *The European Company: Developing a Community Law of Corporations.* Anterp – Oxford – New York: Intersentia, 2003.
Romano, R. *The Advantage of Competitive Federalism for Securities Regulation.* Washington, DC: AEI, 2002.
Ronnmar, M. (ed.). *EU Industrial Relations v. National Industrial Relations.* AH Alpen aan den Rijn: Kluwer, 2008.
Sahpekidou, E. & P. Stagkos. *Law of the European Communities and the European Union I.* Athens – Thessaloniki: Sakkoulas, 2000. (in Greek)
Sahpekidou, E. & P. Stagkos. *Law of the European Communities and the European Union II.* Athens – Thessaloniki: Sakkoulas, 2009. (in Greek)
Scandamis, N. (ed.). *European Law-Texts II. Political Foundations of the European Union.* Athens: Ant. N. Sakkoulas Publications, 2005. (in Greek)
Scandamis, N., V. Christianos & M. Kouskouna. *International and European Law Applications II, Enterprises in Distress and Community Law.* Athens: Ant. N. Sakkoulas Publications, 2003. (in Greek)
Schermers, H., et al. *Free Movement of Persons in Europe, Legal Problems and Experiences.* 1st edn. The Hague: TMC Asser Instituut, Springer, 1993.
Schmidtchen, D. & R. Cooter (eds). *Constitutional Law and Economics of the European Union.* Cheltenham: Elgar, 1997.
Schmitthoff, C.M. (ed.). *The Harmonization of European Company Law.* London: UKNCCL, 1973.
Schmitthoff, C. *European Company Law Texts.* New York – London: M. Bender-Stevens & Sons, 1974.

Shaw, J. *Law of the European Union.* 3rd edn. London: Palgrave Law Masters, 2000.
Shaw, J., J. Hunt & C. Wallace. *Economic and Social Law of the European Union.* London: Palgrave, 2007.
Shuibhne, N.N. *Regulating the Internal Market.* Cheltenham: Elgar, 2006.
Siems, M. *Convergence in Shareholder Law.* Cambridge: Cambridge University Press, 2008.
Sjafjell, B. *Towards a Sustainable European Company Law.* AH Alphen aan den Rijn: Wolters Kluwer, 2009.
Smit, D. & B. Kiekebeld. *EC Free Movement of Capital, Corporate Income Taxation and Third Countries: Four Selected Issues.* AH Alphen aan den Rijn: Kluwer, 2008.
Smits, J.M. (ed.). *Elgar Encyclopedia of Comparative Law.* Cheltenham: Elgar, 2008.
Snell, J. *Goods and Services in EC Law: A Study of the Relationship between the Freedoms.* Oxford: Oxford University Press, 2005.
Snyder, F. (ed.). *The Europeanisation of Law: The Legal Effects of European Integration.* Oxford: Hart, 2000.
Stedman, G. *Takeovers.* Longman Commercial Series. 1st edn. London: Longman, 1993.
Stein, E. *Harmonization of European Company Laws.* Indianapolis: Merrill, 1971.
Steiner, J.L. Woods & C. Twigg-Flesner. *EU Law.* 9th edn. Oxford: Oxford University Press, 2006.
Storey, T. & C. Turner. *Unlocking EU Law.* 2nd edn. London: Hodder Education, 2008.
Toth, A.G. (ed.). *The Oxford Encyclopaedia of European Community Law.* Oxford: Oxford Clarendon Press, 1990.
Toth, A.G. (ed.). *The Oxford Encyclopaedia of European Community Law,* vol. 2. *The law of the Internal Market.* Oxford: Oxford Clarendon Press, 2005.
Tridimas, T. & P. Nebbia. *European Union for the 21st century: Rethinking the New Legal Order*, vols 1 & 2. London: Hart, 2004.
Usher, J. *The Law of Money and Financial Services in the EC.* 2nd edn. Oxford EC Law Library, Oxford: Oxford University Press, 1999.
van Empel, M. (ed.). *Financial Services in Europe.* AH Alpen aan den Rijn: Wolters Kluwer, 2008.
Van Gerven, D. (ed.). *Common Legal Framework for Takeover Bids in Europe.* Cambridge: Cambridge University Press, 2008.
Van Gerven, D. & P. Storm (eds). *The European Company*, vol. 1. Cambridge: Cambridge University Press, 2006.
Van Hooghten, P. (ed.). *The European Takeover Directive and Its Implementation.* Oxford: Oxford University Press, 2009.
Villiers, C. *European Company Law: Towards Democracy?* Aldershot: Ashgate, 1998.
Virgos, M. & F. Garcimartin. *The European Insolvency Regulation: Law and Practice.* The Hague: Kluwer Law International, 2004.

Vaughan, D., A. Robertson & P. Eleftheriadis (eds). *Law of the European Union.* Oxford: Oxford University Press, 2009.

Vogenauer, S. & S. Weatherill (eds). *The Harmonization of European Contract Law.* Portland: Hart, 2006.

Weatherill, S. (ed.). *Better Regulation.* Oxford: Hart, 2007.

Weatherill, S. *Cases and Materials on EU Law.* 8th edn. Oxford: Oxford University Press, 2007.

Weinberg, M.A., M.V. Blank & A.L. Greystoke. *Takeovers and Mergers.* London: Sweet and Maxwell, 1979.

Weiss, F. & F. Wooldridge. *Free Movement of Persons within the European Community.* European Monographs, 2nd edn. Alphen aan den Rijn: Kluwer Law International, 2007.

Werlauff, E. *SE: The Law of the European Company.* Copenhagen: DJOF Publishing, 2003.

Wei, Y. *Comparative Corporate Governance: A Chinese Perspective.* The Hague: Kluwer Law International, 2003.

White, R.C.A. *Workers, Establishment and Services in the European Union.* Oxford: Oxford University Press, 2005.

Wood, P. *Regulation of International Finance.* Law and Practice of International Finance Series, 1st edn. London: Sweet & Maxwell, 2007.

Wood, P. *Law and Practice of International Finance.* London: Sweet & Maxwell, 2008.

Wood, P.R. *Maps of World Financial Law.* London: Allen & Overy, 2005.

Wood, P.R. *Project Finance, Subordinated Debt, and State Loans.* London: Sweet & Maxwell, 1995.

Wood, P.R. *Title Finance, Derivatives, Securitisations, Set-off and Netting.* London: Sweet & Maxwell, 1995.

Wood, P.R. *Comparative Law of Security and Guarantees.* London: Sweet & Maxwell, 1995.

Wood, P.R. *International Loans, Bonds and Securities Regulation.* London: Sweet & Maxwell, 1995.

Wood, P.R. *Principles of International Insolvency.* London: Sweet & Maxwell, 1995.

Woods, L. *Free Movement of Goods and Services within the European Community.* Aldershot: Ashgate, 2004.

Wortley, B.A. *The Law of the Common Market.* Manchester: Manchester University Press, 1974.

Wouters, J. & H. Schneider (eds). *Current Issues of Cross-Border Establishment of Companies in the European Union.* Antwerp: ApeldoornMaklu, 1995.

Wouters, J., J. Stuyck & T. Kruger (eds). *Principles of Proper Conduct for Supranational, State and Private Actors in the European Union: Towards Ius Commune.* Groningen: Intersentia, 2001.

Wyatt, D.A. & A. Dashwood et al. *European Union Law.* 5th edn. London: Thomson Sweet & Maxwell, 2006.

Wyatt, D.A. (ed.). *Rudden & Wyatt's EU Treaties & Legislation.* 9th edn. Oxford: Oxford University Press, 2004.

Wymeersch, E. (ed.). *Further Perspectives in Financial Integration in Europe.* Berlin: Walter de Gruyter, 1994.

Wymeersch, E. (ed.). *Groups of Companies in the EEC: A Survey Report to the European Commission on the Law Relating to Corporate Groups in Various Member States.* Berlin: Walter de Gruyter, 1993.

2. ARTICLES

Andenas, M., T. Gutt & M. Pannier. 'Free Movement of Capital and National Company Law'. *EBLR* (2005): 757.

Andenas, M. 'Member States, Courts and Free Movement of Companies' (editorial). *Comp. Law.* 27 (2006): 1.

Andenas, M. 'Cross-border Establishment in the EU' (editorial). *Comp.Law.* 27 (2006): 33.

Andenas, M. 'European Takeover Directive and the City'. *Comp.Law* (1997): 101.

Andenas, M. 'Free Movement of Companies'. *LQR* (2003): 221.

Andenas, M. 'EU Company Law and the Company Laws of Europe'. *ICCLJ* (2008): 7.

Andersen, D.K. 'The Takeover Directive and Corporate Governance: The Danish Experience'. *EBLR* (2004): 1461.

Angelette, B. 'The Revolution That Never Came and the Revolution Coming: *De Lasteyrie du Salliant, Marks & Spencer, Sevic Systems* and the Changing Corporate Law in Europe'. *Virginia LR* 92 (2006): 1188.

Apps, K. 'Damages Claims against Trade Unions after Viking and Laval'. *E L Rev.* (2009): 141.

Armour, J. 'Who Should Make Corporate Law? EC Legislation versus Regulatory Competition'. ECGI Law Working Paper 54/2005.

Armour, J. & J. Skeel Jr. 'Who Writes the Rules for Hostile Takeovers, and Why? The Peculiar Divergence of U.S. and U.K. Takeover Regulation'. ECGI Law Working Paper 73/2006 and Georgetown Law Journal *Georg'n LJ* (2007): 1727.

Armour, J. & J.A. McCahery. 'Introduction: Improving Corporate Law and Modernising Securities Regulation in Europe'. *JCLS* 3 (2003): 211.

Athanassiou, P. 'Recent Developments in Greek Capital Markets Law'. *EBLR* (2005): 893.

Avgouleas, E. 'The New EC Financial Markets Legislation and the Emerging Regime for Capital Markets'. *YEL* 23 (2004): 321.

Bamford, C. 'Northern Rock and the Single Market'. *Comp Law* 29 (2008): 65.

Baquero Cruz, J. 'Free Movement and Private Autonomy'. *E L Rev.* (1999): 603.

Barber, N.W. 'The Limited Modesty of Subsidiarity'. *ELJ* 11 (2008): 308.

Barnard, C. 'Viking and Laval: An Introduction'. *CYELS* (2008) (Oxford: Hart, 2008): 470.

Barnard, C. & S. Deakin. 'Market Access and Regulatory Competition' Jean Monnet Working Paper 9/01.

Bartman, S. 'Analysis and Consequences of the EC Directive on Takeover Bids'. *ECL* 1 (2004): 5.

Bartman, S. 'Crack the OOC-Code!'. *ECL* 3 (2006): 162.

Bartman, S. 'Corporate Governance: A Challenge to Company Law'. *ECL* 1 (2004): 4.

Baums, T. 'The Regulation of Takeovers under German Law'. *EBLR* (2004): 1453.

Baums, T. & K. Scott. 'Taking Shareholder Protection Seriously? Corporate Governance in the United States and Germany'. ECGI Law Working Paper 17/2003.

Becht, M., C. Mayer & H. Wagner. 'Where Do Firms Incorporate?'. ECGI Law Working Paper 70/2006.

Becht, M. 'Reciprocity in Takeovers' ECGI Law Working Paper 14/2003.

Bebchuk, L.A. & A. Ferrell. 'Federalism and Takeover Law: The Race to Protect Managers from Takeovers' Working Paper 7232, NBER Working Paper Series, <www.nber.org/papers/w7232>, National Bureau of Economic Research, 1050. Cambridge, Massachusetts, July 1999.

Bebchuk, L.A. & A. Ferrell. 'A New Approach to Takeover Law and Regulatory Competition'. *Virginia Law Review* 87: (2001): 101.

Bebchuk, L. & O. Hart. 'Takeover Bids vs. Proxy Fights in Contests for Corporate Control'. The Harvard John M. Olin Discussion Paper Series, Discussion Paper No. 336 10/2001.

Bebchuk, L., J. Coates & G. Subramanian. 'The Powerful Antitakeover Force of Staggered Boards: Theory, Evidence and Policy'. The Harvard J.M. Olin Discussion Paper Series: Disc. Paper No. 353 03/2002.

Bebchuk, L. 'Toward Undistorted Choice and Equal Treatment in Corporate Takeovers'. *HLR* 98 (1985): 1693.

Bebchuk, L.A. 'Reply. Letting Shareholders Set the Rules'. *Harv L Rev.* (2006): 1784.

Behrens, P. 'Annotation: Case C-411/03 SEVIC Systems AG'. *CM L Rev.* (2006): 1669.

Bell, M. 'The New Article 13 EC Treaty: A Sound Basis for European Anti-discrimination Law?', *MJ* (1999): 5.

Benedettelli, M. 'Conflicts of Jurisdiction and Conflicts of Law in Company Law Matters within the EU "Market for Corporate Models": Brussels 1 and Rome 1 after Centros'. *EBLR* (2005): 55.

Bercusson, B. 'The Trade Union Movement and the European Union: Judgement Day'. *ELJ* (2007): 279.

Bergstrom, C., et al. 'The Regulation of Corporate Acquisitions: A Law and Economics Analysis of European Proposals for Reform'. *Col.B L Re* (1995): v. 495.

Berkovitch, E. & M.P. Narayanan. 'Motives for Takeovers: An Empirical Investigation'. *J Fin Quant Analysis* (1993): 347–362.

Bernitz, U. 'The Attack on the Nordic Multiple Voting Rights Model: The Legal Limits under EU Law'. *EBLR* (2004): 1423.

Bernitz, U. 'Special Issue Section on Corporate Governance in Europe in the Light of the Takeover Directive'. *EBLR* (2004): 1350.

Bicker, E. 'Creditor Protection in the Corporate Group'. SSRN Working Paper 2006.

Birkmese, H. 'Regulatory Competition and the European Harmonisation Process'. *EBLR* (2006): 1077.

Bittlingmayer, G. 'The Market for Corporate Control (Including Takeovers)' Online Encyclopedia of Law and Economics. ed. B. Bouckaert & G. De Geest, E. Elgar & the University of Ghent, 725–771. <http://encyclo.findlaw.com/5640book.pdf>, accessed 21 February 2007.

Black, B. & J. Gross. 'Making It Up as They Go Along: The Role of Law in Securities Arbitration'. *Card LR* 23 (2002): 991.

Black, J., M. Hopper & C. Band. 'Making Success of the Principles-based Regulation'. *LFMR* 1 (2007).

Black, B.S. 'Is Corporate Law Trivial? A Political and Economic Analysis'. *NW. U. L. Rev.* 84 (1990).

Bouloukos, M. 'The European Company as a Vehicle for Corporate Mobility within the EU: A Breakthrough in European Corporate Law?'. *EBLR* (2007): 535.

Braunohler, K. 'Hostile Takeovers'. *EBLR* (2001): 308.

Bris, A. & C. Cabolis. 'The Value of Investor Protection: Firm Evidence from Cross-Border Mergers'. *Rev. Fin. St.* 21 (2008): 605.

Burbidge, P. 'Creating High Performance Boardrooms and Workplaces-European Corporate Governance in the Twenty First Century'. *E L Rev.* (2003): 642.

Burkart, M. & F. Panunzi. 'Mandatory Bids, Squeeze-Out, Sell-Out and the Dynamics of the Tender Offer Process'. ECGI Law Working Paper 10/2003.

Burkart, M., D. Gromb & F. Panunzi. 'Why Higher Takeover Premia Protect Minority Shareholders'. *The Journal of Political Economy* 106, no. 1 (1998): 172.

Burkart, M., D. Gromb & F. Panunzi. 'Minority Blocks and Takeover Premia'. ECGI Finance Working Paper 96/2005.

Cain, B. 'Cross-Border Mergers Directive'. *Comp. Secr. R.* 31 (2007): 9.

Carle, F. 'Are French Listed Companies Takeover-proof?'. *ECL* (2007): 154.

Callaghan, H.J. 'Battle of the Systems or Multi-level Game? Domestic Sources of Anglo-German Quarrels over EU takeover Law and Worker Consultation'. (2003) Northwestern University Working Paper, 1–28.

Capriglione, F. 'Freedom of Establishment and Provision of Services'. *EBLR* (2004): 447.

Carruthers, J., Ch. Villiers 'Company Law in Europe: Condoning the Continental Drift?'. *EBLR* 2 (2000): 91.

Chalmers, D. 'Private Power and Public Authority in European Union Law', *CYELS* (Oxford: Hart, 2006): 59.

Chatterjee, R.A. 'The Financial Performance of Companies Acquiring Very Large Takeover Targets'. (2000) *Appl Fin Econ.* 185–191.

Cheffins, B.R. 'Current Trends in Corporate Governance: Going from London to Milan via Toronto'. *Duke J Comp Int'l L* 10 (1999): 5.

Cioffi, J.W. 'Restructuring "Germany Inc.": The Politics of Company and Takeover Law Reform in Germany and the European Union'. *Law and Policy* 24 (2002): 356.

Clarke, B. 'Takeover Regulation: Through the Regulatory Looking Glass'. *Germ L J* (2007): 381.

Clarke, B. 'Articles 9 and 11 of the Takeover Directive (2004/25) and the Market for Corporate Control'. *JBL* (2006): 355.

Clough, M. & N. Forwood. 'The Single European Act and Free Movement: Legal Implcations of the Provisions for the Completion of the Internal Market'. *E L Rev.* 11 (1986): 383.

Coates IV, J.C. 'Explaining Variation in Takeover Defenses: Failure in the Corporate Law Market'. The Harvard J. Olin Discussion Papers Series, D.P. No. 2979/2000.

Coates IV, J.C. 'Ownership, Takeovers and EU Law: How Contestable Should EU Corporations Be?'. ECGI Law Working Paper 11/2003.

Commission Proposal of 2 October 2002 OJ C 45 E, February 2003, I and Explanatory Memorandum OJ C 45 E 25/2/2003.

Coffee, J. 'Regulating the Market for Corporate Control: A Critical Assessment of the Tender Offer's Role in Corporate Governance'. *Col LR* (1984): 1146.

Constantinesco, V. 'Who's Afraid of Subsidiarity?'. *YEL* 11 (1991): 33.

Cumming, D., M. Wright & D. Siegel. 'Private Equity, Leveraged Buyouts and Governance'. J Corp Fin 13 (2007): 439.

Cunha, P. & P. Cadral. 'Presumed Innocence': Companies and the Exercise of the Right of Establishment under Community Law'. *E L Rev.* (2000): 157.

Dashwood, A. 'Viking and Laval: Issues of Horizontal Direct Effect'. *CYELS.* (Oxford: Hart, 2008).

Dashwood, A. 'From Van Duyn to Mangold via Marshall: Reducing Direct Effect to Absurdity?'. *CYELS* (Oxford: Hart, 2007): 106.

Davies, A.C.L. 'The Right to Strike versus Freedom of Establishment in EC Law: The Battle Commences'. *ILJ* (2006): 75.

Davies, P.L. 'The European Community's Directive on Insider Dealing: From Company Law to Securities Markets Regulation?'. *OJLS* (1991): 92.

de Burca, G. 'The Tobacco Advertising Saga: Political Aspirations and Constitutional Constraints' in The ECJ's Tobacco Advertising Judgment CELS Occasional Paper No. 5.

Deakin, S. 'Two Types of Regulatory Competition: Competitive Federalism versus Reflexive Harmonization. A Law and Economics Perspective on *Centros*'. *CYELS* (1999): 231.

Deakin, S. & G. Slinger. 'Hostile Takeovers, Corporate Law, and the Theory of the Firm'. *J Law Soc.* (1997): 124–151.

Decher, C. 'Cross Border Mergers: Traditional Structures and SE Merger Structures', *ECFR* 1 (2007): 5.

De Kluiver, H.J. 'Inspiring a New European Company Law? Observation on the ECJ's Decision in Inspire Art from a Dutch Perspective and the Imminent Competition for Corporate Charters between EC Member States'. *ECFR* (2004): 121.

De Minico, G. 'A Hard Look at Self-Regulation in the UK'. *EBLR* (2006): 185.

Dewing, I. & P.O. Russell. 'Financial Integration in the EU: The First Phase of EU Endorsement of International Accounting Standards'. *JCMS* 46 (2008): 243.

Dignam, A. 'The Globalisation of General Principle 7: Transforming the Market for Corporate Control in Australia and Europe?'. *Legal Studies* 28 (2008): 96–118.

Dine, J. 'The Community Company Law Harmonization Programme'. *E L Rev.* 14 (1989): 322.

Donald, D.C. 'Approaching Comparative Company Law'. SSRN Working Paper (2008).

Donker, H. & S. Zahir. 'Takeovers, Corporate Control and Return to Target Shareholders'. *Int J Cor Gov* 1 (2008): 106.

Doralt, M. 'Cross-Border Mergers: A Glimpse into the Future'. *ECFR* 1 (2007): 17.

Dougan, M. 'Minimum Harmonization and the Internal Market'. *CML Rev.* 37 (2000): 853.

Dougan, M. 'When Worlds Collide! Competing Visions of the Relationship between Direct Effect and Supremacy'. *CM L Rev.* (2007): 931.

Downes, T.A. & C. Hilson. 'Making Sense of Rights: Community Rights in EC Law'. *E L Rev.* (1999): 121.

Drury, R.R. 'Migrating Companies'. *ELR* 24, no. 4 (1999): 354.

Du Plessis, J. 'The German Two-Tier Board and the German Corporate Governance Code'. *EBLR* (2004): 1139.

Durrschmidt, D. 'Judicial Review of Takeover Panel Decisions'. *EBLR* (2005): 1135.

Dyrberg, P. 'Full Free Movement of Companies at the European Community at Last?'. *E L Rev.* 4 (2003): 528.

Ebert, S. 'The European Company and the Level Playing Field of the Community'. *EBLR* (2003): 183.

Ebke, W. 'The European Conflict-of-Corporate-Laws Revolution: Uberseering, Inspire Art, and Beyond'. *EBLR* (2005): 9.

Edbury, M. 'The European Company Statute: A Practical Working Model for the Future of European Company Law Making?'. *EBLR* (2004): 1283.

Editorial Comments. 'Horizontal Direct Effect: A Law of Diminishing Coherence?'. *CM L Rev.* (2006): 1.

Edwards, V. 'The Directive on Takeover Bids, Not Worth the Paper It's Written on?'. *ECFR* 4 (2004): 416.

Edwards, V. 'The European Company: Essential Tool or Eviscerated Dream?'. *CMLR* 40 (2003): 443.

Ehrhardt, O. & E. Nowak. 'Private Benefits and Minority Shareholder Expropriation: Empirical Evidence from IPOs of German Family-Owned Firms'. (2002) *EFA* 2003 Annual Conference Paper No. 809.

Eleftheriadis, P. 'The Direct Effect of Community Law: Conceptual Issues'. *YEL* (1996): 205.
Emiliou, N. 'Subsidiarity: An Effective Barrier against the "Enterprises of Ambition"?' *E L Rev.* 17 (1992): 383.
Engert, A. 'Life without Legal Capital: Lessons from American Law'. (1996) Working Paper Ludwig Maximilians Universitat Munchen.
Enriques, L. 'The Mandatory Bid Rule in the Takeover Directive: Harmonization without Foundation?'. *ECFR* 4 (2004): 440.
Enriques, L. 'EC Company Law and the Fears of a European Delaware'. *EBLR* (2004): 1261.
Enriques, L. 'Company Law Harmonisation Reconsidered: What Role for the EC?' ECGI Law Working Paper No. 53/2005.
Enriques, L. 'EC Company Law Directive and Regulations: How Trivial Are They?' ECGI Law Working Paper No. 39/2005 and *U Penn J Int'l Econ L* (2006): 27.
Enriques, L. & M. Gelter. 'How the Old World Encountered the New One: Regulatory Competition and Cooperation in European Corporate and Bankruptcy Law' ECGI Law Working Paper No. 63/2006.
Enriques, L. & P. Volpin. 'Corporate Governance Reforms in Continental Europe'. *J Econ Persp.* (2007): 117–140.
Enriques, L. 'Silence Is Golden: The European Company Statute as a Catalyst for Company Law Arbitrage' ECGI Law Working Paper No. 07/2003.
European Parliament, Report of 8 December 2003 of the Committee on Industrial, External Trade, and other matters, final A5 0469/2003, 80–82 and 91–92.
Proposal for a European Parliament and Council Directive on Takeover Bids (COM (2002) 534) of 2 October 2002, Explanatory Memorandum.
Enriques, L. & M. Gatti. 'Is There a Uniform EU Securities Law after the Financial Services Action Plan?' (2007) SSRN Working Paper.
Enriques, L. & M. Gatti. 'The Uneasy Case for Top-Down Corporate Law Harmonization in the European Union'. *U Penn J Int'l Econ L* 27 (2006): 939.
Enriques, L. 'Bad Apples, Bad Oranges: A Comment from Old Europe on Post-Enron Corporate Governance Reforms'. *Wak For LR* 38 (2003): 911, 912.
Fama, E. & M.C. Jensen. 'Separation of Ownership and Control'. *J Law Econ* (1983): 301.
Fauvera, L. & M.E. Fuersta. 'Does Good Corporate Governance Include Employee Representation? Evidence from German Corporate Boards'. *J Fin Econ.* (2006): 673–710.
Ferran, E. 'Company Law Reform in the UK: A Progress Report'. ECGI Law Working Paper No. 27/2005.
Ferran, E. 'Regulation of Private Equity: Backed Leveraged Buyout Activity in Europe'. ECGI Law Working Paper No. 84/2007.
Ferrarini, G. 'One Share – One Vote: A European Rule?'. ECGI Law Working Paper No. 58/2006.

Ferrarini, G., N. Moloney & C. Vespro. 'Executive Remuneration in the EU: Comparative Law and Practice'. ECGI Law Working Paper No. 09/2003.
Ferrarini, G. & D. Giudici. 'Financial Scandals and the Role of Private Enforcement: The Parmalat Case'. ECGI Law Working Paper No. 40/2005.
Ferrarini, G. & N. Moloney. 'Executive Remuneration and Corporate Governance in the EU: Convergence, Divergence and Reform Perspectives'. *ECFR* (2004): 251.
Fleischer, H. 'Legal Transplants in European Company Law: The Case of Fiduciary Duties'. *ECFR* (2005): 378.
Franks, J. & C. Mayer. 'Ownership and Control of German Corporations'. *R Fin St* (2001): 943.
Garcia-Riestra, M. 'The Transfer of Seat of the European Company v. Free Establishment Case Law'. *EBLR (*2004): 1295.
Garrido-Garcia, J. 'Company Law and Capital Markets Law'. *RabelsZ* (2005): 761.
Geradin, D. & N. Petit. 'The Development of Agencies at EU and National Levels: Conceptual Analysis and Proposals for Reform'. J. Monnet Working Paper 01/04.
Gesell, H. & P. Riemer. 'Outbound Cross-Border Mergers Protected by Freedom of Establishment: Annotation to the Decision of the Amsterdam District Court (Kantongerecht) 29 January 2007, EA 06-3338 166' (2007) 2 ECFR 308.
Gilson, R.J. 'The Political Ecology of Takeovers: Thoughts on Harmonizing the European Corporate Governance Environment'. *Fordham L. Rev.* 61 (1992): 161.
Giudici, P. 'Private Law Enforcement in a Formalist Legal Environment: The Italian Sai-Fondiaria Case' (2008). ECGI Law Working Paper No. 094/2008, <http://ssrn.com/abstract=1103985>, accessed 19 September 2008.
Goergen, M., M. Martynova & L. Reneboog. 'Corporate Governance Convergence: Evidence from Takeover Regulation Reforms' ECGI Law Working Paper No. 33/2005.
Goergen, M. & L. Renneboog. 'Shareholder Wealth Effects of European Domestic and Cross-Border Takeover Bids' ECGI Finance Working Paper No. 08/2003.
Gordon, J. 'An American Perspective of the New German Anti-Takeover Law' ECGI Law Working Paper No. 02/2002, Columbia Law and Economics Working Paper No. 209 and Harvard Law and Economics Disc. Paper No. 407.
Gormley, L. 'Competition and Free Movement: Is the Internal Market the Same as the Common Market?'. *EBLR* (2002): 517.
Grant, J., T. Kirchmaier & A. Kirshner. 'Financial Tunnelling and the Mandatory Bid Rule'. *EBOR* (2009): 233.
Gravir, G.S. 'Conflict of Laws: Rules for Norwegian Companies after the Centros Judgement'. *EBLR* (2001): 146.
Gross, J. & B. Black. 'When Perception Changes Reality: An Empirical Study of Investors' Views of the Fairness of Securities Arbitration' *J Disp Res* (2008): 349.

Grundmann, S. 'The Structure of European Company Law: From Crisis to Boom'. *EBOR* 5 (2004): 602.

Grundmann, S. & F. Moslein. 'Golden Shares. State Control in Privatised Companies: Comparative Law, European Law and Policy Aspects' SSRN Working Paper Series (2003).

Gutman, K. 'Case Not: Case C-66/04 *Smoke Flavourings*, Case C-436/03 *SCE* & Case C-217/04 *ENISA*'. *Col J EL* 13 (2006): 147.

Hansen, J.L. 'Full Circle: Is There a Difference between the Freedom of Establishment and the Freedom to Provide Services?'. EBLR (2000): 83.

Hansen, J.L. 'When Less Would Be More: The EU Takeover Directive in Its Latest Apparition'. *Col J EL* 9 (2003): 275.

Hansen, J.L. 'A New Look at Centros: From a Danish Point of View'. *EBLR* (2002): 85.

Hansen, J.L. 'Merger, Moving and Division Across National Borders: When Case Law Breaks through Barriers and Overtakes Directives'. *EBLR* (2007): 181.

Hartley, T.C. 'The Constitutional Foundations of the European Union'. *LQR* (2001): 225.

Haynes, A. 'Legal Developments in Debt Securitisation' at W.G. Hart Legal Workshop – Institute of Advanced Legal Studies: 'Transnational Finance and the Challenge to the Law'. *EBLR* (2000): 39.

Heine, K. 'Regulatory Competition between Company Laws in the European Union: The Uberseering Case'. *Intereconomics* 38, no. 2 (2003): 102.

Heiser, K. 'Can Capital Market Law Approaches Be Harmonized with Essential Principles of Company Law?'. *EBLR* (2000): 61.

Hertig, G. & J. McCahery. 'Company and Takeover Law Reforms in Europe: Misguided Harmonisation Efforts or Regulatory Competition'. ECGI Law Working Paper No. 12/2003 and *EBOR* 4 (2003): 179.

Hertig, G. & J. McCahery. 'A Legal Options Approach to EC Company Law' (2006) Berkeley Program in Law & Economics Working Paper Series (University of California, Berkeley) No. 180.

Hillion, C. 'Case Annotation, Tobacco Advertising: If You Must, You May'. *CLJ* (2001): 486.

Hinton, E.F. 'Case Note, *Commission v. France*'. *Col J Eur L* (1999): 477.

Hirt, H. 'Freedom of Establishment, International Company Law and the Comparison of European Company Law Systems after the ECJ's Decision in Inspire Art Ltd.' *EBLR* (2004): 1189.

Hodt Dickens, C. 'Establishment of the SE Company: An Overview of the Provisions Governing the Formation of the European Company'. *EBLR* (2007): 1423.

Hopner, M. & G. Jackson. 'An Emerging Market for Corporate Control? The Mannesmann Takeover and German Corporate Governance'. Working Paper 01/4 Max Planck Institut fur Gesellschaftsforschung (2001).

Hopt, K. 'European Company and Corporate Governance: Where Does the Action Plan of the European Commission Lead?'. ECGI Law Working Paper No. 52/2005.

Hopt, K. 'Takeovers, Secrecy and Conflicts of Interest: Problems for Boards and Banks'. ECGI Law Working Paper No. 03/2002.

Hopt, K. 'Company Law in the European Union: Harmonization or Subsidiarity'. Working Paper Centro di studi e ricerche di diritto comparator e straniero, Saggi, Conference e Seminari 31, (Roma 1998).

Hopt, K. 'Modern Company and Capital Markets Problems: Improving European Corporate Governance after Enron'. ECGI Law Working Paper No. 005/2002, published in *Journal of Corporate Law Studies* 3 (2003).

Hopt, K. & P. Leyens. 'Board Models in Europe: Recent Developments of Internal Corporate Governance Structures in Germany, the United Kingdom, France, and Italy'. *ECFR* 1 (2004): 135.

Howel, B. ' "Companies" Capital and Creditor Protection under the Czech Law: Living on the Edge of Shopping Forum'. *EBLR* (2005): 1415.

Huang, J. 'Hedge Fund Activism in Leveraged Buyouts'. (2008) SSRN Working Paper.

Ichay, F. & M. Schocher. 'The French SE: An Attractive Tool to Facilitate an International Merger?'. *ECL* 3 (2006): 164.

Ipekel, F. 'Defensive Measures under the Directive on Takeover Bids and Their Effect on the UK and French Takeover Regimes'. *EBLR* (2005): 341.

Itzikowitz, A. 'Broadening Access to Financial Services: Competing Imperatives'. *EBLR* (2006): 1241.

Jacobs, F. 'The Evolution of European Legal Order'. *CM L Rev.* (2004): 303.

Jans, J. 'The Effect in National Legal Systems of the Prohibition of Discrimination on Grounds of Age as a General Principle of Community Law'. *LIEI* (2007): 53.

Jensen, M.C. 'Takeovers: Their Causes and Consequences'. *J Econ Persp* (1988): 21–48.

Johansson, M. & L. Sevon. 'The Protection of the Rights of Individuals under the EEA Agreement'. *E L Rev.* (1999): 373.

Johnson, J. & E. Brunet. 'Substantive Fairness in Securities Arbitration'. *U Cinc L* (2007): 76.

Johnson, M. 'Does Europe Still Need a Fourteenth Company Law Directive?'. *Hertfordshire L J* 3 (2005): 18.

Johnston, A. 'The European Takeover Directive: Ruined by Protectionism or Respecting Diversity?'. *Comp. Law* (2004): 270.

Kaisanlahti, T. 'When Is a Tender Price Fair in a Squeeze-Out?'. *EBOR* (2007): 497–519.

Kaldellis, E.I. 'Freedom of Establishment versus Freedom to Provide Services: An Evaluation of Case-Law Developments in the Area of Indistinctly Applicable Rules'. *LIEI* 28 (2001): 23.

Kalss, S. 'The Transfer of Shares of Private Companies'. *ECFR* (2004): 340.

Kamar, E. 'Beyond Competition for Incorporations'. ECGI Law Working Paper No. 42/2005, USC Law Legal Studies Paper No. 05-13, NYU Law and Economics Research Paper No. 05-01.

Kemperink, G. & J. Stuyck. 'The Thirteenth Company Law Directive and Competing Bids'. *CM L Rev.* (2008): 93.

Kershaw, D. 'The Illusion of Importance: Reconsidering the UK's Takeover Defence Prohibition'. *ICLQ* 56 (2007): 267.

Kirchner, C. & R.W. Painter. 'Takeover Defences under Delaware Law, the Proposed Thirteenth EU Directive and the New German Takeover Law: Comparison and Recommendations for Reform'. *Am. J. Comp. L* 50 (2002): 451.

Kirchner, C. & R.W. Painter. 'European Takeover Law: Towards a European Modified Business Judgment Rule for Takeover Law'. *EBOR* (2000): 353.

Kirchner, C., R.W. Painter & W. Kaal. 'Regulatory Competition in the EU Corporate Law after Inspire Art: Unbundling Delaware's Product for Europe'. *ECFR* 2 (2005): 159.

Kjellgren, D. 'On the Border of Abuse: The Jurisprudence of the European Court of Justice on Circumvention, Fraud and Other Misuses of Community Law'. *EBLR* (2000): 180.

Klauberg, T. 'Rules on Takeover Bids in Latvia'. *EBLR* (2005): 1474.

Klinke, U. 'European Company Law and the ECJ: The Court's Judgements in the Years 2001 to 2004'. *ECFR* 2 (2005): 270.

Knook, A. 'Guns and Tobacco. The Effect of Interstate Trade Case Law on the Vertical Division of Powers'. *MJ* 11 (2004): 347.

Knudsen, J.S. 'Is the Single European Market an Illusion? Obstacles to Reform of EU Takeover Regulation'. *ELJ* 11 (2005): 507.

Kolodny, K. 'Protection of Minority Shareholders after a Take-over Bid: The UK and Ontario Compared'. *Comp. Law.* 7 (1986): 17.

Krohn, M. 'Minority Squeeze-Outs and the European Convention on Human Rights'. *EBLR* (2004): 159.

Koehler, N. 'Cross-Border Company Establishment between the UK and Austria'. *EBLR* (2001): 110.

Kroeze, M.J. & H.M. Vletter-Van Dort. 'History and Future of Uniform Company Law in Europe'. *ECL* 5 (2008): 114.

Kubler, F. 'A Shifting Paradigm of European Company Law?'. *Col J Eur L* (2005): 219.

Kumm, M. 'Constitutionalising Subsidiarity in Integrated Markets: The Case of Tobacco Regulation in the European Union'. *ELJ* (2006): 503.

Kurcz, B. 'Harmonisation by Means of Directives: Never Ending Story?'. *EBLR* (2001): 287.

Lamandini, M. 'Takeover Bids and 'Italian' Reciprocity'. *ECL* 5 (2008): 56–57.

Langeroort, D. 'Structuring Securities Regulation in the European Union: Lessons from the U.S. Experience'. ECGI Law Working Paper No. 41/2005.

Lauterfeld, M. 'Centros and the EC Regulation on Insolvency Proceedings: The End of the Real Seat Approach towards Pseudo-foreign Companies in German International Company and Insolvency Law? The Danger of Diverging Developments of the Connecting Factors in Company and Insolvency Law'. *EBLR* (2001): 79.

Leca, C. 'The Participation of Employee's Representatives in the Governance Structure of the Societas Europeae'. *EBLR* (2007): 403.

Lee, J. 'Four Models of Minority Shareholder Protection in Takeover'. *EBLR* (2005): 803.
Leigh French, H. 'Pre-offer Purchases and Partial Take-over Bids'. *Comp. Law* 7 (1986): 66–67.
Lehne, K.-H. 'Working Document on the Proposal for a Directive of the European Parliament and of the Council on Takeover Bids'. COM (2002) 534-C5-0481/2002-2002/0240 (COD), Committee on Legal Affairs and the Internal Market.
Lennarts, M.-L. 'Company Mobility within the EU, Fifty Years on: From a Non-issue to a Hot Topic'. *Utr L R* 4 (2008): 1.
Leyens, P. 'A Framework for Adequate Shareholder Protection'. *EBLR* 2 (2001): 42.
Leyens, P. 'Internal Corporate Governance in Europe: Towards a More Market-based Approach'. *Kyoto J L P* 4 (2007): 1.
Lisauskas, G. & E. Lauraityte. 'Baltic Takeover Practices Already in Line with EC'. *IF L Rev.* (2004): 43.
Lombardo, S. & P. Pasotti. 'The "Societas Europaea": A Network Economics Approach'. ECGI Law Working Paper No. 19/2004.
Long, J. 'Navigating the Maze: Reviewing the Information Disclosure Requirements in the Financial Services Acquis'. *EBLR* (2008): 485.
Looijestijn-Clearie, A. 'Have the Dikes Collapsed? Inspire Act a Further Break-through in the Freedom of Establishment of Companies?'. *EBOR* (2004): 389.
Looijestijn-Clearie, A. 'All That Glitters Is Not Gold: European Court of Justice Strikes Down Golden Shares in Two Dutch Companies'. *EBOR* (2007): 429.
Lσpez-de-Foronda, O., F.J. Lσpez-Iturriaga & M. Santamarva-Mariscal. 'Ownership Structure, Sharing of Control and Legal Framework: International Evidence'. *Corp Gov.* (2007): 1130.
Ludwigs, M. 'Case Note, Case C-380/03 *Germany v. European Parliament and Council of the European Union (*second *Tobacco Advertising* ruling*)* [2006] ECR I-11573'. *CM L Rev.* 44 (2007): 1159.
Manne, H.G. 'Mergers and the Market for Corporate Control'. *The Journal of Political Economy* 73 (1965): 110.
Massimo, M. 'Legal Capital and Limited Liability Companies: The European Perspective'. *ECFR* 2 (2005): 413.
Maul, S. & A. Kouloridas. 'The Takeover Bids Directive'. *German Law Journal* 5 (2004): 4.
McCahery, J. & E. Vermeulen. 'Does the European Company Prevent the Delaware Effect?'. *European Law Journal* 11 (2005): 785 and (2005) TILEC Discussion Paper DP 2005-010.
McCahery, J.A. & E. Vermeulen. 'The Evolution of Closely Held Business Forms in Europe'. *J Corp L* (2001): 855.
McGee, A. & S. Weatherill. 'The Evolution of the Single Market-Harmonization or Liberalization'. *MLR* 53 (1990): 578, 582.
Mengoli, S., F. Pazzaglia, & E. Sapienza. 'Is It Still Pizza, Spaghetti and Mandolino? Effect of Governance Reforms on Corporate Ownership in Italy' SSRN Working Paper (2007).

Menjucq, M. 'French Interpretations and Strategies about the European Company'. *EBLR* (2004): 1275.
Menjucq, M. 'Corporate Governance Issues in France'. *EBLR* (2005): 1005.
Menjucq, M. 'The European Regime on Takeovers'. *ECFR* (2006): 222.
Merkt, H. 'European Company Law Reform: Struggling for a More Liberal Approach'. *ECFR* (2004): 3.
Meulman, J. & H. de Waele. 'A Retreat from Sager: Servicing or Fine-tuning the Application of Article 49 EC'. *LIEI* 33 (2006): 207.
Mitchell, M.L. & K. Lehn. 'Do Bad Bidders Become Good Targets?'. *J Pol Econ* (1990): 372–398.
Mohamed, S. 'Recent Case Law in the Field of Free Movement of Capital'. *EBLR* (2001): 263.
Moloney, N. 'Confidence and Competence: The Conundrum of EC Capital Markets Law'. *JCLS* 1 (2004): 1.
Moloney, N. 'New Frontiers in EC Capital Markets Law: From Market Construction to Market Regulation'. *CM L Rev.* (2003): 809.
Moran, S.J. 'Establishing Establishment: A Modern Chimera. An Investigation into Securing the Right of Establishment for Companies within the Internal Market of the European Community'. *Ir S LR* 15 (2007): 149.
Morkve, C.S. 'The European Company in Scandinavia: Nordea's Transformation to an SE'. *EBLR* (2005): 353.
Morse, G. 'The Takeover Appeal Board Rules on Equivalent Treatment of Shareholders under a Code Offer and the Existence of Different Classes of Shares: Cumbrian Newspaper Group Ltd Case not Applied'. *JBL* 1 (2008): 96.
Mortelmans, K. 'The Common Market, the Internal Market and the Single Market, What's in a Market?'. *CM L Rev.* 38 (1998): 101.
Moslein, F. 'Towards an Organizational Law of the Polycorporate Enterprize? A Comparative Analysis'. SSRN Working Paper (2006).
Mucciarelli, F. 'White Knights and Black Knights. Does the Search for Competitive Bids Always Benefit the Shareholders of 'Target' Companies?'. (2006) Working Paper, <http://papers.ssrn.com/sol3/papers.cfm?abstract_id=910220>, accessed 21 November 2006 (for another version of this paper: F. Mucciarelli. 'White Knights and Black Knights: Does the Search for Competitive Bids Always Benefit the Shareholders of 'Target Companies'?'. *ECFR* 4 (2006): 408–425.
Mueller, D.C. 'The Economics and Politics of Corporate Governance in the European Union'. ECGI Law Working Paper No. 37/2005.
Mulbert, P. 'Make It or Break It: The Break-Through Rule as a Break-Through for the European Takeover Directive?'. ECGI Law Working Paper 13/2003.
The Hon. Lord Justice Mummery. 'Transfers of Undertakings and the Protection of Employment: The UK Courts and the European Court of Justice 1981–2004'. *EBLR* (2005): 471.
Novitz, T. 'Labour Rights as Human Rights: Implications for Employers' Free Movement in an Enlarged European Union'. *CYELS* (2007): 378.

Novitz, T. 'A Clash in EC Treaty Priorities'. *CLI* 6 (2007): 13.

Officer, M.S., O. Ozbas & B.A. Sensoy. 'Club Deals in Leveraged Buyouts'. (2008) Marshall School of Business Working Paper No. MKT 10.

Ogowewo, T.I. 'Tactical Litigation in Takeover Contests'. *JBL* (2007): 589–619.

Oliver, P. & W.H. Roth. 'The Internal Market and the Four Freedoms'. *Common Market Law Review* 41 (2004): 407.

Omar, D. 'Company Law Reform in France: The Economic Imperative'. *EBLR* (2001): 76.

O'Neill, M. 'When European Integration Meets Corporate Harmonization'. *Comp. Law.* 21 (2000): 173.

Orlandini, G. 'Right to Strike, Transnational Collective Action and European Law: Time to Move On?'. (2007) The Jean Monnet Working Paper Series No. 8/07.

Ortino, M. 'The Role and Functioning of Mutual Recognition in the European Market of Financial Services'. *ICLQ* 56 (2007): 309.

O'Shea, T. 'Thin Cap GLO and Third-Country Rights: Which Freedom Applies?'. *Tax N Int'l* (2007): 371.

Pannier, M. 'The EU Cross-Border Merger Directive: A New Dimension for Employee Participation and Company Restructuring'. *EBLR* (2005): 1425.

Pannier, M. & J. Rickford. 'Corporate Governance Disclosures in Europe'. *EBLR* (2005): 975.

Pannier, M. 'New European Company Law and Corporate Governance: The UK and the New Member States'. *EBLR* (2004): 1366.

Papadopoulos, T. 'Legal Perspectives on the Scope of the Tenth Company Law Directive on Cross-border Mergers'. *European Current Law,* No. 10, October 2008.

Papadopoulos, T. 'The relationship between takeover bids and mergers: implications for the internal market of the European Union' International and Comparative Corporate Law Journal vol. 7 issue 2 (2010) p. 1–19.

Payne, J. 'Company Contracts and Conundrums: When Is a Board not a Board and When Is a Director not a Person?'. *ECFR* (2004): 235.

Pelkmans, J. 'Subsidiarity between Law and Economics'. College of Europe Research Papers in Law No. 1/2005.

Pelle, P. 'Companies Crossing Borders within Europe'. *Utr. L R* 4 (2008): 6.

Peter, N. 'The Hypothesis of the European Legal Person'. *EBLR* (2006): 1373.

Poutianen, A. 'Shareholders and Corporate Governance: The Principle of One Share-One Vote'. *EBLR* (2001): 68.

Peter, N. 'The Hypothesis of the European Legal Person'. *EBLR* (2006): 1372.

Pettet, B. 'Private versus Public Regulation in the Field of Takeovers: The Future under the Directive'. *EBLR* (2000): 381.

Prechal, S. & S. De Vries. 'Seamless Web of Judicial Protection in the Internal Market?'. *E L Rev.* (2009): 5.

Prentice, D. 'The Incorporation Theory: The United Kingdom'. *EBLR* (2003): 633.

Raaijmakers, T. 'Takeover Regulation in Europe and America: The Need for Functional Convergence' APF Working Paper No. 01/07, Centre for

Company Law, Working Paper Series, Sponsored by A. Philips Fund, Tilburg University (2001).
Raaijmakers, T. 'The Statute for a European Company: Its Impact on Board Structures and Corporate Governance in the European Union'. *EBOR* (2004): 159.
Raaijmakers, G. & T. Olthoff. 'Creditor Protection in Cross-Border Mergers; Unfinished Business'. *Utr. L R* 4 (2008): 34.
Radwan, A. '25 Thoughts on European Company Law in the EU of 25'. *EBLR* (2006): 1169.
Rajak, H. 'Proposal for a Fourteenth European and Council Directive on the Transfer of the Registered Office or de facto Head Office of a Company from one Member State to Another with a Challenge in Applicable Law: The Legal Issues in the United Kingdom Arising out of This Proposal'. *EBLR* 1 (2004): 44.
Ramsay, I.M., H. Lange & L.A. Woo. 'Corporate Governance and Anti-Takeover Devices'. Faculty of Law University of Melbourne, Public Law and Legal Theory, Working Paper No. 1 (2000).
Reich, N. 'Horizontal Liability in EC Law: Hybridization of Remedies for Compensation in Case of Breaches of EC Rights'. *CM L Rev.* (2007): 705.
Reich, N. 'Free Movement v. Social Rights in an Enlarged Union: The *Laval* and *Viking* Cases before the ECJ'. *Ger L J* (2008): 125.
Reichert, J. 'Experience with SE in Germany'. *Utr L R* 4 (2008): 22.
Reid, A.S. 'The Increasing Europeanisation of Company Law'. *BLR* 7 (2003): 165.
Rickford, J. 'The Proposed Tenth Company Law Directive on Cross-Border Mergers and Its Impact on the UK'. *EBLR* (2005): 1393.
Rickford, J. 'Fundamentals, Developments and Trends in British Company Law: Some Wider Reflections. Second Part: Current British Priorities and Wider Reflections'. *ECFR* (2005): 63.
Rickford, J. 'The Emerging European Takeover Law From a British Perspective'. *EBLR* (2004): 1379.
Rickford, J. 'Current Developments in European Law on the Restructuring of Companies: An Introduction'. *EBLR* (2004): 1225.
Rickford, J. (ed.). 'Reforming Capital'. *EBLR* 15 (2004): 919.
Ringe, W.G. 'No Freedom of Emigration for Companies?'. *EBLR* (2005): 621.
Romano, R. 'The Sarbanes – Oxley Act and the Making of Quack Corporate Governance'. ECGI Finance Working Paper No. 52/2004.
Rogers, P. & A.-S. Cornette De Saint-Cyr. 'Cross-border Mergers (CBMs)'. *ICCLR* 13 (2002): 343.
Romano, R. 'Is Regulatory Competition a Problem or Irrelevant for Corporate Governance?'. ECGI Law Working Paper No. 26/2005.
Romano, R. 'The States as a Laboratory: Legal Innovation and State Competition for Corporate Charters'. ECGI Law Working Paper No. 34/2005.
Romano, R. 'After the Revolution in Corporate Law'. ECGI Law Working Paper No. 50/2005.

Ronfeldt, T. & E. Werlauff. 'Mergers as a Method of Establishment: On Cross-border Mergers, Transfer of Domicile and Divisions, Directly Applicable under the EC Treaty's Freedom of Establishment'. *ECL* 3 (2006): 125.

Rose, C. 'Corporate Financial Performance and the Use of Takeover Defenses'. *European Journal of Law and Economics* 13 (2002): 91.

Rosenzweig, B.A. 'Private versus Public Regulation: A Comparative Analysis of British and American Takeover Controls'. *Duk. J. Comp. Int'l. L.* 18 (2007): 213.

Rossi, S. & P. Volpin. 'Cross-country Determinants of Mergers and Acquisitions'. ECGI Finance Working Paper No. 25/2003.

Rothe, N. 'Freedom of Establishment of Legal Persons within the European Union: An Analysis of the European Court of Justice Decision in the Uberseering Case'. *American University Law Review* 53 (2004): 1103.

Rott, P. 'Minimum Harmonization for the Completion of the Internal Market? The Example of Consumer Sales Law'. *CM L Rev.* 40 (2003): 1107.

Roussos, Al. 'Realising the Free Movement of Companies'. *EBLR* 1 (2001): 7.

Ryan, P.S. 'Case Note Case C-167/01'. *Col J E L* (2005): 187.

Saenger, I. 'Recent Developments in European Company and Business Law'. *Deakin LR* 10 (2005): 297.

Santella, P., E. Baffi, C. Drago & D. Lattuca. 'A Comparative Analysis of the Legal Obstacles to Institutional Investor Activism in Europe and in the US'. (2008) SSRN Working Paper, <http://ssrn.com/abstract=1137491>, accessed 23 September 2008.

Sainz de Vicuna, A. 'The Legal Integration of Financial Services of the Euro Area'. *EBLR* (2001): 223.

Salacuse, J.W. 'Corporate Governance, Culture and Convergence: Corporations American Style or with a European Touch?'. *EBLR* (2003): 473.

Salmon, P. 'Political Yardstick Competition and Corporate Governance in the European Union'. ECGI Law Working Paper No. 38/2005.

Schall, A.L. 'The UK Limited Company Abroad: How Foreign Creditors Are Protected after Inspire Art (Including a Comparison of UK and German Creditor Protection Rules)'. *EBLR* (2005): 1534.

Schindler, C.P. 'Cross-border Mergers in Europe: Company Law Is Catching up! – Commentary on the ECJ's Decision on Sevic Systems AG'. *ECFR* 1 (2006): 109.

Schindler, C.P. 'Discussion Report: Cross-border Mergers'. *ECFR* 1 (2007): 43.

Schoen, W. 'Corporate Disclosure in a Competitive Environment: The ECJ's Axel Springer Case and the Quest for a European Framework for a Mandatory Disclosure'. ECGI Law Working Paper No. 55/2006.

Schon, W. 'The Mobility of Companies in Europe and the Organizational Freedom of Company Founders'. *ECFR* 2 (2006): 122.

Schutze, R. 'Organized Change towards an "Ever-Closer Union": Article 308 EC and the Limits to the Community's Legislative Competence'. *YEL* 22 (2003): 79.

Schwarcz, S. 'The "Principles" Paradox', Duke Law School Legal Studies Research Paper Series, Research Paper No. 205/2008.

Sciara, S. 'Viking and Laval: Collective Labour Rights and Market Freedoms in the Enlarged EU'. *CYELS* (Hart, Oxford 2008).

Sepe, S. 'Private Sale of Corporate Control: Why the European Mandatory Bid Rule is Inefficient'. (2007) SSRN Working Paper, <http://ssrn.com/abstract=1086321>, accessed 24 September 2008.

Sester, P. & J.L. Cardenas. 'The Extra-Communitarian Effects of Centros, *Uberseering* and *Inspire Art* with Regard to Fourth Generation Association Agreements'. *ECFR* (2005): 398.

Sevon, L. 'Making Community Law Efficient'. *EBLR* (2001): 154.

Siems, M.M. 'The Rules on Conflict of Laws in the European Takeover Directive'. *ECFR* 4 (2004): 458.

Siems, M. 'SEVIC: Beyond Cross-Border Mergers'. *EBOR* 8 (2007): 307.

Siems, M. 'The European Directive on Cross-border Mergers: An International Model?'. *Col J Eur L* 11 (2005): 167.

Siems, M. 'The Impact of the European Company (SE) on Legal Culture'. *E L Rev.* 30 (2005): 431.

Simon, J. 'OPA: Divine Surprise ou Faux Semblant?'. *Euredia* 3 (2003): 329.

Sjafjell, B. 'Political Path Dependency in Practice: The Takeover Directive'. *YEL* (2008): 395.

Skog, R. 'The Takeover Directive: An Endless Saga?'. *EBLR* 13 (2002): 301.

Skog, R. 'The Takeover Directive, the "Breakthrough" Rule and the Swedish System of Dual Class Common Stock'. *EBLR* (2004): 1439.

Skouris, V. 'Effet Utile versus Legal Certainty: The Case Law of the Court of Justice on the Direct Effect of Directives'. *EBLR* (2006): 241.

Skouris, V. 'Fundamental Rights and Fundamental Freedoms: The Challenge of Striking a Delicate Balance'. *EBLR* (2006): 227.

Toner, H. 'Non-discriminatory Obstacles to the Exercise of Treaty Rights: Articles 39, 43, 49, and 18'. *YEL* 23 (2004): 274.

Slot, P.J. 'Harmonization'. *E L Rev.* 21 (1996): 378.

Smith, A.J. 'Corporate Ownership Structure and Performance: The Case of Management Buyouts'. *J Fin Econ* (1990): 143–164.

Song, W.-S., T. Gun-Lee & R. Young. 'Foreign Bidders Welcome: Korean Takeover Changes'. *International Financial Law Review* 24, no. 3 (2005).

Spaventa, E. 'From Gebhard to Carpenter: Towards a (Non-)economic European Constitution'. *CM L Rev.* 41 (2004): 743.

Stein, E. 'Lawyers, Judges and the Making of a Transnational Constitution'. *Am J Int'l L* (1981): 1.

Storm, P. 'Cross-border Mergers, the Rule of Reason and Employee Participation'. *ECL* 3 (2006): 130.

Stulz, R. 'The Limits of Financial Globalization' Working Paper 2004, <www.usc.edu/schools/business/FBE/seminars/papers/F_1-21-05_STULZglobalizatio.pdf>, accessed 21 January 2007.

Syrpis, P. & T. Novitz. 'Economic and Social Rights in Conflict: Political and Judicial Approaches to Their Reconciliation'. *E L Rev.* (2008): 411.

Teichmann, C. 'Restructuring Companies in Europe: A German Perspective'. *EBLR* (2004): 1327.

Timmermans, C. 'How Can One Improve the Quality of Community Legislation?'. *CM L Rev.* (1997): 1229.

Tridimas, T. 'The Case-law of the European Court of Justice on Corporate Entities'. *YEL* 13 (1993): 335.

Ugliano, A. 'The New Cross-border Merger Directive: Harmonization of European Company Law and Free Movement'. *EBLR* (2007): 585.

Vaccaro, E. 'Transfer of Seat and Freedom of Establishment in European Company Law'. *EBLR* (2005): 1348.

Vaccaro, E. 'The Italian Company Law Reform: A New European Model'. *EBLR* (2005): 913.

Vajda, C. 'Liability for Breach of Community Law: A Survey of the ECJ Cases Post Factortame'. *EBLR* (2006): 259.

Van Byck, T. 'Case Note: Case C-478/98 *Commission v Belgium*)'. *Col J EL* (2002): 311.

Van Der Elst, C. & L. Van Den Steen. 'Opportunities in the M&A Aftermarket: Squeezing Out and Selling Out'. (2006) University of Gent, Financial Law Institute Working Papers 2006–2012.

Van Der Elst, C. & L. Van Den Steen. 'Squeezing and Selling-Out: A Patchwork of Rules in Five European Member States'. *ECL* 4 (2007): 19–20, 25.

Van Gerven, W. 'Harmonization of Private Law: Do We Need It?'. *CM L Rev.* 41 (2004): 505.

Vaughan, D. 'Factortame and after: A Fishy Story'. *EBLR* (2005): 511.

Vaughan, D. 'Free Movement and Competition Pillars of the Single Market'. *CLI* 4 (2003): 8.

Vossestein, G.J. 'Regulatory Competition in Company Law in the European Community. Pre-requisites and Limits'. *Common Market Law Review* 40, no. 5 (2003): 1304.

Vossestein, G.J. 'Transfer of Registered Office. The European Commission's Decision not to Submit a Proposal for a Directive'. *Utr. L R* 4 (2008): 53.

Vossestein, G.J. 'Companies' Freedom of Establishment after *Sevic*'. *ECL* 3 (2006): 177.

Ventoruzzo, M. 'Experiments in Comparative Corporate Law: The Recent Italian Reform and the Dubious Virtues of a Market for Rules in the Absence of Effective Regulatory Competition'. *ECFR* 2 (2005): 208.

Walker, G. 'European Financial Programme: Content, Structure, and Completion'. *EBLR* (2004): 305.

Ventoruzzo, M. 'Europe's Thirteenth Directive and US Takeover Regulation: Regulatory Means and Political and Economic Ends'. *Tex. Int'l. L. J* 41 (2006): 171.

Ventoruzzo, M. 'Cross-border Mergers, Change of Applicable Corporate Laws and Protection of Dissenting Shareholders: Withdrawal Rights under Italian Law'. *ECFR* 1 (2007): 47.

Vermeulen, E. 'Towards a New "Company" Structure for High-tech Start-ups in Europe'. *MJ* (2001): 233.

Villiers, C. 'European Integration and Globalisation: The Experience of Financial Reporting'. *CYELS* 8 (2006): 109.

Villiers, C. 'The Directive on Employee Involvement in the European Company: Its Role in European Corporate Governance and Industrial Relations'. *I.J. Comp. Lab. L. Ind. Rel.* 22 (2006): 183.

Voermans, W. 'The Quality of EU Legislation: What Kind of Problem, by What Kind of Standards?'. (2008) SSRN Working Paper.

Xanthaki, E. 'The Problem of Quality in EU Legislation: What on Earth is Really Wrong?'. *CM L Rev* (2001): 651.

Waddington, L. 'Recent Developments and the Non-discrimination Directives: *Mangold* and More'. *MJ* (2006): 365.

Waddington, L. 'Editorial: Throwing Some Light on Article 13 EC Treaty'. *MJ* (1999): 1.

Ware, S. 'What Makes Securities Arbitration Different from Other Consumer and Employment Arbitration?'. *U Cinc L R* 76 (2008): 447.

Weatherill, S. 'Harmonisation: How Much, How Little?'. *EBLR* (2005): 533.

Weatherill, S. 'Competence Creep and Competence Control'. *YEL* 23 (2004): 1.

Weber-Rey, D. 'Effects of the Better Regulation Approach on European Company Law and Corporate Governance'. *ECFR* 3 (2007): 370.

Welch, J. 'Tenth Draft Directive on Cross-border Mergers'. *Comp Law.* 7 (1986): 69.

Werlauff, E. 'The SE Company: A New Common European Company from 8 October 2004'. *EBLR* (2003): 86.

Werdmuller, P. Compatibility of the EU Takeover Bid Directive Reciprocity Rule with EU Free Movement Rules'. *BLR* 3 (2006): 64.

Werlauff, E. 'The Main Seat Criterion in a New Disguise: An Acceptable Version of the Classic Main Seat Criterion'. *EBLR* 1 (2001): 2.

Werlauff, E. 'Group and Community: The European Court's Development of an Independent Community Law Concept of the Group and Its Significance for National Company Law'. *ECL* 4 (2007): 201.

Wesseling, R. 'Subsidiarity in Community Antitrust Law: Setting the Right Agenda'. *E L Rev* 22 (1997): 35.

Wessels, B. 'Realisation of the EU Insolvency Regulation in Germany, France and Netherlands'. *EBLR* (2004): 75.

White, R. 'The Citizen's Right to Free Movement'. *EBLR* (2005): 547.

Windbichler, C. 'Cheers and Boos for Employee Involvement: Co-determination as Corporate Governance Conundrum'. *EBOR* (2005): 507.

Winter, J. 'We All Want to Go to Heaven but Nobody Wants to Die'. *ECL* 1 (2004): 4.

Wood, P. Handout-Introduction to the Course of Global Comparative Financial Law, Degree of Magister Juris, University of Oxford, Acad. Year 2005–2006.

Wooldridge, F. & M. Pannier. 'The German Corporate Governance Code: Status and Development'. *EBLR* (2005): 225.

Wooldridge, F. 'The New German Takeover Act'. *EBLR* (2003): 75.

Wooldridge, F. 'Uberseering: Freedom of Establishment of Companies Affirmed'. *EBLR* (2003): 227.

Wooldridge, F. 'The Advocate General's Submissions in Kamer van Koophandel: Further Emphasis on the Right of Establishment'. *EBLR* (2003): 497.

Wooldridge, F. 'Instruments Issued by Italian Public Companies'. *EBLR* (2006): 1181.

Wooldridge, F. 'The Recent Directive on Takeover Bids'. *EBLR* (2004): 147.

Wright, M., T. Simons, L. Scholes & L. Renneboog. 'Leveraged Buyouts in the U.K. and Continental Europe: Retrospect and Prospect'. *J Appl Corp Fin* 18 (2006): 38.

Wyatt, D.A. 'The Growing Competence of the European Community'. *EBLR* (2005): 483.

Wyatt, D.A. 'Community Competence to Regulate the Internal Market'. Oxford Legal Studies Research Paper No. 9/2007.

Wyatt, D.A. 'Constitutional Significance of the Tobacco Advertising Judgment of the European Court of Justice' in the ECJ's Tobacco Advertising Judgment *CELS* Occasional Paper No. 5.

Wyatt, D.A. 'Horizontal Effect of Fundamental Freedoms and the Right to Equality after *Viking* and *Mangold*, and the Implications for Community Competence'. *CYELP* (2008): 1.

Wyatt, D.A. 'Trade, Tax and Takeovers: Can the European Court De-regulate Europe Despite Resistance from the Council and Parliament?'. *CYELP* (2005): 95.

Wyckaert, M. & K. Geens. 'Cross-border Mergers and Minority Protection. An Open-ended Harmonization'. *Utr. L.R.* 4 (2008): 40.

Wymeersch, E. 'Company Law in Europe and European Company Law'. University of Gent, Financial Law Institute Working Paper 2001.

Wymeersch, E. 'The Transfer of the Company's Seat in European Company Law'. *Common Market Law Review* 40 (2003): 661.

Wymeersch, E. 'The Transfer of the Company's Seat in European Company Law'. *ECGI* Law Working Paper No. 08/2003.

Wymeersch, E. 'European Company Law and Corporate Governance: Quo Vadis? Closing Remarks'. *RabelsZ, Bd.* 69 (2005) 787–794.

Wymeersch, E. 'Enforcement of Corporate Governance Codes'. ECGI Law Working Paper No. 46/2005.

Wymeersch, E. 'European Company Law and "Corporate Governance" Quo Vadis?'. *RabelsZ* (2005).

Zetzsche, D. & U. Neack. 'Corporate Governance Reform in Germany: The Second Decade'. *EBLR* (2005): 1033.

Zetzsche, D. 'Shareholder Interaction Preceding Shareholder Meetings of Public Corporations: A Six Country Comparison'. *ECFR* 1 (2005): 107.

Zetzsche, D. 'Hidden Ownership in Europe: BAFin's Decision in Schaeffler v. Continental'. *EBOR* (2009): 131.

Zimmer, D. 'Case Annotation'. *CM L Rev.* (2004): 1127–1140.

Zingales, L. 'The Costs and Benefits of Financial Market Regulation'. Law Working Paper No. 21/2004.

Zumbansen, P. 'European Corporate Law and National Divergences: The Case of Takeover Regulation'. (Book Reviews) [2004] *Wash UL St LR* 867.

Zumbansen, P. 'Spaces and Places: A Systems Theory Approach to Regulatory Competition in European Company Law'. *European Law Journal* 12 (2006): 534.

Index

D

E

F

G

H

I

J

L

M

R

S

T

U

V

W

EUROPEAN MONOGRAPH SERIES

1. Lamm Betten (ed.), *The Future of European Social Policy*, 1991 (ISBN 90-654-4585-4).
2. Annemarie Loman, Kamiel Mortelmans, Harry H.G. Post & Stewart Watson, *Culture and Common Law: Before and After Maastricht*, 1992 (ISBN 90-654-4638-9).
3. John A.E. Vervaele, *Fraud against the Community: The Need for European Fraud Legislation*, 1994 (ISBN 90-654-4634-6).
4. Philip Raworth, *The Legislative Process in the European Community*, 1993 (ISBN 90-654-4690-7).
5. Jules Stuyck, *Financial and Monetary Integration in the European Economic Community*, 1993 (ISBN 90-654-4718-0).
6. Jules Stuyck & A.J. Vossestein (eds), *State Entrepreneurship, National Monopolies and European Community Law*, 1993 (ISBN 90-654-4773-3).
7. Jules Stuyck & A. Looijestijn-Clearie (eds), *The European Economic Area EC-EFTA*, 1994 (ISBN 90-654-4815-2).
8. Rosita B. Bouterse, *Competition and Integration: What Goals Count?*, 1995 (ISBN 90-654-4816-0).
9. René Barents, *The Agricultural Law of the EC: An Inquiry into the Administrative Law*, 1994 (ISBN 90-654-4867-5).
10. Nicholas Emiliou, *Principles of Proportionality in European Law: A Comparative Study*, 1996 (ISBN 90-411-0866-1).
11. Eivind Smith, *National Parliaments as Cornerstones of European Integration*, 1996 (ISBN 90-411-0898-X).
12. Jan H. Jans, *European Environmental Law*, 1996 (ISBN 90-411-0877-7).
13. Síofra O'Leary, *The Evolving Concept of Community Citizenship: From the Free Movement of Persons to Union Citizenship*, 1997 (ISBN 90-411-0878-5).
14. Laurence W. Gormley (ed.), *Current and Future Perspectives on EC Competition Law*, 1983 (ISBN 90-411-0691-X).
15. Simone White, *Protection of the Financial Interests of the European Communities: The Fight against Fraud and Corruption*, 1998 (ISBN 90-411-9647-1).
16. Morten P. Broberg, *The European Commission's Jurisdiction to Scrutinize Mergers*, 3rd Edition, 2006 (ISBN 978-90-411-2474-6).
17. Doris Hildebrand, *The Role of Economic Analysis in the EC Competition Rules: The European School*, 2nd Edition, 2002 (ISBN 90-411-1706-7).
18. Christof R.A. Swaak, *European Community Law and the Automobile Industry*, 1999 (ISBN 90-411-1140-9).
19. Dorthe Dahlgaard Dingel, *Public Procurement: A Harmonization of the National Judicial Review of the Application of European Community Law*, 1999 (ISBN 90-411-1161-1).
20. John A.E. Vervaele (ed.), *Compliance and Enforcement of European Community Law*, 1999 (ISBN 90-411-1151-4).

21. Martin Trybus, *European Defence Procurement Law: International and National Procurement Systems as Models for a Liberalized Defence Procurement Market in Europe*, 1999 (ISBN 90-411-1167-0).
22. Helen Staples, *The Legal Status of Third Country Nationals Resident in the European Union*, 1999 (ISBN 90-411-1277-4).
23. Damien Geradin (ed.), *The Liberalization of State Monopolies in the European Union and Beyond*, 1999 (ISBN 90-411-1264-2).
24. Katja Heede, *European Ombudsman: Redress and Control at Union Level*, 2000 (ISBN 90-411-1413-0).
25. Ulf Bernitz & Joakim Nergelius (eds), *General Principles of European Community Law*, 2000 (ISBN 90-411-1402-5).
26. Michaela Drahos, *Convergence of Competition Laws and Policies in the European Community*, 2002 (ISBN 90-411-1562-5).
27. Damien Geradin (ed.), *The Liberalization of Electricity and Natural Gas in the European Union*, 2001 (ISBN 90-411-1560-9).
28. Gisella Gori, *Towards an EU Right to Education*, 2001 (ISBN 90-411-1670-2).
29. Brendan P.G. Smith, *Constitution Building in the European Union*, 2001 (ISBN 90-411-1695-8).
30. Friedl Weiss & Frank Wooldridge, *Free Movement of Persons within the European Community*, 2nd Edition, 2007 (ISBN 978-90-411-2545-3).
31. Ingrid Boccardi, *Europe and Refugees: Towards an EU Asylum Policy*, 2002 (ISBN 90-411-1709-1).
32. John A.E. Vervaele & André Klip (eds), *European Cooperation Between Tax, Customs and Judicial Authorities*, 2001 (ISBN 90-411-1747-4).
33. Wouter P.J. Wils, *The Optimal Enforcement of EC Antitrust Law: Essays in Law and Economics*, 2002 (ISBN 90-411-1757-1).
34. Damien Geradin (ed.), *The Liberalization of Postal Services in the European Union*, 2002 (ISBN 90-411-1780-6).
35. Nick Bernard, *Multilevel Governance in the European Union*, 2002 (ISBN 90-411-1812-8).
36. Jill Wakefield, *Judicial Protection through the Use of Article 288(2) EC*, 2002 (ISBN 90-411-1823-3).
37. Sebastiaan Princen, *EU Regulation and Transatlantic Trade*, 2002 (ISBN 90-411-1871-3).
38. Amaryllis Verhoeven, *The European Union in Search of a Democratic and Constitutional Theory*, 2002 (ISBN 90-411-1872-1).
39. Paul L.C. Torremans, *Cross Border Insolvencies in EU, English and Belgian Law*, 2002 (ISBN 90-411-1888-8).
40. Malcolm Anderson & Joanna Apap (eds), *Police and Justice Cooperation and the New European Borders*, 2002 (ISBN 90-411-1893-4).
41. Christin M. Forstinger, *Takeover Law in EU and USA: A Comparative Analysis*, 2002 (ISBN 90-411-1919-1).

42. Antonio Bavasso, *Communications in EU Antitrust Law: Market Power and Public Interest*, 2003 (ISBN 90-411-1974-4).
43. Fiona G. Wishlade, *Regional State Aid and Competition Policy in the European Union*, 2003 (ISBN 90-411-1975-2).
44. Gareth Davies, *Nationality Discrimination in the European Internal Market*, 2003 (ISBN 90-411-1998-1).
45. René Barents, *The Autonomy of Community Law*, 2003 (ISBN 90-411-2251-6).
46. Gerhard Dannecker & Oswald Jansen (eds), *Competition Law Sanctioning in the European Union*, 2004 (ISBN 90-411-2100-5).
47. Nauta Dutilh (ed.), *Dealing with Dominance: The Experience of National Competition Authorities*, 2004 (ISBN 90-411-2211-7).
48. Stefaan van den Bogaert, *Practical Regulation of the Mobility of Sportsmen in the EU Post Bosman*, 2005 (ISBN 90-411-2327-X).
49. Katalin Judit Cseres, *Competition Law and Consumer Protection*, 2005 (ISBN 90-411-2380-6).
50. Philipp Kiiver, *The National Parliaments in the European Union: A Critical View on EU Constitution Building*, 2006 (ISBN 978-90-411-2452-4).
51. Alexander Turk, *The Concept of Legislation in European Community Law*, 2006 (ISBN 978-90-411-2472-2).
52. Dimitrios Sinaniotis, *The Interim Protection of Individuals before the European and National Courts*, 2006 (ISBN 978-90-411-2498-2).
53. M. Holoubek & D. Damjanovic, M. Traimer (eds), *Regulating Content: The European Regulatory Framework for the Media and Related Creative Sectors*, 2006 (ISBN 978-90-411-2597-2).
54. Anneli Albi & Jacques Ziller (eds), *The European Constitution and National Constitutions: Ratification and Beyond*, 2006 (ISBN 978-90-411-2524-8).
55. Gustavo E. Luengo, *Regulation of Subsidies and State Aids in WTO and EC Law: Conflicts in International Trade Law*, 2007 (ISBN 978-90-411-2547-7).
56. Eniko Horvath, *Mandating Identity: Citizenship, Kinship Laws and Plural Nationality in the European Union*, 2007 (ISBN 978-90-411-2662-7).
57. Rass Holdgaard, *External Relations Law of the European Community: Legal Reasoning and Legal Discourses*, 2007 (ISBN 978-90-411-2604-7).
58. Jill Wakefield, *The Right to Good Administration*, 2007 (ISBN 978-90-411-2697-9).
59. Dimitry Kochenov, *EU Enlargement and the Failure of Conditionality: Pre-accession Conditionality in the Fields of Democracy and the Rule of Law*, 2008 (ISBN 978-90-411-2696-2).
60. Despina Mavromati, *The Law of Payment Services in the EU: The EC Directive on Payment Services in the Internal Market*, 2008 (ISBN 978-90-411-2700-6).
61. Anne Meuwese, *Impact Assessment in EU Lawmaking*, 2008 (ISBN 978-90-411-2720-4).

62. Ulf Bernitz, Joakim Nergelius & Cecilia Cardner (eds), *General Principles of EC Law in a Process of Development*, 2008 (ISBN 978-90-411-2705-1).
63. Johan van de Gronden (ed.), *The EU and WTO Law on Services: Limits to the Realisation of General Interest Policies within the Services Markets?*, 2008 (ISBN 978-90-411-2809-6).
64. Alina Tryfonidou, *Reverse Discrimination in EC Law*, 2009 (ISBN 978-90-411-2751-8).
65. Mikael Berglund, *Cross-Border Enforcement of Claims in the EU: History Present Time and Future*, 2009 (ISBN 978-90-411-2861-4).
66. Theodore Konstadinides, *Division of Powers in European Union Law: The Delimitation of Internal Competence between the EU and the Member States*, 2009 (ISBN 978-90-411-2615-3).
67. Mattias Derlén, *Multilingual Interpretation of European Union Law*, 2009 (ISBN 978-90-411-2853-9).
68. René Barents, *Directory of EU Case Law on the Preliminary Ruling Procedure*, 2009 (ISBN 978-90-411-3150-8).
69. Yan Luo, *Anti-dumping in the WTO, the EU and China: The Rise of Legalization in the Trade Regime and its Consequences*, 2010 (ISBN 978-90-411-3207-9).
70. Patrick Birkinshaw & Mike Varney (eds), *The European Union Legal Order after Lisbon*, 2010 (ISBN 978-90-411-3152-2).
71. Thomas Gr. Papadopoulos, *EU Law and the Harmonization of Takeovers in the Internal Market*, 2010 (978-90-411-3340-3).